W9-AYD-267

THE PARACHUTISTS

EDWARD KLEIN

The Parachutists

Doubleday & Company, Inc., Garden City, New York, 1981

ISBN: 0-385-12573-9
Library of Congress Catalog Card Number 77-82953
Copyright © 1981 by Edward Klein
All Rights Reserved
Printed in the United States of America
First Edition

For Karen and Alec

THE PARACHUTISTS

FLASHFORWARD

FLASH FORWARD

The priest's face was wrapped from the edge of his eyes to the edge of his collar in a dirty cotton-white beard, and his breath stunk to high heaven.

"You're a damn fool!" he said, each word an assault of full-strength garlic.

The priest knew that whatever he told Albright wouldn't make any difference. Which explained why he was so upset. When he was upset he sputtered, and when he sputtered small pieces of the garlic that he habitually chewed came spewing out of the hole in his beard that was his mouth.

"It's sheer lunacy," he said. Then came the last sibilant spray of garlic and an admission of defeat: "*It's suicidal.*"

But Albright wasn't listening.

Slumped against a marble column on Fisherman's Bastion, Alexander Hamilton Albright gazed down at the smoldering city. It was a horrifying sight and it made him shudder. He could actually feel the trembling along the sides of his arms and in the muscles of his thighs. It was a strange, convulsive sensation and it puzzled him. Despite everything he had been through, he still wasn't used to showing his feelings, even to himself.

There was no doubt about it. He had changed. Not just in little ways, like how he felt about the war. That was to be expected. It went far beyond that. His cool invincible façade had cracked. The sheathing around his nerves had been stripped away. He felt completely exposed. Vulnerable.

It was funny how people always envied him because of his family, his money, his golden-boy looks, all his so-called advantages. That was a laugh. He never put any store in those things. They were accidents of birth, gifts of the gods, the roll of the chromosomes.

As far as he was concerned, the only things that counted were the gifts he gave himself. Poise. Willpower. Self-control. He made of them a shield, his escutcheon.

And now that had cracked, too.

He had to admit it. He was near the end of his rope. His ankle ached more than it had yesterday; the fracture was never properly set. He needed a doctor. The members of the Tchaikovsky Circuit were beyond medical care. They were either dead or worse—in the hands of the Germans. He was tortured by the thought that he was the instrument of their betrayal. They were all volunteers, true, but it was he who led them in the mission behind enemy lines, and he should have known from the start that they were doomed to failure.

"It's my fault," he muttered, as much to himself as to the priest.

The priest put a comforting hand on his shoulder.

"Don't believe what priests tell you," he said. "Guilt is the worst possible motive for human behavior."

Albright was fond of the priest. He owed him his life. The priest had hidden him, fed him, kept his hopes alive. He trusted the priest and knew that the priest wouldn't let him down now.

"I'm counting on you to come through," Albright said.

The priest looked away in exasperation. He reached into the pocket of his black cassock, took out a clove of garlic, and began peeling it.

"It's a demented scheme, but you know I'll do my part," he said.

He bit into the garlic.

"Good," Albright said. "Now, remember, the description of the train and its exact routing must get to Donovan before the train arrives at the Slovakian border. From there until Poland, I want constant reconnaissance. No monkeyshines, nothing fancy, just accurate, steady, aerial reconnaissance. Until the big show at Tarnow."

The priest knew all this already. They had been over it a dozen times. This morning, he went down to the station and personally counted the number of boxcars in the train, noted the markings on the engine and the sidings, the placement of the two *Einsatzkommando* cars. All that was committed to memory. He had been a courier with the underground from the beginning, and he might be old and a bit dotty but his brain wasn't pickled yet.

The problem wasn't in his brain synapses. It was in the connection between the secret transmitter here in Budapest and a whole chain of things that could go wrong—and probably would. Albright was flirting with the impossible. It would take many hours for his message to reach Donovan's OSS office in Washington, and God knew how long for Donovan to make up his mind. What if there were radio interference? What if there weren't enough planes to spare? What if fog or rain made reconnaissance impossible? What if the Germans rerouted the train?

He had presented all his what-ifs to Albright and the only thing Albright had to say was: "What if there isn't a God? Would that stop you from being a priest?"

So by now the priest knew that he was wasting his breath. Albright was going to board the train, and there was nothing left for the priest to do but say a prayer.

"I'll never forget you," Albright said. "Or the smell of your garlic."

The priest laughed.

"And I'll never forget you," he said. "It's people like you, with whom you share a drink and a few jokes, that you really miss—much more than the righteous."

He turned his head so that Albright could not see his eyes and quickly walked away.

Albright watched him go, then looked down from the height of Fisherman's Bastion at the destruction of Budapest below. His city, his lovely Budapest, lay before him dying. He felt the shudder return.

There were times in the past when Albright told himself that particular places didn't count. He had kicked around so much in his life—from school to school, country to country, job to job— that he almost developed an immunity to where he lived. Paris and Rome and Prague—they belonged to everybody. But *Budapest* . . . Budapest belonged to him.

Tattooed on his memory from those years he had lived in Budapest were the names of the streets and the numbers of the trolleys that ran on them; the lyrics of popular songs, including the second verses; the taste of a sauce served in an outdoor restaurant on Lake Balaton; the growl of the engine as the Le Père biplane dipped and soared over the countryside; the smell of the perfume on Madame Madson, the lady who came to teach him piano on Thursday afternoons; the feel of the damask napkins used for official dinners at the American embassy.

Budapest was where he had grown up, stumbled through the sixteenth, seventeenth, and eighteenth years of his life, where he had gradually gathered together the loose strands of boyhood into an image of himself as a man. . . .

Budapest was where his father, who presided regally as American ambassador during those Depression years, taught him how to jump. First from the roof of a garage, then from a platform he had specially constructed on the embassy lawn, and finally from a 125-foot training tower where the parachutes were guided safely to the ground by steel cables. His father taught him everything about parachutes and the law of falling bodies—how, from the moment a man leaps from an airplane, he will continue to fall faster and faster each second until the pull of gravity and the friction of the atmospheric resistance are in perfect balance. There, at the "region of terminal velocity," a man will plunge to earth at a steady rate of a hundred twenty miles per hour—unless he remembers to open his parachute.

They used an Irvin chute on their first jump together. It was Albright's seventeenth birthday, October 19, 1934, and the Budapest airport was deserted as the pilot wheeled out the Le Père. The aircraft slowly clawed its way into the crisp autumn sky.

"Well, how does it look to you?" his father yelled over the noise of the engine.

Albright glanced down, nodded his head and smiled. He was too frightened to risk words. He was determined to control his quivering body, to hide the consuming doubt that took away his breath. His father despised physical cowardice, and Albright would have preferred to jump out of the plane without a parachute rather than betray the slightest wince of fear.

He was a big enough disappointment as it was. Before the family arrived in Budapest, Albright had been expelled from two of the best private schools in America, St. Bernard's and Choate. "Obstreperousness . . . Insubordination . . . Lack of Proper Respect for Authority. . . ." His father and mother could have forgiven that, put it down to healthy high spirits. What they couldn't forgive was his attitude toward their world—their tight, rich, social world. They took *that* seriously.

He didn't even try to fit in. He was a loner and bookworm, an unpredictable, impetuous, quick-tempered boy who was always getting into street fights. He was brilliant at the piano, but he wouldn't perform for anybody, and he was a flop at dances. He would sit for hours and play chess with the caretaker in Greenwich, but he refused to take tennis lessons. He hated neckties, socks, creases in his pants, artichokes, and all the daughters of his mother's friends. He liked fishing, foreign stamps, fast cars, Negroes, and languages.

Above all, languages.

By his second year in Budapest, Albright was already perfectly fluent in Hungarian, a maddeningly difficult language that is totally unrelated to any other tongue spoken by man, except Finnish. He possessed the gift. He learned French from his nurse, Italian from one summer in Rome, Hungarian from his friends, and German from school. He collected old grammar books and dictionaries and taught himself enough Russian to read Tolstoy, enough Spanish to get through Cervantes, enough ancient Egyptian hieroglyphics to grasp the Book of the Dead.

Nobody understood how he did it. His mother had attended a boarding school in Switzerland where she learned to speak French and Italian, and the only time he ever heard her express a positive opinion about him was one evening at a dinner party when she took credit for his special genius in languages. But it was probably more complicated than that. It took an ear for sounds, pitch, rhythm, intonation, stress. A memory that associated those sounds with objects. A mind for grammatical logic. A musical aptitude. A desire to be a different person. A need to express certain emotions that he couldn't find words for in English.

Whatever it took, it was a natural endowment, like a third baseman with a strong arm or a movie star with big tits. He couldn't take credit for being born with it, but it did make a person stop and think. During those three years in Budapest, it made Albright think that he had a chance, an outside shot if he worked hard enough at it, to become not just good at languages, but one of the best linguists who ever lived. Better than Sir William Jones, the eighteenth-century scholar who knew thirteen languages thoroughly and twenty-eight fairly well. Better than Rasmus Christian Rash, the nineteenth-century Danish philologist who was a master of twenty-five languages and dialects and who taught himself Persian—so he could speak it like a native—in six weeks flat. Better even than this century's world heavyweight champion in languages—Edward Sapir, the Yale professor who could speak practically every known American Indian dialect *plus* all the modern European languages *plus* a couple of African languages *plus* Hebrew *plus* Chinese.

Albright thought he could earn a shot at the title. By his seventeenth birthday in Budapest, he already had four languages under his belt. Three more good enough to read. And that wasn't counting Latin and Greek.

His father wasn't impressed. Knowing a few foreign languages was good, maybe even useful later on, but they didn't make the man. That came only through testing yourself physically. In contact sports, big-game hunting, and parachuting . . .

As the Le Père reached two thousand feet over the suburbs of Budapest, his father turned to Albright and said: "Remember what I taught you. Now . . . *jump!*"

Since that October day in 1934, Albright had jumped countless times, but he was never quite able to recapture the passionate joy of that first leap of faith—faith in his father's instructions, faith in his parachute, above all, this new faith in himself. It was a grand self-discovery. He leaped into nothingness and, upon coming safely to rest in a field, he realized that he could control his own destiny. It was a profound lesson for a seventeen-year-old boy.

From that moment, Albright was never again in awe of anything or anybody. Not of his father, not of his family's position, wealth, or power, not of others' expectations, not of anything but his own poise, willpower, and self-control.

Looking across the Danube from his perch on Buda Hill ten years later, Albright watched the destruction of the city and felt a sense of deep personal loss. It was an awesome spectacle, just the kind of chill November day to cheer the soul of a German. The wind whirled the cirrus clouds into fantastic shapes across a dull blue sky, and below, in a panorama that stretched under a smoky haze a dozen miles to the horizon, one of Europe's loveliest cities was being reduced to a submissive heap of rubble.

It had begun this morning, November 23, 1944, in the cold dawn. He heard them coming ten minutes before they were in sight—a distant roar that eventually grew into a deafening earthquake. He went out into the garden of the safe house with the priest and began counting the planes in the massive bomber stream. They were grouped in boxes of four, Lancasters and Stirlings, and he lost track after the twentieth box had dropped its symmetrical stick of bombs. Along with the four-engine bombers, the British sent hundreds of fighter escorts—Hurricanes, Spitfires, Typhoons, Tempests, Mosquitos, Whirlwinds.

The Germans managed to scramble a couple of squadrons of Messerschmitts and Focke-Wulfs, and for a while planes fell out of the flak-pocked sky like soot from a blast furnace. Dozens of parachutes drifted through the inferno. It was all over before seven o'clock, and since then the Red Army had been finishing off Budapest with its long-range artillery and Katushka rockets.

From Fisherman's Bastion, Albright could see that the British and Russians had done a thorough job on the city. But that was nothing compared to the senseless sadism of the Germans. Through his binoculars, he watched as one national monument after another was shattered by the dynamite charges of the retreating Nazis. The bronze chariot above the portico of the Palace of Justice shattered into a thousand galloping pieces. The dome of St. Stephen's Church collapsed, almost in slow motion. Then a succession of dull thuds accompanied the demise of the roof of the Ferenc Hopp Museum, the Archangel Gabriel atop the Millennium Monument, the Renaissance façade of the Opera House. . . .

There was something almost personal in the methodical frenzy with which the Germans demolished the stone and marble. If they could not stamp their own dark image on Budapest, then no historic image, no memory would be allowed to remain. The last to be destroyed were the bridges spanning the Danube: the Arpad and Margit crossing at Old Buda, the Szabadsag and Petofi at the southern edge of the city, the graceful Szechenyi suspension bridge.

By now, the ancient Erzsebet bridge stood as the last link between Buda and Pest. Soon the twin cities would be severed. Time was running out for Budapest, for the Germans, for everyone—including Albright.

The cable railway was still working, but Albright didn't want to call attention to himself and he decided it would be safer to walk. He could have saved himself the trouble. Someone had already spotted him. A short, frail old man had climbed all the way up the hill carrying a baby in his arms.

"*Igazán sajnálom*," the old man said, motioning with his head toward the burning city. "Too bad."

The baby looked dead. Albright didn't know what to say.

The old man fixed him with his eyes. "*Mi a baj?* What's wrong?"

"Nothing," Albright said.

"*Hideg van*," the old man said, looking down at the dead baby. "It's cold."

Albright nodded and moved on. To the old man, he was just another wounded Hungarian officer. One among thousands. Nothing special. Well, perhaps a bit different . . .

It was always that way with Alexander Hamilton Albright. Strangers were struck by something in his physical presence but could never figure out what it was. Though he was nearly six feet tall, he conveyed the impression of compactness, an effortless, natural coordination, all shoulders and chest, no hips. Even limping, he managed to appear athletically graceful, as though he might at one time have been a swimmer or a high jumper or a soccer player. Or, if such an arcane sport had occurred to anyone, a parachutist.

He was good-looking in an unconventional sort of way. For one thing, his jawline seemed too hard compared with the softness of his lips. He was fair and blond but he had dark, Mediterranean eyes. His nose had been broken in a college boxing match and fixed, badly, by a plastic surgeon. It gave his face its special character, its subliminal sense of contradiction. In profile, it looked perfectly straight. Head-on, you could still see the place where the bridge of the nose took a small detour.

Each step down Gellert Hill was an ordeal. Beneath the trousers of his Hungarian uniform, the ankle was throbbing with pain. He stopped to catch his breath at the waterfall and looked at the heroically sculpted face of the statue of Bishop Gellert. The blank stone eyes of the medieval martyr stared back at him.

Those unseeing eyes brought back yet another memory—a visit to this cool grotto ten years ago with a group of his classmates from the *gymnasium*. Apples were in season then, crisp and slightly sour. Nationalism and atheism and faith in man's infinite progress were all in season, too, and the conversation remained vividly sweet in his reminiscence. One of his long-haired Hungarian classmates spat into the eyes of Bishop Gellert and denounced the veneration of saints. Someone declared that science would replace Catholicism.

And then someone said (he could almost hear the rhythm of the expression): "What impresses me most about saints is not their flamboyant self-denial, which is unnatural. But that they make normal people feel so unworthy."

Albright washed away the memory with some water on his face and limped as quickly as he could to the Erzsebet bridge. Across the Danube, on the Pest side, the upper stories of the massive Parliament Building were hidden behind a pall of smoke. Fires raged everywhere, churned by the wind, and the city was a bedlam of fire-engine bells, explosions, collapsing masonry, and the inhaling whistle of incoming artillery and rockets.

He approached the checkpoint on the bridge. A ruddy-faced German lieutenant, his tunic unbuttoned at the throat, cursed the traffic in a Bavarian dialect.

"Hey, gimpy," the German called. "Where the hell do you think you're going?"

He halted the traffic and walked over to Albright.

"Across to Pest," Albright said.

Albright spoke German with a Hungarian accent. Before the war, it used to make his German friends laugh.

"Across to Pest," the German mimicked, not quite getting the intonation right. "Only Germans are allowed to cross."

He looked around for an audience, but the troops in the back of the waiting truck pretended not to pay any attention. Graying at the temples, he looked too old to be a lieutenant; he was probably a sergeant who had received a battlefield commission.

"I must deliver these papers to Lieutenant Colonel Krumey," Albright said, and immediately wondered whether he had gone too far.

Lieutenant Colonel Hermann Krumey was Adolf Eichmann's deputy in Budapest. As such, he was in charge of the "International Storage and Transportation Company"—the Nazi cover name for the extermination program of Hungary's Jews.

"Horseshit!" the German said. "This man thinks I'm a dummy." He was addressing the troops in the truck again. "Colonel Krumey doesn't get messages from Hungarians. Let's see that briefcase."

Albright's heart began to race.

"All right, Lieutenant," he said. "There's no message. I was trying to sneak across."

The troops in the truck were now staring at the two men, waiting to see what would happen next.

"It's my leg," Albright said.

"Let's see," the German lieutenant said.

Albright exposed his ankle, red and swollen, and the German let out a long whistle of sympathy.

"Looks to me like you got a fracture, son," he said.

The bully had suddenly turned paternal. Albright had been right: the man could only be a sergeant.

"There's a doctor I know in Pest," Albright said. "He can fix me up. I want to be in shape to fight when the Russians get here."

"Where's the doctor?"

"Near Berlin Plaza," Albright said.

"You hear that?" the lieutenant said to the driver of the truck. "Let the captain hitch a ride to Berlin Plaza." Then he turned to Albright. "If you don't mind riding in the back with the enlisted men."

Albright thanked him and climbed into the truck.

"Don't worry about those Bolsheviks," the lieutenant shouted up to him. "I was on the Eastern Front. That's where I got this," he pointed proudly with his thumb to his insignia of rank. "They fight like women."

Just then a rocket burst on the side of Gellert Hill.

"What are you waiting for?" the German yelled to the driver. "Move it, move it, move it."

The truck picked up speed as it crossed the bridge and zigzagged around the shell holes on Kossuth Avenue. Along the bank of the Danube, gangs of black shirts were executing Jews and throwing their bodies into the river. The truck turned left in front of the synagogue on the corner of Dohany Avenue, clattered over the tram lines, and came to a stop at Berlin Plaza. The driver honked his horn twice and Albright slid off the back of the truck, favoring his injured leg.

"*Danke,*" he said.

"Kiss the Russians for me," the driver said. "On their red asses."

Albright waited until the truck was out of sight, then entered the waiting room of *Nyugati Palyaudvar*—West Station. It was a cavernous place with a vaulted glass roof and exposed steel beams, and it hummed with empty silence. It had been left unscathed through weeks of Allied bombardment, obviously marked off limits so that the Red Army could resupply by rail, once it conquered the city.

He looked at his watch: sixteen minutes before nine. He did not have much time. He ducked through a door marked *Arnyekszek*—Toilet. He bolted it from inside, opened his briefcase, and took out a pair of trousers, an old shirt, and a baggy gray jacket. He stripped off his uniform, stained in the back with perspiration, put on the old clothes, and stuffed the uniform into the briefcase. Standing on the seat of the toilet, he wedged the briefcase into the overhead flush basin. Water cascaded over the sides and drenched his sleeves up to the elbows. For a moment, Albright was concerned about his appearance until he remembered that where he was going neatness didn't count.

He had an ironic smile on his face when he unlocked the door and stepped out.

It was eleven minutes before nine and the gates leading to the outside platforms were guarded by troops and Dobermans. The dogs pulled nervously on the short leashes, and their ears twitched at each explosion that rocked the city. Once he was on the platform, Albright knew that it would be impossible to escape. The guards and dogs were there to prevent a breakout. But Albright had come to break in.

The old clothes felt loose and comfortable. He stopped sweating. The pain in his ankle subsided. Calmly, he limped through the gate as one of the Dobermans sniffed at his shoes.

"How did you get out here?"

Albright gazed steadily into the face of the guard. He had a bad case of acne.

"I took a pee," Albright said, motioning in the direction of the toilet.

The corporal was clearly bewildered. He looked into the waiting room, as if he expected to see an army rushing in after Albright. Relieved, he said, "Get back where you belong, Jew."

The platforms were packed, edge to edge, with people and their belongings. Thousands were here, a vast congregation, most of them appearing prosperously fat because they wore three and four layers of clothing under their coats. The women sat on their suitcases, hands folded neatly on their laps. The men stood, smoking, querulous expressions on their faces, numb and helpless. The children played with their toys.

There were groups of Gypsies and students. The lame and deformed and insane in hospital garb. Rough-looking men in prison uniforms. Pale, sensitive figures who looked as though they had spent their lives in classrooms or scientific laboratories or in the anti-Fascist underground. But mostly they were Jews.

Hungary's Jews were Europe's last true disbelievers. Though it was the autumn of 1944, though they had heard the rumors and been given repeated warnings, many of the Jews of Hungary refused to believe the fate that was in store for them. After all, while others perished, they survived, the last intact Jewish community in all of Europe. They and they alone endured, and now, in the twilight of the Nazi era, they stubbornly clung to the faith that they would continue to endure—come what may. Thus their cool composure as they awaited the train that would transport them to extermination.

Albright pried his way through the crowds, searching for Ruth.

The clock above the departure sign said four minutes to nine. None of the women looked familiar. The color of this one's hair was wrong. That one's posture was different. She never wore that kind of shoes. He began to grow desperate. He seized a woman by the shoulders, spun her around, stared at her for a moment— then moved on. He made his way to the next platform, ramming his way through the swarm of people. That woman ten yards away . . . It might be her. It wasn't.

It was nine o'clock. At the sound of the buzzer, the German troops passed the order down the platform to load the train. The people picked up their belongings and climbed aboard the wooden freight cars. Ordinarily, the contents of their luggage would be carefully weighed—twenty kilograms each—and checked off against a list of permissible items prepared by Adolf Eichmann's office: two pairs of socks, two shirts, two pairs of underwear, one towel, one cup, one spoon. . . . All valuables were supposed to be confiscated before boarding.

But with the Russians at the gates of Budapest and the Germans in full retreat, these were not ordinary times. And so, as the nervous, understaffed German guard prodded and shoved one hundred human beings into a space intended for six cattle, they did not bother to separate the sexes or search the doomed passengers. The spoils from this train would be collected at the other end.

"Alex!"

It was not the voice he had expected to hear and, at first, he did not recognize his own name being called.

"Alex!"

He turned and ten yards away saw a man who looked vaguely familiar.

"It's me. Joel."

He reached for his friend, his face so swollen and disfigured that he was almost unrecognizable, but Joel was swept by the throngs toward the train.

"Where's Ruth?" Albright cried. "Where's Ruth?"

Joel had already disappeared into one of the freight cars. Albright tried to follow him.

"*Ach*, I think you'll find more room in the next car," a German guard said with mock gentility.

Albright pushed him aside and hoisted himself into the car. The door rolled shut behind him and there was a burst of derisive laughter outside.

Total silence reigned inside the dark freight car. A small, barred window just below the ceiling admitted a weak stream of light and cast the strained faces and bundled bodies in a grotesque chiaroscuro. Desperate for a clue to their destination, the passengers shushed those who breathed too loudly. Someone apologized for coughing. Then there was a sudden jerk as the train shuddered into motion.

Over the sound of the squeaking wheels, Albright heard someone on the platform say: "Tell Colonel Krumey that the last train has left for Auschwitz. They'll be getting some fine Hungarian sausages soon."

As the train ground forward, Albright thought of the boy who had spit in the stone eye of the martyred Bishop Gellert. There was no question about it. He had changed. For the first time in his life, Albright felt completely worthy.

The long train with its body of red boxcars and black head of a locomotive was like a gigantic snake crawling toward Auschwitz. Seventy cars. One hundred people to a car. Nearly seven thousand doomed souls sealed inside the death train. Albright calculated that he had four days before the train reached Tarnow in Poland and would switch onto the branch line for Auschwitz.

Four days to find Ruth among the seven thousand. Four days for Donovan to send his planes. Four days to organize the first mass escape of the war from the ovens of the Holocaust.

PART I

SPRING 1944

CHAPTER ONE

CAIRO
Thursday, March 23

1

Albright crawled out of the cockpit onto the lower wing of the Sopwith Camel and immediately felt the cold blast of air slam against his body. It was a perfect day for a jump. Between the soles of his sneakers and the hard flat earth below stood the thinly stretched fabric on the wing—and fourteen thousand feet of empty cobalt blue sky.

The old Sopwith Camel was a relic of World War I, a rickety, wood-framed biplane with a 110-horsepower Le Rhône engine. At the peak of its performance, it could barely make one hundred thirty miles per hour. But in its antique way, the Camel was an amazing machine. Handcrafted by skilled cabinetmakers, upholstered in blazing orange-and-white-striped linen, armed with two Vickers machine guns and a thousand rounds of ammunition, the Camel was considered in its heyday to be the greatest fighter of them all.

In the hands of a skilled pilot, the Camel had blinding maneuverability and killing power, and during the last two years of the Great War it shot down 1,634 German aircraft on the Western Front. Alexander Hamilton Albright's father had bagged twenty-one enemy planes himself, including a Fokker triplane flown by Lothar von Richthofen, the Red Baron's brother.

Albright crouched on the Camel's undulating wing, his feet together like a high diver, one hand gripping the side of the cockpit, the other a brace wire, the wind and the vibration of the aircraft thrumming through his arms and legs. He had been parachuting for ten years, but this was the first time from a Camel. A 13,500-foot free fall.

He had dried and mended and packed the parachute himself, carefully folding the lightweight Japanese *habutai* silk into the khaki backpack. "The Guardian Angel," his father used to call it. The parachute felt snug and comfortable in its harness as Albright edged along the wing, balancing on the wooden rib supports beneath the delicate fabric. Near the tip of the wing, he grabbed a metal wing strut and stood up straight. The pilot compensated for the extra weight on the starboard side, and the Camel sliced through a lone, wispy cloud.

This, Albright thought, was an aircraft built for performance, not for looks. The Camel was a stubby plane, less than nineteen feet long, and it got its nickname from the ungainly hump that formed a protective cowling over the breech casings of the machine guns. Compared to the sleek beauties of the current war—the Mustang, the Spitfire, the twin-boomed P-38 Lightning—the Sopwith Camel was an aerodynamic toy that looked as though it would rip apart if you played with it too roughly.

Yet for Albright, the plane was a fantasy come true. It seemed that he had been waiting all his life for a chance to jump from a Camel. And like most things that happen to men at war, it was a pure quirk of fate that gave him that chance.

Or was it?

Looking back, Albright recalled his last meeting two years ago with Donovan. Major General William J. Donovan and Albright's father had been friends since the First World War, and Albright had read of "Wild Bill" Donovan's recent appointment as director of the Office of Strategic Services. The OSS was America's first professional espionage organization. Albright hadn't given the story in the *Times* much thought until a phone call from Donovan reached him in the Rose Room of the Algonquin Hotel one day during lunch.

"I want to see you," Donovan said on the telephone. "I hear

you just got back from Europe and saw the whole bloody mess. We can compare notes. Come on over at five."

Donovan lived in a big, comfortable apartment on Beekman Place. From the windows of his library, the East River looked as thick and gray as mercury. The shelves that lined the room were filled with books on the craft of intelligence—histories, biographies, memoirs. But no spy novels. Donovan was dressed in an army uniform with two gold stars on each epaulet.

They hadn't seen each other in years and, as they shook hands, they took a quick mental inventory of each other. For Albright, Donovan hadn't changed much. A stocky man in his sixties with white hair, ruddy cheeks and benign blue eyes, the OSS chief was slumped in a chair as if he had nothing better to do than while away an afternoon with the son of an old friend. What struck Donovan was the way the young man dressed—an old tweed sports jacket, a shirt slightly frayed at the collar, a tie carelessly knotted. He seemed to declare: I come as I am, take me or leave me, I don't really give a damn. Albright had his father's aggressive chin, his mother's sensuous lips, an athlete's build, an artist's tapered fingers, a mop of blond hair that fell over his forehead. And a genuinely warm it's-a-shitty-world-but-why-not-enjoy-it-anyway kind of smile. Donovan had never seen anyone that young radiate more self-confidence. He was tough and charming, vigorous and graceful, earthy and stylish. He looked like a born winner, just what Donovan had in mind.

The butler served drinks—scotch whisky for Albright, tomato juice for Donovan who was a teetotaler. Donovan, who had commanded the famous "Fighting Irish" 69th Regiment during World War I, reminisced lazily about Albright's father and the battle of Château-Thierry more than twenty years ago, about the technological revolution that had occurred in warfare during the intervening years, about the constant nature of the German character, about the global struggle between the forces of good and evil, light and darkness, democracy and fascism. Behind his calm, baritone voice and easygoing manner he left the impression of a man with enormous energy. But only once did he become animated.

"One of my men has come up with this wonderful idea," he

said, sliding forward in his chair. "It's a sort of combination rocket, boom, and parachute with pedals."

Then he eased back into the overstuffed cushions and took a long sip of the tomato juice.

"Well," he said after a moment, "catch me up with what you've been doing."

Albright hesitated. He felt that Donovan was playing cat-and-mouse with him.

"For starters," Donovan prompted, "how old are you now?"

"Twenty-four."

"And what did you do after you graduated from Yale?"

"Well, for starters, I *didn't* graduate," Albright said warily.

"No great crime," Donovan said, covering his embarrassment with a wave of his arm.

"What's the point of the autobiography?" Albright asked. "My father ask you to try to straighten me out?"

Donovan laughed.

"Straightening people out isn't one of my specialties," he said. "Just the opposite. And your father doesn't even know I asked you over today."

Albright didn't believe the second part.

"Well, there's not much to tell," he said. "I think I'm chiefly remembered at Yale for being the best language student they ever had, for losing the light-heavyweight college championship in 1937 by a TKO, and for flunking out in my junior year."

"Why'd you flunk out?"

"General disinterest, laziness, disorderliness, drunkenness, screwing around with girls in the dorm. . . ."

"Okay, I got the picture. What else? Ever go back to get your degree?"

"No. I bummed around Europe and the Middle East, picked up a few more languages—modern Greek, Serbo-Croatian, Arabic. For a while I worked as a simultaneous translator for the League, in Geneva. Lately, I've earned a living, if you want to call it that, as a stringer for the North American Newspaper Alliance."

"I've read a couple of your articles," Donovan said. "Go on."

"I covered the German invasion of Poland and the fall of France. I did some features on life in London under the Blitz."

"Let me ask you this," Donovan said. "You the literary type? I mean, have you been collecting notes for a novel? That seems to be the dream of most young newspapermen I know."

Albright smiled.

"No, I'm not another Hemingway. Free-lancing for newspapers just gets me to the places I want to go."

"Good. Anything else?"

"That about covers it. Not a long autobiography."

"I've heard worse lives," Donovan said. "By the way, do you still parachute?"

"When I get the chance. Which isn't too often."

"I want to offer you a job," Donovan said.

Just like that. Very *sotto voce*. No big intro. He was recruiting men, Donovan explained, for the first important American operation of the war, an invasion of North Africa, and he needed a network of agents for the job. Albright had all the right credentials. He was bright, he was a linguist, he had firsthand knowledge of how the diplomatic service worked, and he had guts.

Albright tried to turn him down.

"I'm not interested in joining a crusade," he said. "I think Hitler and what he stands for stinks, but I'm not the kind of person who stops at the scene of a car accident and picks up the dead body. Life's full of enough unpleasant little surprises, which you can't avoid, for me to go around looking for more trouble. With all due respect, General, I'd suggest you could find other socially respectable men my age who'd be more up your alley."

"I don't give a damn about your social background," Donovan said. "I'd put Stalin on the OSS payroll if I thought it would help us defeat Hitler. Sooner or later, everyone's going to be involved, one way or another, and if you could see beyond your hard nose and realize that you've got something special to contribute, you'd jump at this opportunity."

Then he told Albright about the "Twelve Disciples."

As Albright found out after he went through the six-week training course at the OSS school in Virginia, the "Twelve Disciples" were handpicked by Donovan himself, chosen to serve under the cover of vice consuls in American embassies throughout North Africa. They took their orders from the American ambassador in Algiers, a suave, rich, politically conservative Boston Irishman who also happened to be the OSS chief for all of North Africa. The ambassador had a simple philosophy: the Nazi enemy was evil incarnate and against the Devil there were no holds barred. For the ambassador, they were expected to bribe, cheat, steal, subvert, sabotage, assassinate.

He was their god. They were his "Disciples."

Albright and his fellow "Disciples" did their job well, and on the eve of the invasion, North Africa was ripe for the plucking. There was only one hitch. Within weeks after the successful Allied landings, the ambassador betrayed the entire North African underground which had been recruited and trained by his own "Disciples."

Hundreds of Arab nationalists and pro-Gaullist members of the Free French—men who had risen up on signal and fought bravely alongside the Americans and British—were rounded up and thrown into jail. Albright was in the lobby of the Hotel de Cornouailles in Algiers on the afternoon when American troops stormed in and carted off ten of his best Arab agents.

"Why?" Albright demanded. "Why did you do it?"

The ambassador was standing in front of his desk, a tall, stooped figure in a rumpled suit and a rumpled smile. He didn't invite Albright to sit down and he didn't try to pacify him. Quietly, unemotionally, he just told Albright why.

"Defeating the Germans is only part of our strategy, you know," he said. "The other part is far more subtle. If our victory is to mean anything, we must ensure that the colonial territories we liberate from the Nazis don't fall into the wrong hands."

"The wrong hands?" Albright said. "Wrong like what? Like Arabs who might get it into their heads to demand independence from the British and French after the war? Or like the Free French under De Gaulle?"

"We have to watch that De Gaulle," the ambassador said. "He's accepted thousands of Communists into the ranks of the Free French."

He lifted a pile of papers from his desk and let them fall.

"You know, Albright," he said, "a good agent doesn't let the nature of his enemy fool him. The Nazis might be a bunch of evil psychopaths, but modern wars aren't won on the battlefield by heroes. The real victories are won before and after the fighting. That's what a central intelligence agency like the OSS is for. We prepare the field of battle and we clean up the mess afterward. In our business, there are no moral absolutes."

The ambassador's betrayal delivered North Africa into the hands of the agents of Vichy France. Protofascists. Anti-Semites. The worst kind of colonialists. Men who had sat out the war collaborating with the Germans. This, Albright concluded, wasn't at all what Donovan had described—a battle between the forces of good and evil, light and darkness. Both sides were rotten.

Disgusted and disillusioned, Albright put in for an immediate transfer—and was turned down. He cabled his resignation from the OSS to Washington—and Donovan himself cabled back: ONLY TWO WAYS TO SEVER RELATIONSHIP WITH OSS. DEATH OR DISMISSAL. YOUR RESIGNATION REJECTED. Albright had just turned twenty-five and it taught him a lesson. *Don't get involved.*

He didn't anymore. He went through the motions of his job, shuffled some papers, franked some *laissez-passer*, kept to himself. He received word through the grapevine that one of his fellow "Disciples" in Casablanca had committed suicide and that two other "Disciples" had become alcoholics. A fourth "Disciple" parachuted behind the lines in Italy and was never heard from again. A fifth "Disciple" was sent home because, in the words of a copy of the report that Albright read, he displayed "serious evidence of instability." Gradually, six more "Disciples" were transferred to other theaters of the war.

That left only Albright. The last "Disciple."

Until three months ago when suddenly Albright's transfer came through. But instead of being sent to Britain to help prepare for D-Day, Albright was promoted to captain and shipped clear across the desert of North Africa to Egypt. When Albright arrived in Cairo, in the spring of 1944, all traces of the war had long vanished. The most important capital in the Middle East, a city which had come within days of being conquered by Rommel's Afrika Korps, was now a becalmed, irrelevant backwater of the great global conflict.

On his first day off in Cairo, Albright jeeped out to the airport to arrange for a pilot to take him up for a parachute jump. There at the edge of a scruffy field, half buried in a sand dune, was an old biplane. It was, unmistakably, a Sopwith Camel.

It was also a total wreck. The fabric was weathered to a uniform gray and badly shredded. There were gaping holes in the ply-wood fuselage, exposing its broken frame. Two of the wing struts were bent practically in half, and the propeller was missing. The aircraft had been cannibalized for parts. It was hard to believe that this was the great fighter that had filled his adolescence with dreams of chivalrous glory.

Actually, it wasn't. The Egyptian mechanic explained to him that this particular Camel was not the same Sopwith F. 1 model with which the British and American pilots had scored their kills in World War I. This one was a converted trainer that had been outfitted with an extra seat behind the cockpit and with a dupli-cate set of controls for student pilots. It had never flown in com-bat. No matter. Albright bought the dilapidated Camel on the spot.

He and the Sop Camel were exactly the same age—twenty-six years old—and his colleagues at the Anglo-American Psychological Warfare Branch thought he was "daft" (in the words of the Brit-ish) and "just plain nuts" (as the Americans put it) to buy the old wreck. Albright couldn't have cared less what they thought, and he told them so.

Albright and the mechanic, a tall, bronzed Bedouin named Khattab, hauled the wrecked plane into an abandoned hangar, dismantled the aircraft, took an inventory of missing and broken parts, and set about rebuilding it from the wheels up. The ware-houses of North Africa weren't exactly bulging with spare parts for twenty-six-year-old Sopwith Camels. But Albright had spent the last two years in North Africa and he knew that, if you looked hard enough and were willing to pay enough, you could get any-thing you wanted in this part of the world.

And he had contacts everywhere—Jews in the import-export business, Moroccan smugglers, electricians who could wire minia-ture radio sets or entire power stations, carpenters who could du-plicate the most valuable antiques, auto mechanics who could de-vise any kind of engine, jewelers who did incredible precision work, rug dealers who dealt in most everything but rugs. . . . Albright used the cable facilities in the Psychological Warfare Branch office to wire Benghazi, Tripoli, Tunis, Algiers, Oran, Tangier, Casablanca, and Marakech. Almost without exception, he received replies the next day, but invariably they all began: WISH

EYE COULD HELP BUT REGRET EYE NEVER REPEAT NEVER HEARD OF SUCH AYE CAMEL.

The confusion between the two kinds of camels was cleared up and gradually the necessary parts began arriving on the daily supply flights to Cairo. Whatever Albright's contacts couldn't provide, somehow the Bedouin Khattab miraculously managed to scratch up in Cairo. Albright never asked Khattab for an explanation and the dependable, smug, ever-smiling Khattab never offered one. By the time the rebuilt Sopwith Camel was ready to fly, Khattab had become indispensable. From being a mere mechanic he was now Albright's *suffragi*—his batman, butler, houseboy, cook, chauffeur, and Man Friday all rolled into one.

Now, from the desert near the Pyramids on the outskirts of Cairo, Khattab peered into the sky and watched the tiny speck that was Albright's Sopwith Camel circling overhead.

2

Fourteen thousand feet straight up, Albright stood balanced on the tip of the wing. The wind screamed in his ears, pressed the goggles into his face, whipped the yellow overalls around the rubber bands fastened at his wrists and ankles. He leaned backward, holding on with one hand, and looked down over the edge of the wing at Egypt. It was a vast dun-colored landscape, unmarked except for a thin ribbon of green vegetation along the banks of the Nile. The pilot throttled back on the engine as they came over Cairo and shouted: "Jump!"

Albright hesitated. This was the moment he cherished, the last few seconds before the jump. Nothing could rival this exquisite instant before he released his grip, let himself be swept off the trailing edge of the wing and become, in a split instant, a falling body totally at the mercy of the wind and gravity and atmosphere—and the twenty-eight feet of silk folded into the parachute on his back.

He was filled with sheer joy as he let go and fell backward into the void.

He caught a fleeting glimpse of the tail flashing by and then he was engulfed in a ghostly silence. His body tumbled once, twice, three times, and the sky and earth whirled crazily between his legs. Then by wriggling his body, he straightened himself out, spread-eagle, and plunged straight down in a horizontal position.

He was gaining speed by the second. He felt the skin on his face stretch back over his cheek bones and teeth, he heard the wind pressure increasing to a higher and higher pitch until it became a screech. Suddenly, it leveled off to a monotonous whine. At that exact instant, he experienced a strange sensation, as if an invisible force was slowing his descent. Actually, he had reached that point of balance between the pull of gravity and the resistance of air pressure. He was now falling at a hundred twenty miles per hour. He had attained the region of terminal velocity.

This was the closest a human being could ever come to perfection, he thought. Plummeting face downward, arms and feet spread apart, the music of the wind in his ears, he felt like a man about to embrace the earth.

He was not ordinarily a passionate man. Quite the contrary. He thought of himself as a cool, contained, self-controlled character. But during a free fall, attached to nothing, totally isolated, totally free, he was overwhelmed by passion. A passion that transcended anything he had ever experienced in sex or in the violence of war or in the cerebration of the mind. It must be, he thought, what saints, dope addicts, madmen, and true lovers feel in their most intense moments.

Sometimes it bothered him that he had to risk his life to reach this state of bliss. Friends joked that he had a death wish. He didn't agree. Never, in all of his jumps, had he ever felt the least tempted to succumb to the attraction of gravity and end his life. But maybe there was a kernel of truth in what they said. Maybe he had to defy death to feel truly alive. There were people like that, after all—people who couldn't commit themselves to life, who were somehow incapable of feeling committed to anything.

He imagined that he was like that.

He checked the altimeter on his wrist and saw that he had fallen nearly twelve thousand feet. The total elapsed time of his free fall, according to the chronometer on his other wrist, was 61.5 seconds. He made a quick calculation. Two thousand feet to go. If he pulled his rip cord now, he would fall another fifteen hundred feet before his parachute had a chance to fully deploy. That would leave him a little more than five hundred feet under silk. Five hundred feet was cutting it pretty close, but he decided to wait a few seconds more and cut it even closer.

He could pick out the landmarks of Cairo. The rush-green island of Gezira in the middle of the Nile. The Kaisr-el-Nil steel bridge. The Boulac slum quarter. Shepheard's Hotel on Opera Square. Everywhere, the crimson bougainvillea and the dark-blue jacaranda trees. A carpet of white storks fluttering over the Giza Zoo. King Farouk's gigantic royal yacht, the *Mahroussa*, in its mooring. Mena House standing practically in the shadow of the Great Pyramid. And, directly below, two minute figures beside his jeep.

Now!

He yanked his D-ring and the rip cord jerked free, releasing the pin that fastened the backpack. Four steel ribs, forced open by a compression spring, flung apart, and the little pilot chute dragged out the main canopy. He counted slowly: "One thousand and one, one thousand and two, one thousand and . . ."

There was a bullwhip crack. The main parachute opened and he was jolted violently in his harness. It knocked the wind out of his lungs. He clung to his shroud lines and floated at a gentle ten miles per hour the remaining two hundred fifty feet to earth.

The sand was as soft as feathers. But out of habit, he broke his fall by rolling over on his shoulder and onto his knees. Before he could haul in his parachute, Khattab was there, unbuckling the harness and folding the air out of the billowing silk.

"Nicely done, sir," Khattab said.

In his moments of greatest excitement, Khattab took refuge in his own peculiar imitation of British understatement. Before the war, the Khattab family had been dragomen, or guides, to British tourists, and they had acquired a half dozen English phrases that, they believed, encompassed the entire gamut of foreigners' emotions.

"If I do say so, sir, nicely done."

But Albright could see that Khattab shared his exhilaration. It was reflected in his dark, expressive eyes. Khattab was his suffragi, yes, but he was more than the punctilious servant who woke up Albright every morning with a hot cup of tea and who polished his leather belts and laid out his uniforms. Khattab was a kindred spirit, a friend as only an Arab could become a friend. Empathetic, devoted, loyal.

Albright pulled the elastic bands from his wrists and ankles. "Khattab," he said, "it flew like a dream. We built ourselves one helluva Camel." He let out a whoop. "When we get home, I want you to put some champagne in the frig. This calls for a celebration."

"It's kind of you to say so, sir," Khattab said. "However, with your permission, I made other arrangements for you."

The way he pronounced *ah-rain-ja-ments* made Albright look toward the jeep. There, running toward them through the ankle-deep sand, was Khattab's other arrangements: Philippa Taylor.

She was wearing a long white dress and a bright green scarf in her hair and she looked, as always, stunning. Philippa Taylor was tall and graceful and she was good at things like tennis, waterskiing, small talk, and mixing gin and bitters. Her only problem—*their* only problem—was that she herself didn't mix.

Philippa was the daughter of a British civil servant, long departed, address unknown, and Mme. Badia, proprietress of the Casino de l'Opéra, Cairo's most respectable whorehouse. Philippa had inherited from her father the most exquisitely chiseled Caucasian features, from her mother a skin the color of the Nile at flood. Her mother had sheltered her as a child, sent her to the best available schools in Cairo, and made sure that she spoke English like a duchess. Philippa had never stepped foot inside the Casino de l'Opéra.

It didn't make any difference. As far as Cairo's English-speaking society was concerned, Philippa Taylor was *unacceptable*. She was a *Gyppo*, British colonial slang for Egyptian. Albright couldn't take her to the Gezira Turf Club to watch the afternoon cricket matches from the shaded veranda. He couldn't take her to the parties given by the British resident. When they were together, he was as much an outcast as she was.

He knew it pained her, but Albright had grown accustomed to feeling like an outsider, a permanent alien, and Philippa was, in a way, proof of his separation, his detachment from the world.

They had been sleeping together for almost two months now but, although she always seemed to want him and was glad to share his bed, she was in her pleasant, upbeat way really quite distant too. He knew that she never experienced a full orgasm. She was warm and affectionate and, most of the time, seemed close to letting go, but she never quite did. Something always stopped her. Something held her back. Albright wished he could help her, but he didn't blame himself and, secretly, he really didn't mind.

Otherwise, they were fine. They liked each other's company, laughed at each other's jokes, and knew that when the war was over they'd never see each other again. Love, for both of them, was a fleeting, impermanent, don't-count-on-it-forever kind of thing. A mutual convenience. Neither of them felt used.

She embraced him and whispered into his ear: "You fool. You almost killed yourself. I thought that beastly parachute would never open. You made me die a thousand deaths." She kissed him again. "But you were marvelous."

"I just wanted to see how much you cared," he said.

"Oh, Alex," she pouted. She seemed genuinely disappointed. "You *know* how much I care."

"I was just joking," he said defensively. He felt uncomfortable whenever she became serious, or pretended to become serious. "Let's go get some ice cream at Groppi's." It was the code phrase he used when he telephoned her to come to his apartment at Shepheard's Hotel.

"Is that all you were thinking about while you were falling through the air?"

"Nothing else. The lack of oxygen up there can make a man very sexy, you know."

"You're incorrigible," she said. "I'd love to go to Groppi's, darling, but we can't."

"Why not?"

"Because it's almost five o'clock. You remember, you're invited to dinner at the residence at six-thirty and we decided that this time you really should go."

"I've changed my mind. I want to be with you. I'll call and make some excuse."

"That's very sweet and I'm touched," she said. "But this time I'm afraid you can't."

"Of course I can. The resident can stuff it."

"Not tonight," she said, looking at Khattab.

"What's with you two?"

"Our friend, Khattab, couldn't summon the courage to tell you, darling, but there's a message in your box at Shepheard's that a special guest of honor is coming tonight."

"Who?"

"Your very own boss. General Donovan."

Wild Bill Donovan in Cairo? It didn't make sense. The old man was a restless character, always in motion, always popping in on his OSS agents in the field to boost their morale and receive firsthand briefings. But Donovan had no business being in Cairo. He was a shrewd bureaucrat who knew the value of good public relations, and he was always looking for the main chance. He had scored a big success for the OSS with "Operation Torch"—the North African invasion—and then he had put all his considerable energy and talent into preparing the landings in Italy. Right now, Donovan should have been focusing hard on London, where the Allies were gearing up for the biggest show of all—the invasion of France.

Cairo had long since become a sideshow—and a British sideshow at that. The small OSS operation in the Egyptian capital was presided over by a former vice-president of the First National Bank of Boston and his executive officer, a man who in civilian life had been a senior account executive at the J. Walter Thompson Advertising Agency. Not exactly the OSS's first-string team. Their main job was to run air-supply operations to partisans in the Balkans and provide logistic backup to the British. It was the British Secret Intelligence Service, SIS, that had been given the Middle East as its exclusive sphere of influence for clandestine activities.

SIS jealously guarded its imperial sphere from the Yanks of the OSS.

So Donovan was probably just passing through on his way to somewhere else, Albright thought as Khattab drove them back to Cairo. Still, Albright was annoyed. He had no desire to see Donovan, no desire to talk to him, and absolutely no desire to make excuses for his behavior in Tangier. Donovan probably still harbored a grudge against Albright for blowing the whistle on the shabby outcome of "Operation Torch" and for then trying to resign from the OSS. And Albright could never forgive Donovan for the betrayal of the "Twelve Disciples." Death or dismissal might be the only way out of the OSS, but there was nothing in the rules that said Albright had to be pleasant to Major General William J. Donovan.

The drive into Cairo led them past Mena House, the great Moorish hotel whose famous English rose gardens bloomed on the edge of the desert. The Nile rippled with high-masted "butterfly" boats. At the far end of the bridge, a policeman dressed in starched whites and a pith helmet waved them stiffly on and they entered the city at dusk—the street lights painted a deeply muted blue for the duration of the war, the minarets silhouetted in the sunset, the *muezzin* calling the faithful to prayer over public address systems. The afternoon siesta was over and once again Cairo had become a vast hubble-bubble of noise. Trolley cars strung together in trains of twos and threes roared down Avenue Ibrahim Pacha—men, women, and half-naked children clinging to their sides and perched on their roofs. Dyspeptic camels groaning under their loads and sleek black limousines, concealing ladies of the harem in their flimsy white veils, crept at the same pace through the clogged street. Everyone who had a horn in his car or a bell on his bicycle used it, and those who didn't just shouted.

The sidewalks were aswarm with a vast congregation of different nationalities. Azharites, from the great religious university of Cairo, in black caftans and white turbans. Jews in broad-brimmed fur hats. Greeks and Italians and Cypriotes in western suits. Young British secretaries and shopgirls in beautifully tailored linen dresses. Dragomen in red tarbushes and brilliant rose-colored scarves over their spotless robes. British soldiers in khaki shorts and shirts and befeathered tam-o'-shanters. Their officers in plum-colored jodhpurs.

The riot of color and noise reached its peak in front of Shepheard's Hotel across the street from the white-washed wooden Opera House. In front of the hotel awning was drawn up a motley fleet of armored cars and Army trucks, dilapidated taxis and donkey carts, Rolls-Royces and Cadillacs flying the insignias of generals and air marshals. On the sidewalk, newsboys with dirty bare feet hawked the New York *Tribune*, London *Daily Mail*, and a local weekly called the *Sphinx*. A Circassian with haunting gray-blue eyes, light coffee-colored skin, and sharp, regular features put his performing baboon through its tricks—an endless series of somersaults on a circling donkey. Out of a sense of decorum, the baboon was dressed in a pair of red flannel trousers. Vendors had strewn the sidewalk with crimson velvet cloths on which they displayed their wares: postcards, beads, scarabs, toothpaste, tinned corned-beef hash from Virginia, Michigan oatmeal, big round red tomatoes, British cigarettes, resplendently hand-tooled camel saddles.

Albright kissed Philippa and told Khattab to take her home. He walked up the front stairs of Shepheard's, past the little round tables and white wicker chairs on the terrace, and entered the enormous octagonal reception hall. The light inside was filtered through stained-glass windows and exotic lampshades. Sounds were dampened by thick Oriental carpets. He retrieved his room key from the Swiss concierge and took the open, grille-work lift to the third floor. He was looking forward to sipping a cool gin and bitters in a hot bathtub, and he only hoped that Shepheard's hot-water boilers hadn't broken down again tonight. When he opened the door, he immediately realized that the bath, at least, would have to wait.

He had company.

3

Sitting in facing armchairs in the drawing room were two men. On the left, dressed in summer tans, was General Donovan. He looked as cherubic, avuncular, and as wily as ever. There was a suggestion of a double chin above the half-Windsor knot in his necktie. A half-finished glass of tomato juice was on the table beside him.

The dark young man on the right wore a nondescript pinstriped suit and, if such a thing was possible, an even more nondescript expression on his face. He was pleasant-looking in a melancholy sort of way. Wavy dark-brown hair, a thick straight nose, bright black eyes. His glass stood empty next to an ashtray full of cigarette butts.

"There you are at last," Donovan said, getting up slowly from his chair. "How are you, Alex? It's so good to see you. You're looking better than I expected."

They shook hands.

"Let me introduce you to a British colleague," Donovan said. "This is Mr. Philby. He's with Broadway."

"How d-do you d-do," Philby stammered.

Broadway was the nickname for the British Secret Intelligence Service, whose headquarters were the Broadway Buildings across the street from St. James's Park in London. Harold Adrian Russell Philby, though only thirty-two years old, was the head of the anti-Communist section of British counterespionage. Everyone knew him as Kim Philby. Neither Donovan nor anyone else, however, suspected that he had other employment. Kim Philby was—and had been for more than a decade—a Russian spy.

"Have you g-got any m-more wh-whisky?" Philby asked Donovan.

"Of course," Donovan said.

"S-splendid," Philby said, handing him his glass.

Donovan walked over to the bar in the corner near the shutters and began mixing drinks. "Mr. Philby and I just arrived today from London," he said. "I saw your father before I left and he asked me to send his regards. He's turned into quite a Lothario, your father has. This new American wife of his—what is she? The third? The fourth?"

"Fifth," Albright said, accepting the glass from Donovan.

"Fifth! My God. I don't know how he does it. I certainly couldn't compete with him. But then, we Irish-Catholics aren't supposed to try."

For all his charm, Donovan must have known that he was probing a painful wound. After Albright's mother died of cancer in a Budapest hospital ten years ago, his father began revealing a side of his character that Alex had never seen before. There were women, mostly young, mostly very pretty, mostly flashy Hungarians with polished long nails who looked as if they owned beauty salons. And his father's women usually came mixed with cases of champagne and large, loud parties. That last year in Budapest—when Alex was eighteen—was one continuous round of embassy parties; and rather than witness the drunken revels, Alex would often flee to the home of a Hungarian classmate. Before

Alex went off to Yale, his father married one of those Hungarian ladies with the lustrous red nail polish. The marriage, he learned in a letter, lasted just under six months. Three more marriages—another Hungarian, a Frenchwoman, and an American—were eventually to follow.

Donovan's method was obviously intended to expose Albright's vulnerability and put him on the defensive. It didn't work. Albright had heard that Donovan himself was a notorious womanizer, that he had more to hide in his personal life than in his clandestine activities with the OSS. Donovan was just more discreet than Albright's father, that was the only difference.

"Come sit down and tell me how you like Cairo," Donovan said. "I'm told that it's the ultimate in the velvet rut, made to order for lotus-eaters." It was another subtle dig. "That's not exactly what I had in mind when I sent you here, you know. That wasn't part of my plan."

"I wasn't aware that my transfer here was part of a plan," Albright said.

Philby rose from his chair and went over to peer out the shutters.

"We c-came all the way from London to m-make you a p-proposition," he said. "We thought it m-might interest you."

He didn't sound as if he was trying to be very convincing, yet there was something appealing about his restraint.

"I'm not interested in propositions," Albright said.

He thought he detected Philby make a slight shrug of his shoulders as he mixed himself another drink at the bar.

"I think you'll feel differently after we explain this proposition," Donovan said. "It's potentially the most important hazardous mission of the war. It involves the lives of literally hundreds of thousands of people and it could have an immense bearing on the postwar boundaries of Europe. You'll be given total charge, both politically and militarily, so there's no danger of . . ."

"Betrayal?" Albright said.

"That wasn't the word I was searching for," Donovan said. "I was about to say that since it'll be your show, you'll be able to call the shots from start to finish. All the shots. You'll have complete control."

"I think," Philby interjected, "that I should s-say two things be-fore we lay any m-more of our c-cards on the table."

As he spoke, Philby's stutter seemed to become more and more painful. He convulsively clenched and unclenched his right hand in an effort to articulate his words. His lips worked frantically around the stuck consonants. Yet throughout the struggle, he managed to maintain a warm, winning smile.

"Firstly," he said, "I'm t-terribly fond of your father. He's doing a b-brilliant job of work helping p-plan for the invasion of Europe. Eisenhower's fortunate to have him. B-because of the high-risk n-nature of this operation, I felt m-morally bound to discuss it with your father as a friend. And I'm obliged to inform you that he is m-most k-keenly op-opposed to your accepting this assignment.

"Secondly," Philby continued, "this operation involves a p-para-chute jump behind enemy lines under the m-most dangerous c-conceivable conditions. I know of your reputation as an experi-enced p-parachutist and an accomplished linguist. I'm c-confident that if anybody c-can carry off this affair, you c-can. B-but if you accept the assignment, you'll be p-placed in charge of a group of civilians who have never experienced c-combat and who have n-never jumped from an aircraft in their lives."

"Anything else?" Albright asked.

"Yes, just one m-more thing," Philby said. "I c-can tell you the country into which you would be p-parachuted. Hungary. The ob-objective of the assignment is B-b-budapest."

Philby sat down and unclenched his hand.

"Alex," Donovan said, placing his hand on Albright's shoulder, "you can't refuse. You're perfect. We need you."

Albright looked at Donovan, then across the room at Philby. He felt caught between two opposing forces, two emotions, two gut feelings. He had, he thought, reached his own personal region of terminal velocity.

4

Donovan waited until after dinner to spring his next surprise. They had gathered to watch a movie in the library of the British residence. The room was one of those beautifully ugly sets created by the nineteenth-century designers of the British Empire. Moorish arches. Fluted French furniture. Huge upholstered valances with fringed drapes sweeping to the floor. Walls paneled in dark oak, every square inch covered with intricate Arabesque carvings and inlaid Islamic ceramics. Oval Renaissance ceiling frescoes depicting nymphs and satyrs in violent erotic encounters. Massive chandeliers. A collection of mounted scimitars that had been captured, according to a brass plaque, by General Horatio Herbert Kitchener from the dervishes of the Sudan.

A pair of tall black Nubian waiters in spotless white caftans, bright sashes and tarbushes drifted through the room offering cigars and after-dinner drinks. Brandy for the British resident, an enormously fat man with a small, boyish head that seemed to sit like a trick photograph on top of his body. Scotch and water for Kim Philby who had consumed too much wine at dinner, though it was hard to tell whether he was drunk because of the constant spastic motions that punctuated his stuttering conversation. Tomato juice for Donovan.

Donovan put down his glass and opened a large handworked wooden box next to the movie projector. He removed an object wrapped in a chamois cloth and handed a Colt .45 and a full clip of ammunition to Albright.

"What's this about?" Albright said.

Donovan didn't answer. With visible effort, he lugged an overstuffed black leather briefcase to the other end of the room and propped it against the paneling.

"There's twenty pounds of sand in this briefcase," he said. "Now, Alex, I want you to take a good close look at that gun and then empty the clip into the briefcase."

The gun felt warm from Donovan's embrace.

Albright wrapped his index finger around the trigger guard and shoved the full magazine into the butt. He pulled back the breech slide, chambering the first cartridge. Then he released the thumb safety, pointed the square-tipped barrel at the naked lovers cavorting on the ceiling, and slowly lowered the heavy pistol until his right wrist hooked firmly over his left forearm.

His target shimmered above the sights like a distant mirage.

The three men around the room tensed. Waiting. Set to flinch. Anticipating the explosive assault and brilliant powder flash.

Deep breath. Hold it. Steady. . . .

But Albright's hand wouldn't stop quivering. He took another breath, inhaling deeply, absorbing that intimate association of smell and gun.

Once a gun has been fired, he thought, it comes to resemble an old woman. It never loses its distinctive odor, no matter how many times you clean it. The big boxy gun balanced in his right hand smelled like a .45-caliber Colt Government Model Automatic Pistol. Not anything like its German cousin, the Walther P-38, which struck the olfactory nerve with the scent of iron filings soaked in graphite. The Colt .45 had a sharp, acrid, disreputable smell. Like an old coin in a greasy palm. It reeked of usable power.

Albright felt himself gradually begin to relax. The barrel was now perfectly still. He started to squeeze the trigger.

This particular gun not only smelled familiar. It felt familiar. It had a cool plastic stock. A smooth blue-matt finish emblazoned with a medallion of a colt rearing up on its hind legs. Fixed sights, front and rear. Stirrup trigger scored to improve the grip. Double safeties. The only visible difference between it and dozens of other Colts that Albright had handled was its curious serial number: "X-1." Which meant that, despite its smell and heft and feel, it was *not* a standard-issue Colt. It was an experimental model, the first off the line.

One of Donovan's deadly inventions. Everyone in the OSS had heard about Donovan's addiction to gadgets. Under his prodding, the armorers in Research and Development had designed an arsenal of trick bombs, electric-eye train derailers, wheat-dough explosive powder, high-altitude booby traps, pocket-watch pistols. . . .

"X-1." An experimental model. Death delivered in a slightly altered form. Albright continued to compress the trigger.

Recoil.

Impact.

Sand pouring out of huge hole in briefcase onto polished parquet floor. Smiles from spectators. But something was missing.

There hadn't been a sound.

The .45, which usually made an unholy racket, had discharged its bullet in total silence. There hadn't even been the faint *plup* of a gun equipped with a conventional silencer. The only thing Albright had heard was the click of the hammer striking the firing pin.

"Go ahead, go ahead," Donovan urged. "Don't stop now."

It was hard to believe. Albright inspected the gun again, then fired six more times in quick succession. Six eerily silent shots. Demolishing the briefcase. As a boy on his father's Connecticut farm, Albright had fired air pistols that made more noise.

Donovan was beaming. "What do you think of that!" he said.

"M-m-marvelous," Philby said.

"Sneaky little bugger, isn't it?" the resident said. "But how does it do it?"

"Internal silencer," Donovan said. "Caseless cartridges. Plastic powder. It's the most amazing advance in ammunition design I've ever seen. And my R and D boys did it without sacrificing any velocity. The bullet can still penetrate an inch of pine at fifteen feet."

Donovan sifted through the mound of sand and shredded leather and dug out the seven slugs. He dropped them, one at a time, into Albright's hand. As they fell into his upturned palm, they made a little hollow noise—*clickclickclick*—like the gun.

"It's powerful," said Donovan. "Accurate. Swift. Sure. Deadly. And completely silent."

Clickclickclick.

"The ideal weapon for an assassin."

Albright fingered the spent, slightly misshapen bullets. Then it suddenly dawned on him. *The crazy son of a bitch wants me to kill somebody.*

Who?

He was stunned by the preposterous implication of his own question. What the hell was the difference who? He was a staff officer, not an operative. And there was a crucial distinction. The OSS had a small cadre of men who were trained for that line of work. Albright had met many of the members of Executive Action. They were cut from a special pattern. Strange, silent, fastidious men whose muted neckties invariably matched the color of their socks.

It wasn't Albright's thing. He had never murdered anyone in

his life. Ordered others to kill, sure. Watched it done once or twice, even. But done it himself . . . *personally* . . . no. He had never felt the least desire to try.

"If you're thinking of me, you've got another think coming," he told Donovan. "Why don't you get Mother?"

"Mother's tied up on something else right now," Donovan said.

"Then what's wrong with Jojo?"

"If you need the sensitive touch, you don't put Jojo on it. He knows only one speed. *Vite.* Jojo wouldn't be right for this particular show. Anyway, Jojo's got his hands full back in Washington looking after internal security."

"What's so special about this show?"

"I'll explain while we watch the movie," Donovan said. He motioned to the British resident, who switched off the lights and started to roll the film.

Albright braced himself for a typically slick OSS show-and-tell. Instead, the screen was flooded with the credits for *Hollywood Canteen,* a sappy musical about how all the contract players on the Warner Brothers lot were doing their bit by entertaining GI's on sick leave. Robert Hutton played the clean-cut boy with the two-week pass, and he gee-whizzed and oh-my-goshed his way through a series of introductions to the big-name stars. "I thought you were hungry," Barbara Stanwyck asked him. "I was, ma'am," Hutton replied, "but my stomach sort of jumped into my heart when I saw you." Ten minutes into the movie, Hutton and his dream girl, Joan Leslie, fell in love while the Andrews Sisters serenaded them with "Gettin' Corns for My Country."

Donovan eased himself into a chair beside Albright and said: "The customs inspector in the Azores always insists on having a little look-see at the films we fly over from the States. So we bury our stuff in the latest Hollywood movies. . . . Well, I guess we'd better get started. . . . Would you mind turning off the sound, please?"

Roy Rogers went mute in the middle of "Don't Fence Me In."

Staring at the silent screen, Donovan asked Albright: "What do you know about the situation in Hungary?"

"Not much. Just that some advanced Russian patrols have reached the Jablonica Pass in the Carpathians and are preparing to invade."

"And . . . ?"

"And that we've got some kind of secret understanding with the Hungarians that as soon as Allied units reach their borders they're supposed to pull out on Germany's side and sue for peace."

"Supposed to, but aren't going to," Donovan said. "The Germans got wind of our little deal. Hitler's started moving troops into Budapest."

Donovan took a folded piece of paper from his inside breast pocket and handed it to Albright. "We . . . that is, British intelligence intercepted this message from Himmler a couple of weeks ago."

The message was typed on OSS code stationery and stamped EYES ONLY. Albright read it in the reflected light of the movie screen. It said: "Send down to Hungary the master in person."

Albright looked at Donovan. "Who's the master?"

Philby's voice answered from the back of the darkened room: "A ch-chap by the n-name of Eichmann. Adolf Eichmann."

On the screen, Patty, Maxine, and Laverne broke into a silent tap dance. Suddenly they vanished and the film spliced into a shot of a chalkboard covered with coded numbers, which Albright immediately recognized as belonging to the Intelligence Photographic Documentation Project of the OSS's Field Photo Branch. This was followed by a grainy landscape that had been filmed, Albright estimated, from an altitude of seventy-five hundred feet through an iconoscope.

"This film was taken by one of Hap Arnold's recon units three days ago," Donovan said. "The German military column you see here has just crossed the Austrian border into Hungary. Our research and analysis people estimate that the column is three miles long. That's a helluva lot of trucks when you think of how Germany is desperately short of transport. But this outfit has been given top priority clearance by both the Reich Security Head Office and the Gestapo, IV-B-4. It's been designated *Sondereinsatzkommando Eichmann*. Special Operation Group Eichmann."

The Andrews Sisters flashed back onto the screen again, pompadours shaking, sequined blouses jiggling, grinding out the finale to their number. The resident shut off the projector and turned on the lights. Philby rubbed his eyes.

"It'll be a job of work," he said. "But we think we c-can p-put a t-team in p-place in B-budapest b-by J-june. July at the latest. That would still be in t-time, by our c-calculations, to save m-more than half a million p-p-people."

Albright walked over to the resident, who was rewinding the film, and dragged his palm against the wobbling front reel. It stopped dead and the celluloid snapped apart where it had been spliced. Albright played out about a yard of film, held it up to the light, and peered at it.

Something was fishy, he thought. Eichmann had been slaughtering Jews for six years, at the rate of nearly a million a year. Almost six million Jews. Now Eichmann had embarked on a little mopping-up operation against the last intact Jewish community in Europe, and Donovan was in a lather to stop him. A bit late, to say the least.

"Question," Albright said. "Why the sudden pang of conscience over a few hundred thousand Jews? We've never lifted a finger before to save them. We haven't bothered to bomb the rail lines to the gas chambers. We haven't tried to intercept the deportation trains. We haven't made an effort to organize resistance in the camps. What makes the Hungarian Jews so special?"

He cranked the handle of the front reel and the film flapped in the heavy silence.

"I didn't realize that you'd become such a cynic, Alex," Donovan said.

"I've had lessons from a master. The master himself, you might say. Or maybe you've forgotten North Africa? Or the Disciples? You know, I've got to hand it to you, General. I mean, coming to me like this with your new toy gun and your cock-and-bull story about the Hungarian Jews. It takes nerve. Because I don't believe you give a flying fuck about the Hungarian Jews. . . ."

"Now just a moment," the resident said, dragging his great bulk out of the chair, his face even more boyish-looking now that it was flushed with outraged British decorum. "I insist."

"That's all right," Donovan said. "Let him get it off his chest."

The two men stared at each other across the room, directly under the frenzied gaze of a beautifully painted nymph. Albright found that Donovan was a hard man to stare down. He had the kind of ambivalent pale-blue Irish eyes that were able to communicate two opposing meanings at the same time. *Trust me . . . trust me not . . . trust me . . . trust me not. . . .*

"One thing you should know about me is that I never forget anything," Donovan said.

He reached over and scooped the bullets out of Albright's hand and dropped them into the chamois cloth. He had been waiting all evening for Albright to explode and he was secretly glad that it had finally happened. For it was one of Donovan's basic convictions that whether in war, in the practice of the law, or in the craft of intelligence, a public display of anger was a public admission of weakness.

"There's a little story I want to tell you," he said to no one in particular. "A couple of months ago, Tom Dewey came around and asked me what I thought about his chances of stopping Roosevelt from winning a fourth term. Now you've got to remember that Tom and I go back together in New York Republican politics longer than either of us cares to remember. But I told him that he was out of his mind to run because Franklin's unbeatable. And do you know what he said? He said that the men in his swimming-pool cabinet, fellows like Herb Brownell and Elliott Bell, are convinced that before this campaign's over the President's going to start looking very vulnerable."

He closed the lid of the gun box and scratched the back of his head. It was a gesture he had seen Darrow use in a summation before a jury. People forgot that Donovan was a skilled trial lawyer. One of the best in New York. He knew how to build an argument. The thing was not to rush it. To let the pauses work for you. To allow your listeners to fill in some of the blank spaces themselves.

"There's the matter of the President's health," he said. "To be perfectly candid, Franklin Roosevelt isn't a well man, and the Dewey people know it. The reports we've done at OSS talk about circulatory problems. His doctors want him to take it easier. But it's hard for him because he's worried about Eisenhower's plans for the invasion of France. Ike's run into a snag and he's going to have to delay the Channel crossing. He's had technical problems with getting special amphibious equipment, he's had military problems with Montgomery, and God knows what else. I still think he can pull it off, but Dewey's advisers are predicting a tremendous political backlash at home if Ike falls on his face."

Donovan walked over to Albright and grasped his arm above the elbow. His eyes flashed in their most convincing you-can-trust-me Irish way.

"One of the Germans' greatest weaknesses has been their obsession with what they call the Jewish question," he said. "If we can pull off this operation, Alex, if we can launch a major Jewish uprising in Budapest, if we can create a psychological diversion on Germany's eastern flank and relieve some of the pressure in the west where Eisenhower's betting all his marbles—if we can do that, it would be a tremendous OSS achievement. It could help turn the tide of this war. And it would go a long way toward helping re-elect a great American President."

"You left out one thing," Albright said.

"What's that?"

"The gun. Who's the gun for? Who's the hit?"

"I can only tell you that if you tell me you're interested."

Albright had to admit that he was tempted. It wasn't so much the chance to save the Jews of Hungary that attracted him. It was too late to pretend that much could be done for the Jews. And Albright himself had . . . well, mixed feelings about Jewish people. Not that he considered himself anti-Semitic or anything like that. It was just that he had always thought of Jews as . . . different. Separate. Not like him.

No, it wasn't the Jews and it wasn't even Roosevelt. His father, when he was American ambassador in Budapest, had once taken Albright to meet the President, but all he could remember was Roosevelt's incredibly large head and the leg braces propped up against the big desk in the Oval Office.

What intrigued Albright was the chance to salvage for himself something from this war, the chance to feel once again that his life wasn't a spiritual vacuum. Until tonight, he was convinced that the war had passed him by, just as surely as its dreadful throb of excitement had evaporated from the atmosphere of Cairo. He realized that this Budapest mission, with its grand strategic design and its immense stakes, was his last chance to get back in. And this time he wouldn't be anybody's disciple. He would be in it for

himself. He would put himself to the test. Prove that he could
still perform.

Performance. That was what really attracted him. The sheer act
of throwing himself into action. Everybody lived by a private
code, even if they weren't aware of it, and Albright was deeply
stirred by a romantic ideal of the human capacity for *super*human
performance. It drove him to master yet another exotic language.
Or to make that near-suicidal last-second delay before he opened
his parachute during a free fall. And now it drew him toward
Donovan's mission and the challenge of penetrating Nazi security
and assassinating . . . Who?

"I'm interested," he said.

"That's a good enough answer for me," Donovan said.

"C-congratulations," Philby said.

"Now," Donovan said, "let's talk for a moment about Karl
Adolf Eichmann. . . ."

In the past few months, Donovan explained, Lieutenant Colonel Eichmann had reached the height of his powers. Hitler had
given him a citation for his work in the field of extermination and
had just promoted him to Commander of Security Police in Hungary. He had also been authorized by Hitler to make one of the
most extraordinary offers of the war—to ransom the lives of Hungary's 750,000 Jews in return for brand-new American Army
trucks. One truck for every hundred Jews. Altogether, seventy-five
hundred trucks, complete with spare parts and tires. And Eichmann had given his "word of honor" that the trucks would only
be used against Russian troops on the Eastern Front.

"We've passed word to the Abwehr in Stockholm that we're
ready to do a deal," Donovan said. "But we've just got word back
that Eichmann, and only Eichmann, is authorized to make the
trade."

The Allies, Donovan went on, had no intention of going
through with such a deal. But they saw a golden opportunity to
approach Eichmann with the excuse that they wanted to open negotiations.

This is where Albright and his parachute team came in. They
would be trained at a camp in the Libyan desert, dropped into
safe partisan territory in Yugoslavia and make their way across the
border into Hungary. Once in Budapest they would prepare the

underground. Then, Albright himself would make a direct approach to Eichmann, acting as the Allies' franchised truck dealer.

"We'll air-drop a model truck, a deuce-and-a-half, for you to show him," Donovan said. "After that, it should be quite easy for you to win his confidence."

"And once you've done that," said Philby, "you can pick your moment to k-k-kill him."

5

"How about some ice cream at Groppi's?" Albright said.

It was almost half-past eleven at night, long past Groppi's closing time, but the voice of the woman at the other end of the telephone sounded eager.

"I think that's a smashing idea. I'll be there in about twenty minutes."

"Make it fifteen," Albright said.

He didn't mean it the way it came out. Brusque. Like an order.

"I'll do my best, darling."

Albright looked at the delicately curved mouthpiece of the ancient telephone, the words forming in his mind, but he didn't speak them.

"Is there something wrong, darling?"

"No. Why should there be anything wrong?"

"I don't know. I can just tell. It's something about your meeting tonight with General Donovan, isn't it? That's all right. We don't have to talk about it. We can just pretend that whatever it is, didn't happen."

But Albright knew better. He would have to tell Philippa. Maybe not the whole story, but enough of it to make her understand that she could no longer count on their don't-count-on-it-forever kind of thing. He owed her that much.

He snapped on the light in the bedroom and saw that Khattab had laid out his clothing, belt, and shoes for the next day. It was the uniform that Khattab liked best. A beautiful cotton uniform, custom made at Callacot's, the famous Cairo tailors who had dressed generations of English gentlemen. It always felt strange on Albright, as though it had been cut for someone else and just happened to be his size. It fit him like an undeserved compliment.

Next to his bed, the night table was set with a glass pitcher of ice water, a freshly opened pack of Commanders with three cigarettes sticking out of the unfolded tinfoil, and an American matchbook with the inscription: "Eat at the Bluebird, New Iberia, Louisiana."

American matchbooks weren't easy to come by in Cairo. Albright would have to tell Khattab something, too.

There was, just as Albright had feared, no hot water tonight. He doused himself quickly in a tepid shower, put on the beautifully tailored Callacot slacks, wrapped the face towel around his wet neck, and padded barefoot into the drawing room. He made himself a drink. The whisky tasted wretched.

From the terrace, he could see across the palm groves on Gezira Island all the way to the Pyramids silhouetted in the warm yellow moonlight. Occasionally, a searchlight stabbed into the night sky toward the rising moon. He could hear the sound of the orchestra from the Casino de l'Opéra of Mme. Badia across the square and the steady vibrating rhythm of the drums and pipes from the Arab bands in the Darb Tiab slum quarter. Someone passing near Shepheard's was singing, drunkenly and off-key, "Oh, give me land, lots of land, under starry skies above . . . Don't fence me in. . . ."

And then he heard the soft knock on the door.

She was dressed in a lemon-yellow chiffon gown with extravagantly padded Adrian shoulders and an attached monk's cowl that hid most of her face. He felt the sticky-fresh lipstick cling as he kissed her, and for a moment he was enveloped in the scent of jacaranda.

"Drink?" he asked.

She pushed back the cowl, exposing her lustrous black hair.

"Oh, my poor darling, you look absolutely horrid. Was it that bad?"

"Philippa, I want to talk to you."

"I know, darling, but can't it wait?"

She went into the bedroom and by the time he reached the door, her gown lay crumpled on the worn spot in the Oriental rug in front of the bed and she stood before him naked. Her dark body seemed to glisten against the diaphanous mosquito canopy. She was, he thought, the most stunningly *sleek* woman he had ever seen. A smooth, glossy-brown Egyptian princess.

She ran her hands along the sides of his bare shoulders, over the muscles of his back, down his waist, and began fumbling with the button of the Callacot trousers. She pulled him through the mosquito curtain and down onto the cool sheets, and he felt the most excruciating pleasure as he watched her fingers, the color of mahogany with long isinglass fingernails, stroke him to arousal.

A change had come over her. He had only to touch her to bring forth a long, whispering moan. He had never seen her this passionate before.

"Philippa . . ."

"Please, darling, don't talk. Not a word. First, make love to me. I think I can tonight. I really feel as though this time I can."

She clasped him with such greedy force, using both her arms and legs, that he could hardly move inside her. Yet this time she didn't seem to require any motion, any caressing, any technique. His filling presence seemed to be enough. Just a few practically motionless moments . . .

It was her first orgasm with him, and it shook her so deeply that she became a little hysterical, weeping and laughing soundlessly at the same time. She wiped her tears on his forearm.

"I always knew it would be marvelous, but I never realized how marvelous. You're the best lover in the world, darling. You know that, don't you? The very best lover."

It would have been flattering if it had been true. But it wasn't. She had made a solo flight; she had gone and come back alone. He couldn't bring himself to tell her that he deserved no credit for her orgasm.

For him, their final act of love had been a terrible letdown. He had actually felt the sexual fire go out of him just as she had reached her climax, and he had barely managed to hold his erection long enough to come. He realized that he had never wanted her this way—fully responsive, totally committed, passionately in love. Love like this was a burden. It was more than he could bear.

"Philippa . . ."

"Yes, darling, now you can tell me. You're going away, aren't you?"

CHAPTER TWO

LONDON
Sunday, March 26

1

Kim Philby jiggled the key in the lock of his Primrose Hill flat and a matchstick fell out of the doorjamb.

The cleaners had made a drop.

"Impatient buggers," he muttered to himself.

Immediately he swung around to see if anyone had overheard. But he appeared to be alone. Fog obscured the grated cellar windows of the old Georgian townhouse and scudded down Oppidans Road to the deserted corner of Ainger Road. He picked up the match, broke it in half, and put it in his pocket. Then he shoved the suitcase inside and eased the front door shut.

Standing there in the pitch-dark entrance hall, his back against the stained glass, he cupped both hands over his face as if he was about to vomit, and gave vent to a whispering torrent of profanity. The string of curses spilled from his lips without a single stutter.

Behind his persona of upper-class amiability, Harold Adrian Russell Philby seethed inside with loathing and contempt. His stutter was the dam that held back a passionate misanthropy. When alone, the psychic barrier often burst. All men were faggots. All women cows. All nationalities despicable. Even the country to which he owed his greatest loyalty, the Soviet Union, was the object of his bitter, condescending disdain.

This asinine match game, for instance. He considered it terribly chancy. Unprofessional. Worse, it smacked of cheap melodrama. How many times over the years had he urged a change in the system? There were locks that could be rigged with variable signal turns to control the tumblers. Or color-coded receipts from the cleaners. Or simple marks under the cap of the morning milk bottle. But no, the doltish Cossacks in Gorky Street had rejected all his suggestions.

So the basic agent alert remained as it had since the days of Trotsky's Cheka. Bent matchstick: Communicate with your controller. Straight matchstick: Retrieve your drop.

Philby groped his way up two flights of stairs to the bedroom. A pale moonlight bathed the room. His wife was asleep in her customary position—sprawled diagonally across the bed on her stomach, her nightgown hitched up above the waist exposing her meaty white rear end and a dark patch of vulva. He stared at her genitals. It reminded him of a vicious little animal. Yet he willed himself to have an erection, fantasizing how easy it would be to fuck her in her sleep, like an intruder. And she would probably let him do it. The cow.

First things first, he thought. He had to find the *mipu*.

Why did they insist upon calling it a mipu anyway? The Germans called it that—mipu was the Boche abbreviation for *mikropunkt*. When it came to things scientific, the Russians were forever plagiarizing from their worst enemy. Bloody Russian inferiority complex, Philby supposed. He had filed a suggestion to Gorky Street on that, too. Why not use the more stylish British expression? *Duff*. So-called because it could be sprinkled in the punctuation of typed letters like raisins in a plum-duff pudding. Or if that was a bit too arch, then they could use the perfectly simple American word for it. *Microdot*.

The clothes closet had that nose-stiffening combustible smell of dry-cleaning naptha. He pulled out the brown pinstripe suit, laid it gently across the back of the chintz club chair, and scanned the tag hanging from a button. The sloppy handwriting was new to him. There must have been a change of cleaners while he was in Cairo. A small "Q" was scribbled in a corner of the tag. That meant he was to look in the slit of the silk lining of the left sleeve.

It wasn't there.

He felt anxiety creep into his stomach. His attitude of scornful superiority suddenly shifted, turned. What if he couldn't find the damn mipu? There would be hell to pay. In his mind he began to flagellate himself with the words they'd use against him in Gorky Street. *Stammering ninny. Incompetent bungler.* Words he had heard his father use to describe him.

Philby examined the dry-cleaning tag again. Maybe it wasn't a "Q" after all. Maybe it was an "O." He slipped the tips of his fingers under the collar and felt the tiny splinter imbedded in the felt lining. Relieved, he ran the back of his hand across his forehead. It came away damp with sweat.

He dislodged the microdot with a fingernail and placed it in the fold of his handkerchief. He had dropped a mipu once. Lost it in the shag of the rug. That had cost him an official reprimand on his record in Gorky Street and a reduction in pay of two pounds a week. He hadn't dared reveal that the rug was in the children's room, where he kept the microscope.

As Philby entered the cluttered room down the hall, the boy turned in his sleep. A few feet away the girl lay still, on top of her bunched-up covers, a miniature blond version of her mother. Philby went directly to the desk and turned on the illuminating lamp under the microscope. The tiny six-volt lamp cast a spectral light of slightly greenish hue across the bridge of his nose and into the deep sockets of his black eyes.

The microscope had been a present to his son last Christmas. An elementary compound microscope, quite ordinary-looking, the kind found behind rickety glass cabinets in school laboratories all over England. But this one had been made available to Philby with certain important modifications to suit his special needs. It had a semiapochromat 20X objective. A 10X Periplan eyepiece. An aplanatic substage condenser. He racked up the coarse adjustment and moved the oil-immersion lens into position. He placed a small drop of oil on the front of the objective and a smaller drop on the 0.16-mm cover glass over the microdot. Then, using the coarse adjustment, he moved the objective lens down until the oil on the lens made contact with the oil on the cover glass.

The fine adjustment brought the secret message into sharp focus. There were only four words in his instructions:

BETINCK

TWO

THOUSAND

LEB

"*Prick!*" he hissed under his breath. "Bloody thoughtless prick!"

Philby flushed the microdot and the broken matchstick down the toilet, then went downstairs to the sitting room and poured himself a large whisky. This summons from "Leb." He might have known it. Bloody Lebedev. Never gave a chap a chance to catch his breath. Couldn't hold his water until tomorrow. Had to see him straightaway, at 2000 hours. Eight o'clock. Christ, it was already 2300—eleven o'clock. He would have to bathe and shave and then try to find a taxi in this damn blackout. And go to Betinck Street.

He was absolutely fagged out. The flight from Cairo back to London had taken three days. Three body-jolting days of turbulent weather, and mechanical trouble with one of the engines of the Flying Barn Door. Philby had hardly slept a wink. Donovan was a compulsive talker. He kept congratulating Philby on his promotion to the head of Section IX, the hub of Britain's anti-Communist espionage network. Philby was only thirty-two years old, a prodigy in the craft of intelligence, and since this latest promotion everyone assumed that he was being groomed to take over the top job at Broadway.

He and Donovan had a long layover in Lisbon while the engine was being repaired. So they borrowed the British ambassador's emerald-green Rolls, sank back into the soft velour upholstery, and were driven around the city. Gliding through the dappled shade of the spotless, treelined boulevards, Donovan seemed to find it hard to believe that they were back in a continent wracked by war.

"Deceptive, isn't it?" Donovan said as he pushed the button that sealed off the chauffeur behind a thick pane of soundproof glass.

"Deceptive? I d-don't receive your m-meaning."

"Lisbon. All this. It's deceptive. Looks so tranquil, like nothing's going on, but behind the Iberian façade there's a brutal, permanent war of espionage. A silent war. *Our* kind of war, Kim."

"Ah, yes. I see."

"We speak the same lingo, Kim, and I don't mind telling you that I'm worried. About what comes next, I mean. Damn it to hell, Eisenhower hasn't even completed his planning for the Channel crossing and people are already starting to talk about victory. *Peace*, even. As if there was such a thing as peace. It's the grand illusion all over again."

"Well, it's only to b-be expected, what?" Philby said noncommittally.

"Yes, but do you know that I've been asked to draft a memo outlining a program for dismantling the OSS after the war. Can you imagine? No more mail openings. No more break-ins. No more surveillance. No more dirty tricks. Now if that's not madness I don't know what is."

"Rather p-premature, I'd say."

"Premature? It's goddamn dangerous. Listen, before Eisenhower manages to haul his tail to Paris, the Russians will be sitting pretty in Bulgaria, Romania, Poland, East Prussia. Maybe in all of eastern Europe. Maybe even in Germany. If you ask me, Churchill's got it figured right. After we smash Hitler, we're going to find ourselves face-to-face with a new enemy. Soviet Russia."

"Quite so."

"Now you take Stalin," Donovan said, warming up to a subject that was obviously much on his mind. "Uncle Joe understands. I mean, I admire Roosevelt and all that, but in some respects America's being led by an idealistic dreamer. He's not used to the cut and thrust of international power politics. He thinks he can make Stalin listen to reason. Reason! That's a scream. Everyone imposes his system as far as his army can advance. That's reason."

"Surely, Roosevelt understands th-that."

"You'd be surprised. Let me tell you something. This operation we just laid on in Cairo. Albright's thing. If Roosevelt was aware of all the wrinkles, what do you think he'd say?"

"I haven't the v-vaguest."

"He'd piss all over it. That's what he'd do."

"I t-take it you m-mean Roosevelt hasn't b-been b-brought entirely up to sp-speed on the operation."

"Not on your life. . . ."

"B-but he's aware of it."

"In a general sense, yes," Donovan said. "I sent him a memo. But I'm no fool. I didn't go into all the wrinkles. Not its basic anti-Soviet sting. Listen, Kim, you've got to remember that America isn't Britain. I can get away with certain things that you'd never manage to slip through your Cabinet system. My philosophy at OSS has always been the same: What they don't know can't hurt us. And Roosevelt doesn't need to know that I've hatched a little surprise for his friend Stalin."

By now, Philby's heart was racing so fast that he could barely catch his breath. This blithering idiot, Donovan, was spilling his guts. Absolutely incredible. Not to be believed. All Philby had to do was sit and listen, make a few mental notes. And savor the moment, the delicious taste of deception.

"And Eichmann?" Philby asked. "What will Roosevelt say when he f-finds out about the p-plan to as-assassinate Eichmann?"

"Oh, he knows about Eichmann. But Eichmann's only the hare in the dog race. The chance to catch Eichmann and kill him is what's going to make Albright and his team run. The real key to the affair is Count Teleki."

Teleki?

The name didn't ring a bell. Philby lighted a cigarette. Think fast, Philby, think fast. Teleki . . . Teleki . . . It began coming back. Visual images on a piece of paper. A report in the files of Broadway . . .

Count Pal Teleki. Various ministries in wartime Hungarian governments . . . drafted the "Second Jewish Laws" limiting Jewish participation in certain fields of professional and commercial endeavor to 6 percent and narrowing the existing definition of who is a Jew . . . associated with conservative landholding interests and manufactures . . . arrested earlier this year for advocating the withdrawal of Hungary from the war on the side of the Axis . . . as a consequence, his popularity, which had been only modest, soared . . . now considered a Hungarian national patriot . . . a martyr . . . outspoken opponent of both Nazism and Bolshevism . . . just the man to . . .

"T-teleki. J-j-just the man to lead an uprising."

"Exactly," Donovan said as the Rolls pulled up in front of the airport terminal. "I want Teleki to be in charge of a government friendly to the west when the Russians show up in Budapest."

2

Philby bathed with his wife's Floris soap, skipped the shave, put on the brown pinstripe, and was riding past Lord's Cricket Grounds before midnight.

The taxi swung down Park Road into Baker Street and turned into Wigmore Street. He paid the driver and walked the short block to Betinck Street. The party was still going full blast when he arrived at Lord Rothschild's elegant Marylebone flat.

He could identify certain voices over a scratchy record of Bach's *Passaglia and Fugue in C minor*. The writer John Strachey . . . the ubiquitous Noël Coward . . . the art critic Anthony Blunt. In counterpoint to the nasal Oxbridge buzz, he detected brittle Cockney accents. Apparently, the real fun had yet to begin.

The first person he spotted in the jam-packed entranceway was Guy Burgess, who had "borrowed" the flat from Lord Rothschild almost a year ago and had lived there ever since. Burgess was dressed in a blue velvet smoking jacket, a paisley cravat, and a discreet gold earring clipped to his right ear. He looked, Philby thought, like a pirate. An outrageous plunderer. Which was not far from the truth.

"My dear fellow, how delightful," Burgess said. "Do come have a drink. Listen, I want your opinion. Do you see that young chap over there? The one with the broad shoulders and the spot of mud on his shoes? Well, what do you think? Isn't he an *apparition!* I've fallen madly in love with him and I mean to sleep with him tonight if it's the last thing I do."

"Come off it, Guy. I'm not in the m-m-mood."

Philby had little patience with Burgess these days. They had been up at Cambridge together and Burgess hadn't changed an iota. The smart set still considered him terribly, terribly clever. Too clever by half, Philby thought. Well, the smart set could have him; Burgess was one of theirs. The grandson of an admiral. A brilliant conversationalist. Handsome in the slightly effeminate fashion of a silent movie star. A notorious homosexual who delighted in debauching young boys. Impeccable credentials—except for one thing. The smart set didn't know it, but Guy Francis de Moncy Burgess was, like Philby, a Soviet agent. They shared that secret. And something else. They were controlled by the same man. Bloody Lebedev.

"I must see Lebedev," Philby said.

"Robert, oh, Robert. Do come here, dear boy, and meet my friend, Philby. . . . Look at him, Kim. Isn't he absolutely divine."

"D-damn your eyes. I said I came to see Lebedev."

"Really, old boy, I'm not my controller's keeper."

Philby slipped away and entered the main drawing room. It was immense. Robin's-egg-blue walls, gilt moldings. Decorated with fine French antiques, Renaissance masters. And, Philby thought with scorn, the flowering manhood of the English Establishment. Many of the guests, like Goronwy Rees who was on General Montgomery's staff, and Randolph Churchill, the Prime Minister's son, were in uniform. Brian Howard, a mediocre avant-garde writer, was dressed for a costume ball in a harlequin's outfit with high ruffled collar. His friend, Harold Acton, was sitting on the floor with his legs crossed, deeply engrossed in a conversation with Christopher Isherwood, who had shown up in a cardigan sweater full of holes. Philby recognized a pair of producers from the British Broadcasting Corporation and some of his colleagues from Broadway. One of them was a particularly nasty chap from Special Operations Executive, a skinny, baby-faced assassin by the name of Simon Wood.

All of them were quite social, some very rich, perhaps a third to a half promiscuously homosexual, a few with real talent. They ignored the cluster of working-class boys that Burgess had deposited in a far corner of the room under a massive Titian. Later, at the end of the night, after all the black-market whisky and the cocaine had run out, Burgess would no doubt organize one of his famous stripteases. Philby had stayed to witness the buggery just once. It was enough to confirm his opinion of mankind.

Lebedev was nowhere to be seen and Philby wandered through the sprawling flat looking for him. He found him seated at a writing table in one of the back bedrooms, going through a stack of letters and some photographs. The desk lamp cast a circle of light on the green tooled-leather surface of the table, leaving Lebedev mostly in shadow.

Philby had been taking orders from Soviet controllers for almost ten years, ever since he was recruited as a *nash* during his university days at Trinity College. Simon Kremer . . . Filip Kislitsin . . . Boris Krotov. Each one attached to a different set of initials—OGPU, NKVD, GUGB. By this time Philby should have been used to dealing with different personalities and different commissariats within the vast bureaucracy of the Russian espionage organization. But he wasn't.

This latest controller, this Anatoli Lebedev of the NKGB, was cut from a different cloth. He was the best of the lot. And the worst. Philby despised and feared him because bloody Lebedev had turned out to be his controller in more than name.

The Russian looked up at Philby, then back to the letters.

"The prose of King James and Shakespeare in the service of pederasty," Lebedev said. "How wonderful! And how appropriate, too. Just look here, Philby. Look at these love letters to Burgess. From his latest conquest at the Foreign Office. These letters will come in very useful. And these photographs—even better. Blackmail, you see. Burgess has letters and photos like these of several of your friends. All neatly bundled in rubber bands. Very organized. Very useful, yes? Very useful."

"Indeed," Philby said, glancing down at the compromising photographs of one of the men at tonight's party.

"You yourself are not homosexual, correct?" Lebedev said.

"Correct. I was n-never so inclined."

"Too threatening to your delicate ego, eh?"

"N-not-a-tall."

Lebedev smirked at him from the darkness.

"You are what the French call a *naïf*," he said.

"How so?"

"Well," Lebedev said, collecting the letters and photos into two separate piles, "let us just say that you close your eyes to the truth in order to pursue your disillusionment."

"I'm afraid that I d-don't follow your t-train of thought."

"Come, come, Philby, let's not play games. Is it not true that you have a deep-seated hatred for the British ruling class and everything it stands for?"

"Y-y-yes."

Philby felt once again that he was being put through a recruit's interrogation. This happened quite regularly with Lebedev.

"And even as you mock the conventional standards of your own society, isn't it also true that you look upon my country as the repository of the future hope of mankind. Just answer yes or no."

"I have g-great faith in the Soviet model."

"Yes, of course you have. But you have also conveniently chosen to forget the Great Purges and show trials of the Thirties. Our cynical little pact with the Nazis. Stalin's murderous paranoia. His betrayal of the Revolution."

"This is quite ab-absurd. You're trying to p-p-provoke me."

"You think so? That is what I mean about your being a naïf. But do you know something? I distrust naïfs. They are apt to turn on you, to behave independently, to become an infernal nuisance."

Philby had begun to quiver. The spymaster was reduced to a trembling mess of porridge. Stammering ninny . . . Incompetent bugger . . .

"Now," Lebedev said, "tell me what you've brought back with you from Cairo and I'll tell you exactly how much I value you."

In a matter of a few minutes, Philby expertly summarized his trip with Donovan, their meeting with Albright, the mission of the parachutists to Budapest, and Donovan's remarkable admission that he had cooked up a scheme that was the sole brainchild of the OSS.

"And Roosevelt isn't aware of what Donovan is up to?" Lebedev asked.

"Only p-peripherally. B-but n-not its essential p-purpose, which is t-to throw the weight of the west behind C-count T-t-teleki and create a third force. Between the retreating Germans and the advancing R-r-red Army."

"Incredible!"

"I thought you'd think s-s-so."

"So much for the distinction between democracy and totalitarianism. We have our Lavrenti Beria, America has its William Donovan. Two rogue elephants."

Just then, Brian Howard staggered through the doorway in his harlequin's costume. He was either very drunk or doped or both. He led a frightened and equally intoxicated young boy by the hand. The same young boy Guy Burgess had pointed out to Philby earlier in the evening.

Lebedev made a loud noise in his throat.

"Hu-*loo*," Howard said. "Who's there?"

"This room is being occupied," Lebedev said.

"Dash it," Howard said. "Somebody beat us here. A lech can't find a bit of privacy in this damnable place."

The door closed behind them and clicked shut. Philby went over and turned the large brass key in its lock.

"Well, now, Philby, what do you think? Shall we have a little amusement with General Donovan? One good turn deserves another, yes? He sends this Albright and his team to Budapest to free Teleki from prison. But our agents are already in place. A simple signal. *They* get to Teleki first. Eliminate him. And *poof!* So much for the good general's operation, yes?"

"*No.*"

"No?"

"I think there is a b-better solution. One that would be less c-crude."

Philby had chosen his words with care. It was his turn to be smug. He had given the problem deeper consideration than Lebedev. Controllers had a way of becoming arrogant and sloppy. Philby's plan would make Lebedev realize that there was more to their relationship than simply the controller and the controlled. After all, he wasn't like Guy Burgess, entrapping his homosexual lovers with simpering letters and pornographic photographs. Philby had more polish than that. His art, the art of the master spy, was a grand intellectual exercise, not some crude physical activity. The great practitioners of the art, men like Victor Sorge and Allen Dulles and . . . *yes*, Kim Philby . . . they were the true geniuses. Geniuses in the effortless, graceful, bloodless destruction of other human beings, of whole armies, of entire nations.

"Let the Germans d-dispose of T-teleki for us."

"The Germans? I don't understand."

"I'll explain. It would be a simple enough m-matter for the agents of Soviet State Security, our NKGB, either in Stockholm or in Berne to contact the German Abwehr and b-b-burn Donovan's operation."

"I don't understand what you mean by this word 'burn.'"

"It's an American t-term," Philby said. "Meaning to ruin, abort. Here is a c-case in which we and the Germans share a common c-c-cause. To d-dispose of T-teleki b-before the Americans c-can reach him and free him. Let the Germans do our d-dirty work, then b-boast to the world that they have foiled the American p-plot."

"To what purpose?"

"So that Stalin can fly into a rage, c-complain to Roosevelt that the OSS was c-caught red-handed scheming against its Soviet c-comrades-in-arms. Don't you see? It will give Stalin g-great leverage to use against D-donovan and the OSS. If we handle this T-teleki affair with subtlety rather than c-crudeness, it will be the OSS's first and l-last attempt to staunch the t-tide of revolution in eastern Europe."

"A useful idea. Very complicated, but useful. Yes, I like it."

"Th-thank you."

"No, no, it is I who should thank you, Philby. And apologize for what I said before. I was wrong. You are not a naïf."

There was a knock on the door. Philby opened it and found Guy Burgess standing there. Grinning.

"I say, you two," Burgess slurred. "No fair. You're missing all the fun."

CHAPTER THREE

THE LIBYAN DESERT
Sunday, April 2

1

The British resident arrived at the airport half an hour after sunrise. He hoisted his immense bulk out of the Jaguar convertible. He had already sweated through the armpits of his white suit. His small, boyish face was flushed and he wheezed asthmatically in the oppressive heat of the hangar. A pale blue handkerchief, sopping wet, was clenched in one hand, a suitcase in the other.

Albright signed some papers, in triplicate, and the resident handed over the suitcase with the Hungarian forints. Fifty-five thousand dollars' worth of brand-new forints in unvouchered OSS funds.

"Now, then, here's your map," the resident said. "The training camp is located here"—he stained the map with a moist finger—"less than fifty miles south of Cairo. A bit west of El Faiyum. On Lake Birket. You can't possibly miss it. It's marked Jubilee."

"Thanks," Albright said. "Guess I'll be taking off. See you around."

"You have the gun?" the resident asked.

"Yup."

"And the ciphers?"

"Right here."

"Splendid. Everything seems to be in order. Oh, yes, one last thing, Albright. I wonder if you'd mind terribly doing a favor. Running a young lady down to Jubilee in your little airplane. Be awfully grateful, you know."

The resident didn't wait for Albright's answer, but called out, "Ruth, it's all been arranged. You can come. . . . I say, do you need a hand with that?"

"I can manage, thanks," the woman said.

She was carrying a metal splash can, not much bigger than a pocketbook. From the looks of it, Albright assumed it contained her "piano." The SSTR-5. The newest model of the Strategic Service Transmitter-Receiver, with a built-in fifty-foot antenna.

"She's a pianist," the resident explained to Albright in a hushed, confidential tone. "And you know what they say about pianists. Their life expectancy behind enemy lines . . ."

"I never go by the odds," Albright said. "They're always stacked against you."

Albright looked over at the pianist. She was standing a few yards away in the slanting morning sun, tucking the last few strands of her light brown hair inside an aviator's helmet. She twisted her head to fasten the strap, caught him staring at her and broke into a dazzling smile. Her face was as white as the skin on the inside of Albright's wrist. Framed in the oval brown leather, it looked like an ivory cameo that had survived from a bygone age.

The resident had called her Ruth. An Old Testament name. Albright had stumbled through the Book of Ruth once in the original Hebrew, a language he could read but never learned to speak. He recalled, *Wither thou goest, I will go*. . . . To be ruth*less* was to be without the qualities of Ruth—compassion, pity, mercy. Fine attributes in the Bible. Not much use in war.

Still, he had to admit that this Ruth was as lovely as her name. Prominent, almost Oriental, cheek bones. Almond-shaped eyes, gray-blue. Full bowed lips. A sensitive beauty. At least that was the first impression. But a little misleading, he decided. Because when he stole another look, he saw the face of a woman in her early twenties, still in the process of defining her inner character. A cameo with emerging planes of strength, angles of certitude. Sculpted with an elongated, poignant touch of sorrow. Self-sacrifice. The face of an El Greco.

He didn't think they'd get along. She wasn't his type. All that natural beauty mingled with such feeling and lofty purpose made him distrustful. Suspicious. People like that gave him the creeps.

He didn't try to hide his annoyance. This was probably going to be his last flight in the Sopwith Camel for a long time. And he had looked forward to making it solo. The last thing he wanted was company, especially some gung-ho radio operator who dreamed of glory in Morse code.

Noticing Albright's displeasure, the resident said, "Do try to be decent to her, won't you?"

"Cross my heart," Albright replied.

He gave the resident the finger as the plane lifted off the runway.

At twenty-one hundred feet, the Le Rhône engine emitted a loud, lugubrious *buuurp!* and went into a stall. The Camel shuddered, dropped a couple of hundred feet like a dead bird. Then its heavy nose sank beneath Albright's line-of-sight and the altimeter began doing cartwheels. The old wooden biplane dived straight for the desert.

Albright had stalled the plane on purpose. A barnstormer's prank to give his uninvited passenger the heebie-jeebies. He knew it was a dumb move. Childish. Showing off in front of the new girl like Tom Sawyer. And they hadn't bothered to strap on their parachutes.

Then it suddenly occurred to him that somebody like the resident had probably calculated the odds against him too. Had it all figured out. *Pity about old Albright. Can't last more than a few months behind the lines.* Maybe they'd already chosen his replacement. Well, fuck the nearsighted actuaries of the world. They tried to run things by the numbers. He wasn't playing by their rules. He was making up the game as he went along.

The trick about the plane was to wait until it gathered the speed to produce that frightening banshee wail, wait until it looked as though it couldn't be pulled out of its crash dive, wait some more . . . *then* jerk out the choke and spark the engine. The Le Rhône coughed once, twice, but it wouldn't turn over. The spark wasn't making the jump. He tried again and it worked. As soon as he caught the full blast of air from the propeller wash, he hauled back on the stick and the Camel scooped out of its dive, lifting his stomach into his throat. The plane rolled over on its side, onto its back, rolled again, and leveled off.

Albright squeezed the button on the intercom. "You can open your eyes now."

Ruth looked over her shoulder from the front trainer seat and shouted something that was lost in the wind. He held up his microphone, pointed to her console. She fumbled with the button, then he heard her voice crackle in the earphone beneath his helmet.

"I *loved* it! Can you do it again?"

He should have known. She was one of those. The brave, fearless type. They always confused him, women like that. He admired their courage, but at the same time felt cheated by it. Robbed of his role. They were the most interesting women, but also the most elusive. They asked for the most, but not for what he was willing to give. The brave were eligible to live by their own standards and values, but how were a man and woman to play by two different sets of rules?

The Camel skittered over the palm groves and fields, rousing the bent figures of fellayeen in long white gallabiyehs and veiled women in black robes. In a few minutes they were approaching Memphis and could see the gigantic Step Pyramid of Djoser rising in massive tiers on the opposite bank of the Nile.

"Look. Over there on your left." Her voice sounded as distant as a transatlantic phone call. "Djoser's monument. Isn't it fantastic? Almost six thousand years old. Do you know why the ancient Egyptians always buried their dead on the west bank?"

"Why?"

"Because that's where the sun sets. They lived on the east bank and built the pyramids on the west. One of their names for the dead was 'The Westerners.'"

"Go on, I'm listening."

Actually, he was listening to her accent. The pitch, the rhythm, the intonation. He was willing to bet that she was Hungarian. Still, there was a dissonance. His linguist's ear detected another language, something he didn't recognize, sandwiched between her native Hungarian and her accented English. The filling in the sandwich intrigued him. It sounded as though it was close to, but not quite, Arabic.

"The most important ceremony performed in the Step Pyramid was called *heb-sed*," she continued. "Every few years, the Pharaoh was required to run around the courtyard of the Pyramid. The timing and the course were fixed by the priests, and the Pharaoh had to perform the ritual of regeneration. To renew his life and virility."

"Sounds familiar. Like a typical assignment from the OSS."

"What?"

"Forget it."

He followed the compass south, over the wriggling green garter snake of the Nile, catching glimpses of Dashûr, Barnasht, El Aiyat, El Maharraqa. . . . At Philadelphia, he banked the Camel and headed west into the boundless ocher-colored Libyan desert, checking off the fragile oases with the names on his map: Tâmîya, El Rôda, Sinnûris. . . .

She came back on the intercom. "Crocodilopolis! Could we go down and take a look? I've never seen it from the ground."

"Okay," he said.

He set the plane down on a flat strip of rocky moonscape, and they walked a few hundred yards to the ancient site of Crocodilopolis. Tall mounds of debris marked the seat of worship of Suchos, the crocodile-headed water god. This, too, she explained as she conducted him on a Cook's tour of the devastated past.

The sun had risen to a forty-five-degree angle, a hard disc of blinding brilliance that seemed to bleach the desert landscape into a flat reflecting glass and made it hard to see without squinting. There wasn't a tree in sight. Not a smell of life. Just a powdery taste of disintegration on the lips and a weird distant whispering sound, as of wind through leaves. They spent ten minutes searching for the source of the murmuring noise and finally found it.

Obscured behind a high mound on the outskirts of the ruins was a large oval-shaped depression in the desert. It was half-filled with water, crystal clear, tinted blue by the sky. A few stunted bushes, succulently green with white blossoms, clung to the steep sides of the glittering pool.

She seemed enchanted by the setting.

"See any crocodiles?" Albright said.

"No." She laughed. "But I'll go look."

She slid down the embankment to the edge of the water and

there, as he watched from above, she stripped off her blouse and skirt and shoes. In bra and panties, she dove into the still water.

She swam with extraordinary grace, rhythmically, not athletically. In a totally unselfconscious water ballet. She knifed down to the bottom, toes pointed, ankles together, and dredged up fragments of antiquities, tossed them to the edge near her clothing, dove again for more. Before long, she had collected a small pile of treasure and seemed satisfied. She waded out of the pool, hair streaming down her back, shimmering globes of water collecting at her waist and running in golden rivulets over her hips and thighs.

He didn't feel as though she had put on a performance for him. Her every move seemed spontaneous and unaffected. Yet gazing down at her slim, self-sufficient back, he felt shut out, unnecessary. And he was suddenly seized by a cold, sharp resentment. She was so enclosed. Her independence was like a challenge. He bristled with an erotic anger.

She waved up at him. Saw the rough passion in his eyes. Dropped her arm. He felt exposed, so he loped down the sandy bank to her side, forced a smile and put his hand on her wet shoulder. He wanted to regain his sense of poise and self-control. His detachment.

"What'd you find?"

"Just these."

One of the fragments was from a small statue. An armless human torso with the narrow, pointed snout of a crocodile's head. Its worn lower teeth protruded upward, bulldog fashion. It was carved in a richly veined onyx, inscribed with hieroglyphics.

"Let me see," he said.

He studied the picture writing. Many of the ideograms were chipped or eroded, but he could still make them out.

"'Pay homage to the Westerners,'" he read, "'for they are sacred of Suchos.'"

"You can *read* that?" It was more an accusation than a question.

"A little."

"Why didn't you tell me? I feel like a fool. Reciting my schoolbook history of ancient Egypt."

He could breathe her flesh drying sweetly in the sun. But the sexual attraction was evaporating along with the golden globes of water on her skin. And so was his resentment. He was no longer in her thrall. He had reestablished an equilibrium between them.

"That's all right," he said. "It was a charming history."

"*Charming*," she said, as if he had insulted her. "Please. Who would want to be thought charming? And *this* . . ."

She took the crocodile-headed statuette from his hand and tossed it back into the water. It sank quickly, nestled in the mud of the bottom, and disappeared. Into the dim hidden past. Perhaps for another six thousand years.

"Why'd you do that?" he asked.

"Because I refuse to pay homage to the dead. I don't believe in that. Not since Hitler began . . . *peopling* the whole world with the dead."

She began dressing. Her blouse clung to the wetness of her breasts.

"You see, there's no grandeur in death," she said, agitated with feeling. "Not anymore. Not in *our* time."

She collected her pile of shards and fragments from the ruins of Crocodilopolis and started up the embankment.

"Then, what *do* you believe in?" he called after her.

She looked back, surprised that he had asked. She studied his face for a moment before she gave her answer.

"Survival."

"That's not much to go on," he said. "Survival's a matter of chance."

"Then what do you 'go on'?"

"Me? I believe in myself."

"That's not much either, is it?" she said.

2

No doubt about it. They were lost.

On the aeronautical chart strapped to Albright's thigh, the distance from Crocodilopolis to El Faiyum was indicated by less than half an inch of blank space. Blank because the topographer really hadn't known how far it was and had taken an educated guess. Maybe four miles, maybe five. If the chart was right, it should have taken ten minutes of stickwork from takeoff to landing. But by now, Albright had been tooling around over the Libyan desert for almost an hour. And still . . . nothing.

Let's face it. Less than nothing.

Yes. Endless, flat, monotonous, uninhabited, mind-numbing, yellow-ocher nothingness. In all directions, as far as the eye could see, clear to the curve of the horizon. Empty sky, empty desert, an empty feeling in his stomach. Spooky.

Take it easy. Why don't you relax and look at it this way. You're dipping and soaring like a big unfettered bird. Free.

Free from what?

From the shitty nothingball world down there. That's why you like to fly. Right?

Wrong. Right now, I'd just like to know where I am. That's all. Before I run out of gas. I knew I should have installed a radio in this crate. Then I'd know where I am.

Come on, you know where you are. In your Camel with a pretty girl named Ruth up front in the trainer seat. Now cut the crap and fly.

Pretty girl, huh? Listen, that's nothing. I used to know lots of really beautiful girls. Sleek girls from New York who changed their underpants twice a day and their sheets twice a week. I'd meet them in the bar at the Algonquin. Let's see, what's the telephone number of the Algonquin? Murray Hill seven, four four hundred. Of the Stork Club? Plaza three, one nine four oh. The Copa? Templeton . . .

Will you shut up and pay attention.

Right. I'm concentrating.

No you're not. You're whistling. "Mairzy Doats," for Chrissakes. A little grace under pressure here wouldn't hurt, you know.

Sorry. It just slipped out. I'm okay now.

Yeah? So then how come you're thinking about how Ruth looked in her bra and panties? Wet.

I'll control myself. Promise.

But Albright couldn't turn off the generator of his brain. A lot of pilots were that way. They talked to themselves when they flew solo over the desert or the ocean. Especially when they lost their bearings. It was a terribly unnerving experience because, in the final analysis, the goal of every aviator was to achieve that fine balance of *controlled* freedom. And lost meant you were out of control.

So Albright recited old telephone numbers or whistled new tunes or just thought pleasant thoughts. Anything to fill the dreadful void. He knew how difficult it was to find a ship in the ocean or an oasis in the desert. But with the map that the British resident had given him, it should have been a cinch.

You can say that again. Don't look now, pal, but what's that speck on your windscreen?

With a sudden sense of relief, Albright saw it, tiny and green, no more than a distant stain on the floor of the desert. He kept the nose of the Sopwith Camel pointed steadily at the daub of color, and it continued to grow and spread and swell until it flooded over the windscreen and blotted out the parched desert and rose up into the sky like a majestic green citadel.

He had found what he was looking for. El Faiyum. The first of the fabled oases of the Valley of the Nile.

It was actually an extensive plateau, cooled by its height and watered by underground springs. As Albright banked the plane to prepare for the landing, he saw the silvery glitter of streams spreading in all directions beneath a thick carpet of olive trees. At this time of the year, the shores of the lakes around El Faiyum were a pointillist's bed of wild roses and fruit blossoms. He corrected the direction two degrees so that the nose of the Camel threaded between the blue-tiled dome of a large mosque and the copper-green Cross on top of the Roman Catholic church.

He taxied the plane to a hangar, jumped out, and helped Ruth down.

"Thanks for the ride," she said. "For a while there I thought we were lost."

"Nope, I wasn't lost," he lied. "Just thought it would be fun to take a pleasant lazy Sunday-afternoon kind of drive."

"It's really a marvelous airplane. Thanks again."

"Sure. Any time."

There was a strained moment of silence as they stood on the tarmac beside the fragile-looking biplane. Face to face, so close that they could actually feel the coolness of each other's breath. Yet they avoided eye contact. Not ready to risk exposure and hurt.

"Well . . ." she began.

"Look," he said, "I'm not good at beating around the bush. Maybe we could see each other again."

He didn't know if he really meant it. But there was something about her, something very special, and he knew that if he had half a brain he *should* mean it.

"That's very gal-*lant* of you," she said. She was afraid that sounded sarcastic, so she added, "That would be fine," and wondered if *that* sounded too stilted.

"How will I find you?"

"Well, I guess we'll both be at Jubilee for a while," she said. "It's really a rather cozy place for a training base, you know. I'm sure we'll run into each other."

She stuck out her hand and he shook it.

"I'll find you," he said. "That's a promise."

CHAPTER FOUR

CAMP JUBILEE
Sunday, April 2

1

Only his tiny, yellow pig eyes moved.

Otherwise, the guard stood as stiff as a post beside the locked door. A grim totem of death in his polished knee-high boots, black SS uniform, and phallic field helmet.

The object of the guard's rapt attention was a beefy little rooster of a man strutting around the room. Barely five feet tall in the special shoes with the three-inch stacked heels that the shoemaker had made for him. An oversized trenchcoat was caped over his shoulders and the belt trailed along the bare floor behind him.

The buckle scraped concentric circles around the prisoner, who sat slumped on a stool, scratching forlornly at a flaming red Vandyke beard.

"I repeat. We found your one-time pad. With all the codes."

Trenchcoat's raspy voice filtered through the sound system to a speaker mounted in a corner of the ceiling in the adjoining room. The matching dimples on the back of his shaven head were clearly visible to the two men who watched the performance through the one-way mirror.

"Pad?" the prisoner said. "I know about the pads sewn into ladies' garments. Under the arms. To prevent perspiration stains.

My wife always insisted that our customers use removable pads when they tried on garments in the fitting room. But one-time pads? And codes?"

"There-is-no-record-of-such-a-dress-shop-in-Hamburg!"

The entire sentence modified the interrogator's posture of cocky triumph. He hitched up his trousers with his elbows, elevating himself another inch on the balls of his feet. Then in a different tone of voice, dipped in honey but even more menacing:

"Your whole story stinks of fabrication."

"Ah, you don't know how it distresses me to hear you say that," the prisoner said. "Please remember those horrible bombing raids by the British. My shop, my inventory, my fixtures, the hand-lettered sign outside. All gone. Not a trace. How could there be any records? Why, even the municipal branch of the Gestapo was bombed out."

In the next room, Guido DeVita turned off the speaker and drew the curtain across the one-way mirror.

"What do you think?" he asked.

"Your boy needs more practice," Albright said.

"You don't have to be a brain surgeon to see that," DeVita said.

The camp commander at Jubilee was a spare, sharp-featured man with a mane of white hair that fell naturally into a middle part and hung, like slightly soiled angel's wings, over his ears. Thick, jet-black eyebrows arched over the most hypnotic set of icy blue eyes that Albright had ever seen. He appeared to be in his late forties or early fifties, but the skin on his neck was already crosshatched with lines like the fine crazing under the glaze of old porcelain. Albright noticed that each of DeVita's wrists bore a thin snakelike scar that ran from the base of his thumb across the delta of green veins.

"It's only his first time in the tank," DeVita said. "We put everyone in the camp through the simulated interrogation at least three times. The question is, does he have the potential?"

"The first thing I'd tell him is to ditch the beard."

"What for?"

"Two reasons," Albright said. "The bulls in the Gestapo hate facial hair. Especially beards. It makes them even meaner. And the red beard gives your boy a kind of . . . *Jewish* look."

"I'll be sure to tell him that you think so," DeVita said. "It'll give him a good laugh. He *is* Jewish."

"You're kidding."

Albright parted the curtain and took another peek.

"You're *not* kidding. Listen, people are always complaining about how the OSS doesn't have any Jewish agents. But let me tell you something; it's not because our initials stand for Oh-So-Social. There's a reason for it. Ask our psychologists and they'll tell you that Jewish agents get romantic ideas about paying back the Germans. And the first thing you know they're taking unnecessary risks. Acting like martyrs. Jeopardizing the whole operation. I'm not saying I blame them, but I'd find some excuse to wash out red beard."

"That'd be a problem," DeVita said. "If I did that, I'd have to wash out everybody. Starting with me. You see, all of us here at Jubilee are Palestinian Jews."

Allofushereatjubileearepalestinianjews.

At first, the words were jibberish banging against the tympanic membrane of Albright's middle ear. But gradually he sorted them out. Absorbed their incredible meaning.

Ho-ly shit! A campful of Jewish agents. Now that had to take the goddamn prize. And nobody had bothered to warn him.

Donovan! That dissembling sonofabitch. He'd held out on him because he knew what Albright would say. Nothing fucking doing. He should lead an all-Jewish parachute team into Eichmann's sausage grinder. . . . A joke. A bad, unfunny, sick joke.

But Donovan didn't joke. It wasn't a joke when he had sent Albright to North Africa and then betrayed the Disciples. And it wasn't a joke when he had transferred Albright to Cairo to work on the Anglo-American Psychological Warfare Branch and familiarize himself with the underground in Hungary. No, Donovan always had a carefully worked-out plan. Okay, but then why had the chief of the OSS, an organization that was notorious for its iron policy against using Jewish agents behind enemy lines, chosen an all-Jewish team for this Budapest mission? Did Donovan really want this mission to succeed? Or was he setting Albright up for another fall? What was Donovan's real plan?

Using Jews as agents was the tipoff. It wasn't the religious thing or the cultural thing that bugged Albright. He was at peace with himself when it came to the question of Jews. He could look himself in the mirror and admit, without feeling the least twinge of guilt, that he had an uncomfortable feeling about them. Who wouldn't, coming from his kind of background?

Sure, they made him feel a little queasy. But so did Hottentots and Eskimos and Americans who spoke with southern drawls. And what the hell did that prove? Nothing. The point was he did not resent or envy or fear or hate or despise or wish any ill to Jews. Christ, you had to admire them. They got higher grades in school than the Chinese and were faster on their feet than the Episcopalians, and he didn't give a shit if they went to Yale and joined the New York Athletic Club and bought up all the property in Bronxville.

It was just that they made lousy agents.

Everybody knew that.

Jesus, he'd really stepped into it this time.

2

Guido DeVita watched the shock register. The cool self-assurance on Albright's face crumpled into an expression of numb disbelief.

So, DeVita thought, *that's the way it is, is it? Mister tough guy is ready to risk his life to save some Jews, but to work with Jews . . . ah, that's another matter. Stereotype number one: Jews make lousy fighters, ergo, Jews make lousy agents.*

Not that he's anti-Semitic, heaven forbid. Hitler's anti-Semitic, maybe a few Germans are anti-Semitic. But an American? In this day and age? Never!

Ask him. He'll tell you. He admires Jews.

It's just that Jews are too emotional, too passionate, too . . . Jewish . . . to work behind enemy lines.

He got himself into a mess is all.

But the question is how is he going to get himself out of the mess?

A mind reader he wasn't. But DeVita knew exactly what Albright was thinking. Knew it as surely as if the thoughts were flashing through his own head. DeVita had this uncanny ability. Call it insight, intuition, a sixth sense. Whatever. He always knew.

It had nothing to do with clairvoyance or mental telepathy. It came from talent and training. And that extra dimension of human understanding that had made DeVita a good psychoanalyst.

Not just a good psychoanalyst. A brilliant one. Before the war, he was among the most sought-after psychoanalysts in Europe. He had trained in Vienna with Anna Freud, the great man's own daughter, and like most of the early Freudians, DeVita considered psychoanalysis to be as much an art as a science. In those days, it wasn't enough to know about the wayward Id or the double whammies of countertransference technique. If you wanted to hold your own with Freud or Rank or Ferenczi, you had to know practically everything. Anthropology, mythology, folklore, sociology, law, education, even the occult.

DeVita more than held his own, but eventually, as with most of Sigmund Freud's disciples, there was a falling out between De-Vita and the Founding Father. Their last meeting took place early one chilly fall morning in 1936 in Freud's study at 19 Berggasse. DeVita was ushered into the book-lined inner sanctum by the maid. And there, seated behind the desk with its meticulously arranged collection of Greek, Assyrian, and Egyptian antiquities, was Freud. He wore a tweed suit, stiff white collar, and a ready-made black bow tie, and he puffed with obvious contentment on a fresh cigar from the Tabak Trafik shop near the Michaeler Church.

"*Herr Professor*, I've fallen in love," DeVita said.

"Then why such a sour puss?" Freud said.

"Because the woman is my patient."

A fierce frown from Freud. "Extraordinary. Do I know her?"

"Yes. It's Sarah M."

"The American ballerina who danced *Swan Lake* the other night?"

"Yes."

"Hmmm." Freud stroked his neat white beard. "Tell me, my young Italian friend, have you adopted Ferenczi's outrageous kissing technique in your treatment of women patients?"

"Of course not."

"Then," said Freud, "what leads you to think this is love rather than countertransference?"

"Because I respect her!" DeVita blurted out. "Because she's good and noble and incapable of evil thoughts. Because she throbs with vitality, feels deeply about life, and is brave enough to admit her feelings honestly. Because she admires me and respects my work. And, finally, because I find her enormously attractive."

Freud passed the cigar between his lips and, as he pondered DeVita's words, the smoke clung to his beard as if it had caught on fire.

"You face a difficult choice," he said at last. "You can marry Sarah M. and confirm the worst suspicions of those who charge that psychoanalysis is an unscientific doctrine practiced by sexually obsessed madmen. In which case, you would do our movement great harm and I would be constrained to ask you to remove yourself from Vienna. Or, through a process of introspection, you could analyze the deeper reasons for your feelings toward this woman and, I suspect, recognize that they are being used as a rationalization to discredit and hit out at our movement—*and at me personally!*"

Loyalty or love. Freud or Sarah. It was the most difficult decision of DeVita's life. He was a man of absolute principles and passionate commitments, and until then he had never had to make such an agonizing choice. His dedication to science inclined him toward loyalty. His basic Italian nature drew him toward love. The conflict raged inside DeVita for weeks, filled his dreams, tore at his soul.

In the end, Guido DeVita listened neither to his head nor his heart. But to his dreams. That clouded window on the unconscious mind through which the most profound truths are discovered. And all his dreams conveyed the same message: "Go with Sarah! *She* is the affirmation of your life." And remarkably, one of those dreams even told DeVita where to begin afresh with his new wife and psychoanalytic practice. Jerusalem! The city of hope.

It was there that Guido DeVita had tried to take his own life.

3

The contrast between Guido DeVita and Alexander Albright couldn't have been sharper. On the day before Albright arrived at Camp Jubilee, the Italian psychoanalyst had received a copy of the American's OSS "Proso Profile" that traced Albright's life from the moment of his birth to the present. Complete with the raw data on the Rorschach, Thematic Apperception, Wexler-Bellevue IQ, and half a dozen other psychological tests. As well as in-depth interviews with practically everyone who had known Albright from the age of eight.

The American doctors had done their usual thorough job. The workup had been tabulated and charted and graphed as though Albright was an economic statistic like the gross national product rather than a complex human being. Still, when DeVita was done checking the findings, he was satisfied that the American psychiatrists were basically right. There was nothing seriously wrong psychologically with this boy Albright.

Except the most important thing.

Albright's motivations were all wrong.

There wasn't any moral force behind Albright. He was all action, no purpose. A compulsive performer who was out to prove something personal. He didn't believe in anything beyond himself. And in an agent that could be the fatal Achilles' heel. Because when things became nasty, as they had a way of becoming, an agent needed something to fall back on, an extra reserve of courage that went deeper than guts. Faith in an abstract ideal. A *zetz* from the soul.

And there was another thing that disturbed DeVita. They had sent him a Gentile to do a Jew's work. What could a *goy* know or care about the Jewish cause? DeVita's suspicion of Gentiles didn't come from inspired artistry or profound understanding. It was, even he admitted, a pure unadulterated prejudice. Which gave it the force of a zetz from the soul.

DeVita put aside Albright's file, lay down on his narrow cot. He was still thinking about the aloof, uninvolved American, when he fell into a troubled sleep. And gradually, images began appearing on that clouded window into the truth and Guido DeVita began dreaming. . . .

It is Sarah. Sarah wearing her white wedding dress. But what is this? She is being carried over the threshold of their home on a shady street in Jerusalem by a young British lieutenant. Rust-red blood stains the tulle veil and puffed silk sleeves of the dress and is caked between the fingers of the officer as he places her gently upon the leather couch in DeVita's office.

The soldier begins explaining in his clipped cool way the circumstances of the atrocity. Some words filter through DeVita's mind, disjointed words, as if one of his patients is free-associating. "Demonstration . . . Arabs in the street . . . riot . . . troops . . . tragic accident." DeVita's gaze focuses on Sarah's right foot. A shoe is missing, exposing that thin foot with its graceful ballet dancer's arch. . . .

There the dream suddenly stopped, in a freeze-frame of that exquisitely artistic arch, the support of Sarah's life.

DeVita awoke, puzzled. Except for the detail of Sarah dying in her wedding dress, it was hardly like a dream at all. Because everything else was exactly as it had happened in real life. Then what did the dream mean? What was it trying to tell him? And why had he dreamt it on the night before Albright's arrival?

Sitting there in the dark, he pondered the mysterious workings of his own mind. The process of self-analysis brought back more painful memories. Brutal images cascaded before his mind's eye of the day that his wife died during an Arab riot in Jerusalem. . . .

As soon as the British lieutenant had left, DeVita put a record on his Victrola. A Red Seal of Tchaikovsky's *Swan Lake*. Then he stretched out on the couch beside his beloved Sarah and slashed his wrists. His heart pumped the blood out of his body and it mingled with the blood of his wife.

And God had spoken to him as he lay dying.

"You Italians with your melodrama, you make me want to puke," God had said. "Who gave you permission to commit suicide? So what if your wife is dead? So what if the idea of rescuing individual souls with your psychoanalytic skills no longer interests you? So what if the effort to live in this insane world seems trivial?

"Look around you," God continued. "There are thousands of

souls to save, millions of them, Jewish souls being lost every day in Europe and here in Palestine. Even for a sanctimonious *schlemiel* like you, that should be cause enough to live for."

But it wasn't God talking. It was *Gad*. Gad Yacobi, his oldest and dearest friend in Palestine. This man with a face so expressionless that it looked as though it had been anesthetized with Novocain; this Gad Yacobi was a professor of Oriental art at Hebrew University. He was also known to a few close friends as the chief of Mossad. The Central Institute for Information and Espionage. The secret Jewish counterpart of the OSS, Broadway, and the NKGB.

DeVita was inducted into the Institute a week later. He never touched a woman again. It wasn't a rule of the Institute. It was his own doing. A renunciation. He gave up his four-pack-a-day cigarette habit, his wine with dinner, his record collection of Tchaikovsky ballets, his correspondence with the famous Italian psychoanalyst Eduardo Weiss (which he had intended to publish one day), all his personal belongings, all his personal ambitions.

For the first time since he had broken with Freud, DeVita was able to merge his feelings of love and loyalty into a single, unified higher ideal. Zionism. He became the chief recruiting officer for the Institute, the man chosen to pass judgment on who was worthy and who was unworthy to join the Jewish intelligence organization. And later, after the British reluctantly agreed to train Jewish parachutists, DeVita was sent to Egypt to organize the camp at Jubilee and prepare the most important Jewish rescue operation of the war.

Now, the success of that operation was called into question by one man. Alexander Albright.

4

As he entered the room, Albright was immediately struck by two peculiar things. It was as sparsely furnished as a monk's cell. And it was carpeted, wall to wall, in green. Then he realized that it wasn't carpeting after all. He was standing on a floor completely covered with piles and piles of green paper money.

He instinctively shrank back, like someone who has blundered onto a freshly waxed kitchen floor and left a telltale footprint.

"Come in, come in," DeVita said. "Don't worry about the floor. We can't have our agents using brand-new banknotes, so I spread them all over my office and in a few days they'll be as good as old. It's the most efficient way I know of aging money quickly."

They had finished touring the base and DeVita had brought Albright back to his office for a cup of coffee. It turned out to be *ersatz* coffee, but DeVita dressed it up with condensed milk and real sugar. They sat there blowing into the steaming tin cups for a minute or two without exchanging a word.

Finally, DeVita said: "When are you leaving for Cairo?"

At first, Albright wasn't sure that DeVita meant it the way it sounded. But one look into those icy blue eyes told him that he did.

"I take it that's an invitation to go back where I came from," Albright said.

"That's another way of putting it," DeVita said. "You see, I had a strange dream last night about my wife's death and it's been nagging me all day. I happen to be a trained psychoanalyst, and yet I wasn't able to interpret the meaning of the dream. Then, while I was showing you around the base, it came to me.

"The dream," DeVita continued, "was a warning. It reminded me of the loss of my wife, the person who meant the most to me in all the world, the person who stood for everything good and noble in my life. In my dream, she is wearing her wedding dress, which puzzled me until I reminded myself that when I married her I made a moral commitment."

"What's this got to do with trying to get rid of me?" Albright said.

"I'm coming to that," DeVita said. "You see, to the Americans and the British, the Budapest mission may be just a piece in the overall military puzzle of the war. But to us, the opportunity to save Jews is a moral statement. And my dream was telling me that your cynical, hard-nosed approach is likely to upset the moral applecart. You'd rob the mission of its moral purpose. Forgive me, Captain Albright, but you're the wrong man to lead the parachutists."

5

So it was all over before it began.

As Albright moved across the room toward the door, the carpet of crisp new banknotes rustled underfoot. He figured that he was walking out on more than a million dollars' worth of secret unvouchered funds. One hell of a dramatic exit.

But there was no satisfaction in that. Never before in his entire life had anyone told him that he was the wrong man for anything.

Well, DeVita could stuff his moral crusade. Albright didn't want any part of it. He was grateful to be off the hook. He was a free agent again. Free agent was the perfect expression for it. Because this time—this one time—he hadn't fallen for one of Donovan's Machiavellian schemes. It was Albright's victory.

But what the hell did DeVita mean that he was the wrong *man!*

The truth was that Albright didn't feel any lift from his victory. He had been dismissed, discarded, rejected. And he didn't know what to make of it. He simply wasn't used to dealing with self-doubt. It rocked him physically. He actually felt a bit dizzy. There was a ringing in his ears. . . .

Then he realized that the ringing was coming from somewhere in DeVita's room. A telephone. Distant, muffled, repeating itself over and over like a summons. Albright couldn't have said why, but he hoped that the summons was meant for him. He turned back at the door and waited.

Without taking his eyes off Albright, Guido DeVita reached down behind his desk and opened a small cabinet. Now the telephone, which he kept locked inside, jangled like an alarm clock, demanding instant attention.

"Yes!" DeVita shouted into the radiotelephone.

"Is that you, Guido?"

"What can I do for you, Henry?"

The wireless connection exploded with crackles and pops and DeVita held the phone an inch or so away from his ear. Albright could hear the voice of the British resident in Cairo coming over the other end of the line. The atmospheric interference made it sound as though he was shouting from the scene of a battle.

"Hate to resort to the phone like this, old son, but we've just decoded an urgent cable from the Message Center in Washington and I thought . . . well, why not ring up old Guido and read it to him straight off. Seemed like the most expeditious thing, don't you know."

"All right, then, let me have it."

As DeVita copied down the message, he cradled the phone in the crook of his shoulder, making it impossible for Albright to hear what the resident said.

"Is that it?" DeVita asked. "Okay, hold the wire and I'll dictate an answer."

He put his hand over the mouthpiece and passed the piece of scratchpaper to Albright. On it was printed:

THE MASTER HAS BEGUN TO GRIND THE SAU-SAGES—URGENTLY REQUEST YOU CONTACT MAN FROM THE INSTITUTE—IMPRESS UPON HIM NECES-SITY OF ADVANCING SCHEDULE OF THE TCHAI-KOVSKY CIRCUIT—NEED CONFIRMATION SOONEST —DONOVAN.

DeVita watched the expression on Albright's face while he read the message. Suddenly, the blond American goy looked different to him. *Everything* looked different. Even the great yawning moral gap between himself and Albright had shrunk to insignificance. None of that mattered anymore.

It was one thing to be a purist, but DeVita didn't live on cloud nine. People could say what they might about the obscurantism of psychoanalysis, but they forgot that Freud stressed the importance of reality testing. And Adolf Eichmann, the lives of 750,000 Hungarian Jews, and a quirk of fate that had brought Albright and DeVita together all added up to one thing. A sobering dose of reality.

"Do you understand the message?" he asked Albright.

"Eichmann's begun the deportations to Auschwitz. And Donovan wants us to move up the jump-off date for the Hungarian parachute team."

"That's right," DeVita said. "As usual, we've underestimated

Eichmann's efficiency." He glanced at the phone. "I must give Donovan an answer."

"What're you going to tell him?"

"It depends," DeVita said. "I can tell him the truth. Which is that you and I mistrust each other. That we don't want to work together. And that the OSS and Broadway should find me another man. Which means delaying everything by a month or so. Eichmann can kill a lot of Jews in a month.

"Or," DeVita continued, "I can tell Donovan a lie."

"Such as?"

"Such as that you and I are getting along famously. That we see eye to eye on everything. That you're ready to start whipping your team into shape. And that we'll bust our *tuchuses* to get your team into Hungary ahead of schedule."

It was up to Albright. For the first time since he had been presented with this assignment, he began to picture real people being herded into real cattle cars and dying in real gas chambers. He had seen men die individually, in twos and threes, but until now it had strained his imagination to conceive of hundreds perishing at the same time. He had tried to grapple with the idea, but it had eluded him. The death of a single person could be a tragedy. Mass death was an atrocity that left you grasping for meaning. But now he began to understand.

And he thought, *If I'm the wrong man to stop Eichmann, where in the world is DeVita going to find the right man?*

He bent down and picked up a banknote. He folded it into the shape of a paper airplane and aimed it across the room. It spiraled onto the desk in front of DeVita.

"I'm a lousy liar," Albright said.

"So am I," said DeVita.

They looked at each other across the room, across the million dollars' worth of banknotes, across a million dollars' worth of misunderstanding.

"Good," Albright said. "That means we start off even. Go ahead and lie for both of us."

CHAPTER FIVE

CAMP JUBILEE
Monday, April 3

"You've got to be kidding," Albright said over breakfast the next morning.

He returned the forkful of cold, overcooked scrambled eggs to his plate and stared at DeVita. Across the table, the camp commander went right on eating. He consumed his food the way he did everything else—with total, undivided attention. He was the kind of man who could commit himself profoundly even to cold eggs.

Albright pressed him.

"What do you mean, they're already on the tower? You told me they've never jumped before. They'll break their goddamned necks."

DeVita finished his eggs and carefully folded his paper napkin beside his plate.

"I suppose they just got tired of waiting," he said. "Remember, they've been kept waiting for a long time. Two thousand years."

Albright shoved back his chair and stood up. "Come on, let's go. Maybe we can stop them."

"Lesson number one about Jubilee," DeVita said as he followed Albright out of the swinging mess-hall door. "People here have many virtues. But patience isn't one of them."

They got into DeVita's Land-Rover and took off in the direction of the parachute-training towers. There were two of them, the controlled tower and the free tower, and silhouetted against the early morning sky they looked to Albright like graceful modern pyramids.

"It's just dumb, that's all," Albright said. "Those towers can be treacherous."

He was right. The towers were mortally dangerous if you didn't know what you were doing. The physical and mental development of a parachutist required long, intensive, exacting training. Like a classical ballet dancer. Corny as it sounded, there were similarities between jump school and ballet school. In both, the object was to toughen the muscles while making them ever more supple and responsive. In both, minds were conditioned to perform split-second reflex actions. And after all the pain and sacrifice and agony, there were only two grades that counted in professional ballet and professional parachuting: Superior or failure.

DeVita hunched over the wheel, concentrating on the curve of the road that skirted the perimeter of the airstrip. He swung the Land-Rover through a gate and entered the parachute-training area. A few flat acres of hard-packed ground studded with uneven rows of wooden barracks. Picking up speed on the macadam surface, they flashed by the sweat shed, the rocking-chair suite, the wind machine, the mock tower, the sawdust pit, the rigging hall. . . .

As they approached the towers, DeVita turned to Albright and said: "You know, I have something of a reputation for being a mind reader."

Albright looked at him but didn't answer.

"Let me see if I can guess what you're thinking," DeVita said. "You're thinking . . . what kind of a cockamamie place is this where raw recruits can jump off a tower if they feel like it?"

"I don't know what cockamamie means but you've got the rest right."

"Well, first you have to understand why we named this base Jubilee. Do you?"

"Haven't the foggiest."

"It's from the Bible," DeVita said. "You see, after this war, after liberation, it's going to be like the time when the slaves were

freed and the land was restored to its rightful owners. Traditionally, the period is called Jubilee. In Jewish tradition."

"I'm a little rusty on my Old Testament," Albright said.

"Then how are you on modern European history?"

"Try me."

"All right. Why did the British wait until now to train Palestinian Jews to operate behind the lines in Europe?"

"Is this an open-book test?"

"I'll tell you," DeVita said, ignoring what he presumed was
American sarcasm. "You remember last year's Allied bombing
raids against the Ploesti oil fields in Romania? Well, there was a
massive breakdown in our side's intelligence and entire agent net-
works were rolled up by the Germans. Our side suffered fantastic
losses. Hundreds of pilots were shot out of the sky, and suddenly
the Allies were desperate to rescue those pilots so they could fly
again."

"That makes sense."

"Of course it does," DeVita said. "The only trouble was the
British didn't have a pool of trained agents to do the job, so they
turned to us for help. Now, here's the part you should try to understand. Most Palestinian Jews originally came from eastern
Europe. They speak the native languages, they know the countries
like the back of their hands. And they have another quality that
makes them better material than other agents. Motivation. Every
Jew in Palestine is ready to make any sacrifice—up to and including his own life—for one thing. To defeat Hitler.

"By the time the British finally came to us asking for help, they
had been at war for four long years. Their empire was in a sham-
bles. They didn't care any longer whether Jews who got military
training might someday turn that training against the British
mandate and launch a fight for a national homeland in Palestine.
They didn't care whether Jews would organize uprisings in eastern
Europe, which might, in the process, help speed up the Russian
advance. They didn't care about anything. Except one thing. How
to save their own necks. Some empire, some neck. Isn't that
Churchill's famous line?"

"It's close," Albright said.

"And there's something else you should know," DeVita said.
"Since the beginning of the war, this great British empire has

sent fewer than two hundred parachutists into Nazi-occupied territory. Two hundred in a war that has consumed armies of millions. Yet thousands of Palestinians eagerly volunteered for the assignment. Not hundreds. *Thousands.* All of them knew that their chances of survival were practically nil.

"And I was given the dubious honor of choosing those few who were deemed worthy to go to their doom. I picked two hundred and forty of the best and organized them into small teams of four or five members. Each team is named after the underground network, or circuit, in the country where it will eventually operate. Your Hungarian team, the Tchaikovsky Circuit, is the best of the best."

DeVita brought the Land-Rover to a skidding halt near the controlled tower. It looked, up close, like a giant erector-set model strung with wires and pulleys. Four parachutists were being hoisted by cables to the tower's giant booms that formed a cross two hundred and fifty feet above the ground.

As they rose, the parachutists squirmed like puppets at the ends of their shroud lines. Their chutes were stretched open in metal frames that resembled conical Chinese parasols. Eight sets of guide wires ran from the top of the tower through the loops in the parachutes to the ground. During the descent, the wires guided and controlled the movement of the parachutes.

Albright and DeVita got out of the Land-Rover and watched. There was a loud *clank!* as the first parachute was released from its frame, filled with air, and began to float toward the earth.

"That's Nathan," DeVita said. "He's thirty-two years old. Born in Szeged, a Hungarian city near the Yugoslav border. A mechanic by trade. One of our best demolition men when he fought in the Haganah. Highly reliable. And, if you're interested, a devilish chess player."

Another *clank!*

"Patir," DeVita said. "Only twenty years old, but skilled in ordnance. A bit too intense, perhaps, but he'll be fine when it counts. Tremendous courage."

A third *clank!*

"Gur. Twenty-eight. Born in Belgrade. Fought with General Orde Wingate's Jewish Brigade in Syria. A superb guerrilla tactician. Actually, though he doesn't like to admit it, an intellectual.

His great passion in life is archaeology. Wonderful sense of humor. Tough as nails. And shrewd."

And the last. *Clank!*

"Now, this one is my favorite. Bar-Adon. Twenty-three. Born in Budapest. An expert on all phases of radio operation and repair. A superbly trained cryptographer. Extremely committed to our cause. The spiritual leader of the group."

Spiritual but clumsy, Albright thought.

He watched the last member of the team, Bar-Adon, drift toward the ground. The form was all wrong. The hands weren't placed near the reserve chute. The knees weren't bent. The body was too stiff. The parachute was slipping air, making Bar-Adon swing wildly against the control wires. . . .

Suddenly, Bar-Adon's parachute jerked violently and stopped. Halfway down.

"What's the matter?" DeVita asked.

"Looks like the guide wires got tangled," Albright said.

They glanced at each other, exchanging a single silent thought, then broke into a dash for the control room at the base of the tower. By the time they reached the concrete-block room, the place was a bedlam. A dozen or so trainees were shouting at the mechanics, demanding that they do something to save their endangered comrade on the tower. Everyone was yelling at once, in a variety of European languages. Albright didn't even try to understand what was being said. He surveyed the roomful of faces, picked out the man who looked the most frightened, went over to him, and put a hand on his arm.

"You in charge here?" he asked in English.

"Yes."

"What's your name?"

"Pascal. Lieutenant Pascal."

The young lieutenant was stiff with fear and his eyes were filled with panic.

"Okay, Lieutenant, now I want you to listen to me very carefully. No matter what any of these jokers here tell you, don't touch those cable gears. It looks like just one guide wire got tangled in the frame, but if you try to hoist the chute, all the wires may snap. And your friend up there will drop before the parachute has a chance to open. There's nothing you can do. Do you understand?"

Pascal couldn't talk. He licked his lips.

"Do you understand?"

"Yes, sir," Pascal managed.

"Good. Now, do you have any wire cutters?"

"No, sir."

Albright went outside and the others followed him. Directly above them, Bar-Adon hung helplessly, swaying in the gentle breeze beneath the collapsed chute.

"Get an ambulance," Albright said.

Then he grabbed a rung of the narrow tower ladder and swiftly began climbing. Hand over hand he hauled himself up. Ten, twenty, fifty, one hundred feet. The air grew cooler, drying the perspiration on his neck. The metal rungs of the ladder seemed to yield under the shifting weight of his body. The whole steel structure creaked and swayed over the flat landscape like a ship's mast in a mild sea.

At the top, the tower listed in the wind, bending first to one side, then another, making it difficult for Albright to balance on the smooth surface of the metal girders. As he made his way to the end of the boom, the earth, twenty-five stories below, seemed to rock in perpetual motion. He peered straight down along the sheer perpendicular of the guide wires to the stranded parachutist. He lowered himself to a sitting position on a strut, twisted his legs around a cable, grasped it with his hands . . . and swung the weight of his body over the two hundred and fifty feet of space.

Now Albright began to shin himself down the thick black cable. Ratcheting his hands and legs in ten-foot falls. Until, out of breath, damp with sweat again, the muscles in his shoulders wrenched with waves of pain, he came to the dangling figure of Bar-Adon.

"We can't untangle your cable," Albright shouted. "You're going to have to make it down on your own steam. I'll give you a hand. Do you understand?"

Bar-Adon's goggles were askew and the parachutist's flying cap had slipped forward to the eyebrows.

Tightening the grip of his knees, Albright reached out and grabbed the nearest cable and shifted his body directly underneath Bar-Adon. He wedged his shoulders between the parachutist's legs and hauled himself up until he had Bar-Adon in a piggyback position, feet tucked under his arms.

"Unbuckle your harness," Albright instructed. "When it's loose, slip out, and grab hold of the cable with both hands."

Before Albright had a chance to brace himself, the full weight of the parachutist on his shoulders struck him like a sledgehammer. And entwined together, they dropped down the cable. Albright tightened his grip and the coiled steel slashed into the flesh of his palms and dug into his shins. The combined weight of the two bodies was simply too much for him to control. He decided to take a chance. He released his legs and slammed the soles of his boots against the cable. He caught a whiff of burning leather as, gradually, they slowed their descent and finally came to a stop fifty feet from the ground. Manipulating the pressure of his boots, he "walked" them down to the base of the tower.

They were immediately engulfed by the waiting crowd of parachutists, and Albright was passed from one set of hands to another like a hero at a football game. Guido DeVita, tears of relief in his eyes, grabbed Albright by the shoulders and kissed him on both cheeks.

"Well, well," DeVita said, "maybe you've turned out to be the right man, after all."

"That's high praise, coming from Guido," said a woman's voice.

Albright turned to face her. She stripped off her goggles and flying cap and Albright saw the face of a cameo from a bygone age. It was Ruth.

"Ah, yes," DeVita said. "This is Bar-Adon. The parachutist who owes you her life. Ruth Bar-Adon. This is Captain Albright."

"We've met before," said Ruth. "And you're as good as your word, Captain. You promised you'd find me at Jubilee, but I'm sure you never thought you'd have to go to such lengths. Or heights."

"I'll admit that never occurred to me," Albright said.

"Now that we've been properly introduced," Ruth said, "I hope we can stop all this silly playacting and get on with the war."

CHAPTER SIX

CAMP JUBILEE
Tuesday, April 4

1

As always, Ruth Bar-Adon awoke with the first gleam of dawn. It was the morning after her near-fatal accident on the parachute tower and she lay in bed, her head swimming with thoughts. *And such shameful thoughts, too!* Like how pleasant it would be, just once, to wake in the morning and feel the hard muscular body of a man beside her. Or how much she would enjoy sipping a cool lemonade in the Café Storch in Tel Aviv while holding hands with a man. Or . . .

Why did she torture herself with these impossible fantasies? For a young Jewish soldier in the spring of 1944, it was wrong, it was sinful, this longing for sensual comfort. It was bad enough to catch herself thinking about safe, faraway places. But her secret shame was that she couldn't complete her fantasies without imagining a relationship with a man.

Men! They didn't understand how it felt to be a woman. How could they? Especially during war. Her gender, her physique, her physiology were all wrong. It had taken a man to rescue her from that tower yesterday. And right now she could feel a slight tumescence in her breasts, a stirring in her womb, a languor creeping over her entire body. Her team was scheduled to begin parachute training this morning and, wouldn't you know it, she was about to get her menstrual period.

She resented her body.

Oh, how she yearned to be a soldier! But she did not inhabit the body of a soldier. A soldier, after all, bled from bullet wounds. Not from a healthy uterus.

The soft light that fell upon her face and shoulders came from the small window in the sleeping area of the barracks. The *haver* had insisted that her bed be placed near the window. Air for her health, light to read by, a view to freshen her spirit. These haver, her comrades in the Tchaikovsky Circuit, treated her with special kindness. Dan Gur had put up curtains on the window and divided the room with sheets to provide her with privacy. Saul Patir had found a chest for her clothes and painted it yellow. And every morning Joel Nathan would poke his head around the sheets and whisper, "Ruthie, Ruthie, it's time to get up."

Yes, her haver were tender and considerate. Joel's head would disappear and he would go back to bed and wait while she dressed and used the WC. Until she was decent. That's how discreet these fighting haver were. They treated her like a . . . *woman.*

Which meant that they weren't true haver at all. Because haver in Hebrew meant more than just comrade. It implied equality, a total sharing, a blending of differences. Ruth Bar-Adon never told the men that she had mixed feelings about this treatment, this special regard that was paid to her because of her sex. She knew it would wound their feelings if she objected. It would remind them that they dwelt in separate sexual worlds.

But what a bother, this being a woman at war. She wished she could suspend her menstruation. If only she were as strong as Dan Gur. Or as physically reckless as Saul Patir. Or . . .

If only she were a man.

No, she wouldn't want to be a man. With a sense of exquisite guilt, she admitted to herself that she secretly relished her femininity. Rejoiced in her monthly rhythm. And, worst of all, *expected* special treatment from the men. This terrible truth made her feel even guiltier. She had no right. Not so long as the voices of thousands upon thousands of Jews were calling to her from across the sea. But she couldn't help it. She berated herself for

being weak. For being unworthy of the task to which she had
been called.

She heard the men stirring in their beds on the other side of the
curtain.

Yesterday, when the American captain had looked at her, she
had seen the expression that came over his face. At a moment like
that, a woman knew there was more power in her femininity than
in the strength of ten Dan Gurs. Captain Alexander Albright had
been mesmerized by . . . By what? She hesitated to use the word:
Beauty. Because she did not think of herself as beautiful. No matter how many times people told her that she was. Perhaps because
her mother, who *had* been a great beauty in her day, never told
Ruth that she was one too.

Ruth had been praised instead for her intellect. Her father, who
died when she was six years old, had been a successful playwright,
and everyone who came to their spacious Victorian home in Budapest said that little Ruth had inherited his Oriental almond-
shaped eyes and his talent. The men would kiss her mother's hand
and say, "Ah, you grow more beautiful every year, Madam," and
then they would twirl the ends of their moustaches and turn to
little Ruth and add, "And how is our young literary genius this
evening?" As a child, she put out a mimeographed family newspaper, and some of the most famous writers in Hungary, those
men with the waxed moustaches, contributed articles to it. She
recalled her favorite headline: "Charlie Chaplin Ill From Stomach Trouble, But Has Recovered." At sixteen, she was described
by the editor of a small literary magazine as "the great hope of
Hungarian poetry."

The great hope!

In fact, her mother's reputation as a beauty owed more to her
radiant charm than to her features or her figure. But still, a young
girl with a tinier waist and shapelier breasts and smoother skin
found it impossible to compete against such sophistication. "And
you look lovely, too, Ruth," her mother's guests would say. Always
too. An afterthought. Hungarian *politesse*. True, she was popular
in school, but once on the way home a boy had tried to kiss her,
and when she resisted, he had protested, "You're the prettiest girl
in class!" She called him a liar and ran home crying.

Her hope was to become a literary figure like her father.

Scratching away with royal blue ink on thick white paper at an old, polished desk. What had happened to all the poetry she was going to write? The pure, youthful vision? Where had it disappeared to? *It's still here within me,* she thought, *but it has taken another form. It has been transformed from words into deeds.*

The transformation had occurred shortly before her seventeenth birthday. It was the summer of 1938, and she remembered the argument she had with her mother over a blouse. A beautiful blue blouse, with billowing long sleeves, padded shoulders, three pearl buttons at each cuff, and an attached scarf that tied into a bow at the side of her throat.

"You'll be too hot in the theater," her mother said. "And, anyway, it's too . . . *sophisticated* for someone your age."

But Ruth insisted on wearing the blue blouse to the opening of a revival of one of her father's most popular plays. A gala benefit, marking the tenth anniversary of his death, with the proceeds to go to a scholarship fund for young playwrights. All of Budapest society would be there to honor her father. As she stepped from the open Mercedes in front of the theater that night, Ruth felt as though the whole world revolved around her. There was her father's name on the billboard. Someday, *her* name would be famous too. On book jackets, playbills, maybe even in the credits of Hollywood movies. In her blue blouse, she felt that everything was possible. Even that she could be beautiful.

And no one showed up.

The theater was deserted. Grotesquely silent. Neat little stacks of glossy programs remained untouched beside the entrance to each aisle. A single light blazed on the stage. Mother and daughter stood at the back of the theater, leaning against the purple velvet rail, unable to move or talk. Eventually, the producer, a man named Bela Bartha who had been one of her father's closest friends, appeared on stage in a dinner jacket, his coat folded over his arm, and made a little speech to them alone.

"Go home, go home," he said, his voice cracking with emotion. "No one's coming tonight. Haven't you heard? Why do you behave so ignorantly?" Now he was beginning to weep. "You should read the newspapers. Everyone's talking about it." He was too overcome with grief to speak. He covered his face with his hands, dropping his coat, which appeared like a black stain on the stage.

And in a stage whisper, which carried clearly all the way to the last row, Bela Bartha said: "My dear, lovely ladies, haven't you heard by now? They have passed a new law. It is no longer permitted to produce a play in Hungary that is written by a Jew."

No more plays, no more poetry, no more novels, no more movie scripts, no more newspapers and magazine articles, no more . . . no more . . . no more . . .

The so-called "Jewish Laws," the first of many to come, had been drafted by Count Pal Teleki.

2

"Ruthie, Ruthie . . ."

A face appeared around the side of the curtain.

"It's time to get up."

"Thank you, Joel."

"Ruthie, haven't you heard? Everyone's talking about it."

"No, what?"

"That we're going to leave for Hungary next week."

She took out her diary and wrote: "How strangely things develop. Only a few months ago, I wrote of the idea that suddenly stirred me. Now this morning a haver has come to tell me of the mission being planned. Just what I dreamed of! I feel a fatality in this, just as at the time before I went to Palestine. Then, too, I was not my own master. I was caught by an idea that did not let me rest. I knew that I would enter Palestine, no matter what difficulties were in my way."

When she finished, she slipped the diary back under her underwear in the top drawer of the chest and began to dress. Her uniform, too, distinguished her from Gur, Patir, and Nathan. The men had been issued regular British Army uniforms, so that in the event they were captured behind enemy lines, they wouldn't be shot as spies but would be eligible for treatment as prisoners of war. But the British didn't make Army uniforms for women, so she ended up dressed as a member of the First Aid Nursing Yeomanry. Or, as the insignia on her shoulder patch abbreviated it, FANY.

She ran her fingers over the embroidered letters and smiled. *Fany, shmany.* What difference did it make? It was a uniform. That's all that counted.

Strangely, for someone who had once cared so passionately about her clothes, about her individuality, about her uniqueness, Ruth Bar-Adon had grown to love uniforms. The anonymity, the *groupness* they conferred on her. It had taken some getting used to. After that night at the empty theater, she had joined the Betar Zionist Youth movement and her first uniform was a black-and-white affair that made her feel like a sham. The members of Betar were supposed to be militant Zionists, brave pioneers headed for a brave new land, but as she said good-bye to her mother five years ago in Budapest, she was filled with remorse and guilt and fear. In Palestine, she was given another "uniform"—blue shorts, white blouse, sandals, white cap—but it had taken her months to feel at home with the chicken farmers at the kibbutz in Merhavia. Then, just as she was getting used to her new surroundings, the British issued their infamous "white paper," an official document that practically shut the gates to further Jewish immigration to Palestine. Almost immediately, a savage, three-sided civil war erupted among Jews, Arabs, and British, and Ruth found herself wearing the homemade khaki uniform of the Haganah, the underground Jewish defense force.

And still she thought of herself as a temporary inhabitant of her uniform, a borrowed body for the cause. In her heart, she remained Ruth the poetess, Ruth the talented, Ruth the great hope. Until one day when, quite by chance, she became an unexpected witness to a terrible event that changed her entire life.

It was, she remembered as though it was yesterday, February 12, 1942. Very early in the morning. Still dark. So dark that she woke with a start in her bungalow in Merhavia and realized that a figure was standing over her bed. At first she thought it was an Arab who had pierced the kibbutz defense perimeter and had come to kill her. Then, the figure lit a match and she saw that it was Shmuel, the commander of the local Haganah unit.

"Don't be alarmed," Shmuel said. "We need someone to deliver a message to Tel Aviv. The Arabs in Nazareth are planning a little surprise party for us and we must get reinforcements."

Her instructions were simple. She was to go to 9 Mizrachi B

Street in the Florentine quarter of Tel Aviv, ask for Chaim Weisel, and convey her request: twenty men from Palmach, the elite
strike force of the Haganah. If anyone became suspicious, she was
to say that she had brought Mr. Weisel some *t'filin*, religious
phylacteries, to repair.

The sun was just beginning to tint the peaks of Mount Carmel
over the Jezreel Valley as the lorry pulled out of the kibbutz.
Ruth sat next to the driver and slept most of the way. Three
hours later, they were in Tel Aviv, and Ruth found herself standing in front of the Esther Cinema in Dizengoff Street. The clock
in the ticket booth said ten-fifteen. Down both sides of Dizengoff
Street, outdoor tables under colorful café awnings were jammed
with people drinking Turkish coffee and steaming hot glasses of
tea. She had only a few minutes to make her appointment with
Weisel, and she ducked into one of the narrow, dark streets off
Dizengoff and quickly made her way toward Mizrachi B.

Here were the worst slums of Tel Aviv, mean, squalid alleys of
crumbling concrete houses, stacked with rotting garbage, fes-
tooned with lines of laundry that could never be washed clean,
crawling with dogs and cats and donkeys, a brawling home for the
poorest Jews. Here, in this dark, moist, dangerously inflamed ab-
scess of one of the most elegant Levantine cities, was the heart of
the Jewish revolt. The vital center of a Jewish movement that
fought, simultaneously, against the authorities of the British mandate in Palestine, against the Arabs who wanted to prevent the
creation of a Jewish state, and, from afar, against a Nazi war machine that threatened to exterminate the entire race. By now, the
Jewish revolt had splintered into a dozen bitterly contending factions, but here in the fetid ghetto of Mizrachi B Street you could
find, living cheek by jowl, the men who ran Haganah, Haganah-
bet, Mossad, the Irgun, the Stern Gang, the Palmach. . . . Fortu-
nately, Ruth thought as she climbed the outside staircase of 9
Mizrachi B, her task was only to find a t'filin repairer named
Weisel.

She knocked on the door of the attic flat and entered the low-
ceilinged room. It was empty. She had a sudden rushing sense of
déjà vu until she realized that the deserted scene reminded her of
the vast empty theater in Budapest on the night of her father's
memorial performance. Memorial. Memory. Death. She had a

chilling premonition. Something horrible was about to happen. *Was already happening.* She rushed to the window, which, here in the attic, was flush with the floor, lay on her stomach, and peered down on the street. The British had cordoned off the neighborhood with four Land-Rovers and a squad of helmeted troops. *They had come for her.*

She lay on the splintery floor, frozen in fear, watching the precision of this British counterintelligence sweep, overcome with a feeling of fatality. They would bind and gag her and submit her to torture. Humiliate and degrade her. She had heard about such things. A woman was, naturally, more vulnerable. No! She vowed that, no matter what, she wouldn't break under the torture, that she wouldn't reveal the name of her kibbutz, her mission, not even her own name. *Her own name* . . . Incredibly, she had forgotten her name! It didn't seem possible. It was absurd. How could she forget her own name? But it was true. It had been expunged from her mind by a grim determination to remain true to her cause, her haver, her collective, all of her people in Eretz Israel and in the Holocaust. She felt transformed. She was no longer an individual, a great hope. *She had become a part.* A part of something greater than herself. A name no longer mattered.

All this happened to her in an unmeasurable fraction of a second, not long enough to realize that the British weren't moving in on 9 Mizrachi B, but were converging on the house directly across the alley. Number 8. Gradually, she understood that she was in no danger. Her name was unlocked from the closet of her mind. I am Ruth. The "I" became an observer again. She leaned forward, anxious to learn the identity of the person for whom this British net had been cast.

Two British CID agents clomped up the staircase to the top of Number 8 and broke down the door. The shutters of the flat were open and Ruth could see the agents searching the room. After a few minutes, they threw open the doors of a large wardrobe and pulled out a man who had been hiding there. One of the agents grabbed the man by his long hair and dragged him to the open window, where he was displayed like a trophy to the soldiers below.

"Telephone Inspector Morton," the agent called. "Tell him we've bagged our man and he should come straightaway."

For a brief moment, no one moved. All eyes were on the face of the Jewish terrorist framed in the window. The face had stared at them before. Never in real life, though. Only from posters, thousands of which were plastered all over Palestine. Always with a price over his head. The broad forehead, deep-set eyes, hawkish nose, the ears set back from prominent cheekbones, the soft lips and strong jaw. They had captured Avraham Stern. The most wanted Jewish revolutionary in Palestine. The legendary "Yair," or Illuminator, whose Stern Gang had been conducting a devastating campaign of terror against the British.

Within less than fifteen minutes, Inspector Morton, a squarish-built man with a slight limp, arrived and ordered the other agents to leave him alone with Stern. Even before Morton drew a pistol from his shoulder holster, it was clear to Ruth what he intended to do. She watched as Morton raised his pistol and pointed it at Stern. Stern didn't budge. Didn't say a word. What was Morton waiting for?

Ruth didn't dare breathe.

At the precise instant that Morton shot Stern point-blank in the head, everything went blank for Ruth Bar-Adon. A blindfold was slipped over her eyes, a rag stuffed in her mouth, handcuffs clamped on her wrists. Unable to resist or utter a sound, she was led down the stairs. There, she and her kidnappers waited. She heard shouts. "Jews, they are killing Stern! Jews, they are killing Stern!" There was another shot. Then the sound of engines starting. And then the British were gone.

She was trundled into a car and driven for what seemed like hours through the streets of Tel Aviv. She had no idea where she was being taken or who was taking her there. Or why. Finally, the car came to a stop. She was brought inside. She smelled raw wood and glue. Felt sawdust underfoot. Doors opened and closed. Footsteps came and went. Time crawled by or rushed by. How could she tell? Inner feelings became her only clock. She grew hungry. Needed to urinate. Began to despair.

Then, the blindfold, gag, and handcuffs were gone and, for the second time that day, she was certain she had fallen into the hands of the Arabs. For the man who stood over her was as dark as a Bedouin. He had large coal-black eyes and hair as sleek as seal fur. Gleaming white teeth. He stood with his hands on his hips, his feet wide apart. To her astonishment, she actually found him attractive. Fiercely, frighteningly handsome. Like a black knight in some dreadful fairy tale.

He spoke in Hebrew. A soft, lilting, east-European-accented Hebrew.

"You are a prisoner of LEHI," he said.

LEHI, or *Lohamey Heruth Israel*, the Fighters for the Freedom of Israel, was the proper name of the Stern Gang. A tightly organized, highly disciplined brotherhood of fanatic terrorists, the Sternists knew little and cared less about the war in Europe. They were violently opposed to the tacit Zionist alliance with the British against Nazi Germany. Their sole purpose was to drive the British out of Palestine by force. But now, suddenly, Avraham Stern was dead and a shattering blow had been dealt to LEHI. Ruth realized that she, as a witness to his murder, had been kidnapped by the Sternists as a suspected British collaborator.

"I had nothing to do with what happened today," she said.

"What were you doing in Mizrachi B?" he asked.

"I can't tell you," she said.

"It makes no difference," he said. "We wouldn't believe you, anyway. We have taken a vote. You have two minutes to confess your treason. Names and details. Two minutes."

During the two minutes she was left alone, the door to her dark cell was left open and she could hear the sound of a buzz saw. She assumed she was being held in the office of a carpenter's shop. She tried to remember physical details so that in case she was let go or escaped she could lead the Haganah back to this LEHI hideaway. But there were so many carpentry shops in Tel Aviv, if this *was* Tel Aviv, and it seemed to her unlikely that she would ever escape alive. . . .

The "black knight"—she never learned his name—reappeared.

"Two minutes," he said.

"Two minutes, two days, two years," she said. "I saw the murder but I had nothing to do with it."

He removed his shirt. The skin on his arms and chest was much lighter than on his face. The contrast was so sharp that it looked as though he wore a hood. His large hands grasped her shoulders and yanked her to her feet. He tore open her blouse and clamped his hands over her breasts.

"Are you a virgin?"

She couldn't answer. But she closed her eyes and nodded that she was. At twenty-one, still a virgin. It was a confession, something that she had never admitted to a man before. It was not something to be proud of. For a young girl on a kibbutz to stay a virgin, she thought, was almost unpatriotic.

"Are you sure?" he asked.

"Of course I'm sure."

He looked at her quizzically, uncertain how to proceed.

"The British stand in the way of a Jewish state," he said. "Violence is the only language they understand. Blood for blood. Destruction for destruction. Jews like you who sell out to the British are no better than they are. I tell you this so that you will understand the sentence that is being carried out."

She couldn't believe her ears. Here he was about to rape her as an act of revolutionary retribution and he was delivering an absurd speech. He was trying to justify himself. Trying to whip himself into an autoerotic frenzy.

He threw her on the floor and fell on top of her, fumbling, dragging at her skirt, unzippering his pants, prying open her legs, tearing at her panties, entering her, heaving, shaking tiny drops of salty perspiration onto her lips, hard now inside her, the veins in his neck swelling, his teeth clenched, staring at her. . . .

But unable to come.

He couldn't ejaculate. He could not deposit the seed of his hatred, of revolutionary death and transfiguration, in this girl.

He collapsed beside her, bathed in sweat, out of breath.

"I believe you," he said.

"It's the truth," she said.

"Then what were you doing there?"

She hesitated.

"You must tell me," he said.

"I was there," she said, "to deliver a message to the Palmach for my kibbutz. We are going to be attacked by the Arabs."

"But you said you saw the man who murdered Stern."

"Yes."

"Did you recognize him?"

"No, but I heard his name."

"What was it?"

"Morton."

"Ah, yes," he said. "Inspector Geoffrey Morton. We know Morton. Wait here."

He left and she waited. But he did not come back for three months. During most of that time, Ruth was left alone. Except when she received her meals or was escorted by a member of the Stern Gang to the toilet, she was kept in a form of solitary confinement. At night, the members of the underground gang gathered around their shortwave radio in the carpenter's shop and listened for the mournful tune that was whistled as a prelude to each broadcast. During the long days, she was given pen and paper and she wrote poetry and essays. Three uninterrupted months of writing, not with royal blue ink and thick white paper, but still the most intense period of creation in her life.

And then one day he returned. He had lost a good deal of weight and he looked gaunt and ashen. His eyes seemed larger and blacker than before. The tips of his shoes were splattered with red paint or blood.

"Morton?" she asked.

He shook his head. "We missed. Twice. The last time was close. He must lead a charmed life."

"I'm sorry," she said.

She was shocked at her own words. Sorry? What did she mean? Sorry that Morton was still alive? Sorry that the Stern Gang's orgy of bloody terror was an exercise in futility? Sorry for her "black knight"?

He searched her eyes.

"I've thought of you often," he said.

"Have you?"

"Yes."

She ran her hand over his forehead, an almost maternal gesture, and he shut his eyes. She thought she felt him tremble.

"We must leave here tonight," he said. "You can come with us if you wish."

"I don't believe in what you're doing," she said. Then she added: "I believe in you, but I don't believe in your cause."

"They're one and the same," he said.

"I'm not so sure."

"Come with us and find out."

They left that night, in pairs, each one carrying the tools of the terrorist's trade—a variety of pistols, boxes of ammunition, disassembled parts of a mimeograph machine, wire, timing devices, explosives. . . . There was a silent understanding that Ruth would take the radio. When they reassembled the next day in a safe house in the Hasidic quarter of Petah Tikva, one of the men taught Ruth how to set up the radio, and from then on she was in charge of their precious communications with the outside world. In no time, she was expert at sending and receiving, both by voice and in Morse. It was she who whistled the sad melody of the Stern Gang's anthem before each broadcast, she who sent news of bombings and assassinations, she who whispered instructions for the next attack. Though she never fired a gun, wired an explosive, or pasted up a wall poster, she had become, in the eyes of the men with whom she shared the shadowy world of the terrorist, a part of their mystical bond.

They never stayed in one place for more than a few days. One week it would be a tailor's shop in Mea Shearim in the New City of Jerusalem, the next a dingy hotel room in Jaffa, then a cellar in Haifa. . . . She and the "black knight" were hardly ever alone. But when they could steal a few minutes together, they made love, swiftly, fully clothed, sensitive to suspicious sounds, like hunted animals. They never talked during their lovemaking, but twice after it was over he told her that she was beautiful. And she believed him. He did not lie. She was in love with him. A man without a name. With no kin. No past. Certainly no future. She became impregnated by his ideals, his vision, his uncompromising devotion to a dream, his example of sacrifice.

It was on one of those rare occasions, when they had been alone for almost an hour, that he told her they had to leave their safe house. She had grown accustomed to these sudden moves and, without questioning him, she began to pack the radio while he took a suitcase full of explosives and went for the car.

Unconsciously, she whistled the Stern Gang's dirgelike anthem. She had just come to the part whose words were, "We serve our cause for the length of our lives, a service which ends with our breath," when the explosion blew in the window of the first-floor flat and knocked her to the floor.

She screamed and ran outside, violating one of the cardinal

rules of the terrorist: at the first sign of danger, flee! A crowd had gathered around the wreckage of the car. The entire roof had been blown away by the explosion. In the driver's seat there was a headless lump of flesh. Blood, black as ink, cascaded from the hole between the shoulders.

"What happened to his head?" she heard a little girl ask.

The girl's mother pointed at Ruth.

Ruth Bar-Adon looked down at the gutter and there, staring from coal-black eyes, was the face of her lover.

3

After breakfast, the Tchaikovsky Circuit assembled in the rigging hall. Parachutes hung like sleeping bats from the forty-foot ceiling. A life-size straw dummy, which was tossed out of planes to test the wind before training jumps, lay like a corpse on a table. On the wall there was a plaque with the Rigger's Ten Commandments. "I will keep constantly in mind that until men grow wings their parachutes must be dependable. I will pack every parachute as though I am to jump with it myself, and will stand ready to jump with any parachute which I have certified as properly inspected and repacked. I will remember . . ."

"That reminds me," Gur said, clearing his throat. "Do you know the story about the officer who was going through the ranks asking each man, 'Do you like to jump?' Finally, he came to a Jewish trooper who answered, 'No.' The officer was naturally indignant, so he asked him, 'Then what the hell are you doing in this outfit?' And the Jewish trooper replied, 'Well, I just like to be around people who like to jump.'"

Everyone tried to laugh but, for the first time since they had come together at Camp Jubilee, the members of the Tchaikovsky Circuit had a bad case of the jitters. It was the uncertainty. Not knowing exactly when they would leave, where they would be dropped, who would meet them on the ground, what assignment they would be expected to carry out. It had been made clear to them when they volunteered that the details of their mission would remain a mystery until the last minute. Only one thing was divulged. Their ultimate destination: Hungary.

Each of them had a reason for wanting to go back. Gur, the guerrilla tactician, wanted to link up with the underground. Patir, the ordnance expert, had a consuming ambition to kill Germans. Nathan, the demolition man, dreamed of destroying Nazi installation. And Ruth . . .

Ruth had the most complex motives of all.

"There is something you should know about me," she had told Guido DeVita at their first meeting.

"There is a lot I should know about you before you can be accepted for training," DeVita said.

"Yes, but there is something . . . how shall I say? *Unusual.*"

"What is that?"

"Sometimes," she said, "I hear voices."

DeVita ran his fingers through the thick mane of white hair. "Voices? What do you mean, voices?"

"The voices of my people calling on me to lead them to salvation," she said. "I know this sounds demented, but I think of myself at times like . . . like . . ."

"Yes?"

"Well, like Joan of Arc."

DeVita had heard about Ruth Bar-Adon. How she had lived in the underground for almost a year. How her voice had become famous as the emblem of the Stern Gang's clandestine radio broadcasts. How she had suddenly reappeared one day at her kibbutz in the Jezreel Valley and resumed her old life. How she had published a small book of poetry entitled *Redemption*, which had become an instant best seller. How she had fought in Syria with the Haganah. How she cast an instant spell over men. How, despite all this, she was modest. How . . .

The hows were endless. No one could possibly live up to such a reputation. In any case, as a psychoanalyst and now as the chief recruiter for Mossad, DeVita was more interested in the whys than the hows. But as she walked through the door of his office in Jerusalem, even he had to admit that she made an extraordinary impression.

"You remind me a bit of my deceased wife," he said as they sat down in facing easy chairs. "The eyes and the shape of the face."

"And you, of my father," she replied.

"You are close to your father?"

"He died when I was six years old."

"Then, you can't remember very much about him."

"What I remember is that he was good to me until he died and then"—she paused—"and then he wasn't around."

"Very much like this man in your book of poetry," DeVita said. "What did you call him? Your 'Black Knight.' "

"I never thought there were similarities," she said rather defensively.

"They are quite obvious," DeVita said. "Your father and this man, they are both powerful, idealized figures in your mind. Both are a source of love. Both then abandon you through their deaths. Both . . ."

"You can hardly call being blown to pieces by a suitcase full of explosives abandoning someone."

"Please, don't take offense," DeVita said. "I am not accusing this man, this 'Black Knight,' of some crime. I am only trying to understand how you must have reacted, how you must have felt. Why don't you tell me something about this man."

"Do I have to?" she asked.

"I think it might be useful."

"Well, he was different," she said. "It's hard to explain unless you lived with them. The members of the Stern Gang, I mean. They were like puritans. So pure. So undefiled. So self-denying. Frankly, I never felt worthy of them. I suppose I have too passionate a nature for the life of the ascetic."

DeVita waited for her to continue.

"Listen," she said, "my life with the Sternists is over. It is part of the past. You must accept me for this assignment. I will make a good agent."

"It is almost certain death, you know."

"No," she said, "it is certain *life*."

"What do you mean?"

"It is the voices," she said.

And that was when she told him about her voices, calling on her, as if she were Joan of Arc. She explained that the voices had taught her a lesson, that everyone was destined to die and that what was happening to the Jews of Europe was only the most extreme example of that truth.

"The only response is to grasp destiny by the throat," she said. "To shape life. Not to succumb. To endure."

She did not think it was too late. Hitler had actually done the Jews a grim favor by stripping them of their illusions. Now they knew the truth—that they were not like others, could never assimilate, never down till the end of history, could not make a life as mere individuals. Most important of all, the only thing that could save those Jews remaining alive in Europe was for them to regain their sense of community, of wholeness, to bind together and rise up as one. . . .

"Those of us whom you choose to send back into the flames of the Holocaust will be messengers of that hope."

4

Dressed in a freshly starched uniform, his trousers meticulously bloused over polished jump boots, Captain Alexander Hamilton Albright entered the rigging hall. His presence brought conversation to an abrupt halt.

The members of the Tchaikovsky Circuit unconsciously assumed the military posture of parade rest. Even young Saul Patir —the intense, rebellious Saul whose habitual slouch and lolling head betrayed a disdain for all forms of authority—managed to straighten up. The moment they had all been waiting for had finally come.

Ruth could feel her heart beating wildly.

I'm not dreaming, I'm not dreaming, she thought. *This is really it. This tall, blond American, who looks and acts so different from the rest of us, has been sent to teach us how to parachute. He will give us wings. Wings of . . . hope. . . .*

And Dan Gur, rock-solid, practical, shrewd Dan Gur, thought: *If Guido picked this American, he must be pretty good. Guido knows what he's doing. Of course, everyone can make a mistake, even Guido. Well, we'll know soon enough. . . .*

And Joel Nathan, the "old man" of the Tchaikovsky Circuit,

old and wise beyond his thirty-two years, the stabilizing influence
who had brought them through two months of tough training as a
close-knit unit, Joel thought: *Why do I feel so strange? Am I jeal-*
ous? Jealous of what? That somebody else is taking over?
Schmuck, it's a good thing. You've done as much as you can. Now
it's the American's turn. You should be proud. You're making
him a present of a fine group of people. The best. If he told them
to, they'd jump out of an airplane without a parachute. That's
how eager they are. All he needs is a few gentle words. Just a few
gentle words. . . .

"Shalom," Albright said.

He was lugging a stack of books under his arm and he plunked
them down on a table next to the straw wind dummy. There were
four copies each of *The Art of Guerrilla Warfare*, *The Partisan*
Leader's Guide, *The Housewife's ABC of Home-Made Explosives*
(all authored by the legendary British intelligence agent, Colin
McVeagh Gubbins), and *Paratroops* (Major F. O. Miksche's
landmark study of airborne warfare).

Albright paused, then continued in almost flawless Hebrew: "I
brought along a little reading for your spare time."

They broke into laughter.

Not bad, not bad at all. This American had rescued their
Ruthie from the training tower yesterday and here he was today
speaking to them in Hebrew. And making with the little jokes.
You see, you shouldn't believe everything you hear about American Jews. Some of them, like this one, can get off their fat be-
hinds.

"Before we go any further," Albright went on in Hebrew,
"there are some things you should know about me. First, each one
of you has jumped to a false conclusion. I can't speak Hebrew. I
know you don't believe what I've just told you, so I'll repeat: I
can't speak Hebrew. I taught myself these words that I'm speaking to you now by studying a book. You think that's impossible?
Well, it took me exactly twenty-four hours, and just for your information, the name of the book is Max Reichler's *Hebrew*
Primer, which happens to be available in libraries in most major
cities.

"I taught myself this speech," Albright continued, "in order to
establish an immediate rapport with you, to put you at your ease,

to show you how easy it is to be deceived by someone who speaks your language, and to prove to you that remarkable feats of memory and willpower can be accomplished in an extraordinary short period of time. I expect you to do as well with the books I brought along with me here today."

Saul Patir jammed his hands into his pockets and stared at Albright from the corners of his eyes.

"Now," Albright said, switching into English, "that just about exhausts my conversational Hebrew for the moment."

There was another burst of laughter, this time more restrained.

"The next thing you should know about me," Albright said, "is that I have been given one week to teach you how to leap out of an airplane and land safely with your parachute on the ground. That shouldn't be as hard as it sounds, because if thousands of postadolescent American boys of average intelligence and slightly above average physical coordination can be trained to parachute, so can you. But it isn't as easy as it sounds, either. Because one week is a very short period of time. You're only going to be required to make one jump under actual combat conditions, but your mind and body, your arm and back and leg muscles—and your mind muscles—have to be in shape for a hundred jumps. And one week isn't much time to accomplish that.

"You should also know that in American Army airborne slang, the men who train paratroops are called gorillas. As you might imagine, that is not meant as a term of endearment, and by the time our week of training is over you will understand why. No matter how well you have done in your other training here at Jubilee, each one of you has to pass muster with me before you will be accepted for this mission.

"Finally, you should know—since you will find out eventually anyway—that I am not Jewish. I tell you this because I don't want any misunderstandings. Being Jewish, in my way of thinking, has absolutely no bearing one way or the other on our training and our mission.

"That's all I have to say by way of introduction. Any questions?"

How could DeVita have done this to us? Joel Nathan thought. *This man is an unmitigated disaster.*

The American had said all the wrong things. He had fooled

them with his canned speech in Hebrew, a language which each of them had learned with some difficulty and which they considered almost a sacred tongue. He had insulted their intelligence. He had treated them like raw recruits, refusing to give them any credit for their weeks of training. He had tried to undermine their confidence. He had threatened them with physical hardship, as if they hadn't already been hardened. He had warned them of the pain of failure. He had dismissed their Jewishness with contempt.

Worse than a disaster, Joel thought. *Unacceptable.*

From the moment they arrived at Camp Jubilee with the first wave of Guido DeVita's Palestinian volunteers, Joel Nathan had assumed the role of father-protector of the Tchaikovsky Circuit. If Saul Patir symbolized their daring, Dan Gur their strength, Ruth Bar-Adon their spirit, then Joel Nathan combined in his person all these qualities and was therefore accepted as their natural leader.

No one, least of all Nathan, would have said that he fit the part. He was a slight, almost scrawny man, with a long, thin neck that was punctuated like an exclamation point by an enormous Adam's apple. He had a nervous stomach, which rejected all but the smallest portions of solid food, and to keep from losing weight he consumed gallons of Ovaltine. He had a constant pallor, and even after being out in the desert sun all day, he would turn up at night looking as pale as a sheet.

Not exactly your run-of-the-mill, Hollywood-type hero. Physically, he should have been a washout. But Joel Nathan had been tempered in childhood by a long and painful and humiliating struggle against poliomyelitis which, though it had left him frail in body, had ultimately forged a character that was determined never to succumb. He was a classic case of the sickly child turned into the dauntless adult, a man who was self-confident to the point of recklessness. In another place, at another time, this might have made Nathan a bully, a ruthless competitor devoted to winning at the expense of others. But this wasn't just any place or any time. It was, for Jews like Nathan, a rendezvous with a horrible destiny, and he had sublimated all his steely narcissism into a determination to win the Jewish crusade.

During their first week at Jubilee, Nathan, Patir, Gur, and Ruth Bar-Adon were subjected to a two-day battery of tests to gauge their basic motivation, intelligence, aptitudes, emotional stability, initiative, discipline, leadership qualities, physical coordination, and stamina.

Nathan came out first in the overall rating.

After they had passed that hurdle, they began their training in various forms of small arms, map reading, compass use, field craft, demolition, wireless operation, the use of small boats, the organizing and equipping of resistance groups.

Once again Nathan scored first.

Then they were given specialized training in foreign weapons, mines and booby traps, industrial sabotage and propaganda.

Nathan again.

Nobody seemed to mind. For gradually it became apparent that though Nathan was clearly the best all-round agent in the team, he did not possess a monopoly on talent. Everyone had a special skill.

In the field exercises, which were designed to teach them how to operate under clandestine conditions behind enemy lines, Dan Gur was the most resourceful. A powerful bull of a man with a soccer player's neck and shoulders, Gur was the master guerrilla tactician, quick-witted, clever and tough, always able to find a way to turn the tables on his enemy.

Saul Patir, fidgety, slightly pigeon-toed, boyishly handsome in a fullmouthed sort of way; Saul who always seemed to be on the verge of boiling over from some obscure source of rage; Saul became effortlessly proficient in the art of silent killing. So proficient that he once confessed to Joel Nathan that he was haunted by a constant fear. "Some day," he said, "someone is going to come up behind me and put his hand on my shoulder, just like this, you know, in a gesture of friendship, and I know I'm going to turn and kill him in that split second without even realizing what I'm doing."

And Ruth Bar-Adon was the best pianist, the one who was sent to advanced wireless training, where she was taught to double her speed in Morse to forty words a minute and mastered the latest British codes and ciphers.

After two months of this, they were more than a team. They were like a family. They spent all their free time together in their barracks, which Guido DeVita had turned into a total-immersion laboratory. There they read the latest Hungarian newspapers and magazines, listened to recordings of local Hungarian radio broadcasts, watched films smuggled out of Hungary showing daily life, learned the latest Hungarian jokes, memorized popular songs. They spoke to one another only in Hungarian, wore only Hungarian clothes, ate only Hungarian food, used only Hungarian money, ration cards, pens, pencils, stationery. . . .

Despite the rigors of training, none of them had ever been so happy, so perfectly content.

One evening, Ruth showed Joel a copy of a Hungarian translation of *Anna Karenina* that she was reading.

"Happy families are all alike," Tolstoy wrote; "every unhappy family is unhappy in its own way."

"Were you ever unhappy, Joel?" she asked.

"Ruthie," he said, "what a silly question. Everybody is unhappy most of the time."

"No, I mean were you especially unhappy as a child," she said. "Growing up in your family."

He looked at her for a long moment. He had never told any of them about his poliomyelitis, the shame he had felt being a cripple.

"Yes," he said at last. "From time to time."

"Oh, Joel, I can't imagine you being unhappy as a child," she said. "*Really* unhappy. You're too . . . too strong-willed to let anything make you really unhappy. Not like me. I was desperately unhappy while I was growing up. And, you know, I can't even say why. I just was. I can't even blame it on my mother and father. Certainly not my father . . ."

Tears welled up in her eyes. "My father," she said with difficulty, her throat thick with emotion, "he loved me very much, but . . ."

"Ruthie, that's what childhood is about," Joel said. "It's like here at Camp Jubilee. It's training in how to live with unhappiness."

"Then what did Tolstoy mean by happy families?" she asked.

"Oh, he was talking about adults in the family like us. If you survive childhood, you have a chance at some happiness."

She threw her arms around his neck and hugged him.

"We're going to survive, Joel; we're going to survive," she said. "Won't we?"

They were a happy family because, like all happy families, they had a purpose: to protect, succor, and promote the welfare of each member. But now, suddenly, with the arrival of the American, they began to fear that their short happy life as a family was about to end. And that they were about to begin to be unhappy in their own special way.

CHAPTER SEVEN

CAMP JUBILEE
Wednesday, April 5

1

The sawdust pit was where it all began.

At six o'clock the next morning, Albright led the Tchaikovsky Circuit, double-time, from their barracks to the sawdust pit for calisthenics. They worked in pairs—Joel with Ruth, Dan with Saul—holding each other's ankles while they did sit-ups. Then they spread out—arm's length, fingers touching—for pushups. Then leg lifts. Then roll overs. Then together again for more pushups. Then somersaults. Then deep knee bends. Then more sit-ups. . . .

The sawdust stuck to their perspiring bodies, infiltrated their boots, crept into their eyes and ears, was sucked into their nostrils and lungs.

Then more pushups. More deep knee bends. More . . .

As she lay on her back, preparing for yet another set of sit-ups, Ruth felt faint. The menstrual blood was soaking through the pad between her legs. Cramps—deep, roiling cramps—shot through her uterus, making her wince with waves of excruciating pain. She was determined not to let on, not to give in, not to be vanquished by her femininity.

"One-two . . . one-two," Albright called out.

Finally, it became too much for her, and she collapsed onto her side, her knees drawn up to her chest, her hands kneading her stomach, trying to reach the pain and relieve it. Joel knelt beside her. He didn't know what to do. He didn't even know what was wrong with her. It didn't occur to Joel that this could happen to a woman because . . . she was a woman.

"All right," Albright said, "we'll take a five-minute break."

He walked over to where the men had gathered around Ruth.

"What's wrong with her?" he asked without a trace of sympathy in his voice.

Ruth looked up at him.

"I'm fine," she managed to say. "It's just a little cramp, that's all."

"Good," Albright said. "Then let's get back to the barracks. It's time for showers."

By six forty-five, they were in the mess hall for breakfast. By seven, they were double-timing to the mock tower for jump training.

After they had strapped on their heavy harnesses, Albright ordered them to do ten more pushups. Then he led the way to the top of the thirty-four-foot-high tower and demonstrated the proper exit technique—feet together, knees slightly bent, hands extended over the handles of the front reserve chute, head down. One at a time, they followed, hurling themselves from the narrow door, experiencing the sensation of falling through space and the shock as their straps tugged violently against the overhead trolley tracks that swung them over a hundred fifty feet of hard-packed earth to a pile of sawdust.

Ruth was the last to jump. Wracked by another round of menstrual cramps, she flung herself out the door in an almost semiconscious state. Her legs flailed behind her. She forgot to tuck her chin in her chest, and when the fifteen-foot-long strap leading from her harness was suddenly restrained by the pulley screeching along the overhead trolley track, her neck jerked back violently in a whiplash. She reached for her shroud webbings but couldn't get her hands securely around them because her body was bobbing and twisting like a badly played out yo-yo. She landed in the pile of sawdust with a thud. The wind was knocked out of her lungs.

Albright made her do it again. This time her form was a little better, but she still had trouble controlling her body and her lines at the same time.

She was ordered up the tower a third time. By now, the cramps were like powerful fists grabbing and squeezing the tender, spongy walls of her uterus. The all-encompassing pain made her double up and, because of that, it appeared from the ground below that she had exited in the proper coiled-up body position.

"Better," Albright told her.

She smiled.

"But not good enough. We'll try again tomorrow."

At eight o'clock, they assembled around the wind machine to learn the quickest method of collapsing a chute and disengaging a harness after landing. The machine consisted of an enormous fan framed in a cylindrical casing. It could simulate ground winds of up to fifty miles an hour. They took turns lying in a prone position in front of the machine with their parachutes billowing at the end of their shroud lines. As Albright revved up the machine, the force of the wind in the parachute acted like a sled, pulling the hapless parachutist over the hard-packed ground and rocks. The trick was to use the pull of the chute to raise yourself onto your feet and run around the chute and collapse it.

After a while, the men began to master the technique, but Ruth was still being dragged along, unable to keep her footing. She bounced along behind the parachute and her uniform ripped along her arms and shoulders and tore open at her knees.

Eight forty-five. Filthy, torn, bruised, and weary, they straggled into the rigging hall. It was time for their first lecture. By Captain Albright.

"We'll start with a little history," he said. "There are pads and pencils on the table for you to take notes. There'll be a quiz on this tomorrow morning."

Four pencils hovered over four lined pads.

"The idea of building a parachute," he began, "is older than recorded history. As every textbook on parachuting points out, it goes back to the desire men have always had to fly, to build a device to defy gravity. The first actual attempt we know about happened in the early fourteenth century in China. There are records from the Chinese Imperial court that acrobats gave a parachute exhibition at the coronation of an emperor in the year 1306. Although it doesn't say so in the records, we assume the Chinese were successful.

"In the western world, we didn't get around to parachutes until the time of Leonardo DaVinci, who experimented with parachutes in the sixteenth century. Note: two hundred years or so later than the Chinese. The first successful parachute jump in Europe occurred in 1783 and was accomplished by a Frenchman named Leonomard. An American named Irvin—or Irving; there's some dispute over how to spell his name—this Irvin invented the modern backpack chute for aviators during World War I. A lot of pilots didn't like the idea of using a parachute because they thought it was cowardly. But eventually it caught on and the pilots nicknamed it the Guardian Angel.

"Today's parachutes, like the ones you see hanging in this rigging hall, are essentially a variation and improvement upon the original Irvin chute. They are twenty-eight feet in diameter when fully opened. Each chute contains a hundred and forty panels and each set of five panels constitutes what's known as a gore. In other words, there are twenty-eight separately reinforced triangular pieces, or gores, in each chute. Nowadays, the materials consist mainly of nylon fabric. They used to be made of silk. Japanese silk. But that was before the war.

"Okay, now, your shroud lines are threaded into the canopy along the gores. That means that when your parachute opens there are twenty-eight shroud lines running down to your harness. Those shroud lines are gathered together in four places to distribute the opening shock, and they are attached to specially webbed straps with a breaking strain of four thousand pounds to a single thickness.

"When you make a jump, you'll actually be carrying three parachutes. A backpack main chute. A chestpack reserve chute. And, inside the chestpack, a small pilot chute, thirty inches in diameter, that ensures that the reserve chute is dragged out in time. Of course, you'll only use the reserve chute if your main canopy is defective. If *both* chutes fail to work . . . well, no one's bothered to give a lecture on that contingency yet . . ."

Albright talked on for more than an hour, filling their heads and notepads with all the facts and lore he had stored up over the years about parachutes. Things even he had forgotten he knew.

He didn't want to leave anything out. Normally, a lecture like this would be broken into three or four sessions so that the novice parachutist could absorb one major lesson at a time. But the members of the Tchaikovsky Circuit didn't have that luxury. They had to know everything and they had to know it quickly.

So he threw the whole book at them at once, realizing that he was confusing them as much as he was enlightening them, but hoping that things would sort themselves out as they got to practice what he was preaching. He took them, step by step, through an imaginary jump: How to line up in front of a C-47. How the stick of jumpers enters in reverse order of exiting. What it sounds like as the plane takes off and the wheel carriage is retracted with a thump that makes you think a piece has been ripped off the plane. What it feels like with the icy wind blasting through the open door of the C-47, the jackhammer roar inside the fuselage, the corset-tight parachute harness squeezing you in the bucket seat, the no-turning-back-now fear as the countdown nears for the jump.

The only way to describe the experience was *pure dread*. Like the first time you had sex. Everything that he would teach them, everything they had read, all their fumbling attempts as they groped through their training toward the brink—none of this would really prepare them when it came to doing it. *Actually doing it.* And strangely, the dread was not connected with a fear that the parachute would fail. The dread lay in the fact that once you took the plunge, you were entering a new world, a world for which millions of years of evolution had not prepared your body or your mind, a world for which a lifetime of personal experience had left you ignorant, a world that earthbound man could pass through but never conquer.

One practice jump was all they were going to get before they faced the real thing. And the real thing was going to be a lot harder. Because when they jumped behind enemy lines, they would be loaded down with fifty to one hundred pounds of equipment and they would land in a heavily wooded forest area. By comparison, the flat Libyan desert where they would make their practice jump would be a piece of cake.

So they had to know their stuff. There was no room for the almost perfect. One screw up and the whole team would suffer. In the plane, for instance, there was only one way to hook up their anchor lines to the cable that ran the length of the fuselage so that, when it was time to jump, they wouldn't get entangled in the static line and tear off an arm. There was a wrong way and a right way to handle different kinds of malfunctions of their chutes during descent—like a "Mae West" when the parachute partially collapsed in the middle and billowed out on the sides into two large brassiere-shaped cups. There was a wrong way and a right way to handle a situation where your reserve chute had to be used in the middle of a jump and you weren't falling fast enough yet and you couldn't count on just pulling the D-ring and you had to reach in with your hand, like a surgeon at a difficult birth, and grab the sonofabitch and wrench it out and throw it forcibly into the wind while you were falling through the sky. . . .

And just as they thought they would go stark-raving mad if they had to listen to another word, Albright stopped.

"It's time to break," he said. "You've got half an hour to shower and change, an hour and a half to eat and rest up. We'll assemble back at the sawdust pit at noon."

They groaned at the prospect of another torture session in the sawdust pit.

"I'm glad to see you're getting into the spirit of things," Albright said.

2

Albright waited until they had gone, then went back to his room. He stripped off his clothes and stepped into a steaming-hot shower. When his skin began to develop red blotches, he turned off the shower and, dripping wet, lay on the wood-plank floor and started doing calisthenics. He wanted to exercise away the charley horses that he felt in his arms and legs.

At least, that is what he told himself.

Got to stay in shape, he thought. *Got to stay ahead of them. Can't fall behind. Must show them who's best.*

Soon, his body was lathered with sweat. At one hundred and thirty-seven, he lost count of his pushups. And yet he continued—

up, down, up, down, up, down—in a punishing, self-hypnotic rhythm. He felt he could go on forever. Once in stride, no one would be able to keep up with him. He could outdistance them all.

He changed his position and began doing sit-ups. His sweat-soaked back acted like a suction cup against the floor.

Yes, he could stay ahead of them. Outperform them . . . Then what the hell was bugging him?

He stopped. Lay motionless on the floor. Breathing heavily. *What was it?*

This group was . . . *different.* They didn't really need him. Oh, sure, they needed him to teach them how to parachute. But they didn't need him to teach them *how to be a group.* They were already formed. They had already achieved that sense of unity which was, finally, the goal of all military training. He could see that from the start. That was why they could take anything he dished out—and more. He had watched them this morning as they went through each stage of the training and he had seen that, separately and collectively, *they were already there.* He had envied them their spirit.

They had made *him* respect *them.*

It was supposed to be the other way around.

He blamed it all on the girl. Ruth. It was incredible that she had been able to go on, in spite of the fact that more than once she looked as though she was near collapse. And no one had felt sorry for her. No one had complained that Albright was driving her too hard. No one tried to stop her. Her suffering seemed to spur them on. She gave them hope.

Even he had begun to admire her.

Albright stood up. The sweat had stained the floor in the shape of his body. The dark shape looked like a shadow. Like he had left part of himself behind.

As long as Ruth was around, the group would not belong to him. Physically, she was not up to this mission. Spiritually, she would always be his nemesis. She would complicate his life. Who needed this? Who needed her?

She was the weak link.

Albright decided to tell DeVita he wanted to remove Ruth Bar-Adon from the group.

3

That night, Ruth took out her diary and tried to find the words to express her feelings. She told herself that she would simply let the words flow out of the end of the cheap Hungarian fountain pen that they had issued to the members of her team. Anything. Whatever would come. She wouldn't try to compose nicely turned sentences, nothing literary. She would forget poetry. She was beyond caring how her words would sound to posterity.

Posterity!

She didn't think she could last another day.

Not if Albright kept up this pace. The afternoon training had been, if anything, harder than in the morning. And she had lost so much menstrual blood that she had to call it quits after hanging in her harness for half an hour in the "rocking-chair suite." Albright hadn't said a word, but she knew what he must have thought. She wasn't good enough for the team.

Her pen hovered over the open diary page but nothing came. Not a single word. She was so shattered by the realization of her physical incompetence, her sexual difference, her demeaning failure, that she was mortally afraid to let the words spell out what she thought of herself.

Albright made her feel this way. It was his doing. He managed to destroy, in a single day, the self-confidence that it had taken her a lifetime to build.

And by what right?

After all, she had been a soldier before. During her time with the Stern Gang she had proven herself brave and strong and, perhaps most important of all, able to survive. She had earned her place at Camp Jubilee. She had passed all of Guido DeVita's tests. . . .

And what had this American done? So he knew how to parachute from an airplane. This was such an impressive thing? For this they give you a medal?

The pen touched the page and, without thinking, she wrote:

I HATE HIM.

Before the ink could dry, she slammed the diary shut, slipped it beneath her underwear in the top drawer, and switched off the lamp.

And she was overcome almost immediately by that same haunting sexual need that she had felt so often before. But there was a difference this time. For she could actually visualize in the darkness, under her closed eyelids, the face of a man. A particular man. Albright.

She tried to shake off the image. But it wouldn't go away. It grew larger, like a close-up in a movie. A three-quarters profile of a handsome, golden-haired leading man.

It had welled up and taken shape, without her willing it, from someplace in her imagination—a place that she didn't understand. Because, after all, she *despised* this man.

She felt ashamed that her sexual need was attached to his face. What did it mean? How could she experience this wet pleasure when it was attached to someone who had caused her such pain? It was unnatural. What was wrong with her?

Guido would know the answer. Guido always knew.

Dressing quickly, she tiptoed past the sleeping forms of her haver and made her way through the silent, star-bright desert night to Guido DeVita's quarters. As she expected, the lights were still on. Guido never seemed to sleep. She tucked in her blouse and was about to knock on the door when she heard a man's voice. It was Albright.

". . . hopeless," he was saying. "You should have seen her today. It would have been funny if it wasn't so pathetic. In a pinch, in a tight spot, she's going to jeopardize the whole team. I want her off."

"There must be another explanation for her poor performance," DeVita said. His voice sounded weary, as if the subject was painful to him. "She's one of the strongest women, physically and psychologically, that I've ever tested. There's got to be another explanation."

"There's only one explanation," Albright said. "And that's that you goofed on this one. You let this one slip by you. This girl should have never been accepted for a mission like this."

"I don't believe that," DeVita said. "I've spent hours talking to this woman. She possesses an inner core of certitude about her mission in life that borders on the visionary. I've seen her inspire confidence in others. There's something magnetic about her, something that compels others to follow her. That should be a great asset when you get to Budapest and start organizing the underground." He paused. "Speaking as a psychoanalyst, I might say that she has one weakness. She has a tendency to form romantic attachments to the wrong kind of man. Like you, Albright."

"That's ridiculous," Albright said.

"It's not ridiculous at all," DeVita said. "It's part of the pattern of her life. She forms dependency relationships with men who are not—how should I put it?—not dependable. I wouldn't be surprised if she's falling in love with you. And that her ineptness during training is her way, unconsciously of course, of making sure that you don't return that feeling."

"But I . . ." Albright began.

"Yes?"

"Nothing."

"You were about to say something," DeVita said. "Perhaps something concerning how you feel about her."

"No," Albright said, "I was just going to say that I don't believe in all this psychological crap."

"Come now, Captain," DeVita said. "We've all fallen under Ruth's spell. And it looks as though you have fallen more than any of us."

Ruth did not want to hear any more of the conversation. She walked back under the swarming desert stars to her barracks. What she had overheard made her profoundly depressed. And profoundly happy.

CHAPTER EIGHT

LONDON
Thursday, April 13

1

Anatoli Lebedev fiddled with the heel of the shoe.

The damn thing was stuck and he had to force it open. He carefully folded his message—an original plus two copies—into quarter-inch squares and dropped the three pieces into the secret compartment.

So much for Donovan's Hungarian parachutists, he thought.

He slid the heel back in place and returned the shoe to the closet. His fortnightly drop to Gorky Street was due tomorrow and this message, which contained the information that Philby had gleaned from Donovan, was a bombshell. It was important enough to go all the way up the line to Lavrenti Beria, the chief of the NKGB. And from there . . . who knew? To Stalin himself!

It was the break Lebedev had been waiting for. There was no telling how they might reward him. A promotion to department head . . . his own Zil limousine . . . a comfortable dacha . . . commissary privileges. . . .

On the other hand, some jealous bureaucrat in Gorky Street might get hold of the message and try to bury the whole affair in red tape. Lebedev had seen that happen before. They could set up a committee to report to Beria and, before you knew it, the chair-

man of the committee was taking all the credit. And who would
remember the name of Anatoli Nikolayevich Lebedev?

When you worked for the Soviet State Security Police, you
never knew how things would work out. You never knew.

Lebedev shrugged and walked across the room. He pushed a
shiny brass button on the wall beside his bed. The one that promised to summon the valet. He counted the seconds silently in Russian. *Odin, dva, tree* . . . Before he reached *shezdyesiat*—sixty—
there was a soft, deferential knock on the door.

It never failed. Always before shezdyesiat. No matter that the
valet was bent with arthritis and looked as if he had stepped out
of an illustration for *The Ancient Mariner*. Push the button and
he was at the door in less than a minute. To someone else, this
might not have seemed so important. But to Lebedev, whose life
hung by gossamer threads of uncertainty, the valet's clockwork appearance meant a great deal.

Which was why the knock on the door brought a grin of contentment to Lebedev's broad Slavic face. He had to admit it. Despite everything, he was a lucky man. No, lucky wasn't the word
for it. He didn't believe in luck. Somehow, he had ended up in
London instead of in one of those godforsaken armpits of the
world like Dar es Salam or Karachi or Nanking.

When you stopped to think about it, it was too good to be true.
And it made him wonder. Were they testing him? Giving him
rope to hang himself? Who was behind his transfer to this cushy
job? Who was out to get him? Why? . . .

Someday, Lebedev thought, he would discover that the knock
on the door wasn't the valet but one of his colleagues from the
NKGB. *Lebedev*, this agent would say, *the charade is over. You
will please come with me. We're sending you to the mines of
Norilsk.* . . .

Norilsk was the Siberian camp to which they had sent his sister.

It was a good question: How had he escaped such a fate?
Unlike some brown noses he could name if he wanted to, he had
never been a pet of Beria. Why, during the great purges of 1937
and 1938, he had been denounced and arrested along with his entire subsection in Gorky Street. He still carried the scars of his
"rehabilitation" on his left hand where the fingernails would
never fully grow back in. And even Lebedev had to admit that his

work for the NKGB during the siege of Leningrad was . . . How would one put it? Less than brilliant?

More times than he cared to remember he had been passed over for promotion. And then without explanation, Lebedev had been rushed back to Moscow sixteen months ago and ushered into the top-floor corner office in Gorky Street *where he was greeted personally by Lavrenti Beria.*

He had never seen Beria in the flesh before and the secret police chief turned out to be a disappointment. He was a moon-faced little Mongol of a man with squinty eyes, delicate wrists, and a high-pitched voice. Beria didn't get up from his desk or offer him a hand to shake or even a smile of reassurance. He just sat there, looking at Lebedev, and then he finally said: *"Na nyebo ni oblaka."* Not a cloud in the sky! A line of poetry from . . . Pushkin, perhaps. Beria spouting Pushkin! Now that was a laugh.

For a moment, Lebedev had a chilling thought: *It's a code. A password or something. I'm supposed to give a reply.*

"Yes, Anatoli Nikolayevich, the sun shines on those who do their duty to the state," Beria continued. "And you have clearly done your duty."

Lebedev didn't have the faintest notion what Beria was talking about. But you didn't ask stupid questions when Lavrenti Beria was talking about cloudless skies and duty to the state. You kept your mouth shut and hoped for the best.

It was even better than Lebedev had hoped. On the spot, Beria promoted him to colonel. Gave him the plum assignment in London. Provided him with the "cover" of deputy chief of the Soviet mission in the British capital. Put him in charge of one of the NKGB's most valuable string of agents, including Philby and Burgess.

A superstitious person would have called it a miracle. Ada Nikolayevna, for instance. His sister in Norilsk. She would have called it providence with a capital "P." Meaning that God had willed it so. Ada was a religious fanatic as only a Russian can be fanatic. She saw the capital "P" in everything. If God, through "P," was responsible for all that happened to you, then an absurd world suddenly became sane and logical. Ada was the kind of person who would get down on her knees every morning to thank God for sending her to a Siberian slave-labor camp.

Ah, Ada! Adele! Adelina! My beloved twin sister! If only you could see me now.

She would have enjoyed living with him in London. The civilized manners, the segregation of the classes, the weekends in the great country homes—yes, all this would have pleased her. It would have made her nostalgic for the pre-Revolutionary Russia of their lost youth. In those days, everyone in Russia knew his correct place in the scheme of things. Knew the proper forms. Understood the meaning of the word duty. "P" reigned supreme.

Ah, Ada! You have only yourself to blame.

They could have remained close, as close as when they were children and took baths together and crept into each other's bed at night after their parents blew out the candles. But no! Ada wouldn't listen. She insisted on befriending those effete intellectual types who hung around the ballet school where she practiced. He had warned her. She thumbed her nose at the authorities. She got mixed up with those dangerous elements, people who didn't support the state. He had warned her again. And again. Until it was too late. And what choice did he have? None. He had to turn her in. As an officer of the NKGB, it was expected of him.

Ah, Ada! It was my duty. This you surely can understand.

And so Ada, the one person in the world he loved above himself, loved in ways that would have shocked other people if they had known about it, Ada was shipped off to the *gulag* and he . . . But, no! No one, not even Beria, had hinted that there was a connection between Ada's arrest and his promotion and assignment in London. He refused to consider the thought.

You betrayed yourself, Ada. You and your stubborn belief in "P."

Of course, Lebedev had to admit that with Ada out of the way, so to speak, life was not so complicated. He was less vulnerable to gossip and exposure. After all, people couldn't be expected to understand such a relationship between brother and sister. Even those terrible dreams that used to trouble his sleep had vanished . . . along with Ada.

Still, he missed her. He and Ada would have felt at home together in London. Despite the Depression, despite the Blitz, despite the wartime erosion of certain class distinctions, London remained much the same as before the war when they used to travel there with their parents. Service was still rendered with a smile. It didn't seem to matter to anyone that the smile was beginning to wear a trifle thin. How did Kim Philby put it? "In England," Philby said, "one must always remember that a servant's politeness is only skin deep, but as a member of the privileged classes, it's deep enough for me."

Deep enough for Lebedev, too. Yes, Anatoli Nikolayevich Lebedev considered himself a man who had been blessed by the mysterious circumstances of life. Not by "P" and not by "luck." And not by anything he had done to earn it.

Take his lodgings. Thanks to Philby's influence, Lebedev was able to rent this lovely flat in the Royal Automobile Club in Pall Mall. A German bomb had damaged the club two months ago, but it continued to function as a kind of universal mess and home away from home for hundreds of foreign officers and diplomats. Though some of the members on the board of governors had objected to renting rooms to a "Bolshie," as they put it, the matter was decided in Lebedev's favor because one of the men happened to be sick on the day of the vote.

By now, Lebedev had settled into a comfortable routine. Breakfast in his rooms. Lunch in the Long Bar overlooking the club's Roman-style swimming pool. A session in the Turkish bath, which doubled as an air-raid shelter, on Mondays and Fridays. An occasional game of squash with Amr Bey, the diminutive Egyptian who was considered by his fellow members to be one of the greatest squash players of all time. Theater every Thursday.

All of Lebedev's personal needs were cared for. He had only to call for the chambermaid to get a change of linens. Or the waiter to get tea in the afternoon. Or as now, dressing for the theater, the valet to get a button replaced on his suit jacket.

And always, the valet arrived before shezdyesiat.

"Come in," he called.

"Sir?"

"Norman, I've lost a button on my jacket and I can't find it. Do you think you can come up with a replacement so I can wear it to the theater?"

Norman, who had been with the Royal Automobile Club since it was founded in 1897, shuffled into the room and examined Lebedev's jacket with the missing button.

"I'm sure we can do something for you, sir," he said.

"Good. See what you can do while I bathe," Lebedev said.

He stepped into the bathroom and closed the door, leaving Norman standing there, thinking to himself that the club was going to the dogs.

In the forty-seven years that Norman Wilkes had served as a gentleman's gentleman at the Royal Automobile Club, he had never once been called upon to match buttons for a Communist. If anyone had inquired of his opinion, which of course they hadn't, he would have gladly told them that he thought the board of governors had taken leave of their senses in letting Anatoli Lebedev live at the club. It was one thing to extend honorary membership to foreigners like De Gaulle or Prince Olaf of Norway. It was quite another to let in a bounder like Lebedev. *That* would never happen at clubs like Boodle's or the Atheneum or White's. The next thing one knew, the Royal Automobile Club would throw open its doors to women.

No matter. Wilkes slowly let himself sink down on his creaky old knees and began to search under the bed. Then he went through Lebedev's closet, checking to see whether the wayward button had dropped into the cuffs of the Russian's trousers or into one of his shoes. He picked up each shoe and turned it over and shook it. He was examining the last pair when he noticed that the heel of the left shoe was loose.

For a moment, Norman Wilkes forgot how he felt about anarchists, left-wingers, socialists, and Communists. His forty-seven years of training as a valet told him that this shoe was badly in need of the attention of the cobbler. Why, the heel actually swiveled in his hand. . . .

Dumfounded, he stared into the secret compartment under the heel and saw the three neatly folded squares of paper.

2

A few minutes later, Norman Wilkes was standing in front of the house manager, wheezing heavily and trying to explain how he had come upon the mysterious bits of paper.

"You put the shoe back exactly where you found it?" the house manager asked.

"Yes, sir."

"And you say Mr. Lebedev suspects nothing?"

"How could he, sir? You see, he's still in his bath."

"Yes. Of course. I see."

"If I may say so, sir," the valet said, realizing that this would be the one opportunity to speak his mind, "I feel it is my duty to point out that the staff never quite understood why the club would trust a Russian in the first place."

"I daresay," the house manager replied.

He agreed with Wilkes but, as his superior, he felt it would be improper to admit it. He looked at his desk where the three pieces of paper remained, folded and unread as Wilkes had found them.

"Now, Wilkes," he said crisply, fixing the valet with his eyes, "what about those confounded buttons?"

"Beg your pardon, sir."

"The buttons, man. The buttons. I want a fresh set of matching buttons sewn on Mr. Lebedev's jacket before he's done with his toilet."

"But, sir . . ."

"You go about your duties, Wilkes, and leave these matters to me."

As soon as Wilkes was gone, the house manager looked at his pocket watch, then picked up the phone.

"Ask Lowther to step into my office, will you?" he told the operator.

While he waited, the house manager scribbled a note on club stationery, blotted it, carefully folded it into an envelope and inserted the three bits of paper. He couldn't help but think that it wasn't every day that a house manager bagged a Russian spy. He was licking the glue on the envelope when Lowther arrived, looking handsome and alert in his hall-porter's uniform.

"Lowther, be a good chap and deliver this personally to Mr. Daniels."

"Mr. Daniels is in the billiard room with the Marquis Merry del Val," Lowther said.

"Well, it's frightfully important," the house manager said. "I expect Mr. Daniels will require a car after he's read my note. Have Quinn arrange it with the garage."

Lowther spoke to Quinn, the door-porter, then tracked down Daniels, the club chairman, who had finished his game of billiards and was having a brandy with the marquis in the Long Bar above the swimming pool.

At first, the two men failed to notice Lowther.

"I say, there's old George," the marquis said, pointing down at a swimmer who had just dived into the pool. "Have you heard his latest?"

"Can't say I have," Daniels said.

"Well, it goes like this. What would they call the Bath Club and the Conservative Club if they ever decided to amalgamate?"

"What?"

"The Lava-Tory."

Lowther waited until the two members had recovered from their laughter before he approached with the note on his silver tray.

"Thank you, Lowther," Daniels said, still smiling.

Lowther retreated two steps while Daniels read the note.

"Bother!" Daniels said.

"Bad news?" the marquis asked.

"Rather."

"Pity."

"Yes. You will excuse me, won't you?"

"Naturally," the marquis said. "When duty calls . . ."

As Daniels saw it, his duty was clear. As chairman of the club, his first obligation was to protect his fellow members and their institution. A mistake had been made by allowing this bloody Bolshie to rent those rooms. True. And this bloody Bolshie had now been discovered stuffing a hole in the heel of his shoe with God-knew-what kind of secret guff. True. And if word leaked out, it would cause a terrible scandal and do irreparable damage to the club's reputation. True. And the thing to do was to nip the whole business in the bud. True. And there was only one man who could help him do that with utter discretion.

It was a short ride from Pall Mall to the Broadway Buildings just across the street from St. James's Park Station. The duty officer at the desk escorted Daniels to a small reception area in

Section IX, and a minute later Harold Adrian Russell Philby appeared.

3

Kim Philby's dark eyes shone with exhaustion. His shirt collars curled up at the ends like wilted flower petals. The creases in his trousers—in the crook of the knees and in a V-shape along the groin—showed that he had been seated in one position for hours.

"D-daniels, old m-man," he said with his usual amiable charm. "What on earth b-brings you here?"

"Terribly sorry to intrude, old chap," Daniels said.

"N-nonsense. I welcome the interruption. Scribbling d-dispatches, you know. B-bloody b-bore. What c-can I d-do for you?"

Daniels handed him the envelope containing Lebedev's secret scraps of paper.

"Spot of club business," Daniels explained. "Thought you might lend a hand."

"D-delighted," Philby said.

Philby examined the outside of the envelope with its embossed crest of the Automobile Club. A melancholy smile hid his annoyance with the club chairman. Officious little bugger, he thought. Probably organizing the guest list for another one of his ridiculous topsy-turvy dinners where they start with the coffee and end with the soup and oysters. Well, one never knew what kind of useful information one might pick up at these absurd occasions. Lebedev would expect him to go. . . .

Lebedev!

For an instant—but *only* for an instant—the name of his Russian controller flashed through Philby's mind. Lebedev was, arguably, the most unpopular tenant in the club's history. But Daniels was far too proper to barge into Philby's office to discuss that. It must be something else. Philby didn't give the Lebedev connection a second thought.

"I s-say, Daniels, c-come b-back t-to m-my office and I'll g-give you a whisky. We c-can t-talk there."

"You're sure it's all right?" Daniels asked. "I mean, I expect you chaps have secrets lying about and all that."

"You're n-not some b-bloody spy n-now, are you?"

"One never knows about such things nowadays, does one?"

Philby led Daniels through the rabbit warren of cubicles and offices that made up Section IX, the anti-Communist division of Broadway. Once back in his cramped office, Philby sloshed some water into Daniels' whisky and put his feet up on his desk.

"Well, D-daniels," he said, opening the envelope, "how are things at the c-club?"

Philby never heard Daniels' reply. He was overcome with a wave of nausea the moment he realized what was in the envelope. He had to collect his wits and find out how much Daniels knew. Had Lebedev's message been read by someone competent to understand it? Was Philby's name mentioned in it? Before he could ask Daniels anything, however, the intercom on his desk buzzed.

"Philby here."

"I understand," the voice in the machine said back, "that you're sharing our top secrets in that pigsty you call an office with an old colleague of mine from Sandhurst."

"As usual," Philby said, "your intelligence is excellent, 'C.' "

"Well," the man called "C" said, "you tell Daniels that I serve a better brand of whisky than you do. And a better brand of secret, too. You tell him that, Philby, and you tell him to come down to my office for a drink. And, Philby, you can come along, too."

The inner sanctum of Broadway, from which Stewart Menzies presided over Britain's Secret Intelligence Service, was a square, high-ceilinged room without windows. The lemon-yellow walls were badly in need of fresh paint, and had been that way for more years than anyone could remember. It looked like a cross between an officer's quarters and a university don's drawing room. Pictures in cheap black frames listed in all directions on the walls. A riding crop stuck out of the umbrella rack. The mahogany desk was awash in papers, including many of Menzies' own notes in green ink on blue paper. The smell of a recently extinguished coal fire mixed in the air with an aromatic blend of pipe tobacco.

Stewart Menzies was a former Life Guards officer who had joined Broadway during the First World War and had risen

through that clubby establishment to the post of "C," as the chief
of the service was traditionally called. A decent, simple soldier, he
ran Broadway the way he had once run his battalion, by handing
down orders to his trusted subordinates and expecting those orders to be carried out immediately. In all his years at Broadway, it
had never once crossed his mind that a colleague would disobey or
deceive him. That simply wasn't the way the game was played.
And to Menzies, it was a game. A brutal, fateful game, but a
game nonetheless. His favorite gamesman was Kim Philby, and in
recent months he had taken Philby under his wing with the
thought that someday perhaps the younger man might succeed
him in the post of "C."

Menzies was not alone in his office. He had a visitor. It was the
skinny, almost emaciated, baby-faced man whom Philby had last
seen at Lord Rothschild's flat. The assassin Simon Wood.

"Come in, come in," Menzies called out when he spotted Daniels at the door.

Menzies came across the room like a locomotive gathering
speed and practically swept Daniels off the floor in a bearhug.

"Come in and meet a real hero," Menzies said. "Now, you
know that I don't throw that word around loosely. But this young
chap here has recently returned from the Near East, where he put
on an impressive show."

He turned to Simon Wood and said: "Wood, come meet a
decrepit old chum of mine. Daniels, Wood."

Simon Wood offered Daniels a limp hand to shake.

"I can tell you this," Menzies said. "Wood is one of the best
men they have in SOE."

Daniels looked puzzled.

"Special Operations Executive, you know," Menzies said. "My
God, man, don't tell me you don't know about SOE. It's what all
the novels are written about. The real cloak-and-dagger stuff. Assassinations in the night. Garroting in dark alleys. All that bloody
nonsense."

"Yes, yes, of course," Daniels said unconvincingly.

"Do you realize," Menzies continued, "that chaps like Wood
have one chance in fifty of survival behind the lines. Bloody
awful. Worse than sending men into battle. But Wood always
comes back in one piece, don't you, Wood?"

He gave Wood a hearty slap on the back. From the tight expression on Wood's face, he didn't seem to appreciate the gesture.

It went on like this for the next half hour, with Menzies dominating the conversation, reminiscing about his old battalion, recalling his exploits as a young intelligence officer in the Balkans, regaling the others with gossip about David Lloyd George and Chamberlain and Churchill. He was a natural storyteller and everyone seemed to be having a splendid time. Everyone, that is, except the unsmiling Simon Wood.

Finally, Menzies turned to Daniels and said: "Well, it's not like the old days, eh? Things have changed. For the worse, if you ask me. Not much fun anymore. Everyone's so damn intense nowadays. Even here at Broadway. Like a bloody hospital, an emergency clinic, that's what it is. People don't come around to see us just to pass the time of day. No, indeed. They treat us like physicians at a bloody disaster." He paused and looked hard at Daniels. "What's your problem?"

Daniels turned to Philby, then back to Menzies.

"Some sticky business at the club," Daniels said.

"Well, let's have it," Menzies said impatiently.

Philby reached into his pocket and took out the envelope. As he walked across the room toward Menzies, he sensed Wood's eyes following him.

Menzies devoured the contents of the envelope, then looked up.

"Where did you find this?"

Daniels explained how he had come upon Anatoli Lebedev's secret message.

"You know this chap, Lebedev?" Menzies asked Philby.

"I b-believe we have a file on him," Philby said. "He's d-deputy chief of the Soviet m-mission. We p-put him in the c-club so we c-could k-keep an eye on him."

"Get this message decoded and have someone bring me the file," Menzies ordered. "Daniels," he said to his old friend, "you'll understand if I ask you to leave now. You mustn't mention this to anyone. Even that you came here. Can you trust the servants at the club to keep silent?"

"Of course, Stewart."

"Good. Philby will see you out."

Half an hour later, Stewart Menzies had Lebedev's file and the decoded version of his message on his desk. Philby watched as he read the papers. Simon Wood stood warming himself at a freshly made coal fire.

"See here, Philby," Menzies said at last. "You understand this kind of business better than I do. What do you make of this?"

With a sinking heart, Philby read the message. His eyes scanned the page, then went back over it carefully, word by word.

His name did not appear anywhere. Bloody Lebedev had taken all the credit for himself. Just like Lebedev. Well, this time he was welcome to it.

"It appears," Philby said, looking across the room at Wood, then back at Menzies, "that we have s-stumbled upon one of our friends from G-gorky Street."

For the first time, Wood's face betrayed a trace of interest. Philby could have sworn that the pupils in Wood's eyes actually grew larger, as if they were adjusting to sudden darkness.

Philby's initial relief at not finding himself mentioned in Lebedev's message was mixed with a sense of exquisite dilemma. After months of chafing under Lebedev's contempt and derision, he now found himself in control of his controller. Lebedev's fate was in his hands. Philby could pretend that he did not understand the meaning of the message or . . .

"As I m-make it out," Philby said, "this chap Lebedev has got wind of a Yank p-plan to s-send an OSS team into Hungary to free C-count Pal T-teleki from prison. It appears to m-me that Lebedev b-believes that General D-donovan has c-cooked up a scheme to help T-teleki c-create a p-popular uprising against the Germans with the aid of the J-jewish underground in B-budapest. Lebedev is recommending that his chaps tell the German chaps in B-berne about the whole b-business so that the Germans can d-dispose of T-teleki b-before the Yanks arrive."

"In heaven's name, why?" Menzies asked.

"It's d-devilishly clever, really," Philby said. "T-teleki represents a threat to b-both the Germans and the Russians. A d-dagger in the rear of the retreating Germans. A b-barrier to the advancing Russians and the likely communization of a p-parcel of eastern Europe. B-but the Russians c-can't d-do anything d-directly about T-teleki, who is a rabid anti-C-communist, without admitting that their interests and the interests of the Americans are incompatible in eastern Europe. So they t-turn over the d-dirty work to the Germans, who d-dispose of T-teleki. Then Stalin c-can c-complain to Roosevelt that the Americans and n-not his chaps in the N-NKGB are thwarting the spirit of alliance. It will g-give Stalin a stick with which t-to b-beat the OSS. I d-daresay, knowing how strongly Roosevelt feels about the n-need to p-placate Stalin, it will p-put a c-crimp in the OSS's style in eastern Europe for a long t-time t-to c-come."

As he listened, Menzies did not try to hide his admiration for Philby. This was the kind of man who made Broadway what it was. It only confirmed Menzies in his belief that Philby was by far the best man on his staff. Definitely the leading candidate for the post of "C."

"Complicated piece of business, eh, Philby?" Menzies said.

"Indeed," Philby said. "These things often are."

"If I may make a suggestion," Simon Wood said, coming across the room.

"Of course, Wood," Menzies said. "What is it?"

"Perhaps it would be best if you let me handle this," Wood said. "It's more in my line of business."

4

She had not been there during the first two acts. But as the curtain went up on Act Three, she brushed past his knees in the narrow aisle and took the unoccupied seat on his left. He was immediately aware of her perfume, which reminded him of Ada.

"I hope you don't mind," she whispered to Lebedev. "One can see so much better from here."

"Not at all," Lebedev said.

He was aware of her aroma during the entire act, and as the lights went up for the curtain call, he stole a glance. She was quite young. Not more than twenty-five. Her auburn hair was parted in the middle and pulled back straight into a bun. It was remarkable how much she looked like Ada.

He began moving toward the exiting crowd.

"Oh, dear," he heard her say.

"Is there something wrong?" he asked.

"It's my earring," she said. "I seem to have dropped it."

They spent almost half an hour lighting matches and looking under the seats for the earring. And although they didn't find it, they left the theater together on a first-name basis.

Amanda.

Her name was Amanda.

So close to Ada.

She was a ballet dancer. Her teacher was Russian. She loved everything Russian. The Russians were the best dancers in the world. They composed the best music. Her favorite authors were Tolstoy and Dostoyevsky. She wasn't political, but she couldn't believe all those nasty things people said about Russia. After all, weren't they our allies now? Weren't they fighting those beastly Germans? Russians were the warmest, most soulful, most . . .

They ate a light supper at a nearby restaurant. Afterward, it seemed only natural that he walk her to her flat. She put on a Shastokovich record and brought out a bottle of Chianti which she had bought on the black market and had been saving for a special occasion. While he sipped the wine, she took out a ball of cotton, soaked it in nail-polish remover and stripped away the red coating from her nails. Then she shaped each nail with a long metal nail file.

When she was finished, she stood up.

"Would you mind if I changed?" she asked.

"Please," he said, feeling like a foolish young boy.

He wondered if he was taking a risk being alone like this with a woman. It was certainly not a wise thing for a man in his position to do. It would be considered a violation of the rules by Gorky Street. But he decided to hell with it. He deserved a little diversion. He had just scored a tremendous intelligence coup and a night with this young woman would be his reward.

When she returned, her flesh smelled even more pungently of Ada's perfume. He removed the pins in her hair and it cascaded down her back to her waist. Her dancer's buttocks were firm to his touch. He felt dizzy from the Chianti and the perfume and the young firm flesh.

"Ada," he said.

"Noooo," she cooed into his ear. "My name is Amanda."

"Ada," he said again, and fell unconscious in her arms.

She carefully positioned his head on a pillow of the daybed. She went into her bedroom, closed the door quietly, and dressed. Then she picked up the telephone.

"He's asleep," she said into the receiver.

"Leave the door unlatched," a voice replied. "I'll be there in fifteen minutes."

It took him only twelve minutes.

When Simon Wood entered the flat, he heard Lebedev's labored breathing. He switched on the lights and the girl came out of the bedroom. It was remarkable how well she matched the description in the file of Lebedev's sister.

"How much did you give him?" he asked.

"Enough," she said.

"Okay," he said. "Get out of here. I'll let you know when I need you again."

She left and Wood bolted the door behind her.

Standing over Lebedev, Simon Wood stuffed three tufts of cotton into each of Lebedev's nostrils. He tugged at Lebedev's body until the Russian's head fell backwards over the edge of the daybed. Slowly, Wood inserted his left forefinger into Lebedev's mouth and felt for the soft membrane above the hard palate. With his right hand, he picked up the long metal nail file and brought its tip to the point that he had staked out with his forefinger.

Then he shoved the nail file into Lebedev's brain.

CHAPTER NINE

LONDON
Thursday/Friday, April 13/14

1

Simon Wood stared into space. It was always like this after he had taken a life. He tortured himself with a daydream about food. There was a time, just after he had joined Special Operations Executive, when he tried to force himself to daydream about something else. Sex. Money. Travel. Anything else. But it invariably came back to one thing: food.

And he hated food. Had always hated it. In his early teens, he had been diagnosed as suffering from anorexia nervosa, the wasting disease. A strange malady, usually found among young women, rare in men, in which the victim loses all appetite and, if left unchecked, will starve himself to death. Simon Wood had come close to doing just that a number of times.

Even as an adult, when the affliction was supposed to wane, Simon Wood had continued to despise food. Its look. Its smell. Especially its taste. For him, it was still a daily struggle just to ingest a sufficient number of calories to keep himself alert and in shape. The mere thought of food tended to make him sick to his stomach. But after he carried out an assignment for Special Operations Executive, once the body of his intended victim lay inert, at the very moment when Simon Wood should have been most pleased with himself for eliminating another enemy of King and country, then his daydreams took over and he was plunged into the circle of hell reserved for anorexics. The hell of food.

Now, as he sat in a state of semiconsciousness, his salivary glands were pouring their juices into his mouth. In his mind's eye he poked a fork through a golden flaky crust and saw it disappear into the thick stew of a lamb pie. He raised a piece of meat, piping hot, pungent, dripping with a heavy gravy. He brought it close to his wet lips. He opened his mouth. . . .

A furtive little knock on the door gave him a start and brought him back to reality. It took him a few moments to recover. The imaginary taste of the succulent lamb was still on his lips and his stomach growled in protest. He rose from the easy chair, slightly dizzy, and crossed the carpeted room. He put his ear to the door.

"Who is it?" he asked, his voice hoarse with the emotional strain of his daydream. He cleared his throat. "Who?"

"It's us, 'arry and Phil," a low voice replied.

A second voice, this one with a heavy east European accent, said: "Tell him it's Mompa, the Jewish detective."

Simon Wood opened the door and looked at the two figures standing there in the dim glow of a bare hallway light. One of them was a tall, strapping man with a mop of oily red hair and a flushed beer-drinker's face. He carried a canvas sack slung over his shoulder. The other, short and dark, barely reached to the strings that hung from the opening of his companion's duffle bag. On top of his diminutive body was a large, classically formed head that would have pleased a sculptor. A cigarette burned at the corner of his lips.

"'arry 'ere 'ad an accident with the van," the florid-faced man said.

"Hey, *schmendrick*," Harry said, "you got diarrhea of the mouth maybe?" The cigarette bobbed in his lips as he spoke.

"And that's why we was 'eld up a bit," Phil continued, ignoring Harry. "But like they say, better late than never." He rubbed his large hands together to indicate that he was eager for the task that lay ahead.

"I wondered what delayed you," Simon Wood said. "I must have rung up the disposal unit more than an hour ago."

"It was 'arry's van."

"Enough already with the excuses," Harry said.

"Put 'im in a foul mood, too, it did," Phil said.

"All right, all right, come in," Simon Wood said.

Harry pushed in ahead of Phil. He walked on the balls of his feet, bouncing with each step. He surveyed the room and immediately spotted Anatoli Lebedev's body, the head bent grotesquely backward over the edge of the daybed. Harry turned to Simon Wood and gestured with his thumb at the dead body.

"Where's the gash?" he asked.

"The what?" Simon Wood said.

"The gash. The pussy. The dame. They told us it was going to be a dame."

"There's no . . . woman," Simon Wood said. "Just him."

"We *schlepped* a bag they make for dames special."

"There's been some mistake," Simon Wood said.

Harry took the cigarette from his lips, flicked the ash with a long fingernail on his pinkie, and put the butt back in the corner of his mouth. All his movements seemed too broad and exaggerated for his size. Even his way of speaking—the amalgam of Yiddish and American-gangster slang—seemed put on. Like a young boy trying to imitate an adult.

"Broke his neck?" Harry asked.

"No," Simon Wood said.

"Come on," Harry said, examining the dead man more closely. "If that ain't a broken neck, then I ain't Harry Brodsky. I handled enough stiffs in my time that I should know from a broken neck. You're talking to a licensed mortician, mister. Three countries I got licenses from. Poland, Chicago, and England. From broken necks I should know. It's my business."

Simon Wood was growing impatient and angry with little Harry Brodsky, but for some reason he wanted to put the feisty undertaker in his place.

"Come over here," he said, "and I'll show you something you most probably have never seen before. Not in Poland nor Chicago nor England."

As Harry leaned over the body of the dead Russian, Simon Wood forced open the already stiff jaw and revealed the ugly wound in the soft palate.

"*Oy ya yoi*," Harry said. His childlike hands sprung involuntarily toward his face, slapped his cheeks, and his head shook back and forth in mournful disbelief. "You . . . cut . . . him . . . up . . . into . . . the . . . *brain?*"

Simon Wood nodded.

"I'll tell you something, mister," Harry said, bending down and snuffing out the tip of the cigarette with the sole of his shoe. He pocketed the remains. "You got some imagination. It takes some imagination to think up something so weird that can turn the stomach of Harry Brodsky. In my own business yet."

"'arry," Phil said, "watch what you're saying, lad."

"Shut up," Harry said. "I thought I seen everything. But this brain cutting . . ." He rolled his eyes. "Strictly professional speaking, I'm curious. Why'd you do this?"

"What's the difference how I did it?" Simon Wood asked.

"Plenty difference," Harry Brodsky replied.

"Well, then," Simon Wood said condescendingly, "let's just say that if you know your business, Harry, I know mine."

"But this ain't like business," Harry Brodsky said. "This kind of killing don't look like business to me. It don't take much to kill a human person. You only go to this much trouble if it gives you pleasure."

"Thanks for your professional opinion," Simon Wood said. "Now, how about getting the bloody beggar out of here?"

"Sure, mister. Sure. Come on, Phil."

Harry Brodsky held open the duffle bag while Phil easily picked up the body and stuffed it inside. He had to bend the knees to make it fit. As Harry Brodsky tied the rope, he looked at Simon Wood and said: "I'll tell you something. You keep track of how many people you kill, right?"

Simon Wood didn't bother to answer him.

"Sure you do," Harry Brodsky said. "All you *meshuginas* in Special Operations keep track. So I'll tell you something. Half the men you kill, you shouldn't. *Half.* Maybe more than half. You know why? I'll tell you why. Because most of the time they'd be more use to you alive than dead. And I'll tell you something else."

Phil tugged at Harry's sleeve.

"If you knew your business," Harry Brodsky told Simon Wood, "you'd know that without my telling."

Silence from Simon Wood.

"Come on, Phil. We got to get this stiff in the van so we can get him over to the burner before they shut down for the night."

They closed the door quietly behind them. Simon Wood heard the body bag thumping down the staircase. He peeked between the window curtains and watched them load the van and drive away.

Better off alive . . .

Simon Wood shrugged. *What did Harry Brodsky know?*

He went into the bathroom and looked at himself in the mirror. A pudgy, innocent-looking baby face stared back at him. *Butter wouldn't melt* . . . He reached with two fingers into his mouth and removed the rubber pads between his upper teeth and his cheeks. He stripped off the false, blondish eyebrows and carefully peeled away the adhesive that held his real, darker eyebrows in a horizontal position. He filled the washbasin with warm water and shampooed his hair with the bar of soap. He towel-dried his hair, which without the stiffening egg white and vegetable dye looked thinner and many shades darker than it had just a few moments before. Then he combed his hair and looked at the results in the mirror.

The face that stared back at him now was dramatically different. Older. Leaner. More . . . The word that came to him was "reclusive." Yes, he looked reclusive, wary, distant. It was not an inviting face. He scowled at himself. He had never been particularly fond of his face. His real face, that is. As a youth, he had thought of becoming an actor so that he could assume different roles, different faces. And in a way, he had achieved that ambition. Except that now when he put on a disguise he wasn't acting. He was in deadly earnest. That was the way he killed. In disguise. That was the way he eluded detection, stayed alive. Always in disguise. That was versatility for you. That was imagination.

What did Harry Brodsky know about that?

Yes, imagination. Nowadays, a rare commodity. He didn't think of himself as a particularly ambitious person, but when he compared himself to other men of his seniority and rank in Broadway, he was appalled at how little spunk and drive and original thinking they displayed. Broadway had entered the war at the peak of its power. Never before did it have a larger staff, a bigger budget, a higher reputation. And now, because it had grown old and fat and tired and smug, it was getting trampled underfoot by the bloody Yanks of the OSS. Nobody ever admitted that, of course, but everybody knew it was true. The Americans simply had more cunning, more guts, more . . . imagination. Wild Bill Donovan was more of a scrapper than Stewart Menzies. Donovan relied on his boys in Special Operations, the action boys. For Christ's sake, the OSS was *run* by the covert side, while Broadway had fallen into the hands of the Menzies types, the old-regimental-tie bureaucrats, the Kim Philbys. Why, it was well known that Donovan's OSS was even moving in on Britain's traditional sphere of influence in the Middle East. The Americans had become virtual equal partners in Palestine . . .

Palestine . . .

Jews . . .

Jewish underground . . .

Budapest . . .

That was it! Anatoli Lebedev had sniffed out an OSS plan to create a *Jewish* uprising in Budapest. Not a general uprising by all the underground factions, but specifically a *Jewish* uprising. That was the key to the plan. But the only way the OSS could conceivably organize the Jewish underground in Hungary was to send in a team of Jewish agents. *And the OSS didn't have any Jewish agents.* If they wanted to use Jewish agents, they would have to borrow them. Borrow them from the British, who recently had begun to train Palestinian Jews as parachutists to operate behind enemy lines in eastern Europe. Which meant that the OSS and Broadway were in on the Budapest mission together. Partners. It couldn't be otherwise.

But Stewart Menzies, "C" himself, had never heard of the plan until yesterday.

Harry Brodsky, you smart bastard, you were right.

It was a mistake to kill Anatoli Lebedev.

2

Simon Wood left the apartment and began wandering through the streets of London. It was a pleasant spring night. Too warm for the coal fires that created London's wintry fog. Simon Wood was unaware of the strolling couples passing him on the street. He was so engrossed in his own thoughts that he didn't even hear the warning wail of the air-raid sirens. Soon, he was the only pedestrian. He had no idea where his feet were taking him. But as his mind churned over the questions raised by Anatoli Lebedev, he felt certain that he was drawing closer and closer to the right answers.

Question: How had the Russian obtained the top-secret Allied plan for the mission to Budapest?

Answer: Obviously, from someone high up either in the OSS or at Broadway.

Question: Which was more likely?

Answer: Broadway.

Question: Why?

Answer: Because the Russian secret police apparatus was a notoriously rigid bureaucracy, and Lebedev would almost certainly have been acting under instructions to deal only with British contacts in London.

Question: Meaning what?

Answer: That the Russians had successfully penetrated the highest levels of British intelligence.

Question: What should Simon Wood do next?

Answer: Find "C" and tell him.

"You there! What do you think you're doing?"

A buxom, middle-aged woman in an air-raid warden's tin helmet stood squarely in front of Simon Wood, blocking his way on the sidewalk. She folded her arms across her heaving breast, managing to look both dignified and farcical at the same time.

Simon Wood mumbled an incoherent apology. He looked up, saw the gilt statue of Count Peter of Savoy over the entrance of the Savoy Hotel, and slipped into the darkened lobby. A crowd had gathered in the crimson splendor of the lobby, waiting out the air raid.

He glanced at the big clock over the reception desk. A quarter past ten. The air raid seemed to be a false alarm and would probably be over in fifteen minutes. Where would he find "C" at ten-thirty? At the Atheneum? No, "C" went to his club on Wednesdays. This was Thursday, and on Thursdays "C" always dined at Simpson's-in-the-Strand.

And then it dawned on Simon Wood that all the time he was wandering through the streets of London he was unconsciously making his way toward Simpson's. Part of his mind had been working on the problem—unraveling the Lebedev riddle—while another part of his mind had been working on the solution— finding "C." Simpson's-in-the-Strand was next door to the Savoy Hotel. A minor triumph, to be sure, but another example of the superiority of his mind.

Why had he let Harry Brodsky get under his skin?

He pushed his way politely through the press of people in the lobby and found the grill and the swinging doors that led to the Savoy kitchen. There was an underground passage, illuminated by a few gaslights, that led to the kitchens of Simpson's-in-the-Strand. It was a popular shortcut during air raids and none of the chefs in Simpson's steaming kitchen gave Simon Wood a second glance as he emerged from the tunnel's iron door. He followed a white-clad waiter pushing a silver-domed carving trolley into the vast dining room.

And then it hit him. Hundreds of men and women, all dressed in uniform, were squeezed into the room, devouring Southdown mutton and Scotch beef. The large space reeked of onion sauce and cabbage and sizzling fat. The sights and sounds and smells of the diners slavering over the dripping sides of meat made Simon Wood sick to his stomach. He wanted to run from the place. He was overtaken by panic. He felt he might vomit right there in front of everyone.

He spotted the manager, Mr. Heck, in his starched wing collar and swallowtail coat and forced himself to go over.

"I'm looking for Stewart Menzies," Simon Wood said. "Would you tell me which table he's sitting at?"

"Are you quite all right, sir?" Mr. Heck said.

"Of course I'm all right."

"I see," Mr. Heck said, looking at Simon Wood strangely. "Mr. Menzies hasn't come in tonight."

"That's impossible," Simon Wood said. "Mr. Menzies always dines here on Thursdays. Are you certain?"

"Quite certain, sir," Mr. Heck said. He ran a finger down a list of names on his large, leather-bound reservation book. "Mr. Menzies personally confirmed his reservation late this afternoon. I took the call myself. But he hasn't come in to claim it. I'm afraid I had to give his table away to another party."

Just then, the all-clear signal sounded and the subdued hum of conversation in the dining room was broken by raucous laughter. Without saying a word to Mr. Heck, Simon Wood turned on his heels and fled out the front door.

Outside, he leaned against a parked car and hungrily sucked in the night air. Gradually, the stomach-churning sickness began to disappear. A taxi pulled up in front of Simpson's-in-the-Strand and disgorged a party of four people.

"I'm famished," Simon Wood heard one of the women say.

He got into the taxi.

"Sixty-four Baker Street," he told the driver.

By the time the taxi reached the headquarters of Special Operations Executive, Simon Wood was feeling better. But as he rode the self-service lift to the third floor, he noticed that he had developed a slight tick in his right eyelid. The grubby offices, normally a beehive of activity during the day, were deserted except for the duty officer who was asleep at his desk in the corner under a hand-tinted photograph of His Majesty and the Royal Family.

Simon Wood sat at his desk and rubbed his fluttering eyelid.

"Hello, is that you, Simon?" the duty officer called across the sea of cluttered desks.

Simon Wood didn't answer. He wasn't in the mood for good-natured shop talk. Things weren't going well for him tonight.

"Simon, Simon. It's me. Guiness. I guess you didn't recognize me at first."

Guiness sat on the edge of Simon Wood's desk, his legs crossed, one heel beating against a drawer. Guiness was a new man, just out of training school, and Simon Wood had hardly exchanged more than half a dozen words with him until tonight. He had freckles all over his face and the tops of his hands. Premature creases in his forehead. Pale blue eyes. They hadn't sent him out yet. He was still a virgin.

"What are you staring at?" Simon Wood said, touching his eyelid.

"You," Guiness said, undaunted. "You look . . . normal."

"What did you expect me to look like?"

"They told me you might show up in disguise. I've been expecting it. I mean, I didn't expect to see you looking like . . . you."

Simon Wood took an official-looking form from his desk drawer and began filling it out.

"I say, Simon, is that a Termination Report you've got there? You just do somebody?"

"Do me a favor, will you, Guiness? In fact, two favors."

"Of course."

"Stop beating at my desk with your bloody foot and don't address me by my Christian name."

With a few illegible strokes, Simon Wood completed the particulars on Anatoli Lebedev. He left the space next to "Method Used" blank. At the bottom of the page under "Remarks," he scrawled a note to Travis Epps, the pool secretary, saying that he was taking the customary three-week "post-op" holiday. "Destination?" Blank. He shoved the form in his "Out" box and got up to go.

Guiness slid off the desk and followed him toward the exit. "Have you heard about Graham and Winfrey?" he said. "They bought the farm in France."

Graham and Winfrey were agents who had been with Simon Wood in the original wartime Special Operations Executive class. There had been more than thirty of them to start with. Now, there were five, including Simon Wood. The attrition rate in SOE was more than ten times that of the other branches of Broadway.

"They might send me to take Winfrey's place," Guiness said.

Simon Wood brushed his eyelid.

"Oh, yes, and Simon," Guiness said. "Sorry, old boy, I mean Wood. I suppose you've heard about 'C'?"

Simon Wood whirled on Guiness and grabbed him by the shoulders.

"What about 'C'?"

"They had to take him to the hospital," Guiness said. "I had to call Number Ten myself with the news because there wasn't anybody over at Broadway to handle it."

" 'It'? What's 'it,' you bloody fool?"

"The old angina is what they told me," Guiness said. "But it sounded to me more like a heart attack."

3

As Simon Wood walked sowly back to his flat, he noticed that it had grown overcast. He could tell because the antiaircraft searchlights were making a vain attempt to poke through the heavy cloud cover that had blanketed London. They only succeeded in creating an eerie fluorescent effect over the sleeping city. It was well past midnight when he turned the key in his door.

Once inside, he immediately stripped off his clothes and stepped into a steaming shower. When he had dried himself, he opened the medicine cabinet and took out a leather toilet kit. He checked the contents: permanent wave cream, curlers, hair dye, hair clippers, adhesive, putty. . . . He was about to close the cabinet door when he noticed the bottle of baby oil. He poured a few drops on the palm of his hand, grasped his penis, and masturbated swiftly, mechanically, without passion.

Then he went into the bedroom. He examined himself carefully in the floor-length mirror. Nude, he did not look particularly menacing with his shoulder bones and rib cage poking through his skin. Knobby kneed too. He was probably twenty to twenty-five pounds below the normal weight recommended for a man who stood five foot ten.

He had made a trip to Cairo only a few weeks ago. And now, looking at his emaciated form in the mirror, he knew that he would have to prepare himself again for another journey to the Egyptian capital. It would take him a week to get into shape, to make the transformation. A painful, disgusting, horrible week. But he had no choice. Lebedev was dead. Broadway was compromised. "C" was in the hospital. There was no one he could talk to. No one to trust. He had to act on his own.

He thought briefly of trying a different disguise, but quickly dismissed the idea. It would have to be the same as last time. Everything would have to be the same.

Still nude, he padded into the kitchen and unbolted the door that led into the larder. He snapped on an overhead light. The shelves were stocked with hundreds of tins of black-market food and cases of whisky. He consulted a chart of calorie values pasted to the wall and removed enough food to provide six thousand calories a day for the next week. This consisted of five bottles of scotch, forty cans of lentil soup, a dozen large cans of condensed sweetened milk, half a dozen cans of chocolate syrup, three dozen tins of tuna fish packed in oil, eight large jars of American peanut butter, fourteen jars of pickled avocado, three vacuum-sealed containers of fruitcake, a large tin of tea, and a sack of sugar.

He set his alarm clock for seven-fifteen and went to sleep. When the alarm woke him, he sat on the edge of his bed, still nude, and made a phone call.

"Yes?" the voice at the other end of the line said.

"I should like to place a personal notice in the Cairo *Sphinx*," he said. "The same as last time. It should read: Shimon Wolinsky has important news of PAMT."

Then Simon Wood put on his bathrobe and slippers and shuffled toward his kitchen.

CHAPTER TEN

CAIRO
Saturday, April 22

1

Mme. Badia was in one of her moods again. Her French maid, Solange, had a word for it. *Morosité*. Which loosely translated meant moroseness. Her Egyptian whores called it "Madame's Ramadan," referring to the ninth month of the Islamic calendar when devout Moslems fast from dawn to dusk. And her daughter, Philippa, who had come to live at the Casino de l'Opéra shortly after the departure of Captain Alexander Albright, began to mumble about leaving.

Mme. Badia's moods seemed to come and go without any apparent reason. No one ever noticed that they were invariably linked to the appearance of an obscure item in the Personal Notices section of Cairo's English-language weekly newspaper, the *Sphinx*. It said: "Shimon Wolinsky has important news of PAMT."

The same day that the notice appeared, Mme. Badia took to her bed. Solange was instructed to draw all the drapes, pile extra pillows against the fraying tapestry of the headboard, and set a bedside table with a pitcher of unsweetened lemon juice, a bottle of Bayer aspirin, a stack of Balzac novels, and Madame's most prized possession: an inscribed photograph of the one great love of her life—Philip Arthur Michael Taylor.

"*Regardez*," Mme. Badia said to Philippa, pointing to the inscription with a stubby finger. "'Eternally yours, P.A.M. Taylor, February, 1921.' *Vingt-trois ans.* Twenty-three years since I last saw your father. Ah, *mon petit choux*, you were spared a great deal of pain because you never knew your father. With me, it is otherwise. The true cruelty of time is not that it assaults one's body, though heaven knows that is bad enough. The true cruelty is that it leaves the memories of the heart unscathed."

As she watched her mother light a thin blue candle before the photograph, Philippa was seized by a sharp fear. Was this the future that lay in store for her? Would she spend the rest of her life mooning over the loss of Alex Albright the way her mother had mooned all these years over *her* lost lover? Would her body grow grotesque, her beautifully chiseled features erode, her eyelids disappear under sagging folds of fat?

Philippa felt trapped. Ever since that last night at Shepheard's Hotel with Alex, when she amazed herself by having an orgasm, she had wondered whether any man could make her feel that way again. Since that experience, life seemed empty of meaning. The moment she had trusted a man, fully, completely, with all her femininity, he had abandoned her. Could she ever trust another? Could she ever take the risk? She needed time to think. That was why she had come to live with her mother. For in a whorehouse, even one as respectable as the Casino de l'Opéra, time was meant to stand still.

Everything that had happened at the Casino had happened before. And in exactly the same way. For instance, once the candle was lit before the photograph, Mme. Badia always summoned the conductor of the Casino's orchestra, a fussy little Italian with a head of beautiful, curly gray hair, and ordered him to play only romantic numbers. This season she was particularly fond of "Long Ago and Far Away," and the Italian conductor played it over and over and over again. When the doctor came to take her blood pressure and administer a glass of greenish tonic, he always hummed the music off-key and exclaimed to his patient: "You'll soon be dancing the night through." To which Mme. Badia inevitably replied: "Rubbish!"

Sometimes, Mme. Badia would subsist on her lemon juice and her morosité for an entire week. During this time, the whores would grow unconsolably sad, smearing their mascara with tears and driving away the customers. Finally, such a pall of gloom would fall upon the once-roisterous Casino that even the agents of the European and Egyptian secret services would not bother to show up to keep an eye on each other.

That evening, the Casino would close early and a sign would be hung on the huge wrought-iron entrance gate: "Temporarily Closed for Business." The chandelier over the tiny wooden dance floor dimmed and was extinguished. The bottles of whisky were locked in their glass cabinets. In the wallpapered "apartments" on the second floor, the beds were stripped of their linen and left unmade. And in this cool, dark hush, the string orchestra delivered its poignant rendition of "Long Ago and Far Away."

This was the moment that Mme. Badia had been waiting for.

Now she bestirred herself enough to scribble a note and tell Solange to take it to the Mena House Hotel the next morning. Solange did not know for whom the message was intended, since the envelope only had a room number on it. When Solange returned, she was given the rest of the day off to visit her sister's children. Philippa was sent on a shopping trip to Gezira, an errand that was meant to keep her away from the Casino for two or three hours.

Alone now, Mme. Badia dressed herself in a loose green gown with long sleeves designed to hide the hanging flesh on her upper arms. She took the photograph of Philip Taylor into her private office, placed it on the imitation Louis XV desk, and sat down to wait for her secret visitor. The only sound in the room was the wheezing from her strained breathing and the ticking of the clock in the Parker desk pen set.

It was four-thirty in the afternoon. Without a knock, the door to the office opened. The strains of "Long Ago and Far Away" drifted into the room. A man entered. He was a tallish, lumpy, pear-shaped man, narrow at his stooped shoulders, and heavily padded around the midsection and buttocks. He was bald except for a ring of curly black hair around his temples and back of his head. Beard stubble framed his bow-shaped lips. Beneath the sallow complexion and heavy jowls, you could discern the earlier outline of an innocent-looking baby face.

"*Mon cher Monsieur Wolinsky,*" Mme. Badia said.

"Madame." Wolinsky bowed in the deferential fashion of the cultured European. His fingers played with the rim of his black felt hat. He hung back at the threshold of the doorway, waiting to be invited in.

"Please, please come in and sit down, monsieur," Mme. Badia said. "Perhaps you would like some refreshment? A cup of tea? Coffee?"

Wolinsky came toward her, shuffling his scuffed black shoes over the parquet floor. He held up the palm of his hand in a limp stop sign. "No, no, nothing for me, sank you, sank you." The palm patted the roundness of his stomach. "As you can thee, I am far too fond of refrethments. Yes, my thweet tooth is my vice, madame."

"Ah, yes, I find it hard to resist, too," Mme. Badia said.

Wolinsky sat down, crossed one wrinkled, stained trouser leg over the other. He placed his black felt hat on the edge of the desk next to the Parker desk pen set. He looked at Mme. Badia, but over her head, carefully avoiding meeting her eyes. "It was tho good of you to arrange to thee me again on thuch thort notice," he said. As he spoke, white spittle formed in the corners of his mouth.

"You are looking well, monsieur."

Wolinsky shrugged.

"I manage to thurvive," he said.

"Business is good?" she asked.

He shrugged again. "Tho far thith year I can't complain," he said. "When the Germanth were winning the war, they bought diamondth. Now that they're loothing, they thell diamondth. Either way, I manage to make a thmall profit. And you? Your buthineth ith altho good?"

"*Toujours amour*," she smiled.

"I'm glad to hear that," he said.

"*Alors*," she said. "Now for our *real* business."

"Yeth," he said. He looked around the room. "We are alone?"

"Completely," she said

"No one knowth I wath coming?"

"Not a soul," she replied.

He smiled at her, a yellow-stained smile. With the tips of his fingers, he moved his black hat in a circle on her desk. He could feel the sharp metal wire concealed in the sweatband of the hat.

"Not even your friends in Mossad?" he asked.

"Monsieur Wolinsky," she said, trying to control her impatience, "I do not know how you got this fixed idea that I am a member of Mossad, the so-called Jewish Institute. Whatever information I exchange with you is my own information, obtained through the normal course of doing business here at my Casino. My sources . . ."

"Madame," he interrupted, "your connection with the Institute ith well known to me. You are the eyeth and earth of Mossad. If I sought you were anything leth, I would not be here today."

"Have it as you wish, monsieur."

He took his hands away from his hat and brought out a sealed envelope from his inside breast pocket. He put the envelope on the desk in front of Mme. Badia.

"For you, madame," he said. "The eyeth and earth of Mossad in Egypt."

Her hands shook as she picked up the envelope and tore it open. Tiny beads of perspiration formed a moustache on her upper lip. She removed a lock of hair and a slip of paper from the envelope. She devoured the words.

"Is this all?" she asked, clearly disappointed.

"I'm afraid tho," he said. "Ath I told you lath time, since Mithter Philip Taylor'th stroke, he hathn't been very active. There ithn't much to report."

Wolinsky/Wood looked upon Mme. Badia's sentimental attachment to the past with venomous contempt. He could not fathom her insatiable hunger for news of a man she had loved and lost more than twenty years ago. It was his luck that he had learned of her Achilles' heel. Otherwise, he would never have been able to penetrate the secrets of the Institute. After today, after he squeezed one more secret from her disgustingly fat body, he would no longer be able to use her. Then he would remove the metal wire from his hat and noose it around one of the fatty creases in her neck and . . . But before he killed her, he would tell her the truth—that Philip Arthur Michael Taylor had been dead and buried for these past three years.

"What about his wife?" Mme. Badia asked. "Philip's wife? How is she?"

"About the thame," he said.

"She is still . . . *away?*"

"Yeth, ath you thay, *away*."

"And his son? His son must be old enough for the army."

"He hath nosing to do wis hith son. They haven't thpoken in yearth. His son blames him for what happened to the wife."

"Ah, *pauvre* Philip," Mme. Badia said. "All alone. No one to console him in the twilight of his years. He must suffer greatly."

"Perhapth after the war, you will be able . . ."

"*Jamais!*"

"I thee. Well, it wath just a sought."

"No, monsieur, I am not worthy. I am sure that he would rather forget the chapter in his life in which I took part."

"Yeth, yeth. Now, Mme. Badia, it is time for me to ask a few quethionth."

"Bien."

"Let me thay, madame, that I know the anthers to motht of the quethionth, tho pleath do not prevaricate with me."

"Monsieur, I will answer all your questions, fully and completely. That is our arrangement."

"And I will bring you more information on Mithter Taylor next time."

"Bien."

"We begin. Mossad is training two hundred and forty parachutith thomewhere in thouthern Egypt. That is my first quethion."

Mme. Badia took a deep breath and closed her eyes.

"That is not entirely accurate," she said. "It is the British who are training the parachutists you speak of. Mossad is *supplying* the parachutists. Palestinian volunteers."

"Good. Now, I am interethted in one particular group of these Palethtinian parachutith. There ith one group that ith being trained for a mithion into Hungary."

"*Oui.*"

"And thith group ith an American group."

"Not precisely," Mme. Badia said. "It is trained at British facilities. Supplied by Palestinian Jewish manpower. And led by an American."

"The American. What ith hith name?"

"*Je ne sais pas.*"

"Madame, you thay pa."

"His name is Captain Alexander Albright."

"Fine. You are doing jutht fine. Ath a reward for your co-operathon, I have a thurprith for you. I am going to tell you thomething about Mithter Taylor that you never would have guethed. Now, my next quethion is thith: Who picked Captain Albright to lead thith mithion?"

"General Donovan."

"The general himself? I thee. And where did he do the picking?"

"I do not understand your question."

"How did General Donovan find thith Albright fellow?"

"Albright was here in Cairo."

"The general never met him?"

"General Donovan personally came here to appoint him," Mme. Badia said. "It was a joint decision among the Americans, the British and Mossad."

"General Donovan reprethented the Oh Eth Eth. Who reprethented Mossad and Broadway?"

"Monsieur, the names of members of Mossad are not . . . I cannot tell you any Mossad names. That will have to be a condition of our arrangement. Even if that means you will no longer bring me information of Philip Taylor."

"All right. No Mossad names. How about Broadway? Donovan personally came to Cairo to organize thith mithion. It ith that important. Thomebody mutht have come from Broadway, too. Who?"

"Kim Philby."

"Philby."

Not-to-be-believed! Kim Philby. Philby working with the Russians! At the very pinnacle of Broadway. "C" 's own fair-haired boy. Practically the annointed successor. If "C" should falter, the bloody Russians would have one of their own running Broadway. And once he became "C," Philby would automatically share the most sensitive secrets of the OSS.

"C" was just released from the hospital. They said it was only angina. But who could say how long the old boy would last. And now the only thing that stood in the way of Philby was Simon Wood.

"And now, madame," he said, "it ith time for me to go."

They both stood at the same time. He picked up his black felt hat from the desk and tucked a finger into the sweatband. Mme. Badia came around from behind the desk. He began removing the sharp metal wire. His eyes were on a fatty fold in her neck. She walked toward the door. He followed. Behind her. Just two more steps. Before she turned to say good-bye.

Suddenly, the door burst open and Philippa Taylor rushed into the room. Her dark, beautifully chiseled features were contorted into a mask of sorrow. Tears coursed down her face. She hugged the sides of her arms. She looked desolately at her mother.

"I saw him," she said.

"Who?" Mme. Badia asked.

"Going into the Gezira Turf Club to watch the cricket match," Philippa said. "He was with a girl."

"Who was with a girl?" Mme. Badia asked.

"Alex," Philippa said.

"Oh, no," Mme. Badia said, putting a consoling hand on her daughter's wet cheek.

"Oh, Mother!"

Philippa fell into Mme. Badia's arms.

"He's back," Philippa sobbed. "And I saw him with this girl."

"Oh, mon petit choux."

Shimon Wolinsky/Simon Wood had tucked the metal wire back into the sweatband of the hat.

"Is it Alex Albright?" he said soothingly. "Is that who you mean?"

"Yes," Philippa said, her face buried in her mother's fleshy shoulder.

"Alex Albright in Cairo," Wolinsky/Wood said.

"Oh, Mother, I shall never leave you now," Philippa cried. "Never. I will stay here with you forever."

"Ooo la la, ooo la la," Mme. Badia crooned.

"Here in Cairo," Wolinsky/Wood said. "Who'd have thought it? Well, then, I must be going. Yes. *Yeth*. I mutht be going. Pleath excuthe me. I mutht rush off thraight away. You will excuthe me, I'm thure."

Mme. Badia rocked her daughter back and forth in her arms, crooning softly in her ear. She did not notice when Monsieur

Wolinsky left. And she was only barely aware that the orchestra had stopped playing "Long Ago and Far Away."

2

Simon Wood was in luck.

As he closed the massive wrought-iron gate of the Casino de l'Opéra behind him, he spotted a taxi parked at the foot of the driveway. Both of its curbside doors were thrown open. Wood looked inside. A pile of dirty white rags in the back seat turned out to be the driver curled up in his gallabiyeh for a siesta. Wood shook him awake and offered two pounds over the meter for the trip to the Mena House Hotel. A few minutes later, they were inching their way through the congestion of Cairo's late-afternoon rush hour.

"*Wen-Nabi!*" the driver cursed the traffic. "By the Prophet!"

He was an enormous hulk of a man. His thick chocolate-brown neck glistened with sweat. His shoulders practically filled the entire front seat of the ancient Morris Minor taxi. His white towel-like turban rubbed against the shredded upholstery of the roof. He poked his head out of the window, leaned on the horn with his elbow, and bellowed his frustration.

"Wen-Nabi!"

Then he tucked his head back inside and turned toward his passenger.

"Stuck," he apologized. "Like snot in the nose of an urchin."

"*Malish,*" Simon Wood said in Arabic.

"Malish?" the driver repeated with evident satisfaction. "Oh, yes, sir, that is certainly true." His smile revealed a mouthful of short, babylike teeth set in a mountain of inflamed gums. "You know malish. How do you say in English? 'It can't be helped.' Yes? Ah, sir, you are indeed wise."

The driver turned toward the fly-speckled windshield, mumbling contentedly to himself in Arabic. He glanced in the rearview mirror at Simon Wood's reflection. His passenger was dressed all in black. Even his hat was black. Curious. Very curious.

"Pardon me, sir," he said. "You come from this part of the world, perhaps?"

"No," Simon Wood said. "Why do you ask?"

"It is your features, sir," the driver explained. "I am a student of phrenology, you see, and the shape of your skull, the placement of your ears and your facial features have altogether a certain—how should I say?—a certain Semitic quality. Let me guess. You are a Lebanese?"

"I am a Jew," Simon Wood said.

The driver didn't seem to understand.

"Jew," Simon Wood repeated. "*Yehuday. Yehuday.*"

"Yehuday!" the driver exclaimed. "By the Prophet!"

That should keep the bloody beggar quiet for a while, Simon Wood thought. *But who knows? It might prove useful. If the police should question him later during the investigation, he'll remember me as his Jewish passenger.*

He could hear his stomach growling. The juices were beginning to flow. He felt slightly nauseated. To distract himself, he looked out the window at the tangle of traffic. The little Morris Minor was immobilized between a trolley car and a British Army truck that had been painted black, with gold angel wings on its sides, and converted into a hearse. Malish. It can't be helped. Anyway, as far as Simon Wood was concerned, things were moving very nicely. Very nicely indeed.

Ordinarily, Simon Wood was not one to conceive of life in analogies, but he couldn't help but think of the past nine days in terms of a very complex chess game.

How would he score the game so far?

1. Playing the Russian gambit, Lebedev tries to inform Gorky Street about the Hungarian mission.

2. Wood defends. Takes Lebedev.

3. With his side under assault, it is logical to assume that Philby must counterattack by devising a way of getting Lebedev's original message through to Moscow.

4. Wood blocks Philby, who is now isolated and can thus be picked off easily later in the game.

5. Albright, an unwitting pawn, moves to Cairo positioned for final instructions.

6. Albright must be stopped from carrying out the original Russian gambit, so Wood sweeps across the board. Take Albright.
Mate.

The taxi began moving again. Simon Wood looked down at his wristwatch. It was almost half past six. His stomach seemed to have quieted down. But now he had developed a slight tick in his right eye.

3

It was nearing teatime at the Gezira Turf Club. Set out in buffet style, tea consisted of a dazzling variety of sandwiches, salads, scones, cakes, and breads, and it was presented in lavish colonial style, with Sheffield tea service on pretty tables along three sides of the "El Alamein Room." The fourth side opened onto the awn-shaded terrace, where the club's servants moved expertly among the members and their guests, offering three different types of sherry in pink, long-stemmed crystal glasses. Beyond the terrace, the well-tended lawn and the cricket ground—laid out 180-by-145 yards, the exact dimensions of Lord's Cricket Ground in London—swept to a line of palm trees swaying in a refreshing breeze off the Nile.

Ruth Bar-Adon hadn't raised any objection when Alex Albright suggested that they go to the Turf Club. But she had been full of private misgivings. For her, it was almost like stepping into the hushed coolness of a Catholic cathedral. Pleasing to the eye, perhaps, but an alien, hostile environment whose symbols conjured up all sorts of painful associations. Cross . . . Communion wafers . . . surplices . . . cricket . . . tea . . . Royal Army uniforms . . . The British masters of Palestine were not, after all, exactly her favorite people. She realized that Albright didn't share these associations. He only meant to please her. So she tried to suppress her feelings. Not very successfully.

From their little, round, damask-covered table on the shaded terrace, Albright pointed out the positions of the players on the sunny cricket ground. He explained that the match between the officers and the enlisted men had probably been going on, with leisurely breaks for lunch and afternoon tea, for nearly seven hours. How typical of the British, Ruth thought, to drag things out to the point where boredom became a virtue. Only now, shortly after their arrival, was the match coming to its lethargic climax. The players were dressed in white—white flannel trousers, white shirts with sleeves rolled up to their elbows, white woolen sweaters, and white buck shoes. They looked to Ruth as crisp and fresh as if they had just stepped out of the cool shade onto the immaculate turf. Their unruffled appearance after hours of strenuous exertion made her wonder again why the British strove so hard to make life look so easy.

Albright tried to explain the fine points of the game, but he lost her somewhere between the "silly mid off" and the "popping crease." So their conversation drifted on to other subjects and eventually, without their being aware of it, came to rest on a topic of mutual interest. Themselves.

"Would you mind repeating that?" Ruth said.

To avoid his eyes, she looked down at her foot poking out of the fringes of the fine tablecloth. The straps on her red shoes looked so delicate. She couldn't remember the last time she had worn high-heeled shoes and stockings. She was aware of her garter straps rubbing against her thighs.

"I said," Albright repeated, "'I hope you've enjoyed yourself today.' Did I say something wrong?"

"Of course not," she said. "Except that it's the first time I've heard you express an interest in my feelings."

"I see," Albright said a bit defensively.

He still didn't understand her. All this stuff about feelings all the time. It was like checking your pulse every five minutes. Who could be bothered? For instance, it occurred to him, after it was too late, that she probably hadn't wanted to come to the club because it would remind her how she felt about the British, and that she would blame him for being insensitive.

That was the trouble. Feelings were always getting in the way and complicating things. You couldn't just have a nice time with her, like normal people. But, at the same time, he had to admit that that was what he found so damn appealing about her. She wasn't like other people. Other girls. She made him feel . . . *privileged*. Just being near her. Even during their training at Camp Jubilee. You could tell that she cared. That the mission was the most important thing in the world. And she made everyone else feel that way too. Including him. *She made him feel.*

"There hasn't been much time for feelings these past few weeks," he said.

"That's true," she said. "But I'm glad there's time now."

"Not much," he said. "Just a few more hours."

"It's hard to believe that we're finally going tomorrow," she said. "No more dreaming, no more training, no more uncertainty. We're really going to do it. What's the weather supposed to be like tomorrow?"

"They say it's clear all the way across the Mediterranean," he said. "Perfect for a jump. Are you scared?"

She reached across the table and touched his hand. "You astonish me," she said. "All these questions about how I feel. The next thing you know you'll ask me how I feel about you."

He braided his fingers between hers. She felt icy cold. From fear of tomorrow's jump? From fear of him? He didn't understand it either. It was all too complicated. Why couldn't he just take her to bed? That would simplify matters. A nice straightforward screw, with him on top and her on the bottom, and—*bang*—all the questions would be answered in a couple of minutes in bed. When you had an itch, his father used to say, scratch it. And he was itching for her now.

"I wouldn't dare ask you how you feel about me," he said. "You might tell me the truth."

She began to say something. Leaned forward. Searched his eyes. Then something drew her back and she shifted uneasily in her chair. Their hands slowly parted.

Guido DeVita had given the members of the Tchaikovsky Circuit a twenty-four-hour furlough, and Albright and Ruth had flown up to Cairo in his Sopwith Camel for the day. Just the two of them. Albright had to see the British resident alone, and although he didn't tell her what it was about, Ruth assumed that he received final instructions for the mission. They had the rest of the day to themselves, and it was turning out to be a tender interlude.

Ruth raised her glass and peered at Albright over the pink rim. She had come to notice certain things about him. His straight blond hair, for instance; it looked so neat and trim in the morning after he had wet it, but it never stayed combed when it dried. Or his hands—so strong and masculine, yet expressive and feminine the way they tapered to the fingertips. Or his eyes—dark and hard but, at times, amazingly vulnerable. He didn't look at all like her "Black Knight" from the Stern Gang days (all that seemed like a hundred years ago now). Physically, the two men were almost opposites. Yet there was a resemblance. It was something she sensed, something in both men that was held back, checked, ungiven. Something deep within the characters of the "Black Knight" and Alex Albright that always seemed to be struggling to be . . . born.

"I haven't answered your question," she said. "Yes, I've had a glorious time today. I loved the zoo and I loved the ice cream at Groppi's and I loved the cruise on the Nile and . . ."

"But you don't love it here, though, do you?" he said.

She glanced around the terrace. At the adolescent-looking men in their grown-up uniforms and the big-boned women with their strawberry-and-cream complexions and their buck teeth. It was all so British. So complacent.

Just then, a waiter came by with a tray of clinking glasses.

"I know what you would love," he said. "Another sherry."

"I really don't think I should," she said. "If I have another, I'm afraid I won't wait for you to ask me how I feel about you. And God knows where that might lead us."

"Waiter, two more, medium dry, please," Albright said.

They sipped at their sherries.

"You look different," Albright said after a moment.

"I do?" she said.

"I mean different from the first time I saw you," he said.

"You didn't like me very much then, did you?"

"I thought you were very beautiful," he said, "but I took an instant dislike to you."

"That's honest," she said. "And now?"

"You know, I tried to have you removed from the team," he said.

"Yes, I know."

"Well, do you know why?" he asked.

"I don't think it will do any good to talk about it," she said.

"All right," he said. "But I want to tell you that I think I was wrong about that—about you and the team. I think you've earned your place."

She could hardly believe her reaction to his words. *You've earned your place!* It was as if he had told her that she had a right to breathe, to exist, to go on living. She was absolutely overcome with gratitude. How astonishing! And, she realized, how absurd! Why should she be grateful? Why was his judgment of her so important? What had Guido DeVita said about her? *She forms dependency relationships with men who are not dependable.* Was that really true of her? If so, how sad. How terribly, terribly sad.

You've earned your place. It hadn't been easy for Albright to say those words. But what he said was true. He looked at Ruth, at her beautiful cameo face with its almond-shaped gray-blue eyes against the white skin. Skin whiter than the inside of his wrist. In his mind's eye, he could picture that face, flushed with concentration, as she had hooked up her line inside the C-47 transport plane just before their practice jump over the Libyan desert. And he could see her pushing back her light-brown hair from her forehead, her full, bowed lips parting as she began to recite the coded abbreviations during her final test in shortwave transmission signals: *QRB—Your message regarding broadcast received and understood. . . . QUO—I am forced to stop transmitting because of imminent danger. . . .* And he could visualize her on the Fairbairn close-combat course, proving that she knew how to break someone's neck from behind or that she could deliver a deadly blow by stomping on someone's stomach or that she could aim a mortal stab with a pencil under someone's chin. . . .

There was a murmur from the spectators on the field.

"Watch this," Albright said. "See that fellow there? He hit four sixes in the last innings, but this bowler has a wicked googly."

"A wicked what?" Ruth asked.

"A googly."

"Alex, what in the world is a googly?"

"Would you mind repeating that?" he said.

"I said, 'What in the world is a googly?' "

"No, you didn't," he said. "You said, '*Alex*, what in the world is a googly?' Do you realize that that's the first time I've ever heard you call me by my first name."

"Alex," she said tentatively. Then: "Alex, Alex, Alex . . ."

4

As he changed his clothes, Simon Wood looked down from the window of his room on the rose garden of the Mena House Hotel. Guests had gathered on lawn chairs to watch folk dances. To the beat of drums, two dark-skinned men in flowing gallabiyehs circled each other, brandishing long wooden sticks. They thrust and parried with the poles, beating them together in a counterpoint to the quickening rhythm of the drums. The dancers continued to twirl and leap, slashing with their own sticks, jumping, stomping, twisting. The drums beat faster. The dancers dodged the blows. The drums became a furious staccato. Then, suddenly, one of the dancers collapsed on the ground, in ritual surrender, while the other pirouetted around him in victory.

The audience applauded and Simon Wood turned away from the window. He crossed the room to the dresser and looked at himself in the mirror. He had on a rumpled, blue cotton seersucker suit, white button-down shirt, and blue-and-red rep necktie. He had shaved off the "Shimon Wolinsky" stubble of beard and applied a mixture of aluminum, potassium, and sulfate to his face, which gave his cheeks a chafed, reddish glow. A touch of adult acne was what he was striving for. Then the finishing touches: tiny springs in each nostril, widening his nose. Rubber pads between his upper molars and cheeks, giving him a chipmunk look. Horn-rimmed glasses. A curly strawberry-blond wig. A hearing aid in his left ear attached by a wire to a Zenith amplifier clipped to his breast pocket.

He was carrying a large leather briefcase when he appeared at the concierge's desk in the lobby.

"May I help you?" the young, well-tailored Egyptian behind the desk asked.

"How's that?" Simon Wood said.

He fiddled with the controls on his hearing aid.

"Is there something I can do for you?"

"Sure is," Wood said. "I'd be mighty grateful for a cab. I gotta get downtown in a hurry. See what you can do, will ya?"

He slapped an American five-dollar bill on the desk.

Two minutes later, the concierge personally escorted him to the waiting taxi. As the little Morris Minor pulled away from the hotel, Simon Wood realized that he had drawn the same driver who had brought him there half an hour ago. They drove in silence past the rose garden to the stone gates, where the driver stopped and awaited instructions.

"How long will it take you to make it to the Gezira Turf Club?" Simon Wood asked.

"About twenty minutes. *Insh'Allah.*"

"Listen, I don't have much time," Wood said. "You shave that by five minutes, pal, and I'll double your tip. Is it a deal?"

"Yes, sir."

"What'd you say?"

The driver looked into the rearview mirror and saw his passenger adjusting the control on his hearing aid.

"Yes, sir," he said in his loudest voice.

"Good," Wood said. "Then let's make tracks."

"May I take the privilege, sir, of inquiring if you happen to be an American?" the driver asked as he threaded the taxi through the traffic.

"Just so happens that I am," Wood said. "How'd you know?"

"It is your features, sir," the driver said. "You see, I happen to be a student of phrenology . . ."

5

After the cricket match, the players shook hands all around and strolled across the lawn to the terrace, where they joined the members and their guests at the buffet tables. Everyone seemed eager to congratulate a baldish, middle-aged player by the name of Barnes who, as far as Ruth could tell, had scored something called a "century" during the game. Barnes seemed mightily pleased with himself and clearly enjoyed all the attention.

Back at their table, Ruth watched Albright devour a piece of cake.

"You should try some of the pastry," Albright said.

"Do you know what watching you eat that cake reminds me of?" Ruth said. "Those glass display cases full of cakes at the Vörösmarty Gerbau Café in Budapest. Did you ever go there?"

"I practically *lived* at Vörösmarty when I was a student," he said.

"Really?" she said. "I adored Vörösmarty. Not just the cakes or the coffee or the ice cream. I adored everything about it. When no one was looking, I used to run my hand along the walls. Do you remember the fabric on the walls? Each room had a different-colored wallcovering. Green flocked in the main room. Red in the other. And that wonderful lemon yellow where they used to sell pastry to take home."

"I don't remember the walls," he said. "But I do remember those incredible chandeliers. And all those old people sitting there for hours, almost motionless, like wax statues."

"Oh, I wish I had known you then," she said.

"Just as well you didn't," he said. "You wouldn't have liked me. I didn't wear socks."

"You didn't wear socks?"

"I didn't even have any," he said. "I threw them all away. I thought I was very daring. It was my own little revolution against my parents. Appearances were very important to them. But I doubt very much that my mother even noticed that I wasn't wearing them. All I could claim to have accomplished was getting a few splinters."

"God, my mother would have noticed if I didn't wear socks," Ruth said. "My mother supervised every piece of clothing I put on. We used to have these incredible fights about what I would wear. It seems so silly now. But it wasn't then. I so desperately wanted to grow up and she . . . well, I suppose she really didn't want me to become a woman. It wasn't entirely her fault, of course. There were just the two of us, two women, alone in this large house. My father was dead. And my mother used to have a salon and all these men, important politicians and intellectuals and writers, would come to her soirées. And I guess, looking back, there was this natural . . . *competition* between us, especially as I grew older. Though I'm sure neither of us was conscious of it. But it must have been there. And the more she tried to hold me back, the more I wanted to become my own person. I had dreams of becoming a famous poet one day. And after they started passing laws against the Jews, I thought that if I went to Palestine, I would be free to do whatever I wanted. Free? Look at how strange life is! Tomorrow we start on our mission and I'm returning to Budapest to save my mother. If she's still alive."

Albright took her hand.

"Do you know what DeVita calls you?" he said. "He says you are a Jewish Joan of Arc."

Ruth laughed.

"Guido is a philosopher," she said. "And a man. What he doesn't understand about me is that I am, first, a woman and only second, a Jewish Joan of Arc. Don't you think that I have doubts about myself? Believe me, I often wonder whether I'm really committed to the cause of saving Jewish lives or whether I'm indulging my own selfish romantic fantasy. Someday, I'll let you read my diaries. Then you'll see that my Joan of Arc costume is part of a masquerade."

"I think you're being unfair to yourself," he said. "Everybody has doubts."

"Everybody but you," she said.

"You think so?" he said. "Well, I'm having doubts right now."

"What about?" she asked.

"About whether I can bear sitting here another second without hurling myself across the table and making love to you in front of all these people."

"Now that would be a googly," she said.

They were staring at each other when a waiter approached their table and said: "There is a gentleman who would like to see you, sir."

"Did you tell anyone where we were going?" Albright asked Ruth.

"No."

Albright turned toward the waiter. "Tell the gentleman to join us."

"The gentleman says he would like to see you privately, sir. In the smoking room."

6

It was a small room done in pale shades of rose and blue. The aroma of tobacco clung to the upholstered chairs and sofas. A clock, framed in a gold sunburst, rested on the mantelpiece. A porcelain, life-sized figure of a Dalmatian snuggled on the multicolored Tabriz carpet. A "Do Not Disturb" sign hung from the doorknob inside the room.

"Captain Albright?"

"Yes."

"The name's Wolfe. Sam Wolfe. General Donovan sent me. Put the don't-disturb sign outside so we won't be interrupted."

Albright hung the sign outside, closed the door and turned to face the stranger. He was a porky-looking man with curly red hair and pimples. He wore a hearing aid and, instinctively, Albright made an effort to ignore it.

"This shouldn't take long," Sam Wolfe said. "Come on over here to the sofa and take a load off your feet."

"What does General Donovan want?" Albright said as he eased himself onto the sofa.

"How's that?" Sam Wolfe asked.

He turned up the volume knob on the Zenith hearing-aid amplifier.

"I'm curious," Albright said more loudly, "what the general wants."

"Goddamn fucking hearing aid," Sam Wolfe said. "I can't hear a word you're saying. Fucking batteries must have gone dead again."

He pulled the plug from his ear, detached the wire from the amplifier and unclipped the amplifier from his breast pocket. Albright watched with fascination. It was like watching someone undress in public.

"Excuse me, will ya?" Sam Wolfe said. "I gotta recharge these batteries. I'm sorry about this. I really am. I mean, I shoulda checked before I came here. But this thing never gives you any warning. One minute you're hearing things clear as a bell, the next you're totally blanked out."

As he spoke, Sam Wolfe opened his briefcase and took out a large metal box. He fished into the briefcase again and found an electrical wire, which he plugged into the box. He flipped a switch and a red light glowed on the top of the metal box.

"Good," he said. "The recharger's working."

He flipped off the red light. Then he plugged the other end of the wire into the Zenith amplifier.

"Now," he said, "if you'll just hold this little amplifier for me . . ."

In the next one tenth of a second, Albright saw the red light flash on, felt the electrical charge surge through his hand, up his arm, to his neck, began to grasp what was happening to him. . . .

Sam Wolfe/Simon Wood turned off the sixty-volt transformer. He put away his equipment, closed his briefcase, then checked to see if Albright was still alive. The pulse in the neck was surprisingly strong and regular. He grabbed Albright under both arms and hauled at his body until his head was hanging over the edge of the sofa. From his inside breast pocket, he took out a long metal file. He forced open Albright's mouth and felt for his soft palate. He began to lower his right hand holding the file when something red flashed in his peripheral vision and the instrument flew out of his fingers and across the room.

He swirled around. The red flashed again. The blow caught him on the shoulder and sent him sprawling onto the carpet in front of the porcelain Dalmatian. He looked up and saw a pair of red shoes. Women's shoes. With high heels. He didn't quite understand. Then he saw the red flash again, heel first, coming up from the multicolored Tabriz carpet to the soft, vulnerable place under his chin. . . .

"Alex," Ruth said. "Alex, Alex, Alex . . ."

CHAPTER ELEVEN

BARI
Saturday, April 29

1

Guido DeVita glanced at the luminous dial on his wristwatch. It was nearly 9 P.M. Double daylight savings time. Just minutes to takeoff. He paced in front of the open door of the Douglas C-47 Dakota. On the fuselage above the wing, someone had stenciled the plane's nickname: MISS CARRIAGE.

There was still plenty of light. Low in the western sky, a great orange-red sun ball wriggled on a distant peak of the Apulia mountains. It remained balanced there for what seemed to De-Vita an implausibly long time. Then all at once it melted behind the jagged horizon, and the clouds over the Adriatic Sea were suddenly edged in brilliant gold, drenching the airbase at Bari on the east coast of Italy in the soft pastels of sunset.

DeVita raised his right hand, with its snakelike scar across the wrist, and passed his fingers through his thick main of white hair, which had now caught the colors of the sunset. DeVita had insisted on accompanying the Tchaikovsky Circuit from Camp Jubilee on the hop to Cairo and then to Bari. This ramshackle base was the main transshipment point for Allied supply drops into the Balkans. As an excuse for coming with the team, DeVita had said that he wanted to check personally on all the last-minute details. But that wasn't the real reason.

The real reason was that DeVita was more worried than ever about Alexander Hamilton Albright.

DeVita looked across the cement runway, cluttered with equipment and supplies wrapped in olive-green twill. He spotted Albright, who was standing by the tail of the plane, weighed down with his parachutes. Strapped to various parts of his body were a pistol, knife, grenades, canteen, entrenching tool, rations bag, ammo belt. . . . As he taped a field-dressing kit to the side of his helmet, Albright was deep in concentration. His lips moved silently. He was talking to himself.

Still at it, DeVita thought, nervously threading his fingers through his hair.

This bothered DeVita—this *practicing,* this *trying to remember,* this *making sure he can identify objects by their proper names. Albright must be going through hell. Poor bastard.* DeVita wanted to reach out to Albright, lay on his hands, heal.

No one else seemed to notice Albright as he tested himself. Nearby, Dan Gur was buckling his reserve chute. Saul Patir, a cigarette dangling from the corner of his mouth, was relacing his high-topped jump boots for the third time. Joel Nathan was checking the quick-release device on Ruth Bar-Adon's harness.

In the next few minutes, the Yugoslav crew would finish loading the supplies on the plane and, DeVita thought, the fate of the team would slip irretrievably out of his control. From then on, the success or failure of the mission, the lives of his hand-picked Palestinian volunteers, would depend on their training, their skill, their will to survive and—most of all—their leader. This strange, flawed, wounded American: Albright.

It all finally came down to that. The irony of the situation struck DeVita. He realized that during his months at Jubilee he had grown a bit mystical about this particular mission, as if the course of Jewish history and the ultimate meaning of the Holocaust could somehow be altered by this handful of people—Gur, Nathan, Patir, Bar-Adon. And, of course, Albright. As a psychoanalyst, as a Zionist, as an Italian, as a man who had himself once despaired of life and then found hope, Guido DeVita believed that history was shaped by human behavior, by the force of human character imposing itself on a malleable environment. Of the character of his Palestinians, he harbored few doubts. Of Alexander Albright, he was still unsure. Yes, more unsure than ever.

What DeVita did not realize, or would not admit to himself, was that he had become downright superstitious in the final days before the scheduled departure of the team. When the British resident in Cairo telephoned him a week ago to inform him of Albright's "little accident," he had taken it as an *ominous* sign. DeVita immediately flew up to Cairo to discover Albright, lying in a hospital bed, talking with the British resident. Albright was the only patient in the ward, a long, narrow room that looked as though no one had bothered to paint it since Vicomte Ferdinand Marie de Lesseps built the Suez Canal.

"Guido, old son," the resident said cheerily as DeVita approached. The resident wiped his palm with a blue handkerchief, then extended his hand in greeting. "Awfully good of you to pop up here like this. I was just telling Albright that he has the cheek of old Harry to pull a fast one like this on us."

"Hello, Henry," DeVita said. "How's our boy?"

"Had a bit of a shock, that's all, don't you know," the resident said. "But he'll be all right. Won't you, Albright?"

They turned toward the bed. Albright didn't look as bad as DeVita had expected. A little blue around the lips. Pale. Unshaven. But his blond hair was combed in a neat part and he was propped up on the pillows, his dark Mediterranean eyes alert. He even managed a smile.

"I'm sorry about this, Guido," Albright said. "I feel like a goddamn fool that I let this happen."

"Rubbish," the resident said. "Bad luck, that's all. It could happen to anyone."

"I don't want you to cancel the mission, Guido," Albright said. "The doctors say I'm going to be all right."

"We'll see," DeVita said. "How are you feeling?"

"I mean it, Guido," Albright said. "We can't throw everything away because of this."

"Now, now, no one's throwing anything away," the resident said. "You just need a little time to recuperate."

"We'll see," DeVita repeated. "We'll take things a day at a time. Why don't you tell me what happened."

Albright glanced up at the resident, who turned his incongruously small, boyish head away, to avoid eye contact with him.

So, it's worse than I expected, DeVita thought. *They're holding out on me.*

"Well?" DeVita said.

"I wish I could tell you," Albright said.

The resident picked up the dangling oxygen mask by the side of the bed, seemed to weigh it in his hand, let it drop, took a deep breath.

"In point of cold, hard fact, Guido," he said, "our boy has a touch of amnesia."

According to the hospital records that DeVita read later that day, Albright had been unconscious for about twenty minutes after he received the jolt of electricity. On the way to the hospital, he awoke in a clouded state, dazed and groggy. The doctors administered oxygen, after which Albright fell into a deep sleep for ten hours. Upon awakening, the records noted, Albright had been "incontinent," but he quickly gained control of his bowels and bladder.

DeVita read on with a sickening feeling in his stomach: "Since we do not know the dosage of the electricity nor the duration of the trauma, the long-term prognosis must necessarily be somewhat guarded. We cannot state whether there has been any damage to the tissue of the spinal cord. It can be stated, however, that the patient exhibits the symptoms of a retrograde amnesia, since he cannot remember events for an hour or two *preceding* the electric shock and he has some difficulty with the names of common objects. . . ."

The next day, Albright was up and around, and the day after that he was told that he could be discharged from the hospital. But DeVita noticed that Albright had not *recovered* in the true meaning of that word. There was something different about the American. Nothing that DeVita could put his finger on. But he detected it in Albright's voice, in his gestures, even in the way Albright chose his words. It seemed as though the shock—not only the electric shock that had convulsed his body and brain, but the shock of having brushed so close to death—had profoundly affected Albright. It was, DeVita thought, as though the shock had erased and then redefined the edges of Albright's personality.

This disturbed DeVita. One of his basic assumptions about life was that people change slowly, if they change at all. He believed that with a little insight and understanding it was generally safe to make predictions about human behavior, since most people behave within a predictable range. It had to be that way; otherwise, human affairs would be chaotic. And, for better or worse, he had come to count on Albright's range.

Now, that was no longer possible. The change in Albright was most noticeable when, late on the afternoon of his last day in the hospital, Ruth Bar-Adon came to visit him. Brown shadows were falling through the windows across the row of beds in the corridorlike room. Ruth was dressed in a simple white blouse and a pleated skirt. She had obviously gone to a great deal of trouble to fix her light brown hair, which was swept up from her neck and arranged in a bouquet of curls on the top of her head. She placed her hand against Albright's cheek and DeVita noticed that her nails were freshly shaped and filed. Albright held her hand next to his cheek for a long moment and murmured something to Ruth which DeVita did not catch.

They treated each other with such tenderness that DeVita would have sworn that they were lovers, though he doubted that they had had the opportunity to make love . . . yet.

The "old" Albright, DeVita thought, would not have been capable of demonstrating such sensitivity with a woman. But this seemed to be a new Albright, or at least an *altered* Albright, a more human Albright, a more outwardly vulnerable Albright. *It's an improvement*, DeVita thought. *A definite improvement.* But Guido DeVita was not at all certain that, improved or not, this was the Albright he had hoped for. He hadn't been searching for a *sensitive* man. He had wanted a leader with that extra *zetz*, with faith in the cause.

And then there was Ruth to worry about. She had killed a man, as swiftly and professionally as she had been taught to on the Fairbairn close-combat course at Camp Jubilee. Who could tell what this experience had done to her? Could she kill again? Would she hesitate at a moment of peril? Could her haver depend on her? *That* was the essential question.

DeVita could no longer be sure. All he knew was that Ruth and Alex had each had the opportunity to save the other's life—he at the parachute training tower, she at the Gezira Turf Club—and that their mutual bond was now stronger than anything they could possibly feel toward the other members of the team.

How would this affect the mission?

DeVita wondered. He wondered about all of this and, most of all, about who had tried to kill Albright. And why. No answers turned up in the next few days. Through a cooperative taxi driver, a couple of the boys from Broadway managed to track the route of the assassin back to his hotel room at the Mena House, but there the trail seemed to go cold. Some of the clothing and the disguises that were discovered in the assassin's suitcase bore the traces of having been made in Britain. But others came from America. Still others from Germany. The wigs were Swiss, the briefcase Italian, the theatrical cosmetics were made in Sweden. At the mortuary where the body was laid out for inspection by the agents of Broadway, the OSS, and the Institute, identification proved impossible. As a last resort, DeVita turned to his most reliable agent in Cairo. The chief paymaster of the Institute. Mme. Badia.

She came hobbling into the cool room where they kept the dead bodies, leaning for support on the arm of a beautiful, dark-skinned young woman whom DeVita had never seen before. *One of her prostitutes*, DeVita concluded. Mme. Badia stood before the embalmed corpse. For a few moments, she stared impassively at the waxen baby face, the bowed lips, the brutal scar on the throat where someone had crushed the dead man's trachea. Then she turned to DeVita.

"*Je n'ai jamais vu cet homme*," she said.

"You are certain?" DeVita asked.

"Of course," she said.

"Perhaps you would recognize him in one of his disguises," DeVita said.

"Perhaps," she said.

"Come to the office and I'll show you the clothing we found," he said. "Also, I want you to meet someone."

They had to climb a set of steep stairs and Mme. Badia, supporting herself on the shoulder of her beautiful young companion, grunted as she took the steps one at a time. As they entered the office, Philippa Taylor immediately recognized Albright standing before the window. Instinctively, she drew back, slipping from her mother's grasp, and for a moment Mme. Badia lost her balance and would have fallen if DeVita had not rushed to her side.

Albright looked across the room at the sleek, glossy-brown young woman, and he saw the pain sweeping her face. He knew her, of course, but her *name* . . . For an instant, he could not remember. Then it all came back to him. Philippa. *Philippa.* Memories piled upon memories. He recalled her weeping with joy in bed, wiping her tears on his forearm, whispering to him that he was the best lover in the world. And he remembered what a burden he had felt on their last night, when he suddenly realized that she was in love with him.

And now he did not know how to react. He had never misled her about their don't-count-on-it-forever kind of thing, and yet he had hurt her, deeply, and he wished that he could make amends, heal the wound. Then it occurred to him that the kindest thing he could do was say nothing, to acknowledge her only with his eyes, to leave her in peace. So he bowed his head and said nothing.

And because he was busy helping Mme. Badia into a chair, Guido DeVita missed this silent communication.

DeVita opened the suitcase on the desk and took out a black suit, black hat, and black shoes. But Mme. Badia, who had seen her daughter's reaction and who had instantly understood that the young man across the room was the American who had broken Philippa's heart, was too upset to concentrate on the articles of clothing. And in that same instant, memories of *her* lost lover, Philip Arthur Michael Taylor, flooded Mme. Badia's mind and she thought: *How would I behave in Philippa's place?*

DeVita said something, but Mme. Badia did not hear him. To compose herself, she let her eyes settle on a faded photograph of King Farouk in uniform and fez that hung on the bilious-colored wall.

"You may have seen the man dressed in this costume," DeVita was saying.

"*Non, jamais,*" Mme. Badia insisted.

"I want you to be certain," DeVita said. "This is very important to me. And to Mossad."

If I acknowledge the truth, Mme. Badia thought, *it will open up the past. How this dead man has come to visit me over the years. How I have betrayed Mossad by exchanging secrets for little locks of hair. And not only my past. Philippa's as well.*

"I am certain," Mme. Badia said.

"Mother!" Philippa cried. "*Please.*"

"What is it, mon petit choux?"

"Nothing," Philippa said. "It's nothing. I'm sorry. But . . . I just wanted to tell you that I'm feeling better. Much better. Now that I'm here and have seen . . . I mean, it's not as bad as I thought it would be. It's not bad at all. Really, one mustn't live in the past . . . one mustn't pretend. It doesn't work."

Mme. Badia looked at her daughter, then at DeVita. The little half moons that she had crayoned over her shaven eyebrows seemed to collapse into flat lines.

Not pretend. What a thought! Her whole life was built upon pretense. The gaiety of the Casino, the desperate long-distance longing for Philip Taylor, the sheltered respectability for Philippa, the secret work for the Institute—it was all part of the same make-believe.

She stood and straightened her dress over her wide hips. She picked up the black hat and examined it thoughtfully. She shrugged, emitting a long wistful sigh, almost a whistle.

DeVita decided to take a chance, a psychological shot in the dark.

"Don't do this for me or even for Mossad," he said. "Do it for yourself. It is something you have needed to do for a long time."

Mme. Badia nodded heavily.

"I knew the man as Wolinsky," she began. "Shimon Wolinsky. We first met . . ."

2

In a few more minutes, it would be completely dark. The aquamarine lights twinkled down the runway at Bari, their parallel lines converging in the distance like an arrow pointing out to sea, east toward Yugoslavia. The last of the equipment, Ruth Bar-Adon's SSTR-5 radio, was loaded on the plane. The pilot, a clean-shaven, dark-eyed young man dressed in a cheap leather coat and

Russian-made flying cap, leaned out of the doorless portal. He shouted in Serbo-Croatian to Dan Gur, the Yugoslav member of the Tchaikovsky Circuit.

Gur acknowledged the pilot with a wave, then walked over to Guido DeVita and clasped his shoulders with both hands.

"It's time," Gur said.

DeVita fixed Gur with his icy blue eyes. The two men were about the same height, but Gur seemed twice the size in his parachutist's gear.

"I'm counting on you," DeVita said. "Especially you, because you fought with Wingate in Syria and you've actually experienced battle. You know the value of caution."

"Caution is my middle name," Gur said.

"Good," DeVita said. "Don't tempt God by trying to be a hero." He held up a finger. "That's a warning."

"That reminds me of a story," Gur said.

He looked over his shoulder at the airplane, turned back to DeVita, and began to smile.

"There's still time," Gur said. "There's always time for a story. Let me tell you this one."

DeVita knew there was no use trying to stop Dan Gur when he wanted to tell one of his stories.

"In the mountains of Hercegovina," Gur began, "there was this old couple who had been married for more than sixty years, and one day someone asked the old woman the secret of such a long-lasting marriage. The old lady thought for a moment, and then she said: 'It's not such a secret. On the day we were married more than sixty years ago, my husband hired a horse and carriage to take us home from the church. We went a little way down the lane and the horse stopped and refused to go on. My husband got out of the carriage, walked up to the horse and said, *"That's one."* After we had gone a little farther down the lane, the horse stopped again, and again my husband got out of the carriage and he told the horse, *"That's two."* After a while, the horse stopped again. This time, my husband got out of the carriage, walked up to the horse and pulled out a pistol and shot the horse dead right through the head. I couldn't believe my eyes. I shouted at my husband, "I can't believe that you've done such a horrible thing on our wedding day. You're a monster!" And my husband turned to me and he said, "That's one." ' "

They laughed and hugged and kissed, and then Gur walked toward the plane.

Saul Patir was next. He stood awkwardly in front of DeVita, slightly pigeon-toed. The muscles in his jaw throbbed. His large brown eyes brimmed with emotion.

"I'm confident that you'll do well," DeVita told him. "You've *already* done well. If I had a son, I'd want him to be like you."

"Thank you for choosing me, Guido," Patir said. "I will make you proud."

Then Joel Nathan came to shake DeVita's hand.

"Have faith in us," Nathan said.

"I wish I could go with you," DeVita said.

"You *are* going with us," Nathan said. "In our hearts."

Now it was Ruth Bar-Adon's turn, and she smiled at DeVita. And all he could do was smile back. They clasped hands and nodded repeatedly at each other. She turned to go.

"Ruth," DeVita called after her.

"Yes, Guido."

"Do you remember the first time we met in Jerusalem?" he said. "And we talked about your 'Black Knight' and your father and your feelings about men."

"Yes."

"Well, I would like to give you a little piece of advice," he said. "Call it professional advice, if you wish. If you haven't slept with Albright yet, don't do it until this mission is over. There isn't time now for me to explain. Just take it on faith. It wouldn't be good for you."

"I think I'm falling in love with him," Ruth explained.

"I know," DeVita said. "That's why I'm warning you not to go any further. I wouldn't want to predict the consequences for the entire team if you commit yourself fully to this man and if he then fails to meet your needs. It could be dangerous. I am being utterly serious."

"I know you're serious, Guido," she said. "But I think you're being ridiculous, too. I don't even understand what you're talking about."

"I know you don't," he said. "Just promise me you won't sleep with him."

She thought for a moment, then said: "I can't make such a promise."

"Then," he said, "I'll have to give you an order. As your superior in Mossad, to which you have taken an oath of allegiance, I am giving you a direct order not to sleep with Albright."

"I can't believe this conversation," she said. "An *order*? Not to sleep with a man?"

"That's correct," he said.

She made a face.

"All right," she said finally.

"Good," DeVita said. "Now, you should know that I left a little surprise for you on the plane. You'll find a box of cold chicken with some matzoh and a bottle of wine."

"That was very thoughtful of you, Guido," she said, still angry.

He looked to her as though he was close to tears. She had never seen him this way before.

"It's nothing," he said, shaking his head, fighting back the tears. "Just think of how this noble gesture is going to make me look when it comes time for me to write my memoirs."

"Oh, no, Guido," Ruth said, beginning to feel the tears on her own cheeks washing away the anger. "It will appear in *my* memoirs."

DeVita walked with her to the plane, and he and Albright supported her on each elbow as she climbed heavily up the little ladder and disappeared inside. Albright clambered up after her, then turned at the door to look down at DeVita.

The starboard engine coughed loudly—once, twice, three times—and the propeller thrummed powerfully alive.

"How are the headaches?" DeVita asked.

"All gone," Albright lied.

"And the memory?"

"Seems fine," Albright said. Which was the truth. Though he didn't know if it would stay fine.

"That's a good sign," DeVita said.

"Yes, I know," Albright said. "Have you heard back from London yet?"

"No," DeVita said. Which was a lie.

A message had, in fact, reached him just a few hours ago from London. Kim Philby, the head of the anti-Communist section of British counterespionage, reported that Broadway had made a positive identification from the fingerprints of the man who had attempted to kill Albright. The man's name was Simon Wood. He was a member of the British Special Operations Executive. A killer-agent. One of those. But Philby cabled that Simon Wood must have also been a double agent. That was the only explanation he could offer.

". . . We must therefore assume," Philby's message read, "that Gorky Street fully informed of mission of Tchaikovsky Circuit and that Russians may be prepared to take measures of their own in Budapest. That, regretfully, leaves you delicate decision to proceed or cancel. For our part, we will understand if you cancel on ground mission has been compromised. However, should you opt to proceed, we prepared to offer full support and cooperation. Please advise. All best. Philby."

The port engine sputtered and then caught, and the C-47 vibrated down its entire length and strained against its brakes.

"What about Mme. Badia and the girl?" Albright asked from the door of the plane.

"I had them put under house arrest," DeVita said. "We have to find out how badly they've compromised Mossad."

"The girl can't possibly have been involved," Albright said.

"How can you know?" DeVita asked.

"*I know*," Albright shot back.

"Why? Because you had an affair with her? You had no right to withhold that from me."

"I was worried about . . . how it might look for her," Albright said.

There it is! He has changed, DeVita thought. *Suddenly mister tough guy has gone soft on me. He's more worried about his old girl friend than about his mission. This is like some cosmic joke. What a time for God to play jokes! I can't count on Albright. I can't count on Ruth. I can't count on Mme. Badia. And now Philby sends me this cockamamie message.*

DeVita did not accept Philby's explanation that Simon Wood had been a double agent working for the Russians. DeVita was an expert on these matters, and from what he learned from Mme.

Badia, Wood had not behaved like a Russian agent. If he had been working for Gorky Street, Wood would have asked Mme. Badia for certain specific information: the size of the Tchaikovsky Circuit, its date of departure, its port of debarkation, its drop zone in the Balkans, its crossover point into Hungary, its contact in Budapest. . . . *But he had not asked any of these questions.* Which was curious, to say the least.

Even more curious were the questions that Wood *had* asked. Who ordered the mission? Who picked Albright? Who, in particular, represented Broadway?

Kim Philby represented Broadway.

How on earth could the name of Kim Philby be of any use to the Russians? It couldn't. Gorky Street already knew that Philby was in charge of the anti-Communist section of Broadway. The names of section heads in competing secret services were usually the worst-kept secrets of all. And yet, Philby's name seemed to be all that Wood was after.

What did that mean? What kind of cosmic joke was this?

A mechanic in overalls ducked under a wing and removed the triangular wooden blocks from the wheels of the plane. He signaled to the pilot, then waved DeVita out of the way of the prop wash.

As he watched the plane rumble down the airstrip between the rows of aquamarine lights, DeVita suddenly wished that he could cancel the mission. He had a guilty premonition that he was sending the entire team to a certain death. He felt it in his bones. Insight, intuition, a sixth sense—call it whatever you want. He always knew these things.

The airplane lifted off into the darkening sky. And as he watched it disappear, Guido DeVita said out loud to himself: "You really are a schlemiel, you know. You could be wrong. You could be totally wrong, and everything could turn out fine."

PART II

SUMMER 1944

CHAPTER ONE

TITO'S HEADQUARTERS
Saturday, April 29

1

Albright was numb.

From the brutal cold. From the constant metallic vibration. From the deafening racket of the engines. From being strapped and buckled and squeezed into full combat gear for more than two hours. From the adrenalin that was pumping fear and confusion into his stomach.

This was it. His chance. His *last* chance to salvage something from the war. And he didn't know—*didn't have the faintest idea—*what he was supposed to salvage.

What the hell was he doing here?

Albright was so numb that he had lost all feeling in his toes and fingers. He had lost touch with his thoughts. He was unaware when the plane plunged into a thick cloud bank, tossing and yawing and losing altitude, and he didn't notice when it broke free of the storm over the island of Vis, awash in the shimmering Adriatic.

In this state, he did not see Saul Patir get up, lurch to the bathroom in the tail of the plane, and find that he could not squeeze through the narrow doorway in his bulky parachutist's equipment. He did not hear Dan Gur tell one of his stories. Nor Joel Nathan inquire of Ruth Bar-Adon if he might have another piece of chicken, please.

Albright remained like this, in suspended animation, until the light bulb beside the doorless exit suddenly glowed red.

"Four minutes," the navigator shouted.

The parachutists stood beside their bucket seats. One by one, Albright, Bar-Adon, Nathan, Patir, and Gur wrapped the static lines around their left wrists and hooked up to the anchor cable that ran overhead along the length of the fuselage. They shuffled in tight formation to the door.

Albright could feel Ruth's breath, hard and warm, on his neck.

Was that it? Maybe it was Ruth that he was supposed to salvage from the war.

He leaned forward, his legs braced wide apart, his arms tensed on either side of the exit, and stared down into the night.

Under a clear moon, he could make out the foamy cataract of the Pliva River and the brooding outline of a medieval fortress fifteen hundred feet below. This was Jajce, temporary headquarters of the Supreme Staff of Josip Broz Tito's partisan army.

The plane banked into a turn, then leveled off and headed toward a field.

A sharp buzz . . . The green light . . . A tap on the back . . .

He hurled himself out of the door and felt his internal organs—stomach, spleen, liver, lungs—pitching toward his throat, resisting the force of gravity. . . .

. . . *two, three* . . .

. . . and he heard the ripping as the fifteen-foot-long static line tore off the back cover of his parachute, and the slurping sound of the parachute unfolding and filling with air, and the snapping of the break cord that connected the top of the chute and the static line, and then . . .

. . . *whack!* . . .

. . . the incredible whiplash jolt, the shock of four G's, as the canopy spread fully open, all twenty-eight reassuring feet in diameter, billowing full of air, swaying back and forth, and then . . .

. . . *silence*. No sense of motion. An exquisite stillness. Utter fulfillment.

All in less than five seconds.

He looked around and could see no one, not even the shape of another parachute. He was all alone. For a moment, he was filled by a sense of déjà vu; he realized that he was experiencing the same sense of satisfaction that he felt ten years ago when he made his first jump from his father's La Père biplane. But it wasn't quite the same. Things had changed. *He* had changed. Still, suspended here, hanging over this moonlit field in Bosnia, he felt a surge of confidence. This was more like it. The numbing fear was gone. Yes, he still had faith in the things that really counted. Poise. Willpower. Self-control.

Or did he?

Now the field began to rise toward him very quickly and he tucked in his knees, brought his elbows close to his body, assumed a fetal position, braced himself for the landing. He was whirled about by the force of the ground wind. The wind was stronger than the meteorologist had predicted. This was potentially dangerous, especially for inexperienced parachutists.

If only they remember what I taught them.

His mind was on the others as he hit the ground, at an angle, blowing forward, but his legs absorbed the shock and he somersalted on a shoulder and began spilling the air from his chute. In a matter of seconds, he had slipped out of his harness and was fumbling for his pistol.

Where were the others?

It was darker on the field than it was during the descent, and it took a few moments for his eyes to adjust. Then he saw that Joel Nathan and Saul Patir had landed only a few dozen yards away. And over to the right, Dan Gur was drifting toward the field. *In absolutely the wrong position.* Feet wide apart, elbows akimbo, head rigid. And Albright began to run toward the spot where Gur would land.

He could almost feel the thud of Gur's awkward landing, and he whispered as loud as he dared: "You okay?"

"Sure," Gur said. "Where's Ruth?"

Albright looked around.

No Ruth.

Nathan and Patir came running toward them.

"Where's Ruth?" Albright asked them.

They looked at each other, then off toward the tree line.

"I don't see her," Nathan said.

"Shit," Albright said. "She have the radio?"

"No, I've got it," Nathan said, patting the silver splash can with the SSTR–5.

"And the batteries?" Albright asked.

Again, dumb looks. No one said anything.

"Who's got the batteries?" Albright repeated.

"Screw the batteries," Nathan said. "Where's Ruth?"

"I want to know whether we've got to find Ruth *and* the batteries, or just Ruth," Albright said.

"I think they were with her," Patir said.

"Think or know?"

"They were with her," Patir said. "She's got them."

"Okay," Albright said. "Let's ditch the chutes."

Swiftly, wordlessly, they buried their parachutes and entrenching tools in the soft, spongy earth, filled in the holes with their hands and tamped down the small mounds with their boots. Then they removed their rifles from the long khaki sheaths and began walking warily toward the tree line.

At that moment they realized for the first time that they were not alone. Standing in the shadows of the fir trees were the indistinct figures of perhaps a half dozen men. Though their faces and uniforms were hard to make out, it was possible to see the dull sheen on the barrels of their weapons reflecting the moonlight.

Saul Patir dropped to a knee and drew back the bolt of his rifle. The hollow click was instantly answered by the sound of a half dozen rifles being cocked in return.

"*Putz!*" Dan Gur hissed under his breath at Patir.

Gur reached over and carefully lowered the barrel of Patir's weapon. Then he slung his own rifle over a shoulder and moved forward. Toward the unknown figures. Albright covered him from behind.

One of the men moved out of the shadows of the trees to meet Gur. A garrison cap with a red star rested on his head at an angle. Bandoliers of ammunition crisscrossed his chest and a holster dangled from a belt over his groin. A leather coat was thrown over his shoulders. Despite the costume, however, he looked like an improbable soldier. Sallow, slight of build, looking at the world through metal-rimmed glasses, he appeared to be out of place on the edge of this Bosnian forest.

A *headman, not a muscleman,* Gur thought. *Beware.*

"Death to fascism!" the stranger said.

"Death to fascism!" Gur replied.

"I am Rankovich. Of the *Odeljenje zastite naroda,* the Department for the Security of the People. Partisan."

"I am Gur. Counterintelligence. British Army."

"*Stari* sent me to greet you," Rankovich said.

Not a bad welcoming party, Gur thought. Stari, or "the old man," was Tito.

As Rankovich spoke, his men shouldered their rifles and sauntered forward. Most of them were dressed in garrison caps and heavy woolen uniforms like Rankovich, but some of them had swathed their heads with rough scarves so that only their moustaches and hard eyes were visible to Gur. Standing back, on either side of a tree, were two women, young peasant girls wearing handwoven dresses open to their navels. Their black hair, Gur noticed, was greased with butterfat.

"We welcome the British," Rankovich said. He adjusted his glasses by pushing against the metal bridge piece with a forefinger. "Stari awaits you."

"We've run into a problem," Gur said. "One of our team drifted off course during the parachute descent and we must make a search. We can't leave with you until we find our comrade."

"Out of the question," Rankovich said.

"Perhaps you don't understand," Gur said.

"I understand perfectly," Rankovich said. "But you are in partisan territory, operating under partisan authority, and my instructions from Stari are to bring you back to headquarters directly. We can't risk wandering around the woods. Even standing here and talking like this is dangerous. There are no front lines in our kind of war. Just us and the Germans."

"We must look for our comrade," Gur said.

"I beg to differ," Rankovich said. "Your comrade must look for *us.*"

Albright approached Rankovich.

"Listen, my friend," he said, "we're not going anywhere until we make a search."

Gur motioned to Albright in a gesture of introduction.

"This is *our* stari," he said. "Captain Albright."

"Death to fascism!" Rankovich said.

Albright didn't respond.

"In this kind of war," Rankovich said icily, addressing both Albright and Gur, "it's the group that finally counts, not the individual. Any one of us—or any one of you—is expendable. I'm sorry, but that's the way it is."

Gur looked at Albright with an expression that said, "Let me handle this." Then he turned to Rankovich.

"The way we see it," he said, "is different. The group is important only because of the security it gives to the individual that *he* is important—and won't be abandoned thoughtlessly."

There was some murmuring among Rankovich's men. Gur could tell that they approved of what he had said. Rankovich pushed at his glasses. A brittle smile crossed his face.

"All right," he said. "We'll look."

"You'll see," Gur said, trying to lighten the moment, "great successes are made up of small failures."

The partisans joined the parachutists in a skirmish line and began to walk upwind. The two young peasant girls trailed behind, balancing enormous sacks of supplies on their heads. As soon as they passed through the line of fir trees, they found themselves in a thick birch forest. They came upon a small stream that had been turned by the spring rains into a ribbon of mud, smooth as chocolate icing except where deer had left their sharp tracks. Across the stream, the forest was even thicker and the moonlight hardly penetrated the foliage. Tree trunks that had been snapped by storms and by the rot of age lay along their path. The splintered sides of the trees sprouted saplings and flat earlike mushrooms of sulphurous yellow.

Albright found a narrow path that wound its way around thick rococo roots and under moss-covered ledges. There was an opening that led into a thicket and then down through a long tunnel of snapping branches to a swift, wide stream. Along both banks, primroses blossomed where the sun had managed to penetrate the forest. And there, in the middle of the stream, he saw Ruth.

She was standing waist deep in the water, trying to unravel the parachute lines that were caught on a log. The splash can with the radio batteries was strapped over her shoulder. She looked at Albright and shrugged with disgust at her predicament.

"Ruthie, Ruthie!" Joel Nathan shouted, and he plunged into the water to help her.

"Now I see," Rankovich said, joining Albright at the edge of the stream. "Your comrade is a woman. This, I suppose, explains why it was important to jeopardize so many lives to find her. We partisans don't make such distinctions between the sexes. Men and women are treated equally in our army. We would have left her behind. We've learned a great deal in the war."

Ruth waded out of the stream, shivering wet, her uniform clinging to her body, and Albright couldn't help but think back to the afternoon when she had swum in the crystal-clear desert pool at Crocodilopolis. He remembered her gracefulness, her spontaneity, her independence. Why had he felt such a resentment toward her then? Why had she made him so angry? Looking at her now, he couldn't begin to explain why. Those feelings seemed to belong to a different person.

He turned toward Rankovich.

"I once seriously considered leaving this woman behind," Albright said. "But, you see, I've also learned a great deal in the war."

2

It was well after midnight when Rankovich dismissed the partisan escorts and led the five foreign parachutists past the tailor shop on the main street of Jajce. Even at this late hour, the tailor and the baker next door were doing a brisk business. The narrow dirt road that ran through the center of town was thronged with people—rawboned mountaineers, Moslem women in pantaloons, officers on big sorrel horses, and groups of inebriated soldiers singing a favorite partisan marching song, "Little raindrops, don't fall on me. . . ."

"They're making enough noise to wake the devil," Dan Gur whispered to Joel Nathan.

"Or the Germans," Nathan replied, his Adam's apple bobbing furiously in his throat.

"Same difference," said Gur.

"So what was the big *tsimis* about leaving Ruth behind in the woods because they were afraid of a surprise German attack?" Nathan said.

It was in Rankovich's nature to listen in on other people's conversations. But since Nathan and Gur were talking in Hebrew, a language he couldn't understand, no less identify, Rankovich grew suspicious. He wanted to ask them what language they were speaking, but decided against it. *They're probably talking about me*, he thought. *I'll find out. I always do.*

Just then, the sound of applause came from the Theater of National Liberation across the street, where a play called *The People's Representative* was being performed. Rankovich stopped and took out a box of Russian cigarettes. He offered it around to the parachutists. Saul Patir extracted a cigarette with its long cardboard filter, and the two of them lit up as the crowd swarmed out of the theater. Dragging at his cigarette, Rankovich noted something that had escaped his attention before. Practically all of the soldiers who emerged from the theater had female companions hanging on their arms.

Not that Rankovich had anything against female companionship. The sexual fire in men was stoked by the dangers of war, and Rankovich, like most of the top members of Tito's staff, had a mistress. But as the chief of OZNA, the Department of Security of the People—the secret police and counterintelligence all rolled into one—it was his business to notice these things. And what concerned Rankovich was change. Even subtle change like this holding of hands between men and women in public.

In the old days, it would have been unthinkable. But a lot of other things would have been unthinkable too. The perimeter defenses around the town weren't up to snuff the way they used to be. Discipline between the men and their officers had deteriorated to the point where no one bothered to salute when they passed him here on the street. The faces of the partisans were growing . . . soft. Everywhere you looked, you saw a creeping sensuality, a libertinism. Could it be that after five years of bloody sacrifice, the partisans were losing their Spartan thirst for revolution?

If so, Rankovich knew who to blame. Davorjanka Paunovich. "Zdenka," as everyone called her. It was she who had the greatest influence over Tito now. She was Tito's secretary, his closest companion, his mistress. And Rankovich had concluded that it was Zdenka who was responsible for melting the iron in the soul of the revolution. Rankovich stabbed a finger against the frame of his eyeglasses. *Zdenka should be taken out and shot!*

He led the parachutists through the crowded street. Below the fortress, they came to the entrance of a little underground church that had been built into the side of a hill by the Bogumils during the Middle Ages. Here, on a raised platform next to the partly hidden portal of the church, was a large, heroic bust of Tito that had been sculpted out of clay by a partisan artist. *Another of Zdenka's ideas*, Rankovich thought. *Trying to make Tito as important as the big boss, Stalin.*

"You will please wait here," he told Albright.

Rankovich entered the barracks next to the church, giving the sentry a clenched-fist salute as he went by. It was stifling hot inside; the sheet-metal stove in the corner was popping. An aide played with the dial of a shortwave radio, which emitted a sharp crackle while the stove popped. At the end of the room, standing in front of a new wall map that Rankovich had never seen before, was Zdenka herself. She looked up, saw him, and her eyes narrowed with cold hostility. Her fingers were tucked, in a curiously intimate gesture, under an epaulet on the shoulder of the man at the desk. Stari. The Old Man. Josip Broz Tito.

Tito had changed, too. His face, with its broad forehead, sunken cheeks, and deep-set burning eyes, had grown less impressive. There was a certain coarseness to it now, the reflection of Tito's new self-indulgence and, *yes*, self-importance. The body had filled out, becoming *ordinary*. That sinewy tension was gone. The ascetic bone of the head and the body was gradually disappearing under the flesh of narcissism.

Now, Tito alone among the partisan leaders had a private cow for the milk he drank with his coffee. He alone ate on silver— silver that had been captured by the Germans, then recaptured by the partisans at considerable loss of life. Tito grew upset if he lost at chess, so his companions purposely threw games to please him. And it was said that Tito suffered from insomnia and would spend the long mountain nights at his desk, practicing variations of his signature.

"They are here," Rankovich announced. "The parachutists have arrived."

"Ah, Zdenka, look who's come," Tito said. "It is Arso! And doesn't he look as though he's been playing with mud pies. That's what happens when you send an intellectual into the forest."

Zdenka avoided looking at Rankovich. They had not exchanged a word in months. But Tito, ignoring her silence, bounced out of his chair and came across the room to greet his comrade. It was always a shock to see Tito stand up, for his large head led one to expect a taller man.

"Look, Arso," Tito said, brandishing a sheet of paper. "Zdenka and I have been working on this diagram of the seating arrangement for tonight's dinner, and I'll be damned if we can figure it out. We've got the Supreme Staff—Bakarich, Milutinovich, Kardelj, Vukmanovich-Tempo, Djilas, you, me, and Zdenka. That makes eight. Then there are the five parachutists. Thirteen. We can't have thirteen. So I suggested we invite a couple of the women—Mileva and Ljubinka. But Zdenka says that if we invite Mileva and Ljubinka, we've got to invite Zelenka, and you know how Ljubinka feels about Zelenka. They can't stand the sight of each other. . . ."

Tito went on like this for a minute or two, mentioning the names of various women patriots, trying to work out who should sit next to whom. Finally, he threw up his hands.

"You and Zdenka do it," he said. "I'm going to change my uniform. I'll meet you two in the banquet hall."

He stalked out, followed by his aide, and Rankovich and Zdenka found themselves alone. The stove continued to pop.

Finally, to break the silence, Rankovich asked: "Was there any news on the radio tonight?"

"The same," Zdenka said. "A lot of talk about the Allies opening a second front. In Italy or France. Just a lot of talk."

"I see," Rankovich said.

He looked around the room, feeling increasingly uncomfortable in her presence.

"There was a time," he said, "when you and I were never at a loss for words."

"That was a long time ago," she said. "Times change."

"That's true," he said. "But some things don't change. I see that you still rinse your hair in tea. I can tell by the reddish color."

She touched her hair, then quickly dropped her hand.

"That's a new map on the wall there, isn't it?" he asked.

"As a matter of fact, it is," she said.

"What's the scale?" he asked.

She looked for a legend in the corner of the map.

"It doesn't say," she said.

"Anyway, it's useless," Rankovich said. "The scale should be much larger. There's not enough detail."

"Do you think so?" Zdenka said. "I'll tell the Old Man what you said. You see, he obtained this map especially for you, Arso. And he has even taken the trouble to trace your route from here" —she pointed to Jajce—"to the Hungarian border, here."

"*My* route?"

"Yes," Zdenka said. "The Old Man has decided to put you in charge of the escort guard that takes the parachutists to the Hungarian border. In your absence, Comrade Djilas will be entrusted with the task of running OZNA."

"*Djilas?*" Rankovich said.

He could hardly believe his ears. Milovan Djilas was his friend, true, but Djilas was a party propagandist, a poet-at-war. What did Djilas know about secret-police work? And why was he, Rankovich, being asked to play nursemaid to the parachutists on their way to the border? It didn't make sense. Or perhaps it did. Djilas didn't like Zdenka any more than Rankovich did, but he was more artful in hiding his contempt.

"So, you finally found a way of getting me out of your red hair," Rankovich said. "Well, I'll refuse to do it."

"I don't think you understand," Zdenka said, picking up a sheet of paper from Tito's desk. "I typed up this order today, and just before you came in, I had the Old Man sign it. You'll be going, Arso, whether you like it or not."

3

Arso Rankovich drank too much at dinner.

He hardly touched the macaroni and tomato sauce that was served as a first course. He picked at the bread, which was baked from pears and barley. And he only stared at the cook's *pièce de résistance*, a trout stew. By the time the guests had finished dessert—a pudding made of sugar and rice—he had consumed more than half a bottle of Serbian brandy.

"This goddamn floor stinks of kerosene," he said, leaning across the table and addressing his remark to Ruth Bar-Adon. "They clean the floor with kerosene, you know. How can you eat food when all you can smell is kerosene? Kerosene! That's the holy truth!"

Ruth shot a glance at Albright, pleading for help, but neither of them knew what to say.

From the head of the table, where he sat next to Zdenka, Tito had watched with mounting anger as Rankovich became drunker and drunker. Now, he hooked his thumbs in his belt and shoved his chair away from the table.

"Arso!" Tito called down the length of the table.

"Yes, *khoziain*," Rankovich replied, using the Russian slang for "boss," a word that was universally attached in the Communist world to only one man: Josef Stalin.

There was an immediate silence around the table, as Tito and Rankovich stared at each other from opposite ends. Then, slowly, from somewhere deep in his belly, Tito began to chuckle, then to laugh, and the Yugoslavs sitting at the table laughed along with him, breaking the pustule of tension.

"Khoziain, is it?" Tito asked. "You'd better not let Stalin hear you call me that. He's patented the name. But really, Arso, you're going to give our British friends here the wrong impression. Think of what they're going to report back to our friend Winston Churchill.

"And let me say this," Tito continued, leaning forward and obviously warming up to an after-dinner speech in honor of his foreign guests. "These brave, young people seated with us tonight around this table are proof that a new fact has entered the calculations of war. We partisans remember the time, not so long ago, when we asked the Prime Minister of Great Britain for arms and Mr. Winston Churchill sent us food instead. We partisans remember the time, also not so long ago, when we asked the Prime Minister of Great Britain to renounce the discredited King of Yugoslavia and Mr. Winston Churchill gave four Liberator airplanes to the royalist airforce—airplanes that, some day after the war, may be used against our women and children. Yes, we remember those days, but now, thanks to our patriotic victories against the forces of fascism, Mr. Winston Churchill has, if I may be permitted to say so, changed his tune. It is to *us* that he is now sending arms. To *us* that he is now lending his airplanes. And it is to *us* that he has entrusted the lives of these young people who have parachuted into our midst.

"And why the sudden change, you may ask," Tito went on. "Not only because of our victories against the fascists. But also because we are entering the desperate final chapter of the war. A chapter, my dear Comrade Arso Rankovich, that requires a *fresh viewpoint!*"

And here Tito slapped his hand down on the thin boards that had been nailed together for a dining table. The glasses shook and he stood up.

"No more are we the reviled and ignored band of hunted revolutionaries in the mountains!" Tito shouted. "Mr. Winston Churchill, Mr. Franklin Roosevelt, and everyone else have been forced to recognize that we partisans will play a decisive role in shaping the coming world order. They recognize that we are not merely Stalin's men, Stalin's puppets. Khoziain, you called me, Arso. Yes, I am khoziain. There isn't only one khoziain anymore. Let there be two khoziains, five khoziains, twenty khoziains. After the war, those of us who have stood up and been counted will be our own khoziains. We will shape our separate roads to socialism, our own destinies."

And Tito sat down. Arso Rankovich waited a few moments, then he stood up, a bit shaky from all the brandy, and began to speak.

"I meant no offense, of course. Neither to our friends here nor, it hardly goes without saying, to you, our leader. Stari. Khoziain, if you will. Or, as I prefer, simply: Tito."

"Good beginning," Gur whispered in Hebrew to Nathan.

"Yes," Rankovich continued, pushing at the frame of his eyeglasses, "I recognize that the shifting tides of war bring with them new necessities. But allow me to point out two facts. First, a good Communist is flexible enough to change his tactics, but he never changes his overall strategy. Lenin himself pointed out that it is permissible to make a pact with the devil himself, so long as it is in the interest of Communist goals.

"But this is precisely what concerns me. I detect a dangerous tendency, a *revisionism*, if you will, as our Communist ideals and goals—which brought us through this war so far—are beginning to take second place to what you refer to as a fresh viewpoint. And what is this viewpoint? What is it if not an effort to de-emphasize our Communist discipline, our Communist ideology, our Communist solidarity in return for some vague chauvinist dream of . . . respectability. *Men* do not seek respectability. That is a *woman's* impulse."

At this, Edvard Kardelj and Milovan Djilas, the two men closest to Tito on the Supreme Staff, shot up from their chairs. But Tito motioned them back.

Zdenka stared murderously at Rankovich.

"Yes," Rankovich said, "I fear that our good Serbian brandy has lubricated my tongue with excessive candor. These things would normally not be appropriate to say in front of guests, except that it brings me to my second point. You remember that I said I wanted to point out *two* facts. So . . ."

He picked up his glass and drained the brandy remaining at the bottom.

"So. This soft, womanish impulse toward respectability," he went on, "inevitably leads to a self-imposed blindness. You said, Comrade Tito, that Churchill has in the past done this to us or that to us, but now, as a token of his new trust and acceptance, Churchill has sent these five parachutists. But this is not the case. They have not been sent by Churchill. Not in the least. They are not even British."

"What is this rubbish he is talking?" Zdenka said, turning to Tito. "He is drunk. Why do you let him go on like this?"

Tito looked at Edvard Kardelj and Milovan Djilas, searching for a sign that they supported Zdenka. But although Tito had learned long ago how to interpret the slightest expression on his comrades' faces, this time he could not tell what they were thinking. He realized that Rankovich's attack was directed at Zdenka and, through her, at himself. And he decided, from political instinct, that he would ignore Zdenka. To shut up Rankovich now would make Tito appear weak and afraid. This Tito could not permit.

He nodded for Rankovich to continue.

"Good," Rankovich said, readjusting his eyeglasses. "I will put one question to our foreign friends here and we shall see if I am right." He turned to Albright. "What language is this you speak among yourselves?"

"I speak eight or nine languages," Albright said. "Which one do you have in mind? French? Italian? Hungarian? English? German? Arabic? Greek? Serbo-Croatian? *Ima li neko koji govori engleski? . . . francuski? . . . nemachki?*" he said in Serbo-Croatian. "Is there anyone here who speaks English? French? German?"

"I'm afraid," Rankovich said, "that most of us do not share your linguistic gift. But what of your comrades? This young fellow, for instance?" He pointed at Saul Patir. "What is your native language?"

"My *native* language?" Patir said. "I was born in Hungary, but I am a Jew and now my native language is *Hebrew.*"

A smile of triumph broke out on Rankovich's face. He raised both arms, palms outward, took a slight bow, and sat down. Then he blew a kiss of exaggerated courtliness at Zdenka.

It took Albright a few minutes to explain to Tito and the Supreme Staff how it was that Mr. Winston Churchill had come to send them a team of Jewish parachutists. Tito listened in silence, his arms crossed over his chest.

When Albright had finished, Tito glared darkly around the table until his eyes finally settled on the comrade for whom he felt the most brotherly attachment. "Djilas," he said. "What do you think?"

With his long, triangular-shaped face, prominent ears and pensive eyes, Milovan Djilas looked more like a young instructor in a college than a seasoned guerrilla in a mountain hideaway. Yet, in his own way, he was shrewd and cunning and, above all, fiercely independent. Of all the members of the Supreme Staff, only Djilas had been able to cross Tito and get away with it. Like an indulgent elder brother, Tito always seemed to forgive Djilas and even prize him for the courage to speak his mind.

"Well, Tito, as you know, we have spoken of this Jewish question before," Djilas said. "And my fundamental views remain unchanged. The Jews, largely because of their own attitude, are a people apart, a separate people, who choose to dwell in the midst of others. And yet, we as partisans have accepted them as part of our own people in our terrible struggle against fascism. That is why I have argued against setting up special Jewish units like the Czech units or the Magyar units. And you have agreed with me. Both of us have felt that a Jewish unit would act like a magnet for the bloodlust of the Germans and the Ustashi fascists. Not only that. A Jewish unit would be apt to take excessive and dangerous risks in pursuit of mindless revenge. The same concerns must apply to these Jewish parachutists."

As he listened to Milovan Djilas' precise and well-organized words, Albright felt as though he was hearing his *own* words coming back to haunt him. He recalled the first time he had met Guido DeVita. They had watched a red-bearded trainee at Camp Jubilee undergoing simulated Gestapo interrogation, and Albright had told DeVita that Jewish agents were dangerous because they got romantic ideas about paying back the Germans. *Wash him out*, Albright had told DeVita. And now, Djilas and Rankovich and the rest of them were trying to wash out Albright. Because they thought *he* was a Jew.

"Thank you, Djilas," Tito was saying. "We are presented with quite a dilemma. You are all Jews. We can't change that fact. And we can't change the fact that many of our partisans are illiterate peasants who, quite frankly, don't like Jews. I, myself, was only recently forced to dismiss a lieutenant when his men discovered that he was *partly* Jewish. It seems plain to me that you can't travel through partisan-controlled territory flaunting your Jewishness.

"On the other hand, I am a political leader and my fellow political leader has asked me to guarantee your safe conduct across our war-torn country. So I say, if you must speak among yourselves in

Hebrew, call it another language. Call it whatever you want. You're part of the British Army. You can pretend that you are from . . . Wales! Yes, from Wales. And the language you speak is Welsh."

"*Welsh!*" Albright exploded. "What kind of joke is this? It's all right with you if we die as Jews, but we can't live and fight as Jews? Nothing doing."

"Permit me," Joel Nathan interrupted.

He rose from his chair, reed-thin, pale, his Adam's apple bobbing in his throat. A plateful of sugar-and-rice dessert lay uneaten before him.

"We all appreciate the passionate words of our leader, Captain Albright," Nathan said. "After all, what's the use of being a Jew if you don't feel passionately about it? I would say that Captain Albright has demonstrated tonight that he is a good Jew."

Ruth put a hand over her mouth and coughed loudly.

"But," Nathan continued, "the genius of the Jewish religion is that there are all kinds of good Jews. And they rarely agree. I would further say that the Orthodox branch of Judaism, to which my parents belonged and to which I owe my ability to forgive God this war and His other little pranks of history—Orthodox Judaism is, above all, the fine art of discernment. Discerning the important from the unimportant. So on this question, I say, why not Welsh? We'll still be speaking Hebrew, but if someone wants to call it Welsh, who's to call him *pisher?* Let it be Welsh. And we will be Welshmen."

This was not at all what Albright had expected from Joel Nathan. He was in a state of utter confusion. Just when he thought he understood what it was like to *feel* Jewish, he suddenly realized that wasn't enough. You had to *think* Jewish. He sought the eyes of the other members of his team. Each, in turn, returned his look and nodded—Gur, Patir, Bar-Adon.

"We came all this way to save lives," Ruth said, "not to save face."

Tito seemed pleased.

"But just tell me one thing," Ruth said to Tito.

"What?"

"What is the name of the capital of Wales?"

"Rankovich," Tito commanded, "you got us into this mess. And you're an expert on geography. What's the capital of Wales?"

"I believe it's Cardiff," Rankovich said.

"Then, I propose a toast," Ruth said, raising her glass. "*Next year in Cardiff!*"

The Jews laughed.

And even though they didn't understand the joke, the Yugoslavs laughed along with them.

4

"Why do you think Rankovich hates Tito's woman so much?" Albright asked Ruth.

The parachutists were sitting under a beech tree near a little fire, comparing notes on Tito and the dinner. Across a field, a group of armed men and women sang a folk song and danced the *kolo* around another fire.

"I don't know," Ruth said. "Maybe he's jealous. Maybe Tito stole her away from Rankovich and Rankovich still loves her."

"That's a poetic thought," Nathan said. "Yes, I like that idea."

"Ach," Gur said. "Maybe Rankovich hates her because deep down inside she is, essentially, hateable."

Just then, one of the partisan girls who had been dancing the kolo approached them. She had draped a coarse blanket over her shoulders like a shawl and she carried a leather flask of wine.

"Please," she said and offered the flask to Ruth, who accepted it and squirted some of the bitter wine into her mouth.

"We heard of your arrival," the girl said, "and we wanted to extend a warm welcome to the Welshmen who represent Winston Churchill."

"News travels fast around the campfire," Gur said.

"Since I am a woman," the girl said, "I can say things that our men cannot. We are proud that Winston Churchill has sent such a beautiful woman to us. Until now, we partisans thought that the women of the British empire were soft. But now we see that, like the Yugoslav women who fight alongside their men, the women of the British empire are idealistic and brave as well as beautiful. Thank you."

"Thank *you*," Ruth said, shaking the girl's hand.

"Well," Gur said after the girl had left, "I'm going to bed and dream of all the good times I used to have back in Wales."

"Yes, it's late," Nathan said.

Patir yawned and got up to join them.

They went off and Albright poked at the fire. There was little left but a pile of embers. The young men and women across the field wandered off together into the night. Ruth became aware of the chilling stillness and she leaned her head against Albright's arm.

"It's all been too much for one day," she said. "I've parachuted into Europe, I've been converted into a Welshman, and I've heard you speak as though you were one of us. A Jew."

"You know," Albright said, "when we found you in that stream with your parachute caught on the log, I thought about that time when you went swimming in Crocodilopolis. You looked very beautiful when you came out of the water, all dripping wet, and I remember the smell of your skin drying in the desert sun."

"Do you remember how angry I was with you?" she said.

"We were both angry," he said.

"But I was so silly to throw that beautiful little statue back in the water."

"Do you remember what you asked me that day?" he said. "You asked me what I believed in. And I told you that I believed in myself. And you said, 'That's not much.'"

"Did I? I'm sorry."

"No, you were right," he said. "It isn't much. I realized that tonight at dinner."

"You mean when you told off Tito?" she asked. "You were splendid, you know."

"No, it was what you said," he replied. "About saving lives, not saving face. *You* were splendid."

"Then we were both splendid," she said.

"We're *all* splendid," he said. "Nathan and Gur and Patir and you and me."

"Yes, but especially you and me," she said.

"Ruth?"

"Yes."

"I want to make love to you tonight."

"Now *that's* really splendid," she said, "because I want to make love to you tonight, too."

He got up and kicked dirt into the fire, and then they walked a few dozen yards through the forest to a lean-to, where he spread out their blankets on the pine needles and soft earth. As he helped her undress, he heard the buzz of a German airplane in the distance.

Their hands and feet were cold, a nervous, clammy cold.

"I'm sorry I'm not wet yet," she said.

"Don't be sorry," he said. "I'm not hard yet either."

"Maybe it's because of what Guido told me," she said.

"About me?" he asked.

"No, about me," she said.

"What did he tell you?"

"Later," she said. "I'll tell you later."

He kissed her breasts, sucked gently at her nipples, and then he slowly slipped down over her belly until his nose and mouth were buried in downy hair and his tongue found her clitoris. She raised her knees until the arches of her feet were resting on his shoulders, and she threw her arms over her face and moaned.

He cupped her buttocks with his hands, raising her off the ground, rubbing her clitoris up and down the cleft of his tongue, inhaling her smell, swallowing her juice, hearing the quickening sounds of their lovemaking. And as his tongue caressed her, he could feel his penis, hot against his belly, creating a long trough in the blanket.

And each time his teeth brushed against her clitoris, he could sense her rising closer and closer to an orgasm, and when he thought she was almost there, he smoothed back her hair and gently exposed her clitoris with his two thumbs and softly took it between his lips and sucked at it, and sucked at it, and she began to come.

Her hands encircled the back of his head, pulling him into her, bringing his nose and his mouth and his cheeks and his chin into the velvet wetness, a gurgling hot spring, and he drove his tongue in as deep as it would go, and he felt her feet pushing against his shoulders, her legs twisting, her buttocks shuddering, and his hands reached up and found her nipples as her whole body shook violently.

They lay there for a few moments. And after she had recovered, she got on her hands and knees, facing toward his legs, and took his penis in her mouth while she caressed him under his scrotum. With his eyes closed, he moved his hand over the contours of her ankle, the inside of her knee, the back of her thigh, and between her legs. And when he inserted his fingers, she gasped, her mouth still encircling his penis, and that sound and the sudden cool rush of air between her lips and the tip of his penis and the sense of their mutual ecstasy and her slow sinking movement down on his fingers and her hand moving up and down the lubricated shaft of his penis—all this happening at once brought on the first faint sign of the onrushing juggernaut of his own orgasm. And he stopped her.

He lowered her on her back, kneeled between her legs and moved toward her, his penis guiding itself into her up to its hilt. And he felt something he had never felt before. The walls of her vagina were filling, growing, expanding, pressing themselves in a fluid, gentle vise all along the length of his penis, enclosing it in an unseeable and inexpressibly beautiful kiss.

And once again, this time from less far away, he felt the juggernaut of orgasm rushing upon him, with its own force and its own logic, totally out of his control, and from the way she embraced him, he knew that she could sense it too. He didn't have to ask. She was ready again, precisely timed to his exact moment, and as he was overcome, bereft of any poise or any willpower or any self-control, bursting out of himself, transfigured, really, from resisting flesh to willing spirit, they met and came together.

CHAPTER TWO

THE PLIVA RIVER
Sunday, April 30

1

Someone must have lit a fire during the night. Yes, that was the explanation. . . . Thoughtful. But how strange. It doesn't give off any heat. Just that crackling noise, like cellophane crumpling next to your ear, and the sharp pop! pop! pop! *of the sap in the wood boiling into steam and exploding.*

Ruth Bar-Adon liked the *idea* of a fire. The comforting coziness. The sense of safety . . .

But where is the warmth? How can you have a fire without heat?

Ruth turned in her half-sleep, seeking out the warmth. Yearning for that elusive safety. Her hand brushed against the hair on Albright's chest. She felt his belly, warm and hard, the smooth appendix scar, rising and falling in rhythmical breathing.

Pop!

Pop!

Pop!

I must be dreaming, she dreamed.

"Ruthie! Wake up. It's me. Have you heard?"

This was no dream. It was the voice of Joel Nathan, her *haver*. She sat up, covering her breasts with a blanket, wondering what Joel must think finding her here like this next to Albright. She was concerned especially about what Joel would think. The noise from the fire—*or whatever it was*—was louder now. And then suddenly there was an awesome crashing sound in the forest, as though a crazed animal was tearing through the leaves and branches. And at the exact moment of the explosion, she knew.

We're being attacked.

"Tito and his staff have been evacuated," Nathan said. "The Germans . . . they're crawling all over the place . . . they've even dropped paratroops. . . ."

Albright was up, pulling on his underwear, his pants.

"What's going on?" he said.

"Germans," Nathan said.

Ruth was dressing. Forgetting her nakedness. Forgetting Joel.

Dan Gur came running, shouting: "Come on!"

Another explosion. The earth shook. Leaves fell out of the trees. Dust was rising everywhere. Machine-gun fire. Smaller explosions, grenades. Shouts. Screams. Roaring explosions . . .

"Howitzers."

"Where's Saul?"

"Who's got the radio?"

"There's Saul."

Mounted on a horse, Saul Patir appeared through the birch trees, galloping through the curtain of dust, an enormous smile plastered on his boyish face.

"Where the hell did you get the horse?"

"Do you have the radio?" Albright asked.

"Here, here, I've got everything," Patir said, looking down at his companions from the commanding height of the saddle.

"Listen, friends," Gur said, "we've got to split up. It's a lot safer that way. Ruth can go with Saul on the horse. Joel, you go with Alex. . . ."

The forest was rent open again by that animal-crashing sound and they threw themselves on the ground as the shell exploded thunderously, spewing rocks and dirt where they lay.

"There's a place," Gur said. "About seventy miles north of here. It's a small village called Banja Luka. It's got a big mosque. We'll meet there. Under the clock tower."

Albright looked at Ruth. He did not want to lose her now.

"We're not splitting up," he said. "I want everybody out of

here together. We stay together. Saul, get off that goddamn horse. You make a perfect target from a thousand yards away. You take the radio. Joel'll take the batteries. Okay? Come on, follow me, but don't bunch up."

The others looked at Gur, their trusted friend, their haver, the master guerrilla tactician. This wasn't practice field craft at Camp Jubilee. This was the real business.

"We listen to Albright," Nathan decided.

"Okay," Gur agreed. "But we don't go *that* way. You always advance *toward* the explosions, not away from them. The Germans are walking in their howitzers, a few dozen yards at a time, and if we move toward the impact, they'll overshoot us."

"Let's hope so," Albright said, and he began running directly toward the ear-splitting roar of the next explosion.

2

Ridiculous thoughts came to Ruth as they ran through the woods.

God is punishing me because I slept with Alex. If we get out of this alive, I promise I won't do it again until the mission is over.

Absurd thoughts.

That dead girl over there under the tree is the one who brought me wine last night. What happened to her leather flask?

Unthinkable thoughts.

I'd rather die than be raped by a German.

Ruth had no trouble keeping up with the men. But her mind seemed to tarry, lingering over details . . . the dead littered the forest floor in groups of twos and threes, never singly . . . the bust of Tito had disappeared from the front of the church . . . Tito's cow had been left behind. . . .

Partisan soldiers were falling before her eyes. Everywhere, she passed bleeding, moaning, cursing men. Bullets and pieces of shrapnel whistled overhead, thwacking into the sides of trees. Here and there, a few men stood their ground, firing their rifles in the direction of the advancing Germans. But the Germans seemed to be advancing from all sides at once, and most of the partisans tried to scurry for cover behind the trunks of trees that were smeared with the blood of those who tried before them and didn't make it.

As she ran behind Albright, slaloming between the trees, Ruth noticed that the forest was thinning out and that there was more and more sky visible overhead. Soon, there was no forest at all. Just trees that had been felled and stripped of their branches and cut into long logs. They had entered a logging camp. Now they were in the open, completely exposed, still running, heading up a rutted road between flattened acres of logs, inhaling the aroma of freshly cut wood and sap, meeting up with packs of retreating partisans, the explosions behind them, all that death and blood behind them. . . . Up ahead at the top of the hill came a low, steady, mechanical growl, and Ruth imagined that the noise was made by an advancing column of German tanks, that they had run right into the mouth of the animal.

They reached the top of a treeless bluff and looked down into a narrow canyon. It was a rather steep drop of about two hundred feet to the Pliva River below. The river was running fast, swollen by the spring rain, and this was the source of the low growl that Ruth had heard. The entire side of the mountain on which they stood had been smoothed into a concrete-hard sliding pond by the thousands of logs that had been pushed over the bluff and rolled down to the water to be carried off by the river.

"Are we safe here?" Ruth asked.

"For a little while," Albright said.

"Look, there's Rankovich," Gur said.

Arso Rankovich stood in the center of a small group of men, gesturing across the canyon. He seemed to be in charge, although there was not much left to be in charge of. Albright took a rough head count of the partisans. Maybe sixty people had escaped the Germans' surprise attack.

He walked over to Rankovich.

"What do you think?" he asked.

Rankovich did not seem surprised to see him.

"Who can think?" he said. "I stopped thinking back there. We've lost more than a hundred good men. They almost got Tito this time. It was very close. Very close."

"Can we make it over the river?"

"Out of the question," Rankovich said. "Our scouts say that General Löhr has thrown all five of his German divisions against us. He's dropped a brigade of paratroops to the south and he's got the Seventh SS Prinz Eugen Division with a battery of howitzers over there." Rankovich pointed north across the river to the other side of the canyon. "Tito's heading west for Dvar. That's where we're going."

"What about us?" Albright said.

"What about you?" Rankovich replied. "You want to come with us, come."

"We've got to go north toward the border," Albright said. "To Hungary. Tito promised last night that you'd take us there."

"That was last night," Rankovich said. "Today's today."

"How are we going to make it alone?" Albright said.

"Sorry," Rankovich said.

"I'll bet," Albright said.

Rankovich turned away and addressed a young, ruddy-faced partisan standing nearby.

"Tell the men we're moving out in five minutes."

"What about the wounded?" the young partisan asked.

"Leave them behind," Rankovich said.

"I understand, but they want to keep their weapons."

"For heaven's sake, why?" Rankovich said.

The young partisan pointed a forefinger at his temple and lowered his thumb.

"They know what to expect as German prisoners."

"Give them each a hand grenade," Rankovich said. "We need the rifles."

"They're not going to like that. They'd rather die with a bullet fired from their own weapon. Like Communist heroes."

"Listen," Rankovich said, "most of them aren't even Communists. One grenade each, that's it. This isn't the time to worry about communism."

3

Just as Rankovich's depleted band of partisans began to move out, the howitzers of the Seventh SS Prinz Eugen Division opened up with a thunderous roar from across the Pliva River. At first, the shells fell far short, smashing into the side of the canyon, gouging deep craters into the smooth face of the log slide a few dozen yards above the bank of the river. But then the shells began to climb up the steep face of the canyon, and the whole cliff shook with their impact.

"They're finding our range at the top here," Dan Gur said. "They'll be right on top of us in a couple of minutes."

"*Germans!*"

The warning was shouted by one of the wounded partisans left behind by Rankovich.

Saul Patir spun around and began firing, wounding two Germans coming up over the bluff.

"Look at their uniforms," Nathan said. "Paratroops."

"Where're the rest?" Patir asked, kneeling, hunched over his rifle.

"They're scouts," Gur said. "Don't worry, the rest of them will be here soon enough."

The canyon reverberated with the howitzers.

"Listen," Gur said, "I think I have an idea. Howitzers are useful weapons but they have their limitations. They work like this." He made a plane with the fingers of his right hand. "They can fire like this"—his hand pointed at an upward angle—"or like this"—he lowered his hand until it was parallel with the ground—"but they can't fire like this"—and he pointed his hand at a sharp angle at the ground. "If we make a break for it down the log slide just as the shells reach the top, the Germans won't be able to reverse the angle of their guns and follow us all the way down to the river."

Joel Nathan looked at Albright and nodded.

"Sounds crazy," Albright said, and he looked at Ruth.

She nodded, too.

"Okay," Albright said.

And so they waited, flat on their bellies, at the edge of the steep, treeless bluff as the German howitzer shells reached closer and closer.

"Right after the next volley," Gur said.

It seemed as though the shells were exploding in their faces as they leaped over the top of the canyon and raced down the smooth, slippery side of the mountain. Albright went first, Gur following, and the rest following him, and the Germans on the other side must have immediately spotted them, for the howitzers suddenly stopped firing as if they were stunned into silence. And during those few precious seconds of surprise, Ruth was aware of her own harsh breathing, the clopping of her parachute boots against the hard-packed mountainside, and the crescendo of the Pliva River roaring up from below.

Patir fell, rolled, tumbled back onto his feet, hardly losing his stride.

They were halfway down. Not a shot had been fired at them. Behind her, Ruth could now hear a few shouts of encouragement from some of the wounded partisans left behind to die.

Then all at once the Germans let them have it. Rifles, machine guns, mortars, howitzers—everything they had was concentrated on stopping the five figures loping down the side of the canyon. The air seemed to be sucked out of Ruth's ears by the concussions from the exploding shells.

The howitzers were following them down.

The side of the mountain was erupting into geysers of pulverized stone. Bullets stitched patterns into the smooth hillside.

And the howitzer shells were at their backs.

Then, out of nowhere, two German airplanes, Stukas, squeezed in single file through the narrow gorge, the screaming engines echoing off the cliffs, and first one, then the other dropped bombs, the pilots climbing steeply out of the way, and the first arc of bombs exploded in the middle of the river, and, seconds later, the next arc of bombs smashed directly into the side of the mountain.

The wrong side.

The German side.

The pilot had mistakenly bombed his own troops.

And by now Albright was in the swift-rushing river, yelling to the others. Then Gur. Then Nathan. Then Patir. Then Ruth. Clinging to logs. Floating down the rain-swollen Pliva. Rushing past the German position on the cliff, from where a thick gray column of smoke rose into the clear morning sky.

CHAPTER THREE

NEW YORK
Monday, June 5

1

Donovan grabbed the phone on the first ring and switched on the bedside lamp. The gold hands of the Mark Cross alarm clock were just beginning to overlap on the roman numeral XII. The voice on the phone would begin precisely at midnight. Not a second before.

Waiting on the edge of the bed, one bare foot resting on the instep of the other, he stared at the framed photograph of his daughter, Patricia. All in white, at her first communion, holding the bouquet of white violets that would remain eternally unwilted in the photographic emulsion.

He could feel the old pain and the sorrow returning. Donovan was a man of iron self-discipline, but he had broken down and cried like a baby on the day he buried his daughter. His radiant Patricia, so full of promise, had been snatched away in the bloom of life, and her death had been the greatest tragedy in Donovan's life.

It was like that, Donovan's life—promise turning to tragedy. Sometimes, he felt like Job in the Bible. Forever being tested by senseless affliction. As though he were guilty of some grave and unpardonable sin.

This seemed to be his constant destiny.

As a young man, he had come home from World War I wearing the Congressional Medal of Honor, the Distinguished Service Cross, and the Distinguished Service Medal—one of the most-decorated heroes in American military history. The world—especially the political world—was his oyster. His career soared until he ran as the Republican candidate for governor of New York State and was buried in the 1932 Democratic landslide. It was a bitter disappointment to him that he never achieved high elective office.

His personal life was an even greater disappointment.

As a promising lawyer, he had married Ruth Ramsey, a Buffalo socialite who brought him social position and family. He made millions of dollars and insulated himself from the shifting winds of fortune. But then, the one person for whom all this position and money was intended, his beloved Patricia, died. And though nothing could have saved their daughter, Donovan and his wife blamed each other. Their marriage was indelibly stained by this guilt, and they had not slept together as man and wife since the day of Patricia's funeral.

The only thing that was left to Donovan was the OSS.

As a respected adviser to Presidents, he had created the Office of Strategic Services, built it into a model central intelligence agency using every modern management technique, including a new invention called the ENIAC computer. His 30,000 men and women, mostly academics and business-school types with a few savages thrown in to handle the black-bag jobs, could find out anything he wanted to know about anybody anywhere in the world. He had come to think of himself as a sort of latter-day oracle of Delphi. All-knowing. All-powerful. In a modern nation at war, information was power. And by that measurement, Major General William J. Donovan had become the second most powerful man in America after the President of the United States.

And now, like the biblical Job, he believed he was in danger of losing this last thing, too. For Donovan was expecting bad news.

Very bad news.

"Good evening, General," the voice on the phone began.

It was a calm, powerful baritone, much like his own voice. Benevolent and undramatic, but with an air of absolute authority. And what it told him was even worse than he had expected.

Donovan listened, unable to interrupt. These nightly EOS's— estimates of the situation—were delivered by shortwave radio with electronic voice recording. Another Donovan innovation. The estimates were wired in from all over the world, then relayed to him on a scrambler phone here in his apartment on Beekman Place.

When the recording stopped, there was a sharp hum, and Donovan eased the telephone receiver back on its cradle. Softly, so as not to make any noise and disturb his wife, who slept near him in the room.

He made an entry on the note pad attached to the base of the telephone.

Code Yellow. Cabinet C. Drawer 6.

Midnight June 5.

Rider from Washington.

Operation Overlord set to begin in 24 hours.

EOS. 60–40 success, depending partly on weather.

Risk. Failure could set clock of victory back two years.

Privately, Donovan thought that Eisenhower's odds at Normandy were far better than 60–40, but it was always prudent to err on the side of caution with these yellow EOS's. Yellow was for the first layer of secrecy—the official files—and Donovan never knew when he might be required to produce them during a congressional committee hearing as proof of the OSS's infallibility.

He tore off the sheet of paper and, in his neat handwriting, began another entry.

Code Blue. Cabinet F. Drawer 17.

Midnight June 5.

Lancer from Washington.

Phone tap on Senator Vandenburg to Senator Sparkman regarding Foreign Affairs Committee vote on OSS charter.

EOS. 70–30 chance of revocation.

Risk. If vote goes as expected, entire OSS apparatus could be dismantled within months after end of war.

The blue EOS's were the second layer. For limited internal distribution among a handful of top OSS officers. Strictly speaking, it was illegal for the OSS to spy on American citizens. That was

the job of the FBI. But Donovan had never paid much attention
to this distinction.

On a third sheet, Donovan wrote:

Code Red. Cabinet L. Drawer 3.

Midnight June 5.

Mother from London.

Security check on Philby continuing.

EOS. 40–60 chance of his being a double agent.

Risk. OSS agent system in Europe imperiled.

Red was for the third and deepest layer. Threats to the security
of the OSS. Code Red was for Donovan's own personal files. He
could not bring himself to believe the allegations against Philby,
allegations that originated with Mossad, the Jewish secret intelligence organization. But what if it were true? What if Philby was
in fact a Russian spy?

As he pondered that question, Donovan folded the three sheets
of paper and put them in three separate manila envelopes. Yellow.
Blue. Red. In the morning, the envelopes would be dispatched by
courier to three different filing systems in the basement vaults of
the OSS at Twenty-fifth and E. streets in Washington. Only Donovan and one other person—Allen Dulles, the OSS's European
chief in Switzerland—knew the secret of the coded cross-references.

Donovan switched off the light.

"Everything all right?" his wife asked.

"Nothing to worry about," he said. "Sorry I woke you."

"Go back to sleep," she said. "You need your rest."

"You too," he said.

He heard her turn in her bed. Ruth Ramsey Donovan, his wife
of thirty-one years, the woman who had brought him old family
money and social position. And, for a while, love. It had been a
long time since he had needed her for any of those things. Now
they had their own lives, their own friends, their own lovers. They
lived in different systems, and even William Donovan could not
fathom the complex secrets of their coded cross-references.

He lay back on the pillows, his eyes wide open, thinking in his
orderly, logical lawyer's way. If Ike made it across at Normandy,
the war was all but won. And if Senator Vandenburg had his way,
peace would mean the end of the OSS. But what if Philby really

was a Russian spy? Right up there at the pinnacle of the British Secret Service. Who could tell where other Russian spies might turn up? The Russians could be anywhere. *Everywhere.* And who would be there to stop them if there was no OSS?

Yes, he thought, he was forever being tested.

Then, growing sleepy, his mind skipped back in a mystifying series of associations to a dim past, and he thought of the words in the official citation that he had received with the Congressional Medal of Honor for bravery near Landres and St. George, on the western front in France, in October 1918. "Donovan," it said, "moved erect from place to place in full view of the enemy, reorganized and heartened the men. As spurts of dust went around him and shells broke in the vicinity, he cried out: 'See, they can't hit me and they won't hit you!'"

That was the difference between Donovan and the biblical Job. Wild Bill Donovan of the Fighting Irish refused to succumb.

"They *can't* hit me," he said out loud.

"What?" his wife asked. "What is it?"

He didn't answer. She had already fallen back asleep.

And there in the darkness, alone with all the old pain and the sorrow, Donovan resolved to put up the fight of his life for the OSS.

His lips moved silently over the words: "They can't hit me and they won't hit you."

2

At ten-thirty that morning, Donovan drew the venetian blinds, casting his book-lined library into sudden darkness.

"Holy Mary, Mother of God!" he said. "Will you *please* sit down. You're making me nervous."

"I'll stand, if it's all the same," Francis Spellman said. "My hemorrhoids. They're acting up again."

"Suit yourself," Donovan snapped.

"Anyway," Spellman said, "I thought we were supposed to be on our way to Hyde Park to talk election-year politics with the President."

"Let the President wait," Donovan replied.

From across the shadowy room, the Archbishop of New York could not see Donovan's face, but he could tell from the choked tone of voice that something was wrong. Worse than wrong. Donovan was clearly on the verge. On the lip of some great foolishness. Something dangerous.

They were the best of friends, Francis Joseph Spellman and William J. Donovan, two poor Irish boys who had become princes, one of the Church, the other of the Establishment. Two birds of a feather, and the one always knew when the other was out of whack.

This was the way Donovan got when he fell off the wagon and put aside the tomato juice for hard liquor, which happened only rarely, maybe once or twice a year. Or when somebody forced him into a corner, pushed him into making a choice he didn't want to make.

They were alike that way too, Spellman and Donovan. Once put on the defensive, all their easygoing Irish charm fell aside and the toughness, the meanness underneath showed through.

Right now, the director of the Office of Strategic Services was having trouble suppressing this brutish side of his nature. And that was the danger signal.

Donovan hunched over a movie projector in the middle of the room, fiddling with a sprocket spring.

"Okay," he said, "I think I've got it working now. You ready?"

"Sure," Spellman said. "I trust this movie's been approved by the Legion of Decency."

"Listen, Frank," Donovan said, ignoring the wry attempt at humor, "this movie couldn't get past a pair of Jewish lawyers for the ACLU. I want you to understand what you're going to see. I figure that, in an order of magnitude, this ranks as the third-most-important secret in the possession of the OSS."

"So why are you showing it to me?" Spellman asked.

"Why? Because some stupid sonofabitch in my organization went ahead and filmed this without any authorization, and now I don't know what the hell to do with it. I'm in a pickle, Frank. A goddamn *moral* pickle. I don't know what the *right* thing to do is. You're good about these things. I've always thought of you like my conscience, a little birdie on my shoulder whispering yes or no into my ear. And I know I can trust you."

"Yes," Spellman said, "that's something we have in common. We're both trained to keep secrets."

"I'm not farting around here, Frank," Donovan said. "I'm being deadly serious."

"Oh, I can tell that," the archbishop said. "Whenever you get like this, Bill, you start acting obnoxious and insulting."

There was a moment of silence.

"Sorry," Donovan said.

"Apology accepted," Spellman said. "Now, let's see your little movie. I'll consider it a secret of the confessional."

Donovan switched on the projector and Spellman looked across the room at the illuminated screen. The images that flickered there seemed to have been photographed by a telephoto lens through thick foliage and a curtained window. The subjects were two women. Their grainy figures were often obscured by the leaves and the curtain blowing in a soundless wind.

The woman facing the window was large-boned and squarish, almost muscular. She had the heavily padded body of a woman golfer or gym teacher. She wore her dark hair knotted in a severe bun. As she approached the other woman, a reassuring smile spread across her strong, masculine face.

The woman with her back to the camera reached out with her arms. She was nude.

Spellman stared at the screen, riveted with fascination. He grasped his gold pectoral cross as he watched the large woman facing the window slowly unbutton her blouse, slip it off, and unhook her brassiere. Her nipples were remarkably small and firm for a woman of her size and age. She looked to be in her fifties.

"Lorena Hickok," Donovan offered by way of explanation.

"Who?" Spellman asked.

"Lorena Hickok," Donovan repeated. "You know, the one they call Hick. She used to be a reporter before the First Lady took her under her wing."

"You mean that friend of Eleanor's?"

"That's the one," Donovan said.

"Almighty God!" Spellman muttered.

Lorena Hickok put her hands under the other woman's arms

and lifted her to a standing position. The two women embraced. Exchanged a long kiss. Then Lorena Hickok slowly sank down until she was out of sight, while the other woman stood, her head thrown back, mouth open. Suddenly, the standing woman seemed to rise into the air, then fall. Actually, she was being lifted bodily by her companion, turned completely upside down, her legs dangling, being carried away from the window, out of range of the camera's prying lens.

"Well, Frank?" Donovan said, shutting off the projector and turning on a table lamp. "What do you think?"

"Who's the other woman?" Spellman asked.

"We're not sure," Donovan said. "We think it's another newspaper lady, but we haven't been able to make a positive identification. But that's not the point. Let me put it to you this way. Out of the fifty million voters in this country, how many do you think would have trouble identifying Lorena Hickok as the friend of Eleanor Roosevelt?"

"Are you implying that Eleanor's a . . . . a lesbian?"

"I'm not implying any such thing," Donovan said. "In fact, I'd be willing to bet that she's not. She probably doesn't even know what lesbians do to each other. But just the fact that you asked me that question proves this film is dynamite."

"You want my advice?" Spellman said. "I'll give it to you. Burn it. Destroy the film right away. Then forget it."

"That's the trouble," Donovan said. "I can't."

"What do you mean, you can't?"

"I asked you to help me make a moral choice," Donovan said.

"That's what I'm trying to do," Spellman replied.

"The hell you are," Donovan said.

"Now I *know* you've taken leave of your senses," Spellman said. "Bill Donovan, do you realize what you're saying? You're not outraged by what those two lesies are doing on that screen. You're looking for a way to strike a blow against Franklin Roosevelt. But let me tell you something. You may ruin Roosevelt. But you may also succeed in destroying yourself along with him."

Donovan yanked open the louvers of the blinds and the sparkling reflection from the East River spilled through the slanted slats. In the sudden light, he squinted at the plump, rosy-faced archbishop. His friend. His confessor.

"That," Donovan said, "is exactly the choice I've got to make."

3

"You're a dumb Irishman, Bill Donovan."

The words, the first Spellman had managed to utter since they crossed the Henry Hudson Bridge, were meant as an expression of tender concern, but they came out sounding bitter and angry.

The two old friends were seated in the back of the archbishop's limousine, as far apart as they could get, one dressed in black clerical garb, the other in a white silk summer suit. The three-ton Fleetwood was sailing as smooth as a yacht up the Saw Mill River Parkway into the summer green of Westchester County. The two men, engrossed in the prospect of seeing Franklin Roosevelt at Hyde Park, were oblivious to the children who stared out of the back windows of passing cars at the big Caddie with its NYA-1 license plate.

"*I'm* dumb?" Donovan said. "Did you keep your eyes open when I showed you that movie?"

"Let me tell you something," Spellman said, shifting uncomfortably on a little silk cushion. "As a young monsignor, I spent seven years in the Vatican's Secretariat of State. After that experience, there isn't anything about the sexual proclivities of men and women in power that would shock me."

"You're a black-hearted liar and you know it," Donovan said. "You'd like to pretend that you're just a jaded old priest, but I know you too well to buy that, Frank."

"Bill, will you listen to me?" Spellman said, placing a hand on Donovan's knee. "You know, my father once gave me some good advice. He told me, 'Frank, always go with the people who are smarter than you are and, in your case, it won't be too difficult to find them.'"

"Very amusing," Donovan said, not amused.

"It was good advice," Spellman said. "I thought you were one of the smart ones. But I see I was wrong. What you're contemplating—blackmailing a President—why, that's not so smart, is it? Do you think Roosevelt's just going to sit in his wheelchair and let you get away with it? He'll fight you back, fight you dirty, and he's got plenty to fight with. And do you think the bosses and the labor unions and the Negroes and the Jews are just going to let you destroy the Democratic Party? And even if you're dumb enough to think that, what in the name of the Lord Jesus makes you think that anybody in his right mind would touch your dirty movie with a ten-foot pole?"

Donovan stared vaguely out the window as the limousine reached Hawthorne Circle.

"I've considered all that," he said. "The trouble is you left out one important thing. Roosevelt's a sick man who's gone soft. Soft in the body and soft in the head. And time's running out."

He looked at his watch, then at Spellman.

"One more secret for the confessional, okay?"

"Of course," Spellman said, clasping his hands as if in prayer.

"This is the big one," Donovan said. "Secret number one on the hit parade. In about fifteen hours from now, the largest amphibious force ever assembled in history is going to hit the beaches at Normandy, and unless Ike really screws up, which is a possibility, knowing him, everybody's going to clap and cheer and say that the invasion of France is a great victory for Roosevelt's war strategy."

"Thank God we're finally going to do it," Spellman said. "I'll say a prayer for our boys tonight."

"You'd better say a prayer for all of us," Donovan said. "Because as far as I'm concerned, D-Day could spell *doom* for the democracies of the west."

"Come on," Spellman said, "you're not telling me that you oppose the invasion of Europe."

"No, I'm not telling you that," Donovan said. "But I am saying that the strategy behind it is suicidal. Churchill understands that. I don't understand why we don't. Listen, Eisenhower's planning on pouring two million men into France in the next few weeks. Hitler's armies will be forced to wheel around and face west. That's going to leave a big fat hole for the Russians to pour into the east and conquer the heart of Europe. There's your victory. A prescription for winning the war and losing the peace. We're just preparing the stage for another round, another war, against the Russians."

"I'm sure Roosevelt understands the Russian threat," Spellman said. "Everybody understands *that*."

"Frank, you don't get it," Donovan said. "Roosevelt doesn't understand diddly shit. Communism doesn't hold any terror for that man. He thinks he can handle Stalin. You won't believe this, but the President has ordered me to suspend all clandestine OSS operations in eastern Europe. You want to know the reason? As a political signal of our good intentions to Stalin. And that includes a big show that I've laid on in Hungary. I'll tell you something. This one group of parachutists that I'm sending into Budapest has the potential to organize an enormous underground uprising that could put a pro-American government into power. They could stop Stalin in his tracks. Now, you tell me. Should I call that off?"

"I can understand how you feel," Spellman said. "If it's just this one operation, maybe I can put in a good word with the President. After all, there are a lot of Catholics in Hungary."

"It's not that simple," Donovan said. "A number of weeks ago, all the major agencies in Washington were ordered by the White House to submit a memo for transition planning after the war. So I outlined a program for what I thought was a sensible plan for the OSS. I feel strongly that we're going to need an espionage organization that is independent of both the military and the diplomatic service. Well, my plan has been killed. Dead as a doornail. Some crap from the State Department about it being immoral for America to be in the espionage racket after the war. Embarrassing if one of our spies gets caught. And as you might expect, the goddamn generals in the Pentagon are trying to grab the whole thing for themselves. If that happens, you can kiss an effective, centralized intelligence agency good-bye. You can kiss America good-bye, too."

That last phrase—*you can kiss America good-bye*—struck a responsive chord in Spellman. He looked out the window. The traffic had thinned considerably since the limousine had turned off onto Route 9. Well-tended lawns and large, wood-framed Victorian houses lined both sides of the road.

Kiss *this* America good-bye?

This was *his* America.

Spellman had driven this route before, mile after mile, hour af-

ter hour, through Westchester, Putnam, Dutchess, Orange, Rock-
land, Sullivan, and Ulster counties, through the parkways and
roads and streets and lanes that crisscrossed the 4,417 square miles
under the jurisdiction of the Archdiocese of New York, under *his*
jurisdiction. And each time he had come this way, he had mused
about his plans, after the war, to build *more* churches, *more*
schools, *more* colleges, *more* seminaries, *more* hospitals, *more of
everything* for the million and a half Catholics who inhabited his
blessed patch of America.

Yes, he had his transition plan for after the war, too.

By temperament, Spellman was an organizer, a builder. He had
come from modest beginnings and was, in his own eyes, a living
example of the American promise. He had taken his father's advice and gone with the smart people, good advice, practical advice,
effective advice, and now from the pinnacle of power of the
richest Catholic see in the world, he had become what all serious
men of affairs become—a conservator.

Like Donovan, another Irish Catholic boy who had made it the
hard way, different, but just as hard and just as big, Spellman per-
ceived America as both a promised land *and* a bulwark, a mighty
fortress against the Visigoths of the twentieth century—the bar-
baric, godless Communists.

He thought Donovan was going too far with this blackmail
stuff, but he could empathize with him. Spellman was beginning
to have his serious reservations about Roosevelt, too. Why, just
yesterday, he had received a personal note from his friend, Eu-
genio Pacelli, the Pope. The man who had appointed him as head
of the Archdiocese of New York. The smartest of the smart. It
was clear from the words in that message that the Holy Father sat
in the Vatican a heartbroken and crushed man.

And wasn't that Roosevelt's fault?

Despite the Pope's fervent pleas during the final days of the Allies' Italian campaign—pleas that had been personally conveyed
to the President by Spellman himself—American airmen had
bombed the Abbey of Monte Cassino, strafed a Vatican convoy
near Chiusi, inflicted heavy damage on the Papal Basilica of St.
Lawrence-Outside-the-Walls, and actually attacked the Pope's own
villa at Castel Gandolfo. Now, thanks be to God, the Eternal
City had finally fallen to the Allies, but Spellman could foresee a

long and cruel occupation of Rome by the Americans and the British.

And that could mean only one thing. A protracted occupation would bring more suffering to the people and play right into the hands of the Communists. Italy, the Vatican, the Universal Church, Spellman's Catholic America—all this was suddenly at stake.

Maybe Donovan was right about Roosevelt. Maybe the President had gone soft. Well, that's what they were on their way to Hyde Park to find out.

Donovan might have the secrets. Spellman had the Catholic votes.

The Fleetwood turned onto River Road and passed Saint James Episcopal Church in Hyde Park. And there, around a bend, was Crum Elbow, the white-columned Roosevelt mansion perched on a commanding rise overlooking the Hudson River. The chauffeur slowed the limousine to a crawl as it crunched onto the sweeping drive between rows of majestic oaks.

"Tell me, Bill," Spellman said, "you've trusted me this far with your secrets, and you've listed them as one and three. I'm curious. What's number two? For the confessional."

"It's the clincher," Donovan said.

"The clincher?"

"That's right," Donovan said. "There's a guy in British intelligence named Kim Philby. Best man they've got in that organization. Brilliant spy. In charge of their anti-Communist section. He's being groomed to take over the whole shebang when the big cheese retires. I've worked hand-in-glove with him on every major show of the war, including the Budapest operation."

The limousine pulled up in front of the mansion. Close like this, the building looked less imposing, run down, in need of paint. Gus Gennerich, the President's secret service bodyguard, came out of the house, followed closely by a wheelchair carrying a smiling Franklin Delano Roosevelt.

"This man, this Philby," Donovan said, "is arriving next week in America. Part of an exchange program, you might say. We're sending over one of our top guys to London."

"I'd like to meet him," Spellman said, waving back at the President.

The chauffeur opened the back door.

"I'll arrange it," Donovan said, stepping out. He looked back into the automobile at the archbishop. "Philby will be around for a while. You see, we have reason to believe that Philby may be the most important Russian spy ever to penetrate our intelligence. And if we're right, the Russians have already begun to destroy us."

CHAPTER FOUR

HYDE PARK
Monday, June 5

1

Franklin Roosevelt maneuvered the open touring car up the winding drive toward the top of Dutchess Hill. It was a shiny new Ford. Blue as his eyes had once been. It was specially fitted with manual devices for the accelerator and brake. He took such delight in showing off his skill that Gus Gennerich had to hang on for dear life from the running board. Every once in a while, the President stuck his Bakelite cigarette holder between his front teeth and reached down at his side to pet Fala, the black Scottie whose nose nestled on his shriveled right leg.

"Glorious day!" Roosevelt declared.

"Beautiful, absolutely beautiful," said Spellman, who sat up front with the President, on the other side of Fala.

"Great day for a picnic, don't you think?" Roosevelt said.

"Sure is," Donovan said from the back.

Actually, Donovan thought it was a lousy day. One of those hot and humid summer afternoons along the Hudson River Valley, filled with thunder ricocheting off the surrounding hills. As the Ford leaned heavily into a curve, Donovan glanced at the broad green lawns and ivied stone columns of the Roosevelt ancestral estate receding beneath Dutchess Hill. In the distance, over a stand of poplar trees, he could see two sailboats skimming the river in the shadows of the Palisades.

This was Roosevelt's America—serene, unspoiled, manageable. It wasn't Donovan's. The landscape of his life resembled more the battlefield at Château-Thierry in World War I, littered with the bodies of men he had vanquished to get where he was. But like most men who make it on their own, he did not resent the rich and powerful. He was all in favor of privilege—now that he was among the privileged.

Donovan had no intention of disturbing Franklin Roosevelt's tidy world. He knew it would be folly to try to use that lesbian movie to blackmail the President. Roosevelt was far too tough to be muscled around like that. No, Donovan didn't want to destroy Roosevelt; he wanted to use him.

That's where Spellman fit in. The way to reach Roosevelt in this election year was through votes. And Spellman had a hell of a lot of votes. Roosevelt *had* to listen to Spellman. So Donovan had put on his crazy-man act, threatening to blackmail the President, with the hope that this would goad Spellman into acting as his friend in court.

The car skidded to a halt in the gravel driveway at the top of the hill and Gus Gennerich jumped off the running board and opened the driver's door. The President's chauffeur, Monte Snyder, who had driven up to the stone cottage earlier with the servants, was waiting with the wheelchair. With his powerful arm and shoulder muscles, the President hauled himself into the chair, then tugged at the crease in his trousers to lift one paralyzed leg onto the other.

"Hello, I see Franklin got you here in one piece," Eleanor Roosevelt called in her wavering soprano.

The President's wife stood at the door of the porch, dressed in a long, shapeless shirtwaist dress, blue with white letters of the alphabet printed all over it. Her hair was held in place by a matching band. She waved a long-handled barbecue spatula.

"I hope you like hot dogs," she said. "Because that's what we've got."

"As long as they're kosher," said Rabbi Stephen Wise, who stepped out of the doorway behind Mrs. Roosevelt.

"Hello, Wise," Roosevelt called to the rabbi. "Glad you could make it to our little picnic. But let's not rush things. First things first. *Cocktails!*"

Inside, next to the fieldstone fireplace, a tray of bottles and glasses and cocktail utensils lay on a low table. The President began mixing a pitcher of martinis. Nearby, a colored butler from the White House staff was putting the finishing touches on the dining table, which displayed plates of smoked turkey, several different kinds of hams, salads, baked beans, and an enormous strawberry shortcake.

Roosevelt served his guests, then lifted his glass.

"Well, we've got a real celebration going here today," he said. "And why not? The news from Ike is good: the plans for the invasion of France are coming along fine. The news from Judge Rosenman is good: the polls show that I'm far out ahead of Mr. Dewey. The news from Eleanor is good: my children are behaving themselves for a change. And the news from Dr. McIntire is good: the results of my latest physical exam dispel all those silly rumors that I'm a sick man."

"If I may be permitted," Spellman said, "I'd like to propose a toast, as well as a short little prayer." He stood. "To Franklin Roosevelt and the continued health of our leader and our democracy, which are one and the same thing. *To a fourth term!*"

"That's very kind of you, my friend," Roosevelt said. "It's a strange thing, this fourth-term business. When I was five years old, my father took me to the White House to visit President Cleveland. Eighteen eighty-seven, I think it was. Anyway, Cleveland wasn't well, and he turned to me and he said, 'My little man, I'm going to make a strange wish for you. It is that you may *never* become President of the United States.'"

"Hot dogs are ready," Eleanor announced to the laughing group of men.

Over lunch, the President began to feel slightly ill, but he was used to these spells of dizziness and passing clouds of depression, and he was determined to hide his infirmities from his guests.

"Now that we're entering the decisive stage of the war," he said, when the strawberry shortcake was served, "I'm going to campaign for a bigger victory at the polls this fall than in all the other elections. We don't want just to beat Dewey; we want to bury him in an avalanche. Our country needs a government with a clear mandate. We're going to need the Jewish vote and the Catholic vote in the big cities more than ever before. It's going to mean a lot of work. I'm counting on my friends."

Spellman put down his fork and flicked some imaginary crumbs from his black trousers.

"I'm just a parish priest, not a politician," he said, looking down modestly, "but I think you have a potential problem with the Catholics and I think you should know about it."

"I know *all* about it," Roosevelt said, lighting a cigarette at the end of his long holder and flashing a mischievous grin. His teeth did not have their familiar white sparkle anymore. "I hear I've got your Irish up. That's why I asked you here today. Okay, let me have it, Spelly. What's on your mind?"

"Italy's on my mind, Mr. President," Spellman said. "Italy and the Holy Father and this endless war against the Germans. Italy lays prostrate, the Holy Father weeps for his flocks, the Catholic populations of Europe are bombed and starved, and twenty-five million American Catholics ask, 'Why?' Why must the resources of the United States continue to be used to extract a pledge of unconditional surrender from Germany? Why do we insist on bloodthirsty revenge? Why do we have plans to dismember Germany, to wreck all of its mines and factories, to extort six and a half billion dollars in reparations, to convert Germany into an agricultural and pastoral country? Why do we want to tear the heart out of Christian Europe, leaving a vacuum for the barbarous Russians, the wild beasts of communism, to rush in?"

Spellman paused, looked directly at the President, then added: "*The Pope is worried about communism.*"

"Oh, Spelly," Roosevelt said, tossing his head, "the Pope is *too* worried about communism. You know, Russia has need of protection, too. She's been invaded twice. That's why we shall give her part of Poland and recompense Poland with part of Germany."

"But it's immoral to uproot people like that," Spellman replied. "You can't take away their homes and their churches and even their cemeteries."

"Don't worry," Roosevelt said, "I know how to talk to Stalin. He's just another practical man who wants peace and prosperity."

"He's not just another anything," Spellman said. "He is different. You can't trust him. He'll never cooperate."

Roosevelt turned with a patient smile to the others.

"Arguing with the archbishop," he said, "reminds me of what Averell Harriman once said about Endicott Peabody of Groton. 'Peabody,' Harriman said, 'would be an awful bully if he weren't such a fierce Christian.'"

"Why don't we go down to the pool?" Eleanor said.

"Good idea," Roosevelt said. "It'll cool us all off."

2

Water bugs scudded over the Hyde Park pool as Franklin Roosevelt, dressed in a blue-and-white-striped tank top and dark blue swimming trunks, slid into the deep end. Eleanor lowered herself backward on the ladder. Rabbi Wise, broad-shouldered and trim, jumped in, head high, somehow managing to keep his neatly combed hair dry—until he found himself engulfed in a Roosevelt family tradition. Water polo.

The President was in his element. Water was the great equalizer for a man whose legs had been paralyzed for the past twenty-three years. He moved through the heated water powerfully, leaping for the ball, catching it in midair, hurling it toward the imaginary goal at the end of the pool, calling out instructions, laughing, absolutely dominating the physical contest.

From a pair of wicker chairs at poolside, Spellman and Donovan watched the one-man show. They had taken off their jackets as a concession to the Hyde Park informality, but they had both firmly declined to join the swimming party. Tall glasses of iced lemonade sweated on a white wrought-iron table between them. A few yards away, Gus Gennerich sat next to two telephones—a direct line to the White House switchboard and a radiophone for overseas calls.

Spellman glanced over at Gennerich to make certain that he couldn't be overheard, then turned to Donovan.

"You were right about Roosevelt and communism," he said. "And now with this fellow . . . what's his name? . . . Philby . . . uncovered as a possible spy . . ."

He shook his head, heavily.

Donovan didn't say anything.

"But you were wrong about FDR being a sick man," Spellman said. "He looks as fit as a fiddle to me."

"Don't let looks deceive you," Donovan said.

"Oh?"

"It's highly unlikely, even if he gets reelected, that he'll live to serve out a fourth term," Donovan said.

"But I just read in the *Times* . . ." Spellman began, then caught himself. "I've got a feeling that I'm about to hear another secret. Number four."

"A couple of months ago," Donovan said, "there was a secret medical conference at the Bethesda Naval Hospital, in which eight specialists discussed the President's health. They reported high blood pressure, advanced arteriosclerosis, fluid on both lungs —which has since disappeared—and congestive heart failure— which hasn't. Roosevelt's been ordered to cut down on his time in the Oval Office to four hours a day. He's been taking digitalis, phenobarbital, and something called enteric-coated aminophylline."

"As bad as that?" Spellman said.

"Uh-huh."

"If the truth ever got out, it would be as damaging as that movie you've got," Spellman said. "Even more so."

"I've been thinking about that, too," Donovan said.

Spellman looked at Donovan, at those ambivalent pale-blue Irish eyes, eyes that everyone found impossible to fathom because they were capable of communicating two opposing meanings at the same time. *Trust me . . . trust me not. . . .* And Spellman, who had taken his father's advice and gone with the smart people, who had survived and flourished in the Byzantine atmosphere of the Vatican, who was in line for a cardinal's red hat after the war, who had amassed more power than any American Catholic prelate in history—Spellman suddenly realized that William J. Donovan wasn't so dumb after all.

"Bill, what is it you want from me?" Spellman asked.

"What do you mean?"

"I mean, one secret for the confessional I can understand," Spellman said. "Two, maybe. But four? In one day? What's the deal?"

"There's no *deal*," Donovan said. "Of course, you might like to send a confidential summary of some of this stuff I've told you to the Vatican. Make you look awfully good. As long as you keep me out of it, I'll leave what you say to your discretion."

"And in return?"

"In return," Donovan said, "I want you to do us *both* a favor. Do you know why Rabbi Wise came up here today?"

"For the same reason I was asked," Spellman said. "The big-city vote in the campaign."

"Right," Donovan said. "The rabbi and I have been talking. Very interesting man. He's going to make a proposal to Roosevelt here today. Certain military operations he wants Roosevelt to authorize. You'll see. Anyway, all I want you to do is make it very plain to the President that you support the rabbi. That the *Catholics* support the *Jews*. It will make Wise's proposal politically irresistible."

3

"We have known since the summer of nineteen forty-two that the Nazis had a plan to exterminate the Jews of Europe," Rabbi Wise said. "And yet, for almost two years, we have done practically nothing to stop them. Now we have the opportunity."

They were sitting at the edge of the pool, arrayed in an irregular circle of chairs. Sprawled on the warm grass, Fala was gnawing on a steak bone near the President's wasted legs. Eleanor's hair was wrapped in a towel. Rabbi Wise reached into a briefcase, took out some papers, and handed them to the President.

"What's this?" Roosevelt asked.

"Two things you should see," Wise said. "An aerial reconnaissance photo of the death camp at Auschwitz, clearly showing the location of the gas chambers and the crematoria. And an analysis based on the eyewitness testimony of two escapees from Auschwitz, which argues in favor of the United States Air Force bombing the key rail routes and the mass-killing installation itself."

"Oh, I've seen all this stuff," the President said, letting the papers drop to the grass.

There was a subtle change in his voice that alerted Eleanor that something was wrong. She looked over at her husband. How was it possible? Five minutes ago, he was laughing and romping in the swimming pool. Now, suddenly, he looked haggard, limp, almost cadaverous.

Eleanor signaled Gus Gennerich with her eyebrows. The body-guard got up and walked over to his boss. He rearranged the terry-cloth robe that Roosevelt had thrown over his shoulders. The President looked up at Gennerich, a thin gray film clouding his eyes. The look of a sick man.

"Maybe everybody would like to take a rest down at the Big House," Eleanor said.

"What's that?" the President said. "Nonsense. I'm fine. We're all fine. Dammit, Eleanor, you can't interrupt a political discussion. We're talking about votes! This is important. Tell the butler to bring some drinks. Some of the hard stuff. And some cigars. Now, Wise, you go on. I want to hear what you've got to say."

The rabbi looked at Eleanor, who nodded for him to continue.

"For the first time during the war," Wise said, "we have un-contested air supremacy in Europe. General Eaker's Flying Fortresses in Italy aren't tied up with the coming invasion in France, and those planes and others with the Fifteenth Air Force in Italy are within easy striking distance of Auschwitz. We have the means to interdict the rail lines between Budapest and the death camp. We have the means to knock out the mass-murder apparatus with a large-scale saturation-bombing mission.

"Today, and every day that we delay, twelve thousand Hungarian Jews are deported by train to Auschwitz," Wise continued. "These pitiful victims are the remnants of the Jewish communities of Europe. Nearly six million have already died. Hungary contains most of those who are left. If Auschwitz is bombed, a few thousand Jewish inmates may perish in the attack, but they are condemned to a hellish death anyway. The Nazis would not have the resources to rebuild the destroyed gas chambers. Hundreds of thousands of lives will be saved. And America will be praised for its humanitarian act for generations to come."

Just then, the butler arrived with a fresh tray of cocktails and a box of cigars.

"Help yourself," Roosevelt said. "You know what Al Smith always says about liquor and cigars. He says if you can get a group of . . ."

The President abruptly lost his train of thought and could not go on.

"I believe," Eleanor interrupted as loudly and firmly as she could, trying to save her husband from humiliation, "I believe that the War Refugee Board is considering just such a proposal as you suggest, Rabbi."

"It's gone beyond that," Wise replied. "It's been kicked up to the War Department, and they've turned it down flatly because they claim it would mean diverting air resources that are essential to the war effort. But these planes in Italy that I'm talking of are being used right now to bomb industrial areas and oil targets just thirty or forty miles away from Auschwitz. They're practically operating over Auschwitz now. We can bomb the death camp and the rail lines if we want to, and without hurting the war effort. But it's going to take a direct order from the President."

"Well, I don't know," Eleanor said. "I've always thought that it was important in this country that the Jews as Jews remain unaggressive and stress the fact that they are Americans first and above everything else. As far as possible, I think they should wipe out in their own consciousness any feeling of difference by joining in all that is being done by Americans. But a special presidential order to bomb Auschwitz would only emphasize the difference between . . ."

"*Eleanor!*"

"Yes, Franklin."

The President rubbed his eyes with the backs of his hands. He seemed to be emerging from his torpor.

"My dear," he said, "I know that whenever you hear the word 'humanitarian' used, you feel a compulsion to do something good immediately. But a proposal to divert vast aerial armadas engaged in decisive operations elsewhere against the Axis is a complicated business that deserves a bit of sober reflection. Don't you agree?"

"Of course, Franklin," she said. "As a matter of fact, that was the point I was trying to make."

"You know," Roosevelt said, turning to Rabbi Wise, "I've been wanting to make a gesture in the direction of the European Jews. Let me think about what you said."

Archbishop Spellman cleared his throat.

"May I add my clerical voice to that of Rabbi Wise's," he said. "American Catholics would applaud a gesture of this kind to save Jewish lives. After all, isn't that why we are fighting this war? For humanitarian purposes. Yes, we Catholics would approve heartily. It would be very popular among Catholics, Mr. President."

When he finished, Spellman looked over at Donovan.

"Good," Roosevelt said, struggling to his feet.

Gus Gennerich rushed over with his crutches. When Roosevelt had steadied himself, he turned to his guests.

"Now, hasn't this been a glorious day?" he said. "Why don't you all go down to the Big House with Eleanor. I have a couple of things I want to talk over with General Donovan. We'll meet you down there."

After the others had left, Roosevelt said to Donovan:

"I can't give the Jews what Rabbi Wise is asking for. We can't spare the bombers. What do you think the Jews will settle for? From a political point of view, I mean."

"Hungary," Donovan said.

"What do you mean, Hungary?" Roosevelt asked.

"Lift your ban on OSS operations in eastern Europe," Donovan said. "I have a parachute team ready to go into Hungary. Let them organize a Jewish uprising against Eichmann in Budapest."

"The Russians will never stand for it," Roosevelt said. "I've given Stalin my word that we won't interfere with the Red Army in eastern Europe."

"Hang Stalin!" Donovan said.

"Well," Roosevelt said, "I'll think about it."

"Good," Donovan said.

"You really think this one operation in Budapest would satisfy Wise and Spellman," Roosevelt said.

"Yes, I do," Donovan said.

"Curious," Roosevelt said. "Such a big political payoff for one little operation. But what if I say no?"

"I don't understand," Donovan said.

"What if I don't give you the green light?" Roosevelt said.

Donovan shrugged.

"Oh, come on, Bill, don't look so surprised," Roosevelt said. "Tell me. What will you do?"

"I really don't understand, Mr. President, what you're driving at."

"I'll tell you what," Roosevelt said, slipping into his wheelchair. "I understand you have some motion pictures of a friend of Eleanor's that I might be interested in. Edgar Hoover says I shouldn't lose the opportunity to make them part of my home-movie collection. Why don't you make sure that I get the original print and all duplicates by tomorrow morning? By then I should know how I'll decide about that little show of yours in Hungary."

CHAPTER FIVE

CHECKPOINT KIKINDA
Tuesday, June 6

1

Anton Bebler cursed the weatherman.

After a week of steady rain, the radio had been promising a change. This morning on the seven o'clock news, the Kraut announcer had predicted a perfect day. Glorious "Führer weather." But instead, a big glutenous drop of rain had just splattered across the windshield of Bebler's Mercedes truck.

"Dumb Krauts!"

He shifted into overdrive as the canvas-covered rig crossed the Danube and headed north, passing a row of salmon-pink stucco houses, toward the darkening horizon.

"Assholes can't even get the weather right," he muttered to himself. "Look at those fucking rain clouds. It's going to pour again."

Sure enough, just as he uttered those words, the skies opened up and torrents of rain began lashing the tall fields of sunflowers on both sides of the macadam road. He pulled off on the shoulder and stopped, took off his new black-market shoes and socks, and got out. He walked around to the back of the truck and checked the contents under the canvas. Four regulation *Wehrmacht* coffins.

The truck had been sitting in front of his father's garage for the past week, and the canvas top was saturated with water. It leaked along its seams. A few drops hit the wooden coffins, but most of the water dripped onto the metal platform grille that was raised two feet off the bed of the truck. The length and width and depth of the coffins, the size of the screws used to secure the lids, the number of holes per square meter in the platform grille—everything was according to the specifications in the Wehrmacht contract. Rain or no rain, the four dead German officers in Anton Bebler's truck would arrive in Budapest all nice and dry.

Back inside the cab, Bebler dried his feet and laced up his pointed-toed shoes. Then he switched on his wipers and opened a side vent to prevent the windshield from fogging over. Actually, he didn't mind the driving in the rain. He had made this trip from Belgrade to Budapest so many times that he could practically handle the road blindfolded. No, it wasn't the driving he minded. What pissed off Anton Bebler was that bad weather kept hitchhikers off the road.

Especially female hitchhikers.

The wipers couldn't cope with the volume of water and he leaned over the wheel, staring at the liquid distortion of the road. It was coming down so hard now that he could hardly make out the towering haystacks, piled by the Serbian peasants into shapes that resembled barns, that dotted the flat landscape. Somewhere not too far up ahead must be the looming onion dome of the old Greek Orthodox church in Ĉenta.

It was in front of the Ĉenta churchyard that Anton Bebler had made his first pickup. That was almost a year ago, when Bebler had just turned seventeen and qualified for a license to drive his father's truck. Since then, "Tony" (a nickname Bebler had pinned on himself) had picked up no fewer than thirty-seven girls along the Belgrade-Budapest highway. He knew it was exactly thirty-seven because he kept a careful record in a little book, with precise notations of the date, location along the road, description of the girl, and (in his own crude boyish code) whether he had succeeded in persuading her to give him a hand job.

Sex on wheels, so to speak, was not without its perils, since sections of the road on both sides of the border were known to be occasionally interdicted by the anti-Fascist underground. But Tony

Bebler felt that he operated with a certain degree of immunity, thanks to the words stenciled in foot-high block letters in three languages (Serbo-Croatian, Hungarian, German) on the side of the black Mercedes truck: BEBLER & SON MORTUARY CARTING COMPANY.

Whether these words had anything to do with his good fortune Bebler couldn't say. But certain facts spoke for themselves. Fact number one: he had never been stopped by the underground guerrillas. Fact number two: he had scored eight times—or, as he often boasted to the German border guards at Checkpoint Kikinda, "I've got nearly a twenty percent jerk-off rate."

That average, he now thought with a twinge of self-pity as he passed over the Tamis River bridge in Ĉenta and sped toward Zrenjanin, would not be improved by this rain-soaked trip.

As luck would have it, a freight train was passing through the center of Zrenjanin just as Bebler arrived, so he switched off his motor in front of the flashing red warning lights and settled down with a cigarette for the long wait. He watched through the watery murk as the phantom shapes of the boxcars passed in dull, wriggling colors before him. He had heard rumors about the contents of some of these boxcars—wild, improbable stories about human cargo being sent from all over Europe to vast Nazi murder installations in Poland and Czechoslovakia and Germany. Anton "Tony" Bebler, a confirmed cynic at seventeen, was ready to believe almost anything about the Nazis, but he didn't believe any of *that* crap.

"Propaganda," he said to himself out loud, using a word whose meaning he had only recently learned.

He rolled down the window to toss out his cigarette and stared in utter disbelief. *It wasn't possible*. Not more than ten yards away stood the rain-drenched figure of a woman. She was all alone, holding a small shiny metal suitcase over her head for protection. She wore a cotton dress which, Bebler immediately noticed, clung provocatively to her thighs and ass and formed a faint mound over her cunt.

"Number nine," he said, his heavy teenager's lips forming into a kind of smile.

He beeped his horn and she came over.

"Want a lift?" he asked.

She nodded and smiled.

Never before had Tony Bebler seen such beautiful almond-shaped, gray-blue eyes. He *had* to get her into his truck.

"Where you headed?" he asked.

"Budapest," she said.

"You a bohunk?"

She didn't understand.

"Hungarian? Magyar?"

"Magyar," she repeated.

"Okay. Hop in."

She walked around the front of the truck, and as she climbed in, Bebler noticed that the rain was beating down more heavily than ever. It occurred to him that he should probably recheck the coffins in the back of the truck. But just then, the caboose of the train trundled past and he reached for the starter button. He couldn't wait to get his beautiful new Magyar conquest on the road.

His number nine.

2

In the back of the truck, the rain pounded out a deafening tattoo on the canvas, and water sluiced in along the seams. The four pine Wehrmacht coffins, lashed securely to iron bolts in the platform grille, remained steady as the truck lurched forward over the railroad tracks. But one of the men, who had slipped under the flap unnoticed during Bebler's long stop, lost his balance and fell.

Joel Nathan stifled a cry of pain.

"You all right?" Albright whispered.

Nathan nodded, caught his breath and said: "Banged my shin. And my goddamn screwdriver fell through the grille."

"Here," said Dan Gur. "I'll get it for you."

He unlatched the grille and swung it open.

"Dammit," Gur said. "There's three or four inches of water down here."

"Can't be helped," Albright said. "We don't have much time. Let's unscrew these coffin lids."

The truck swerved sharply right, then began picking up speed. Soon, they would pass the turnoff on the road that led up the side of the mountain to the abandoned bee farm where they had been hiding out. From there it was only about a mile to the border checkpoint at Kikinda.

As he worked on loosening a screw, Saul Patir said: "I hope Ruthie will be all right."

"I don't think the kid will try anything funny until after he's through the checkpoint," Albright said.

"I hope you're right," Patir said.

So do I, Albright thought. *So do I*.

Alexander Albright was worried about Ruth. Not only whether she could handle this teenage masher, Tony Bebler, but whether she could handle the tougher job that lay ahead. The doubts about Ruth Bar-Adon, doubts he thought he had buried back in Camp Jubilee, began cropping up again. He had never seen her as edgy as she was this morning when he woke her up for the call from London. Maybe it was the accumulated lack of sleep. Maybe it was the anticipation of more bad news when she got London on her radio set. Maybe it was . . . *them*. Or, more accurately, her feelings about *him*.

It was still dark when he woke her and, while she washed, he stepped outside the squeaky door of the one-room cabin. Raindrops clung like tiny light bulbs to the edge of the overhanging roof, but it had finally stopped raining. That was something to be grateful for, he thought. For almost a week, they had lived with rain and mist and fog and mud and clothes that resolutely refused to dry. Their hideaway on the side of the mountain beside the river had become a damp bog, further depressing their soggy spirits.

From the porch of the cabin, Albright could see the deep purples of the night gradually shading into the gray-blues of the dawn all across the Danube valley. For a fleeting moment, he felt as though the world had come to a kind of grand balance—between night and day, wet and dry, cool and warm, rest and motion. But that feeling almost immediately evaporated as he thought of all the things that had gone wrong with their mission—the ambushes, the hiding, the hunger, the long night marches.

And all the things that had gone wrong between them.

He had tried to talk to her about it, but it didn't do any good.

"Guido was right," she had said. "We should never have slept together."

"What does Guido have to do with us?" he asked.

"He warned me," she said.

"Warned you about what?"

"I don't really know," she answered. "About . . . I don't know. But he was right. Don't you see? I don't want your love now. Not *now*. Not while we're out here, in this cabin, on this mission, waiting, waiting. I don't want to be . . . *swallowed up* by your love. I was swallowed up before. When I was with the Stern Gang. A woman in a war is always facing two dangers. The enemy and the men who are her comrades, her haver. Even her haver want to swallow her up because she is a woman. I don't want you to think of me as a woman while this is going on. I want you to think of me, to treat me, as Ruth. Not as a woman but your comrade-at-arms. I want to be left alone *to fight*."

He had not understood.

Guido?

Did Guido DeVita still think that Albright was the wrong man?

After waiting a few more moments on the porch, Albright went back into the cabin and adjusted the blackout curtain over the window that was set in the door frame. Even with all the windows closed, he could hear the traffic on the road beyond the river. It never let up. Day and night, German military traffic went back and forth across the border checkpoint at Kikinda a mile or so away. At certain times, freight trains came thundering through the valley on a rail line that ran parallel to the river and the road, and then the whole side of the mountain shook and the antenna on Ruth's shortwave-radio transmitter quivered for some time after the noise stopped.

"How much time now?" she asked.

"Two more minutes," he said, sitting beside her at the table.

She suddenly took one of his hands.

"Alex, what are we going to do?"

He was taken by surprise and didn't know what to say.

"This is insane," she said. "This waiting. The same message every night."

"Oh, *that*," he said.

"What did you think I meant?" she asked.

"Nothing," he said.

"What's wrong with them?" she said.

"Maybe we'll get the green light tonight," he said.

"Maybe we will," she said, "and maybe we won't, but I don't think we should wait any longer. There are thousands of people dying in Budapest while we wait for their green light."

"I know," he said.

"You weren't there in Prenj when we met that group of Hungarians who had crossed the border," she said. "You and Dan were out somewhere getting supplies. You should have been there. They told us what was happening in Hungary. They had *seen* it with their own eyes. This wasn't like the reports we've heard on the BBC. These were eyewitnesses. They saw the deportation of the Jews. One of them had even escaped from Auschwitz."

"Ruth," he said, "we've been all over this before."

"But you weren't there," she said. "In Prenj we heard with our own ears what this man had seen at Auschwitz. He himself, not a Jew, had been forced to help throw the gassed bodies of Jews into furnaces. He had touched the dead bodies of Jews."

"Ruth . . ."

"And I kissed those hands. Kissed them because that was the closest I could come to touching those dead Jews myself. Their burning flesh. Oh, Alex, you wouldn't have believed what he told us in Prenj while you and Dan were away. I wished you had been with me . . . with us."

"I wish I had, too," he said. "I'm sorry I wasn't with you, Ruth. I'll try never to leave your side again."

He stroked her hair.

"It's almost time," he said. "Maybe tonight . . ."

"I've almost stopped hoping," she said, switching on the radio.

She began broadcasting her call letters on the preset frequency. Her monitor in London replied with instructions on which code was in use this time. From memory, Ruth began sending in that code, repeating the request she had made for the past six nights: "We at border awaiting orders to cross stop Please query go ahead stop"

Alex watched Ruth's face as she listened to the coded answer coming through her earphones.

"*My God!*" she cried.

She turned and threw her arms around his neck and kissed him. "We can go!"

"When?" he asked.

"Wait. I'll ask."

She tapped out the question and listened.

"As soon as we want," she said.

Alex climbed the ladder to the loft, and as Ruth signed off she could hear him waking the others and telling them the news.

"Wonderful."

That was Dan Gur's voice, low and sleepy.

Then Ruth heard Gur ask: "What's today?"

Joel Nathan said: "I think it's Monday."

Saul Patir said: "No, it's Tuesday."

Gur: "You sure?"

Patir: "Sure I'm sure. Three days ago was Shavuos."

Gur: "Since when are you getting religious?"

Patir: "None of your business. Just take my word for it. Today is Tuesday."

Gur: "That's good."

Nathan: "What's so special about Tuesday?"

Gur: "You tell them."

And Alex Albright explained: "You remember. Dan's gone over the plan. Tuesday's the day that Anton Bebler drives his truck over the border."

3

"Another slice of bread, perhaps, Wisliczeny?" the major said. "It's good to sop up the gravy with."

"*Danke,* but I couldn't," SS Haupsturmführer Dieter von Wisliczeny said, slapping his stomach. A burp escaped his thin, bluish lips. "Oh, excuse me," he said, delicately bringing his napkin to his mouth and nodding gravely across the table. "So much good food. So excellently prepared. And is it really true, as they say, that you bake all your own bread yourself?"

The major wasn't certain whether he had detected a note of sarcasm in Wisliczeny's voice, or whether it was just the derisive tone that Wisliczeny employed in all his conversation. It was said of Dieter von Wisliczeny, who was Adolf Eichmann's deputy in Hungary, that he was worse than the master murderer himself. What this "worse" meant nobody ever explained. The major hoped he wasn't going to find out today.

"All my own bread!" the major replied. "No, no. Not *all* of it. Just when I feel like it. This sour dough is one of my favorites. I do insist that you have another slice."

The major began sawing off a slice. Nearing sixty, he was still a handsome military figure. His impeccably tonsured hair had turned snow white at the temples. His dueling scars blended into the florid coloration of his cheeks. The slight stoop of his shoulders was the only thing that marred an otherwise perfect posture. As he approached retirement after more than forty years of service in the German Army, however, the most remarkable thing about Major Karl August Schneider was the degree to which the bachelor-soldier had come to resemble his own eighty-one-year-old mother with whom he lived and who now sat nodding off to sleep, at the far end of the dining room table.

Major Schneider speared the thick-crusted bread with the knife and handed it to Wisliczeny.

"You know," the major said, "a man must have a hobby. Some antidote to the harsh rigors of the military life. Something less Wagnerian and more . . . *Mozartian*. So, baking bread is mine. What is yours, Wisliczeny?"

"Mine?"

Haupsturmführer Dieter von Wisliczeny seemed genuinely surprised by the question. He made a teepee with his fingertips while he considered his answer. Then he said:

"Ridding the entire world of Jewish scum."

Major Schneider picked up his napkin and carefully folded it along the creases. He placed it neatly beside his plate.

"That is not a hobby," he said. "That, Wisliczeny, is one of those idiotic Nazi obsessions."

At the end of the table, the old lady—chin on chest, mouth

agape, a physical premonition of her son's onrushing old age—snored loudly.

Wisliczeny fastened the top button of his tunic, straightened in his chair, and said:

"Colonel Eichmann warned me about you, Schneider."

"Did he?"

"Yes. He said you were from a different era. That you were shaped by the epoch between the wars. 'Epoch between the wars' were Colonel Eichmann's exact words to me before I left Budapest. I didn't understand what he meant then, but now I see. Homemade bread indeed! *Mozart!* Now I understand why, despite your distinguished war record, you were placed in charge of this border garrison here at Kikinda and were passed over for promotion."

"For forty years," Schneider said, "I have carried out my duty to the *Faterland*. Or don't they teach that concept any longer in the new Nazi army? Are you all so busy killing Jews and Gypsies and Polacks and all the other *Untermenschen* that you forget the sacred calling of the soldier?"

"You would have us allow the Jews to pollute the Reich?" Wisliczeny asked.

"I would win the war," Schneider said. "I would not divert precious resources to this program that you and Eichmann are running. Think of what our army could have done with the transport, the manpower, the steel that you have siphoned off into this racial miniwar against the Jews. And you go on! Even as our army bleeds on the steppes of Russia and braces for the inevitable onslaught across the English Channel!"

"Major," Wisliczeny said, "the inevitable has occurred today."

"What do you mean?"

"I mean just that," Wisliczeny said. "This morning, Eisenhower's forces crossed the Channel. The invasion of Europe has begun."

"Then we are finished," the major said, looking down the table at his sleeping mother.

"No," Wisliczeny said, "we will fight and triumph and hurl Eisenhower back into the sea. But in order to defeat Eisenhower in the west, we must be firm here in the east. And that is why I have come here with a personal request from my superior, Colonel Eichmann."

"If it has anything to do with aiding you and Eichmann in this idiotic final solution . . ."

"It has nothing to do with that at all," Wisliczeny said. "It is a matter of honor between German officers. We have received word through intelligence channels that a group of Allied agents, led by an American OSS officer, may soon try to cross the border from Yugoslavia into Hungary. Among the primary objectives of this group is the assassination of Colonel Eichmann, after which they intend to lead a general uprising of the Jewish population of Budapest. We were a bit concerned about disclosing these facts to you, since it is well known how you feel about the final solution, and we were, frankly, worried that you would not be receptive to our suggestion."

"Suggestion?"

"Yes," said Wisliczeny. "We would like you to agree to augment your border garrison with a special SS detachment provided by Colonel Eichmann. Of course, this is a bit out of channels, you understand, but Colonel Eichmann is . . ."

"Pissing in his pants," said Schneider. "I always knew he was a coward. Well, you can tell Colonel Eichmann that he has nothing to fear. No one can possibly sneak across the checkpoint here at Kikinda. Come, Wisliczeny, I will show you."

He stood up, clicked his heels and led Wisliczeny out of the room.

Outside, the rain had not let up, and the two trench-coated figures made their way down a long, winding path, which was bordered on both sides by wind-lashed beds of colorful geraniums, and through the gate to a large blockhouse. As soon as they entered, the soldiers snapped to attention.

"This is central control at Kikinda," Schneider explained, ignoring the water that dripped off his cap onto the shoulders of his trench coat. "All traffic, both ways, is monitored here. If you look through this observation window, you will see that each vehicle must pass through three stages—documents, search, and interrogation. Traffic controllers in this control room provide a double safety measure by listening in through microphones to each of these stages. That is what these six men do here. At the first sign of anything out of the ordinary, the vehicle in question is pulled into a fourth stage—the alert stage. And there a special team of my best men put it through the wringer."

Major Schneider turned to the soldiers, who were still standing rigidly at attention, some of them with earphone lines trailing down their backs. He addressed a lieutenant.

"How are things today, Karp?"

"Very quiet, sir," Lieutenant Karp replied, blinking nervously.

"No problems?"

"None, sir."

"Tell me, Karp, what do you think the chances are of an unauthorized person getting across the checkpoint undetected?"

"Zero, major."

"Thank you. At ease!"

Major Schneider turned on his heels.

"Come, Wisliczeny, I'll show you how it works."

It was now nearly one in the afternoon, and the rain came down as hard as ever. Under the lowering sky, traffic was backed up for hundreds of yards on both sides of the border. Six vehicles were undergoing inspection simultaneously—three going north to Hungary and three going south to Yugoslavia. Swarms of green raincoated border soldiers buzzed around each vehicle. Instructions blared from loudspeakers.

Suddenly, a pulsing, bleating horn split the air with its urgent warning.

"Ah, you're in luck," Schneider said to Wisliczeny. "We have an alert."

From all around them, the sound of boots echoed on the damp pavement as the special team converged on the vehicle in the alert bay. The area was lighted by brilliant flood lamps. Gates were slammed shut fore and aft, and the vehicle was raised on pneumatic skids so that its undercarriage could be inspected. It was then lowered and Lieutenant Karp ordered the driver out.

On the side of the truck, Wisliczeny noticed, was the stenciled inscription: BEBLER & SON MORTUARY CARTING COMPANY.

The door on the driver's side swung open as the truck came level with the ground and the pneumatic lift emitted a loud exhaling hiss. A polished, pointed-toed shoe emerged. Then a leg with a muddy trouser cuff. Then the driver himself—a tall, athletically built young man with a mop of blond hair and a confident smile.

"What's all the fuss?" Alex Albright asked in German, heavily laced with a Serbo-Croatian accent.

"Where's Tony?" Lieutenant Karp demanded to know. "The boy who always drives the truck?"

"You mean Anton?" Albright asked. "He's sick. Old man Bebler asked me to make the run for Anton today. If there's any problem, you can phone him. Here, he gave me his office number in Belgrade."

Major Schneider approached.

"Problems with this man's travel documents?"

"No, sir," Karp replied. "His documents are in order. But his passenger lodged a complaint against him with our inspectors."

"What kind of complaint?"

Lieutenant Karp walked around to the passenger side of the truck, opened the door, and Ruth Bar-Adon stepped down. She was weeping.

"This young woman," Lieutenant Karp explained, "says that the driver offered her a lift back at Zrenjanin and then, when he got her into the truck, made an indecent proposition."

"Is that true, young lady?" Major Schneider asked.

"Yes," Ruth said, sobbing.

Schneider looked at Wisliczeny and shrugged his shoulders. "Not a major smuggling case, I fear," he said. "Wish we could have put on a better show for you."

Suddenly, Albright was shouting: "Well, for Christ's sake, Anton does it all the time, and he told me that you guys at the border knew all about it and never bothered him and that you even know what his goddamn jerk-off average is and . . ."

"Quiet!" Major Schneider ordered. He turned to Karp. "What's he talking about, Lieutenant?"

"It's true what he says about Tony," Lieutenant Karp said. "Anton has boasted to us about his . . . exploits. But the women have never complained."

"Well, young lady," the major said, "what do you want us to do? Do you want to press charges? If we arrest this fellow as a sex offender, it's off to a labor camp with him, you know."

"As long as he promises to be good until we get to Budapest,"

Ruth said. "Now that you've scared him, I'm sure he'll be all right."

"You're a lucky fellow," Schneider said to Albright. "This girl is willing to give you another chance. Can I count on you behaving yourself?"

"Yes, sir," Albright said, looking contrite.

"Good," Schneider said. "But don't forget; if you try anything, I'll hear about it. Now, get out of here."

Albright and Ruth were halfway back in the truck when SS Haupsturmführer Dieter von Wisliczeny called out: "Wait! What if this is all a trick? A diversion. An effort to avoid a thorough search of the truck. Major Schneider, please be so kind as to order your men to search the contents of the truck."

Major Schneider looked at Wisliczeny and for a moment considered refusing his request. The rain dripping off their officers' hats formed a kind of veil around their faces as they gazed into each other's eyes. Schneider assumed that a search would turn up nothing and would thus end in a modest humiliation for Wisliczeny. But then, if his men did find something—almost anything, even something quite minor—*that* could be used as an excuse by Wisliczeny to wreck Schneider's last two or three years in the army before his retirement. Worse, if the truck were let go without a search and were later discovered to have contained the team that was sent to assassinate Eichmann, it was a certainty that Wisliczeny would have Schneider shot.

"Search the truck," Schneider told Lieutenant Karp.

Karp and two of his men leaped onto the back of the truck and disappeared under the canvas. Seconds later, Karp stuck his head out and announced: "There are four Wehrmacht coffins. And there may be a problem."

"What is it?" Schneider asked.

"The screws that hold down the coffin lids have been loosened."

Major Schneider shot a hard look at Albright.

"Impossible," Albright said.

"Open the coffins!" Schneider shouted.

"You can't do that," Albright objected. "It's against regulations. It's . . . it's sacrilegious."

"*Open them!*"

It required a search to find a screwdriver, but one was finally located and handed to Lieutenant Karp who went to work on a coffin lid.

"Nothing abnormal in this one," Karp shouted out of the back of the truck. "One dead body."

Major Schneider noticed that a smirk had formed on Wisliczeny's face.

"Nothing wrong in the second one," came Karp's muffled voice.

Wisliczeny nodded at Schneider: "The next one or the one after that. Something or someone will be in there. Mark my words."

"Number three is okay!"

By now, everyone around the truck—Schneider, Wisliczeny, Albright, Ruth, the guards—stood practically motionless, waiting for the final report from Karp.

The lieutenant jumped off the truck, blinking nervously as he approached the major.

"Each one of the four coffins contains the uniform-clad body of one dead German officer," he reported, unable to contain an extended blink of satisfaction.

"Nothing else?"

"Nothing."

"Good," Schneider said, turning to Albright. "Get this truck the hell out of here." Then, to Wisliczeny: "You see, we know our business here. Coffins are an outmoded smuggler's trick. No one would be foolish enough to resort to that."

4

Across the border in Hungary, Ruth looked over at Albright and said:

"I was just thinking. What if that German lieutenant had dropped something, like his screwdriver, through the holes in the grille, and what if he had opened the platform to retrieve it?"

"That's funny," Albright said. "That's exactly what happened to Joel when he got on the truck."

She looked at him to make certain that he was serious, and she saw that he was.

"Well?" she said.

"Well, what?"

"What would have happened?"

Albright shrugged.

"One of our boys would have bitten off his fingers."

CHAPTER SIX

BUDAPEST
Tuesday, June 27

1

"You made me love ya . . . I didn't wanna do it . . . I didn't wanna do it . . ."

The singer in black face was belting out a convincing imitation of Al Jolson. White gloves clasped at his chest. Eyes rolling devilishly. Legs braced wide apart. Voice all up in his throat, sounding reedy and moist. Like an old Victrola record.

Which was where the sound was coming from. He was lip-synching to a scratchy old record that wobbled around a turntable at the edge of the stage.

And the audience loved it.

There were nearly two hundred of them, mostly in their twenties and thirties, well groomed and dressed, and they sat at the small, rickety tables smoking cigarettes that reeked of Turkish tobacco and drinking the specialty of the house—purple sloe gin fizzes. They stared in rapt devotion at the spotlighted Jolson figure rocking on the narrow stage.

". . . Gimme gimme gimme gimme what I cry for . . . you know ya got the kinda kisses that I die for . . ."

On his knees now, he crooned the last high note, or rather the voice on the record did, and the audience sprang instantly to its feet and gave him a wild ovation. It was a manic reception, and it went on and on and on until they collapsed in exhaustion back into their chairs and fell silent.

The performer stepped forward and licked his white minstrel lips. The cigarette smoke whirled in the footlights around his legs.

"Is that the best you can do?" he challenged them.

They broke into appreciative laughter.

"You know," he said, rolling his eyes, "you can be replaced by Aryans."

More laughter. Louder.

"In fact," he continued, segueing into an exaggerated German accent, "ve haf speshul little conzentrashun kemps for pipple like you."

By now, the entire room was shaking with laughter. The young people were bent over their tables, slapping their thighs, red in the face with diaphragm-convulsing laughter.

"Oy, I can't stand it," a woman complained, and her words provoked even more laughter.

"Tell him to stop or I'm going to piss in my pants," said a man sitting nearby.

And then with a gesture of his gloved hand, the performer calmed them down and said: "Enough! I'm sure you've all heard the news on the BBC today. For those of you who haven't: there is talk—*just* talk, mind you—that our foreign minister has asked the German ambassador to withdraw the Gestapo from Hungary."

His words were received in silence. A perfect silence. Not a single cough or a scrape of a chair leg.

"Perhaps," he said, his voice becoming soft and caressing, "perhaps Eichmann will leave us alone now at last."

From the corner of the room, there suddenly came the desolate sound of a woman sobbing.

"Well," he said, his face reflecting the sadness in the woman's sob, "when you go home tonight, you'll have something to pray for. You have been a wonderful audience and I love you for it. Good night!"

He blew them kisses with both hands and they responded with another long round of applause. The house lights went on and they got up, tugging at the clothes that clung to their damp bodies. And a long deep sigh of resignation seemed to escape from ev-

eryone at once. A profound sadness was in their eyes as they
tramped out of the door of the nightclub like a procession of condemned men and women.

For this was the famous "Poodle," a dingy cellar club on Sip
Street near the old Pest synagogue. It was the last legal public
place of entertainment for Jews in Budapest. A bizarre escape
valve provided by the Germans. And even as Adolf Eichmann and
his deputy, Dieter von Wisliczeny, scooped up thousands of them
each day, packed them into boxcars and shipped them off to
Auschwitz, the survivors continued to show up every night at the
"Poodle" to drink purple sloe gin fizzes and to laugh until their
bellies hurt at the gallows humor of Sandor Kovacs.

Kovacs was their last link to sanity.

In six short weeks, since mid-May, Eichmann and Wisliczeny
had outdone themselves. They had managed to exterminate more
than half of the 750,000 Jews of Hungary. The other half had miraculously escaped. So far. But if Eichmann and his deputy continued at their murderous rate, the surviving Jews would all be
dead before the end of summer. Most of them could not absorb
this fact and they tried to find ways of pretending that all this
wasn't happening.

One way—one of the best ways—was Sandor Kovacs.

Back in his cramped dressing room, Kovacs bent over the sink,
stuck two fingers down his throat, and vomited his guts out. Then
he poured himself a whisky, and began removing his makeup. Beneath the black face, he had pale smooth skin and a very light
shadow of a beard that looked as though he did not need to shave
very often. As he combed his fine hair, it took on a lacquered
sheen, almost like a toupee. Before the war, Sandor Kovacs had
been one of Hungary's best-known stand-up comedians, and he
still retained a certain vaudeville sleekness.

His wife entered the dressing room and saw him studying his
reflection in the mirror.

"A Jewish gigolo gone to seed," she said.

She still found him physically irresistible.

"Come here and give me a kiss," he said. "My adorable *shiksa*."

She bent over and kissed him on the top of his head, and he
reached around and squeezed her behind.

"Sandor," she said, pretending to reproach him.

"Nice," he said, keeping his hand on her behind.

She was a tall, big-boned woman, a bit swarthy and not at all attractive, but Sandor Kovacs had been faithful to her throughout their marriage. More than faithful. He had been her ardent suitor for more than twenty years. His Gentile wife.

She removed his hand and said: "They're waiting outside for you."

"I don't like it," he said. "Meeting them here."

"I told them you wouldn't," she said. "But you know Hammer. He says that with the Gestapo crawling all over the Poodle, this is the last place they'd suspect."

"Well, Hammer makes the rules," he said, wiping off the last traces of his makeup. "Show them in."

A moment later, she returned with two men.

Kovacs remained seated, looking at his visitors in the mirror. One tall and blond. The other a short, heavyset man whose face was swathed in a dirty cotton-white beard. The one with the beard reached into his pocket, took out a clove of garlic, and began peeling it.

"This is the American," he said, biting into the garlic. "Albright."

"Albright," Kovacs said, nodding to the mirror. "How do you do?"

"If you really want to know, he doesn't do too well," the bearded man said. "You've kept him and his people waiting in that safe house for almost three weeks."

"Don't blame me; blame Hammer," Kovacs said. "You know Hammer. You never can be too careful." He moved his eyes to Albright's reflection. "We had to be sure you weren't followed when you crossed the border." He motioned to the bottle of whisky on the dressing table. "A drink?"

"No thanks," Albright said.

Kovacs freshened his own drink.

"That's some show you put on out there," Albright said.

Kovacs turned around, looked directly at Albright, and said: "You disapprove?"

"It's not my business to approve or disapprove," Albright said. "I'm just surprised."

"Surprised?" Kovacs said. "What? That people would rather laugh than cry?"

"Sandor, *please!*" his wife said.

"Let's drop it," Albright said. "I'm here to see Hammer."

"How much did you tell him?" Kovacs asked the bearded man. "Nothing."

"I can't help you there," Kovacs said to Albright. "No one sees Hammer. Not even me. For all I know, someone called Hammer may not even exist. Like everyone else, I just get my messages from him. And I do what he tells me. Hammer, whoever he—or *they*—may be, is the name of the head of the entire underground organization here in Budapest. The Tchaikovsky Circuit. I am merely one of the leaders of the Jewish underground. A little part of the whole. A very little part. And a *shrinking* part."

He looked over at his wife and sipped his drink.

"In any case," he continued, clearing his throat, "your mission falls under my jurisdiction, such as it is, and so you will have to deal with me. That is my understanding from Hammer."

"That's going to pose a problem," Albright said. "Because my instructions are to deal with Hammer. And only Hammer."

"You know the Yiddish expression, '*S'vil gurnich helfin*'?" Kovacs asked. "It means you can cry your heart out but it won't do you any good. So, if you want to talk business, you've come to the right man. If not . . . Well, we're both wasting our time."

Albright considered Kovacs for a long moment.

Finally, he said: "You tell Hammer that I said this. He's making a big mistake. The last time anyone tried to organize a major uprising against the Germans was in Warsaw, back in forty-two. And we know how that turned out. The Polish underground rose up, and the Red Army simply halted its advance on the outskirts of Warsaw and sat on their asses while the Germans wiped out the entire underground."

"That won't happen here," Kovacs said.

"Don't be so sure," Albright said. "It was a bloodbath in Warsaw because no attempt was made to coordinate the uprising with the west. I was sent here to make sure that you get the arms and ammunition that you need this time in Budapest. But I'm not going to make a move until I personally talk to Hammer."

"You're out of luck," Kovacs said.

"It's not *me* who's out of luck," Albright replied. He turned to the bearded man. "Let's go."

"Father," Kovacs said, standing and putting a hand on the bearded man's shoulder. "Talk to him. You're a priest. Make him understand."

"I left my collar at home," the bearded priest said. "And, anyway, since you asked, I think he's right. There's a lot at stake. He should meet Hammer."

The priest ducked under a rack of costumes and followed Albright out the door.

After they had left, Kovacs' wife closed the door.

"What are you going to do, Sandor?" she asked.

"Come," he motioned to her. "Give me a kiss."

She came near and he folded her in his arms. He pulled her down onto his lap, cuddling his swarthy, big-boned wife as though she were a delicate little girl, and crooned into her ear: "You made me love ya, I didn't wanna do it, I didn't wanna do it. . . ."

"Sandor, be serious. What are you going to do?"

"What else?" he said, nibbling on her ear. "We'll leave the decision up to Hammer."

She wriggled in his lap, making herself more comfortable.

"When?" she asked.

"Right away," he said.

She put her arms around his neck and rested her head on his shoulder.

"Oh," she said, sounding disappointed. "Do I have to go now? It's so nice like this with you, Sandor."

"Sweetheart, I know," he said. "But rules are rules and you're my only contact with Hammer."

2

Albright followed the bearded priest down a steep flight of wooden stairs into a dim basement kitchen of a house on Uri Utca.

"Wait here," the priest said.

Albright watched the priest disappear up the steps and looked around the dank basement room. Across the flagstone floor, partly hidden in the shadows of the wall, he saw a young man holding a machine pistol. Hammer's bodyguard? The young man stood between a massive five-foot-high hearth and a door, which Albright figured led to a garden and the back streets of the Castle district of Old Buda. Above, Albright could hear the traffic rumbling on the loose cobblestones and the church bells of St. Stephen's marking the hour. Eleven at night.

"I'm waiting for Hammer," Albright said.

The young man looked at Albright but did not reply.

"Does Hammer know I'm here?" Albright said.

Still no reply.

Albright sat down at a white metal folding table to wait. The only light in the room came from an unshaded lamp resting on the table.

When the church bells struck a quarter past the hour, he looked up. The young man had not budged from his post.

Half-past eleven . . .

A quarter to twelve . . .

At midnight, the young man opened the back door and left. A moment later, three men, all older than the first, entered and searched the room. One of them turned off the light on the table and then Albright heard them leave too.

Twelve-fifteen . . .

Twelve-thirty . . .

"Good evening."

Albright had not heard anyone come in. He couldn't be sure, but the voice sounded like a woman's.

"I want the light on," Albright said.

The light went on.

It *was* a woman.

It was Sandor Kovacs' wife.

Albright quickly glanced around the room. They were alone. He looked at Kovacs' wife, the bare light bulb casting her swarthy face into a mask of highlights and hollows. She wore a dark-blue beret, a scarf tied at her throat, and a thin green cardigan sweater, unbuttoned. Her hands, large-boned with curved double-jointed fingers, rested on the table.

"You're Hammer?" Albright said.

"I'm Hammer," she said.

"You'll excuse me if I'm a little skeptical," he said.

"It's natural," she said.

"Your husband told me a few hours ago that he's never met Hammer," Albright said.

"As far as he knows, he hasn't," she said. "It's for his own protection that he doesn't know."

"That's still not good enough," Albright said. "I need some *proof* that you're really Hammer."

"It was a serious mistake for you to insist on seeing me," she said. "You can link our two organizations at the top. That's a violation of our rules. You've put not only me but the entire Tchaikovsky Circuit into jeopardy. Hundreds of people. Now you ask me for proof that I am Hammer."

She stood up and walked around the room. At the foot of the stairs, she turned and looked back at Albright.

"All right," she said, "here is proof. You were trained at a British base south of Cairo called Jubilee. The commander of your base is a man named Guido DeVita. Your team departed on a Yugoslav plane from Bari on April twenty-ninth. . . ."

Slowly, relishing the meticulous details of the movements of the Tchaikovsky Circuit, she traced its route from Jajce in the mountains of Yugoslavia across the plains to the checkpoint at Kikinda.

". . . Now that you're in Budapest," she continued, "you asked to see me to work out the details of your assignment. Once you have your proof that I am who I say I am, you will tell me that you've been sent here to assassinate Eichmann, to rally the Jewish underground, and to supply and coordinate a general uprising in Budapest against the Germans. Did I leave anything out?"

"Those are my instructions," Albright said.

"Those are *not* your instructions," she said.

Albright hesitated before he said: "What the hell is that supposed to mean?"

Hammer returned to her chair and took two deep breaths.

"Captain," she said, "you don't want to understand, do you? It must be clear to you that I know all about your mission. So I would suggest that you listen to me very carefully. Your instructions were given to you with a clear purpose. Imagine for a moment that you had been captured by the Gestapo. Eventually, like everyone else, you would have talked. Everyone talks. And what would you have told them? Exactly what you just heard me say. This business about Eichmann and so forth. You believed it because General Donovan wanted you to believe it. It was for everyone's protection."

Albright felt himself flush with anger.

The bells of St. Stephen's sounded a quarter to one.

"There isn't much time," Hammer said.

"I'm listening," Albright said.

"The situation here in Hungary is very complex," she said. "The underground is not only divided into a Jewish group and a national-patriotic group, but within those groups there are many factions. We have our political differences. But basically there is a pro-Communist and an anti-Communist faction. I am personally anti-Communist. So is my husband, Sandor. Our concern is that the Russians are already at the gates of Budapest. And they are in the process of setting up a puppet government in Debrecen, east of here. The Hungarian Government can see the writing on the wall and they've sent a memorandum to Berlin demanding that Eichmann and the Gestapo be withdrawn immediately. Hungary is finished and our ministers don't want to be held responsible for Eichmann's acts against the Jews.

"So," she continued, "you can see we are at a critical turning point. Now, before the Germans totally collapse—which we believe is only a matter of weeks away—and before the Russian puppets move in, we want to set up a government that is friendly to the west. We must move now if we're going to have some leverage in the formation of a postwar government here in Budapest. We need a leader who can rally all the anti-Communist forces, a man who is an acknowledged patriot, someone who has the reputation of being both anti-Fascist and anti-Communist. This man, we believe, is Count Pal Teleki.

"I'm sure you know of him," she went on. "He was a well-known minister before the war, when you lived here as a young man. Count Teleki is being held by the Gestapo under house arrest. You and your group have been chosen to free him. This will be a clear sign that the Americans and the British are behind Teleki. After that, you will help coordinate supply drops for Teleki's popular revolt. *That* is your mission."

As she spoke, an image slowly began to form in Albright's

mind. It was an image of General Donovan. Donovan and his pale-blue Irish eyes. Those eyes that communicated two opposing meanings at the same time. *Trust me . . . trust me not. . . .*

Donovan had done it to him again.

"Listen," Albright said, the anger rising in him like molten lava, "this Teleki. I remember him. He's the one who drafted the edicts against the Jews. He's a goddamn anti-Semite. The worst kind."

"That's right," Hammer said.

"You're some piece of works, lady," Albright said. "What do you think your husband's going to say when he hears about Teleki? The Hungarian Jews will never rally around Teleki. And the members of my team. They're all Jews. They'll never agree to free Teleki."

"They don't have any choice," she said. "Anti-Semitism is as Hungarian as chicken paprika. The Hungarian people will trust Teleki *because* he's an anti-Semite. And the Jews will go along because they have to. I don't like it any more than you do. Don't forget, I married a Jew. But Teleki's the lesser of two evils. Ask the members of your team. See if they don't want to go through with it."

"What about the plan to assassinate Eichmann?" Albright asked.

"There is no plan," she said.

From St. Stephen's came the sound of a solitary bell striking one o'clock. Hammer stood up. The young bodyguard with the machine pistol slipped into the room through the back door and doused the light.

In the darkness, Hammer said: "Forget it."

3

But Alexander Hamilton Albright could not forget it.

After he and the priest arrived back at the safe house, Albright went to his room and took out the gun that had been given to him by Donovan. The X-1 Colt. The gun Albright had planned to use to kill Adolf Eichmann.

He had not handled the gun since leaving Cairo. It still had that acrid, disreputable smell, like an old coin in a greasy palm. The big boxy gun felt cool and smooth in his grip. The little colt reared up on its hind legs on the medallion. Eager. Eager to be used.

"Fucking Donovan," Albright said out loud.

Donovan had tricked him again. Tricked him with this gun. Tricked him into believing something that was not true. Was never meant to be true.

Or had he?

After all, Albright had known Donovan for a long time. He had personally experienced Donovan's duplicity, his betrayal of the "Twelve Disciples." He knew the way Donovan's mind worked. Wheels within wheels. Plans within plans.

So why had he believed Donovan?

Why?

Because, Albright thought, the idea coming to him with sudden clarity, *I wanted to.*

I betrayed myself.

And looking down at the experimental gun, one of Donovan's deadly inventions, Albright realized a truth. The problem wasn't with Donovan and those hypnotic, ambiguous eyes. The problem was with himself. It was he, Albright—*not* Ruth, *not* the Jewish members of his team—who had been the romantic about war. This need he had, this self-absorption with performance, this obsession to prove himself, to be quicker, smarter, braver, better . . . *worthier*—it was all this that had drawn him toward Donovan's mission and the challenge of assassinating the master murderer, Adolf Eichmann.

Not once had Albright considered the deeper commitment, the *moral* purpose of the assignment. All he had thought about was himself.

So Guido DeVita had been right after all. Albright had been the wrong man to lead the parachutists.

Had been.

But no longer.

Now Albright understood.

There was a soft knock on the door.

"Yes?" he called.

"It's me, Ruth."

"Come in."

She sat down next to him on the bed.

"How did the meeting go with Hammer?" she asked.

It occurred to him, looking at her in profile, her hair falling so thick and brown and lustrous onto her shoulders, that he should tell her the truth. That Donovan and the British and Hammer's underground all had their own purposes, and that they did not really care about the fate of the surviving Jews. Nobody cared.

And it occurred to him to tell her that he loved her. With that physical passion that a man feels for a woman, of course. But more. He loved her as Ruth, his fighting comrade, as his haver.

And it occurred to him to tell her that he had struggled with his conscience and made a fateful choice.

But he decided not to burden her with all of that. He would tell her later.

Instead, he placed his fingers gently on her chin and turned her face to his.

"We're going after Eichmann," he said.

CHAPTER SEVEN

VISEGRAD
Saturday, July 1

1

Karl Adolf Eichmann held his bandaged hand.

He had a low threshold of pain, and the sharp features of his long, thin face were contorted in a wince of deep discomfort. He hoped the others wouldn't notice. Even more than physical pain, he feared being thought unmanly.

"I'll be all right," he said to the four men, his words slurred by the night-long bout of drinking. "Don't worry about me. Go ahead and play."

Lucky for him, he thought, that it was only a superficial wound. But how foolish of him to have petted a strange dog. He couldn't imagine what possessed him. It was not like him to take such silly risks. Well, it served him right. It was a useful warning: *Above all, caution!*

Through an open window, he heard the dog yelping in protest as it was dragged outside into the courtyard. Scuffling on the gravel. Then a shot. Then silence.

Eichmann was bathed in a sudden warm feeling of reassurance, and a smile formed on the thin red line of his lips. One more danger eliminated. One fewer of this world's creatures to concern himself about. Now he could go on with the evening, content and secure in the company of his friends. The pain subsided.

Assembled here in this snug game room in Visegrad, at a country estate outside Budapest, were the four men Eichmann trusted above all others in the world. Over there, chalking up his billiard cue, was the tall, ramrod-stiff figure of Dieter von Wisliczeny, the one who had cleansed Slovakia and Greece of their Jewish scum and who was now his chief deputy in Hungary. And there, standing beneath the shelf of silver horse-show trophies, was Hermann Krumey, corpulent and bespectacled, the one they called the "bloodhound of Vienna." And there, next to Krumey, refilling his champagne glass, was blond, effeminate Theodore Dannecker, the one who had distinguished himself by exterminating the Jews of France. And there, leaning over the green baize table, taking careful aim, was Siegfried Seidl—like Eichmann, as dark as a Gypsy or a Jew—lately of Theresiendstadt and Bergen-Belsen.

All first-rate men.

Idealists.

The cream of the Third Reich.

Together, they formed the inner core of *Sondereinsatzkommando Eichmann*, the Eichmann Special Operation Unit.

The door of the game room opened and their Hungarian host, László Endre, entered, an expression of utter mortification on his florid alcoholic's face.

"My dear Eichmann," Endre said, "how can I apologize!"

He examined Eichmann's bandaged hand.

"It's nothing, nothing," Eichmann said.

Endre was clearly worried. As the official in charge of the Jewish affairs section of the Hungarian Interior Ministry, he had made a point of befriending Eichmann. The two of them shared a love of fine horses, strong drink, and submissive women. And a hatred of Jews. Endre didn't want an accident like this to destroy such an important relationship.

"In all the world, I never imagined that one of these dogs would do such a thing," Endre said. "I have had the dog shot."

"I heard," Eichmann said coldly.

"But Endre," Hermann Krumey said, taking off his glasses and cleaning them with a handkerchief, "I didn't know that you kept dogs here inside the villa."

"I don't normally," Endre said with a sheepish smile. "The dogs are part of the entertainment I put together for tonight."

"Entertainment?" Eichmann said.

"For later," Endre explained. "If the colonel wishes. Along with the girls . . ."

Wisliczeny dropped his billiard cue on the table, placed his hands on his narrow hips, and burst out laughing.

"Bitten by a sex-starved dog!" he said.

Eichmann was not amused and his large, stuck-out ears turned crimson.

"We will see," Eichmann said. "Now, Endre, we have some private business to attend to. Leave us for a while. I will call you when we are finished." Then Eichmann thought of one of his rare jokes. "Don't shoot all the dogs before we're ready."

After Endre had left, Eichmann popped another bottle of the champagne they had been drinking, a 1931 Louis Roederer Cristal, and filled his comrades' glasses to the brim.

"I received a message today from Reichsführer Himmler about our operations," he said. "That is why I asked you to come here tonight. To discuss this message."

"Did the Reichsführer mention the health of Hitler?" Siegfried Seidl asked, drawing closer. "How is Hitler?"

"I will come to that in a moment," Eichmann said. "But first, Reichsführer Himmler's orders. He wants us to immediately cease the extermination program against the Hungarian Jews. He expressly forbids us from carrying out our plans for *eine eintaetige Grossaktion*, the great final knockout blow against the remaining Jews in Hungary. He has ordered me to withdraw and return to Berlin."

Eichmann let this astonishing news sink in. Then he added: "Himmler apparently believes Germany is finished. *Kaput*. And he thinks Germany will receive better conditions of surrender if we leave the remaining Jews alive."

"Surely, Himmler is not serious," Wisliczeny said.

"I think he is altogether serious," Eichmann said. "But"—and here he paused—"I want all of you to know that I have no intention of obeying his order. For the first time since Himmler himself swore me in as a member of the SS in 1932, I intend to disobey him."

The others were shocked into silence.

"If Germany collapses," Eichmann explained, "at least we will be able to say we achieved something. We will have completely wiped out the Jews of Europe. Defeat does not frighten me. By November, December at the latest, we will have finished with our job here in Hungary. And if it comes to that, I will leap laughing into my grave because the feeling that I have six million Jews on my conscience will be, for me, a source of extraordinary satisfaction."

"Disobeying Himmler is sedition," Hermann Krumey said.

"Naturally," Eichmann went on, ignoring Krumey, "I would welcome your support in carrying out our plans for the great final knockout blow. I don't think Himmler will try to stop us."

"It's sedition, you know," Krumey said.

"And then there is Hitler to think of," Seidl said.

"I think I can answer both of your concerns," Eichmann said. "As for Himmler, he seems quite preoccupied these days with other matters. Indeed, the word in Berlin is that Himmler is laying plans to push Hitler aside and assume the role of Führer himself."

"Impossible!" Wisliczeny said.

"Impossible?" Eichmann repeated. "No, my friends. Unlikely, yes. But not impossible. These are desperate times. Everything is possible. For us, too. For I am of the opinion that Himmler's plans will ultimately fail. Hitler will act. He will stop Himmler in his tracks. And once that happens—and this goes to your question, Seidl—Hitler will look around to see who stood on which side. Who, in short, stood up for the Führer. Hitler always rewards the steadfast, the loyal, and the pure. And for Hitler, there is no mission purer than the Final Solution."

"Eichmann!" Wisliczeny said, stepping forward to embrace him. "I am with you! After this, Hitler will appoint *you* Reichsführer."

"Yes," Seidl agreed. "You will replace Himmler and become the second most powerful man in the Third Reich."

Eichmann smiled.

"Well, that is a bit premature, don't you think?" he said. "I want you to know that I am not motivated in this by any personal ambition. I just want to make sure that I can count on you."

Wisliczeny looked around the room and then said to Eichmann:

"You can count on us. In fact, I will rush back to Budapest this instant to speed up our plans for the great final knockout blow."

"Splendid," Eichmann said. "You can take my personal car and escort guard."

Theodore Dannecker, who had remained silent all this time, spoke up:

"But Wisliczeny, you will miss Endre's entertainment with the dogs and the girls."

"Ah," said Wisliczeny, flush with pride and purpose, "it will be worth missing if I can kill a few more Jews."

2

Due north of Budapest, the road from Visegrad followed a sweeping bend of the Danube River for a few miles and then entered a dense forest of white birch that was inhabited by storks, spoonbills, and purple herons. It was only a second-class road, but it had recently been repaved and graded by the Germans. Behind the wheel of the six-liter Mercedes 320, Eichmann's chauffeur, SS Oberscharführer Hans Becker, was doing almost ninety miles per hour on its new macadam surface.

In the rearview mirror, Becker could see the skull and crossbones of the SS on the cap of Dieter von Wisliczeny who sat in the back seat of the open touring car. Falling farther and farther behind them were two sets of jiggling headlights. Wisliczeny had brought along his own escort guard as well as Eichmann's.

These SS officers weren't as brave as they looked, Becker thought. Ever since Reinhard Heydrich, the chief of the Security Police, was assassinated in Prague two years ago, the other SS bosses had lived in mortal fear for their lives. They wouldn't even step out of doors for a breath of fresh air without a full complement of guards. It was ridiculous, Becker thought. The successful attack on Heydrich's car had been a one-in-a-million shot, and the underground wouldn't be stupid enough to try and repeat it.

SS Oberscharführer Hans Becker wasn't afraid. And to prove it, he took a sinister satisfaction in gunning the six-liter Mercedes engine and trying to outrun the smaller, slower cars that trailed behind with the escort guards.

Becker knew this road well, having driven Colonel Eichmann out and back from László Endre's country estate practically every Saturday for the past four months. Soon, the road would pass out of the birch forest and start the long descent to Budapest. And then, where the steep hill joined the road coming from Eger to the east, it was necessary for Becker to apply the brakes and slow the big Mercedes to a crawl so that he could negotiate the sharp hairpin bend.

The trees began thinning. The road took a dip. The Mercedes headed down the hill. The speedometer edged past ninety-five miles per hour.

"Tell me if I'm going too fast for you, Haupsturmführer Wisliczeny," Becker said, turning partly toward the back.

Wisliczeny's reply was inaudible in the wind.

Becker turned further toward his passenger. Wisliczeny was braced rigidly in his seat, clearly frightened by the speed and the lengthening gap between Eichmann's car and the escorts.

Not so brave, Becker thought.

And in the brief moment that his eyes settled on Wisliczeny, Becker missed the signal. The two pinpricks of light flashing down at the bottom of the hill at the hairpin bend.

3

Dan Gur pulled the cork on the Thermos and took a gulp of the *sumadija* tea. It was sweet and hot and generously laced with brandy, and it felt reassuring going down. He had been waiting in the dark for more than three hours, and although there was a warm breeze tonight, he was chilled.

He felt like telling a joke.

He lay in the mint-scented scrub brush at the side of the road, listening to the crickets and the self-pitying bleats of a flock of sheep from a distant farm. His mind kept wandering, drifting back. Vivid pictures flashed through his mind. Snippets of a life of a soldier. One after another, he saw other places he had waited in ambush—in Aleppo with Orde Wingate's Jewish Brigade . . . in Hebron with Dayan . . . in the narrow, walled alleys of the Old City of Jerusalem. . . .

Twenty-eight years old and he had already spent nearly a third of a lifetime waiting. Coiled to strike. Prepared to kill or be killed. A hell of a life! An animal's life! Filled with blood and pain and death. Between the killing—in the long, empty spaces of waiting—Gur had desperately sought to reassert his humanity, his nonanimal nature, his personhood, with jokes. Wry, bitter jokes.

It was these jokes that made people think that Dan Gur was an uncommonly brave man. How else to explain someone who made you laugh one moment and was ready in the next to lay down his life? A cool customer, this Dan Gur. Fearless. A superb guerrilla fighter.

If only they knew!

Killing was the easy part. It was the mind that played malicious tricks. And the goddamn anticipation. It got worse each time. What had been a pleasure eight years ago with Wingate in Aleppo, a challenge five years ago in Hebron, just bearable three years ago in Jerusalem, had now become a terrifying ordeal. Because Gur had been through it all. He knew what it was like. There wasn't any horror that his imagination could not conjure up. All the things that might happen. The stupid little mistakes he had seen made by braver men than he, and the swift and lethal retribution that always followed.

He thought of something that Wingate used to say. "If you know the risks and can take precautions, the operation should be a snap. It's only when you don't know exactly what to expect, that you're in trouble."

He took another slug of the sumadija tea.

His place of hiding was halfway between the crest of the hill and the juncture of the roads at the hairpin bend. In his musette bag were two primed grenades. British made. No. 73 antitank weapons with black bakelite fuses and polar ammon gelatin dynamite. They weighed four pounds apiece. Big mothers. Made a hell of a hole in armor plating. They should make chopped liver out of Eichmann's car.

But where was Eichmann's fucking car?

It's only when you don't know exactly what to expect . . .

Then he saw it coming.

The powerful headlights from the Mercedes stabbed two broad beacons straight into the night sky, then yo-yoed over the top of the hill and focused sharply on the blacktop road.

Gur had counted on there being two cars—Eichmann's and the escort's.

If you know the risks . . .

Eichmann's big Mercedes came barreling down the hill. A furious machine-beast with firelit eyes scorching a path toward Gur. His hand reached toward his musette bag. He was tempted to make his move now. His stomach began churning. His heart beat in his ears. His forearms tingled as if something were plucking at his nerve strings. He was supposed to wait for the escort.

Then, just as he thought he couldn't wait a second longer, another set of headlights seemed to come flying over the top of the hill in hot pursuit of Eichmann's car.

The operation should be a snap . . .

Gur let out his breath. This was what he expected. Two cars. This was what he *wanted* to see. The nerve-racking anticipation that was stoking inside him for three hours exploded into action. He turned and blinked his flashlight.

Twice.

Across the road, about ten yards farther down the hill, Ruth Bar-Adon and Joel Nathan saw Gur's signal. They had been waiting, too, almost touching shoulders in the underbrush. Their MK 11 9-mm Sten guns lay by their sides. A starter's pistol, loaded with a phosphorous flare, was tucked inside Joel's belt.

They had been talking, almost without stop, for the past three hours. Mostly about their plans for after the war. How they were going to bring their families to Palestine. And at one point, Joel said:

"You know, Ruthie, you once asked me about my childhood and I didn't give you a straight answer. As a matter of fact, I had a very unhappy childhood. I had polio. For a long time, they didn't think I'd ever walk again. I was such a sickly runt! But I fooled them, didn't I? I walked all the way back to Hungary so that I could be with you here tonight."

"Oh, Joel," she said, "I'm glad you told me."

"Why?" he asked.

"Because you must have wanted to tell someone for a long time. And now you don't have to think about it anymore."

It was at that moment, just as Joel was about to reply, that he spotted Gur's signal.

"Two cars!" he whispered.

Without thinking, Joel reached for the pistol. Then, recalling their plan, he snatched away his hand. He rolled over on his back, took out his flashlight and, holding it between his legs, relayed the signal toward the bottom of the hill.

"Two!" Saul Patir said to himself.

Saul was stationed on the far side of the road, just around the hairpin bend. He looked across the road at the moving shadow that was Alex Albright. Two blinks. Albright returned the signal back up the hill.

Perfect. Everything was going according to plan. Saul watched as Albright wheeled out the BMW motorcycle and leaned it behind a thick old oak tree where it could not be seen from the road.

Saul pulled back the bolt action on his Sten and crawled on his elbows and knees to the gravel shoulder of the road. Lying there, he realized that, whatever happened, it would all be over in the next minute or two. It was the moment he had been dreaming of.

This was his chance to kill Germans! And yet, strangely, he felt drained of all emotion. The anger that had consumed him for so long was suddenly missing, gone, evaporated. In its place, he felt a kind of soothing warmth spread over his body, as though a narcotic were taking effect. He had no idea what it was going to be like, actually killing another human being, but he experienced a wonderful sense of release. He was twenty years old and he was going to find out.

Behind the oak tree, Albright thought about Gur. Maybe he should have taken Gur's position. Maybe . . . It was too late for maybes. Now it was Gur's move.

At the midpoint of the hill, Gur lay motionless, his forehead touching the minty earth, feet flattened and splayed, holding his breath. Eichmann's six-liter Mercedes thundered past, trailing a hailstorm of pebbles and stones. Gur looked up and a small stone bounced off his cheek, stinging him. He touched his cheek, glanced at his fingers—no blood. Not yet, anyway. He reached into his musette bag and extracted two long, cylindrical grenades. He waddled in a crouch to the side of the road. There, he bent down on one knee and waited.

The escort car was about three hundred yards away, its headlights not yet within reach of Gur's crouching figure. He could hear the growing crescendo of its engine and, near him, on the other side of the road, the shuffling steps of his comrades, Joel and Ruth, taking up their positions. He figured he had five more seconds.

He was reminded of a joke.

Later.

Four . . . three . . . two . . .

At the bottom of the hill, the lights from Eichmann's car illuminated the undersides of the leaves, turning the canopy of tall oaks at the hairpin bend into a dimly lit tunnel. Saul Patir could hear the wheels grabbing the road and the gears shifting down.

Third . . . second . . . first . . .

The light grew brighter. The car crunched slowly around the turn. Saul could see the face of the driver, Hans Becker, behind the windshield.

Where was Gur!

Saul looked anxiously across the road, searching out Albright. What should they do? He felt helpless, panicky, very young.

Where was Gur!

Gur stood in the full glare of the onrushing headlights at the middle of the hill, balancing the grenades in both hands. From deep in his stomach, a growl began to form. The growl of an animal. Enraged. About to attack.

The driver of the escort car saw the standing figure at the side of the road, slammed on his brakes, sending the automobile into a screeching skid.

"Now!" Gur bellowed.

Joel Nathan raised his pistol and fired the illumination flare directly at the hood of the car. It exploded off the grille in a blinding flash. Night became day. The hidden became exposed. Joel and Ruth rushed forward, firing their Stens.

The first bursts smashed through the windshield, chewing through the cheekbones and eyesockets of the driver. His hands dropped instantly from the wheel and the car careened to the left. Straight for Gur.

"Dan!" Ruth shouted.

But too late.

The left fender caught Gur at hip level, tossing him into the air. He flew over the front of the car, his arms stretched out like wings, the grenades still firmly in his hands.

Dan Gur landed in the back seat, and the car disintegrated in a towering red-and-yellow explosion. The shock waves knocked Joel and Ruth unconscious.

They never had a chance to see the third car topping the hill.

The noise startled Hans Becker as he guided Eichmann's Mercedes through the hairpin bend. Brake? Speed up? What was he to do? Regulations said he was to get his ass out of here as quickly as possible. He stamped on the accelerator. The wheels spun, burning rubber. Then he saw the figure of Saul Patir. Coming out of nowhere. Rushing right at the headlights.

"Attack!" Becker shouted to Dieter von Wisliczeny.

The car began picking up speed.

Becker ducked behind the dashboard just as the bullets from Saul's Sten stippled ragged holes in the front-seat upholstery.

Now, Wisliczeny was kneeling in the back, firing his Luger.

Braver than I thought, Becker thought.

The car came alongside Saul, not more than three feet away, and Saul and Wisliczeny were firing point blank at each other. Their bullets struck at almost the same instant. Wisliczeny's bullets tore through Saul's abdomen, severing his renal artery, and he slumped down in a gusher of blood. Saul's bullet shattered Wisliczeny's collarbone, spinning him back onto the seat.

The car swerved wildly as Albright gunned the motorcycle out of its hiding place and chased after the taillights of the Mercedes.

Hans Becker straightened up behind the wheel, turned to see the damage in the back seat, and instead saw Albright's motorcycle drawing parallel with the car. The motorcycle rider had a big boxy gun in his hand. One of those American Colts. Becker did not hear the gun discharge, but he felt a strange, wet sensation in his back. He fell forward onto the steering wheel.

Perched on the motorcycle seat, Albright looked down into the back of the Mercedes and saw the black uniform of the German officer. Albright raised the X-1 Colt. He fired two more silent shots into the man he thought was Adolf Eichmann.

Albright christied the motorcycle to a stop. Seconds later, the Mercedes smashed into a stone kilometer marker and turned over on its side.

An abrupt silence. Albright listened. Nothing. Then the sound of distant voices.

In the middle of the hill, the third car drew to a stop between the smoldering wreck and the prostrate bodies of Joel Nathan and Ruth Bar-Adon.

"Are those two still alive?" the sergeant in charge asked.

"Yes," a corporal answered.

"Good," the sergeant said. "We'll take them in."

PART III

FALL 1944

CHAPTER ONE

BUDAPEST
Thursday, October 19

1

A cold autumn sunlight leaked through the windows of the Vörösmarty Café. The coffee house was filled with the sticky sweet aroma of baking fruit tarts and the sting of camphorized winter uniforms fresh from their mothballs.

It was not yet ten in the morning. Most of the customers were black-shirted members of *Nyilas,* the dreaded Arrow Cross. Hungary's home-grown Fascists. They were in boisterous spirits, still celebrating the lightning coup d'état that installed them in power three days ago.

Barely audible over their vulgar shouts and laughter were the sounds outside. In the far distance, the deep rolling thunder of Russian artillery. And closer, marching bands, sharp and rhythmic, parading through the streets of the city.

The door of the café opened, letting in the discordant sounds—fife and drums . . . rumbling artillery . . . marching feet. . . . A short, barrel-chested German, in an SS officer's uniform, stood, framed in the doorway, in a shaft of pale sunlight.

Conversation stopped. A German had become a rare sight in Budapest since the summer, when Adolf Eichmann and the Gestapo had been ordered withdrawn from Hungary. But now, with the Arrow Cross coup, the Germans were invited back to finish the job they started. The extermination of Hungary's remaining three hundred and fifty thousand Jews.

The German looked around and spotted a blond young man sitting alone. He walked to the marble-top table and peered down at the man from behind a pair of round spectacles.

"Herr Albright?" he inquired.

"Yes," Albright said.

"Krumey," he said, introducing himself.

Lieutenant Colonel Hermann Krumey had replaced Dieter von Wisliczeny as Eichmann's chief lieutenant in Hungary. Two men could not have been more different. Wisliczeny had been stiff and dry, with a kind of sadistic humor. Krumey, on the other hand, was a swaggering, beer-swilling egotist. He was known to keep his mistress, a flamboyant redhead named Eve Kosytorz, in the most expensive apartment in Budapest. And he liked to brag that her apartment was stocked with stolen Jewish loot.

Krumey did not wait to be invited to sit down. He removed his cap and gloves, but not his coat.

"Is everything in order about the truck?" he asked.

"Yes," Albright said.

"When will I see it?"

"The drop will be made as you were informed," Albright said. "At noon."

"Good," Krumey said. "That gives us some time. We can get acquainted. I like to talk."

Still looking at Albright, Krumey snapped his fingers and a waitress appeared at their table. Krumey looked her over. She was pink and plump, with rolled-down white socks and heavy calves, and just the hint of a peroxided moustache. He patted her on the rear and ordered two coffees.

When she had gone, Krumey surveyed the customers in the room.

"Ah, the Arrow Cross," he said. "They remind me of when I was young in Germany in the early Thirties. What is your opinion of them, Herr Albright?"

"They're a worse bunch than you Germans," Albright said.

"How fascinating," Krumey said. "That's almost exactly what Colonel Eichmann said to me the other day. And it's true. They are. You see, we Germans kill with purpose. For a principle. The Arrow Cross kill for pure . . . lust."

He unfolded a neatly pressed handkerchief and dipped an end into Albright's glass of water. Then he removed his spectacles and began cleaning them.

"The Arrow Cross leader," Krumey said, "this Ferenc Szalasy, do you know him?"

"Only by reputation," Albright said.

"A beast," Krumey said. "Do you know what he told Colonel Eichmann? Just yesterday, after we got back. He told us that we had been too easy on the Hungarian Jews. We hadn't killed them fast enough to suit him. Sending them off in trains and all that. Can you imagine? *Him* telling *us* how to deal with Jews! But he may have a point. We're short of transport. Not enough trains and trucks to go around. Szalasy wants to march the Jews off to the camps. On foot. Death marches, he calls them. I can tell you, this does not please Colonel Eichmann, who has an orderly mind."

Krumey examined the lenses of his glasses with his nearsighted blue eyes and slipped the frames around his ears. He watched the waitress return with two chipped demitasse cups and a plate of assorted fruit tarts. She flinched at the muffled sound of the distant Soviet artillery. She was so nervous that she almost spilled Krumey's coffee.

Albright found himself feeling sorry for her.

"Didn't this room used to have green fabric on the wall?" he asked her. "Before the war, I mean?"

The unexpected question just made her more flustered. She glanced anxiously across the room at an Arrow Cross officer who was standing beneath a chandelier near the glass display cases.

"I'm sure I wouldn't know," the waitress said, and hurried away.

"Scared," Hermann Krumey observed. "It's interesting how everyone's suddenly scared. If the Hungarians had their way, most of them would surrender to the Americans. But they know the Arrow Cross won't do that. Now, it's only a matter of time before the Russians arrive. It's the end for Hungary."

"And you Germans?" Albright said. "How do you feel about the end?"

"Oh, we Germans are good at the end," Krumey boasted. "*Götterdämmerung* brings out the best in us."

Krumey picked up a sticky apple tart and took a large bite. With his mouth full, he said: "By the way, I understand today's your birthday. My felicitations."

It didn't surprise Albright that the Germans had done their homework on him. That was part of this elaborate arrangement. After all, Eichmann had been waiting for months for an answer to his extraordinary offer—Jewish lives for American trucks—and he couldn't be expected to deal with a person who was an unknown quantity. Albright knew that Eichmann had been given a thick dossier on him. Albright's birthday would be the least important piece of information in that file.

What surprised Albright was that *he* had forgotten what day it was. Completely slipped his mind. Maybe it was because he had never set much store in birthdays. If anything, Albright remembered October nineteenth as the anniversary—ten years ago here in Budapest—of his first parachute jump. From his father's Le Père biplane. That was when life for him really began. When he leaped into nothingness and realized that he could control his own destiny.

He was twenty-seven years old today, and he felt as though he had suddenly lost those ten years, had regressed to a kind of adolescent helplessness, was no longer in control of his destiny. Something terrible had happened to him on that dark night last July when he went after Eichmann and shot Wisliczeny instead. He wasn't the same man who trained and led the parachutists. Two of his comrades—Dan Gur and Saul Patir—were dead. Two others —Ruth Bar-Adon and Joel Nathan—were captured by the Germans. He didn't even know if they were alive. To make matters worse, Albright learned that Dieter von Wisliczeny had miraculously survived his wounds.

And he had lost Ruth.

Sitting here in the Vörösmarty Café, thinking of Ruth, who used to run her hands along these walls when they were covered with green-flocked fabric, Albright recalled a luminous moment they had shared. . . . They were at the Gezira Turf Club, watching a cricket match. He told her that she was beautiful and that she had earned her place on the team, and she called him by his

first name, and they began to fall in love. . . . All that seemed so
long ago—a lost moment in time, like the feeling after his first
parachute jump.

The things he counted on to pull him through—his poise, his
willpower, his self-control—had failed. And yet he must go on.
Find Ruth. This truck deal was a long shot. He would be going
up against the Germans stripped of his armor. Naked unto his enemies.

Hermann Krumey was working his way through a third fruit
tart.

"Herr Albright," he said, "perhaps it is time we talked business.
I believe you know who I am. I was in charge of the action in
Vienna. I personally supervised the slaughter of the children of
Lidice. I am, perhaps, after Colonel Eichmann, the world's
foremost authority on extermination camps. And now I am here
in Hungary.

"We have, of course, investigated you," Krumey continued.
"We know it was your group that tried to assassinate Wisliczeny.
We know that you tried for more than three months to make contact with the Hungarian underground, and that they avoided you
like the plague. We know that when Ferenc Szalasy pulled off his
coup, the Jews of *Vaadah Ezra va Hazalah*, the so-called Council
for Assistance and Rescue, suddenly saw the handwriting on the
wall and asked you for help. For American help. And we know
that you contacted Washington. We have verified that you have
instructions to make a deal."

Krumey pursed his lips, waiting for Albright to react.

"Go on," Albright said.

"Now then," Krumey said, "we are prepared to sell you Jews.
Not the whole lot—you wouldn't be able to handle all that. But
you could manage half or more. Goods for blood; blood for goods.
You can take them wherever you can find them. From the ghetto
of Kassa, from the camps on the Ronyva River, from the disposal
depots of Tizhorod, Tesco, Beregszaz, Felsoviso—from wherever
you want. Whom do you want to save? Men who can beget children? Women who can bear them? Old people? Children? It is
simple. You know what we want. Trucks. Army trucks. Twenty-
five hundred American Army trucks in return for—what shall we
say?—a quarter of a million Jews. It is a fair exchange, yes? And

these trucks would be used by us only on the eastern front. Against the Russians. Our common enemy. We will give you our word of honor on that."

"Let's leave out the crap about honor," Albright said.

Krumey stiffened.

"Don't try to insult me, Herr Albright. My honor is sacred to me. I could have you shot right now."

"Not if you want your trucks," Albright said.

"Then you are prepared to go through with the deal?" Krumey asked.

"My instructions are to deliver a two-and-a-half-ton model of a truck at noon today," Albright said. "From then on, it's a question of negotiations. Between me and your boss. Eichmann."

"One truck for every one hundred Jews," Krumey said. "Those are our terms. Take it or leave it."

"I'll leave it," Albright said. He stood and wrapped his scarf around his neck. "Have a happy Götterdämmerung, Krumey."

He headed for the door.

"*Wait!*"

The Arrow Cross customers fell silent, looked up at Albright, then at Krumey. The plump waitress with the peroxided moustache stood in the middle of the terrazzo floor, holding a tray of tarts.

Krumey got up and walked over to Albright. He put an arm around the taller man's shoulder.

"Let's talk this over," he said. "There's always room for compromise between reasonable men. And you will find *me* a lot more reasonable than Colonel Eichmann. My car is waiting outside. As a matter of fact, a friend of mine, a very attractive woman, is waiting for us in the back seat. Perhaps you have heard of her. Eve Kosytorz. A great beauty. Very charming. She is quite well known in Budapest."

"All right," Albright said.

"We can discuss this on the way to the delivery point in Eger," Krumey said. "I am eager to see your truck. You don't want to throw away the chance to save the lives of a quarter of a million people, do you?"

"No, I don't," Albright said. "But I also want to discuss with you the lives of *two* people. A young woman and a man. They're friends of *mine*. You may have heard of them."

As they walked across the sunny square toward Krumey's car, they could hear the rat-tat-tat of the snare drums and the xylophones rapping out a cheerful march.

Albright wondered what the German would say when he found out the truth. Albright could not deliver twenty-five hundred American Army trucks. He couldn't deliver even one.

2

Ruth Bar-Adon shared the cell with two other prisoners. A curly-haired nine-year-old boy named Stephan. And Frieda, who was blossoming into a woman at twelve. They had just begun their daily composition lesson when Ruth heard the footsteps coming down the corridor.

"What's the matter, Aunt Ruth?" Stephan asked.

"Nothing, sweetheart," Ruth replied. "Why?"

"You look so . . . pale," Stephan said. "Doesn't she look kind of funny, Frieda?"

Frieda made a face.

Ruth had insisted on these daily lessons, but Frieda fancied herself too grown-up for such childish pursuits. After all, she had been in prison since she was ten years old and she liked to think that she was smart enough already.

"She's just scared, silly," Frieda said. "Can't you tell?"

The footsteps stopped in front of the door.

Frieda was right. Ruth was scared. They hadn't come for her for a long time, almost three weeks, but she could feel herself beginning to tremble. She recalled all the things they used to do to her. The iron chair . . . the straps . . . the whip . . . the club . . .

A key turned in the lock.

And the men. There were always three, four, even five men at a time. The defilement was the worst part.

She had stopped menstruating. Something she had once ardently wished for—that she did not inhabit the body of a healthy woman—had finally come to pass. Her mind had rebelled at the repeated sexual violation and her body had obeyed. She had become genderless. Infertile. Insensate. She had suspended her life as a woman. She existed now only as a soldier.

The door began to open. Stephan drew closer to Ruth. Frieda pretended she didn't care.

In the three and a half months since her capture, Ruth had told her interrogators only two things: her Hebrew name and her original nationality, Hungarian. They had assumed, correctly, that most Allied women agents were radio operators, and that Ruth's codes would help lead them to other Allied agents. And so, they had beat her until she was unconscious in an effort to extract the secret transmitter codes that were locked away in her head.

She was kept in a windowless cell, eight feet by two feet, without a mattress, without a latrine, without water. She never knew when they would wake her, snatch her from the filth, take her to the room at the end of the corridor, strike her with hard instruments, rape her, demand the codes.

During those first weeks, she dreamed constantly about the codes. *QUO—I am forced to stop transmitting because of imminent danger.* . . . She even dreamed that she was talking in her dreams, divulging her secret codes. And she would wake up drenched in a guilty sweat.

She did not know what had happened to Joel Nathan. Or whether Alex Albright was still alive. And, if alive, whether he was trying to find her, to save her. And just when she felt as though she was totally abandoned, completely forgotten, no longer able to resist, they came for her . . . and took her out of solitary confinement and put her in a cell with a dozen or so men.

That was in August.

A tall, pale man entered the cell. He looked sickly, as though he had left his bed with a fever. "Come with me. My name is Peter Hein. Arrow Cross secret police."

In August, the heat and stench in the crowded cell had been overpowering. But there were two buckets, one for drinking water, the other for a latrine, and Ruth felt as though she had landed in the lap of luxury. She quickly learned otherwise. The daily ladle of thin gruel that the guards called a meal was no better than before, and when she was roused early in the morning for roll call, Ruth would sometimes find a corpse, blue and rigid, by her side. No one objected when she, the only woman, helped carry the dead body down the three flights of steps into the brick courtyard to be loaded onto a horse-drawn wagon and carted away.

Other men, Jewish men, took the place of the dead. One of these, a frail new inmate, came in September, and Ruth immediately recognized him as Bela Bartha, the theatrical producer who had been her father's good friend. They had not seen each other for six years, since that night when the Hungarian authorities, acting on Count Pal Teleki's anti-Semitic edicts, had canceled the gala benefit performance of her father's play.

It was a few hours before Bela Bartha, numbed by his arrest, noticed Ruth among all the male prisoners. He came over to her corner of the cell.

"Is it possible?" he asked. "Is it you? Ruth Offenbach?"

"You must be mistaken," she said. "My name is Bar-Adon."

"But you look so much like Ruth Offenbach," he said. "The daughter of my friend. There is an amazing resemblance."

"I'm sorry," she said.

The next day, they came for Bela Bartha, and when they threw him back into the cell, broken and practically unconscious, he whispered to her, "I didn't tell."

That was in the first week of September.

She followed Peter Hein, the sickly Arrow Cross secret police officer, down the long corridor. In the dust of the windows were the six-pointed Stars of David that she had traced as an encouragement to other prisoners across the courtyard. So they could see that they were not alone. Through the closed windows, she heard, clear and unmistakable, the stirring sounds of a parade.

The torture of her father's frail friend continued almost daily. And on September twenty-sixth, the eve of Yom Kippur, when they called out his name again, Bela Bartha turned to Ruth. His eyes were filled with remorse for a sin he knew he would never be able to atone for.

"I can't stand the thought of physical pain any longer," he told her.

The next morning, before Bela Bartha returned, Ruth was moved to yet another cell—this one cleaner than the others and occupied by Stephan and Frieda. She immediately became friends with little Stephan. Frieda felt displaced by the new woman, resentful, jealous.

That was almost three weeks ago.

Here, the food ration was better and Ruth's wounds began to heal. Rumors reached her that the Hungarian Government had withdrawn from the war, severing its alliance with Germany, and that all the prisoners would soon be freed. Frieda scoffed; she had heard such rumors before. But the guards turned almost civil, bringing them soap and towels, and the rumor mill said that the guards were trying to befriend prisoners who would be called upon to testify after the war about their treatment.

Then, three nights ago, Ruth's hopes were dashed. She heard that Bela Bartha had died. And that the Arrow Cross had staged a coup d'état to keep Hungary in the war on the side of Germany.

Had Bela Bartha revealed her name?

Would the torture now resume?

"*Wait here*," *Peter Hein said.*

He left her alone in the familiar, high-ceilinged room at the end of the corridor. It was empty. The iron chair was gone. Only the four bolts that had held its legs remained fastened to the floor. The walls had been scrubbed clean of the smears and stains of blood. The place reeked of disinfectant. Somehow, the room felt even more sinister to her than before.

She kept her eyes fixed on the far side of the room. It was there, through a narrow door, that her tormentors always entered and left. That door assumed for her a kind of awesome mystique. What new secrets lay behind it now?

When it finally opened, the tall, pale figure of Peter Hein reappeared. This time, he had a knowing smirk on his feverish face.

"There's someone here who wants to see you," he said, stepping aside.

The woman who entered had a proud, almost regal bearing. She was dressed in an expensive dark purple suit, with matching black gloves and hat. Her lips parted. She tried to raise an arm from her side, but it seemed to be weighed down by an invisible force.

It took Ruth a moment to let in the astonishing fact.

This was her mother.

"Are you hurt?" her mother asked.

"No," Ruth said.

She raced across the room and fell into her mother's arms.

"Oh, Mother!" she cried. "Don't stay! Don't look at me! I can't bear your pain."

Her mother ran her fingers over the marks of torture on Ruth's face and neck.

"Why are you here?" she asked. "Why aren't you in Palestine? What brought you here?"

Ruth could not bring herself to answer. What could she say? That she had responded to the call of voices? That she was a messenger of hope? That she had returned to save her mother? Such words would sound foolish. Her mother wouldn't understand.

Clinging to her mother's bosom, Ruth felt like a young girl again. Why *had* she come back to Budapest? Why *had* she brought her mother so much pain? Her willfulness had always been the cause of her mother's sorrow. Suddenly, Ruth remembered a fight they had had over a blue blouse with billowing long sleeves. Oh, why had she insisted on wearing that blouse to the revival of her father's play? Why hadn't she listened? Why hadn't she stayed in Palestine?

"Was it worth *this* to come back here?" her mother asked. "Was it worth risking your life?"

Ruth looked into her mother's face, once so proud and radiant, now so desperately sad. How could this woman be expected to understand? And then Ruth realized that it wasn't important whether her mother understood. Or agreed with her. *Or approved.* Her mother hadn't come here to pass judgment. Her mother loved her. Had always loved her! And, in a puzzling association of images, Ruth saw her mother and pictured Frieda, just twelve years old, waiting for her back in their cell. *Poor Frieda, she needs me*, Ruth thought. *I have become to Frieda like a mother. I have come back for . . . Frieda.*

"Yes," Ruth said softly to her mother. "For me it was worthwhile."

Her mother began to sob, and suddenly Ruth felt the older woman's body begin to give way, to crumple, and she tried to prevent her from slipping to the floor.

She looked up, saw Peter Hein watching impassively from the door.

"Can't you help?" she said.

The tall Arrow Cross officer swept Ruth's mother into his arms and carried her through the door. Ruth hesitated to follow.

"Come!" he ordered.

Ruth stepped through the awesome passageway and found herself in a narrow and dusty office that contained a desk, a leather arm chair, a sagging sofa, and a wall of bookcases. Heavy gray drapes hung over a double casement window, which had been left ajar. The room was filled with the loud martial music of a parade passing by on Tatra Street below.

Ruth looked through the window. A little boy, not much older than Stephan, led the procession. He was dressed in an Arrow Cross uniform and bore a green silk banner with black tassles. He was followed by a contingent of the Arrow Cross. Behind them strutted the snare drums, bass drums, fifes, xylophones. Bringing up the rear was a frightened band of forty to fifty men, women, and children, yellow stars pinned to their left breasts, carrying rolled-up blankets and suitcases. On both sides of the street, crowds cheered on the parade and hurled curses at the Jews.

"I always say there's nothing like a good parade," Peter Hein remarked over Ruth's shoulder. "Don't you agree?"

Ruth spun around and slapped his face.

He looked at her with cold contempt.

"You don't like parades?" he said, touching the crimson mark she had left on his feverish cheek. "Too bad. Because we have organized dozens of such parades all over the city. Just for you Jews. And you're not even grateful. A shame! We want to give you some fresh air. An opportunity to exercise your limbs. A nice hike in the countryside. From Budapest to the Austrian border. A mere one hundred and twenty miles or so to a camp in Strasshof. But if you don't like parades, someone else will have to take your place."

He glanced at Ruth's mother, who lay on the sofa.

"Perhaps *she* could go in your place," he said.

Ruth went to her mother's side.

"What do you want from her?" Ruth demanded, cradling her mother in her arms. "She hasn't done anything."

"She will be all right if you cooperate," Peter Hein said. "If you give me your codes."

Ruth looked at her mother.

Peter Hein stood over the two women and said:
"*I want the codes!*"

3

The city had begun to die.

Squeezed in the back seat of the car between Hermann Krumey and his expensively perfumed mistress, Eve Kosytorz, Albright could see signs of the terminal disease. Down both sides of Benczur Street, some shops were already boarded up. Others had been smashed and looted. Families were working in relay teams to empty their homes and load their possessions onto cars and wagons. The sick were being evacuated from the Swedish Hospital. The dead, many bearing yellow stars, clogged the gutters and lay like sleeping vagrants in piles of colorful fall leaves.

Krumey's car negotiated the turn onto Tatra Street and stopped in front of the municipal prison.

"What's the matter?" Eve Kosytorz asked.

"Nothing to worry your pretty head over," Krumey said. "It's just one of those Arrow Cross parades."

Albright watched the macabre procession. At the head of the march was a small boy dressed in a miniature Arrow Cross uniform. The band went by. Then the pathetic caravan of Jews. A short old man stumbled and fell, and before he could struggle to his feet, he was set upon by a crowd and beaten. He did not get up.

The car made its way into the heart of Pest and passed by the Astoria Hotel on Rakotzi Street. The hotel had been cordoned off by a ring of barbed wire and antiaircraft guns. Eve Kosytorz let out a long sigh.

"Oh, Hermann," she said, "look at that. Do you remember the dinner-dance we gave at the Astoria? And those lovely jewels you gave me to wear that night?"

"Of course, my dear," Krumey said. "You looked magnificent. Everyone said so."

"Is all that really over?" she said wistfully. Then, touching her coiffed red hair, a frightening thought occurred to her. "What will become of me when you leave Budapest?"

"Why on earth should I leave Budapest, my sweet?" Krumey said.

"I don't want to be left here to die," she said, pulling the collar of her fur coat around her throat. "You'll take me with you, won't you, Hermann?"

Krumey glanced at Albright, forcing a thin smile, then back at his mistress.

"Don't disappoint me, my darling," he said, an edge of menace in his voice. "I promised Herr Albright that you would bring a touch of gaiety to our trip today. You don't want to bore him with depressing thoughts, do you? Look outside. Such a beautiful autumn day. Clear and crisp. You can see the sun glinting off the gold dome of the Royal Palace on Buda Hill. Think of how glorious it will be in the Matra Mountains around Eger. We'll stop and have some refreshments by a stream, and then Herr Albright's plane will come and we'll watch the beautiful canopy of the parachute floating down to the earth with a wonderful, shiny new American Army truck. Isn't that so, Herr Albright?"

"Absolutely," Albright said.

"And you, my plum," Krumey said, reaching across Albright and patting Eve Kosytorz on the cheek, "you will be present at this historic occasion. You will live to tell your grandchildren about our great exchange. Our *humanitarian* exchange. This truck of Herr Albright's could be the first of thousands. All equipped with spare parts and conditioned for a winter campaign against the Russians. We will be doing the Americans a great favor by smashing the Bolsheviks before they reach the Danube. And they'll be doing us a great favor by taking hundreds of thousands of Jews off our hands. It couldn't be better, you see."

"Yes, Hermann," she said. "But what if . . . Don't be angry with me, but what if we get all those trucks and we still can't stop the Russians?"

Krumey thought a long time before answering.

"At least," he said, "I will have made the effort. It will be proof to the Americans that there is such a thing as an *honorable* German. That should count for something even if . . . the worst comes to the worst. Herr Albright will remember that Lieutenant

Colonel Hermann Krumey acted honorably. Won't you, Herr Albright?"

That's what the bastard is counting on, Albright thought.

It was time for the rats to think about deserting the Nazi ship. Krumey was scared. He knew that the war was lost. This stuff about a winter offensive against the Russians—who were rolling through Poland and Galicia and Romania—was all bullshit. Even while he was helping Eichmann prepare the final knockout blow, eine eintaetige Grossaktion, against the Jews, Krumey was anxious to score points with the Americans. Before the end came. So that later they would absolve him for turning Vienna into a slaughterhouse and for murdering the children of Lidice.

It had been a mistake for Albright to ridicule Krumey about his "honor." For as long as Krumey was demented enough to believe that he could get away scot-free after the war, Albright had to play along. It was his only chance. The chance he had been waiting for.

Until three days ago, Albright had practically given up hope. He had been cut cold by the underground for disobeying the order to free Count Pal Teleki. He went to the Poodle, but Sandor Kovacs refused to see him. Hammer disappeared into thin air. Only the priest stuck by his side. And when the priest, nervously spewing pieces of garlic, suggested one day that Albright move to a new safe house on the Pest side of the city, Albright found out just how ostracized he was. There were rumors, the priest told him, that the underground had voted to "discipline" the American.

From then on, Albright was hunted by the Germans *and* the underground. Alone, the priest kept him alive.

Then, on the night of the Arrow Cross coup, the priest came to him in the new safe house on Buljovsky Street and told Albright that Sandor Kovacs was dead. Shot by the Arrow Cross while he was doing his Al Jolson number at the Poodle. Hammer fled the city. A bitter dispute had broken out in the underground between the pro-Communist and anti-Communist factions. Only the Jews of the Vaadah Ezra va Hazalah, the Council for Assistance and Rescue, still clung to the slender hope that the Americans would come to their salvation.

"The Council wants to see you," the priest told Albright. "They're ready to bury the hatchet."

"Where—in my back?" Albright said.

"No, they're desperate," the priest said. "They know there's no stopping Eichmann now. They're ready to ask for help wherever they can find it. It's either you or the Russians."

Albright blew up.

"It's always the Russians!" he shouted. "Who the hell's this war being fought against? The Germans or the Russians?"

"Good question," the priest said. "I'd hate to have to make a choice in whose house to be a guest—Hitler's or Stalin's."

Albright studied the priest's face.

"All right," he said. "But on two conditions. I won't meet them here. I don't want them to find out about this place. And I want you to be present during the meeting."

Disguised in the uniform of a Hungarian Army captain, Albright followed the priest through the dark streets of Pest, aswarm with Arrow Cross troops bent on a rampage of plunder and terror. At one intersection, the crowds were so thick that no one could pass. The Arrow Cross had stripped a man naked and was forcing him to clean the sidewalk with his tongue. His teenage son watched helplessly, shouting, "Father, don't let them do that to you! Refuse! Get up, Father!"

At the Danube, Albright and the priest crossed by foot over the Szechenyi suspension bridge and trudged up Gellert Hill into the precincts of Old Buda. From this height, they could see the brilliant flashes of Russian artillery lighting up the horizon. Here, on a narrow street, they came to a yellow stucco house with a romanesque arch over the front door.

When they entered, a young woman with thick, dark eyebrows looked them over, then led them up two flights of stairs. She rapped on the wall. A trapdoor, concealed in an elaborately stenciled ceiling, swung open and a ladder was lowered.

Three men sat at a table at the end of the attic near a window with a large exhaust fan. Two of them were dressed alike. Tweed workers' caps. Rough clothes. Heavy shoes. They were not much over twenty years of age, Albright guessed. The third man was a good deal older and wore a well-tailored double-breasted suit.

"Well, we made it," the priest said, out of breath, as he hoisted himself up from the ladder.

"Have you explained to your friend why we asked him here?" one of the young men said to the priest.

Albright detected the guttural consonants of a foreign accent in the man's Hungarian. Polish? Slovene? Russian?

"No," the priest said, "I thought I'd leave that to you."

The young man came over to Albright. He removed his tweed cap. It was a gesture of unconscious politeness and it seemed out of place in this setting. His brown hair was clipped short, close to his skull, revealing a scar that ran like a half-completed part along the side of his head. His lips were heavy, dry, almost white. He was Albright's height and he looked directly at him from very large, deep brown eyes.

"Time is short," he said. "I will explain. The Council has been in radio contact with a Mossad representative in Istanbul. Eichmann is expected back in Budapest tomorrow, the eighteenth. The deportations will resume. We must do everything in our power to stop them. Our best hope now is to respond to Eichmann's pending offer to ransom Jews. He is asking for many American Army trucks. Mossad understands the gravity of the situation. Your commander in Mossad, Guido DeVita, has gone to Washington. He has an appointment to speak to General Donovan of the OSS on our behalf. In the meantime, we want you, as an American, to open talks with the Germans until we can get a firm answer on the trucks."

He looked hard at Albright.

"Am I going too fast for you?" he asked. "In the underground, we develop a tendency to speak in shorthand. We also sometimes forget our manners. I haven't introduced myself. My name is Tarnofsky."

"Russian?" Albright asked.

The question seemed to catch Tarnofsky off guard.

"My father was Russian," he said. "My mother is Hungarian." He paused, then added: "I am a Hungarian citizen."

"Look, Tarnofsky," Albright said, "let me tell you something. You'll never get the trucks. Nobody—not even DeVita—is going to convince Donovan that he should send trucks to the Krauts."

"There are three hundred and fifty thousand Jews left in Hungary," Tarnofsky said. "They can be saved. All the Americans have to do is make a gesture. Even *one* truck, at this stage, would buy time. The Germans are desperate for transport."

"You can't count on Donovan," Albright said.

"*Tarnofsky!*"

It was the other young man at the table.

"What did I tell you?" he said. "You're wasting your time with this American. What have the Americans ever done for us? It's the Russians we have to deal with now. They're in the catbird seat. Let me do what I suggested. I know one or two of the Russian NKGB agents here in Budapest. They'll find ways to help."

"We took a vote in the Council," Tarnofsky said, "and it was decided by the majority to go to the Americans, not the Russians." He placed his cap firmly on his head and added with a fierce intensity: "I don't want the Russians mixed up in this!"

Listening to Tarnofsky, a young man with a Russian name, a Russian accent, a Russian father, who nonetheless spoke so passionately *against* the Russians, Alex Albright was struck by the puzzling contradiction. What did it mean? Why did it fascinate Albright so? And this, in turn, made him suddenly aware of his own complex feelings. The struggle he had been waging with his own inner conflicts. *His* name, *his* language, *his* father.

Thoughts of his father flooded Albright's mind . . . the regal ambassador . . . a man who despised physical cowardice . . . who was never impressed by Albright's personal achievements. A restless, essentially unhappy spirit, his father. A man who couldn't slake his thirst for love with five failed marriages.

And Albright thought of his own unquenchable desires. His gift for languages. His wish to be a different person. To express parts of his emotions that he couldn't find words for in English. To *not* be his father's son.

And all these feelings now seemed strange to him, distant, futile, as though they were no longer attached to him.

Instead, everything appeared simple, of a piece, whole. It all fit together. The great global crusade against Nazi Germany, Donovan's involved plots to thwart the Russian takeover of eastern Europe, the Council's last-ditch plan to save three hundred and fifty thousand Jews, Albright's burning need to rescue Ruth—*it all fit together*. It was encompassed in this wild, farfetched scheme to trade Eichmann trucks for Jews.

"Okay, let's forget the Russians," Albright said. "They'd only screw you in the end, anyway. Isn't that right, Father?"

The priest tried to contain a smile of satisfaction.

"But what makes you think the Germans are going to deal with me?" Albright asked Tarnofsky. "They probably know that it was my people who tried to assassinate Wisliczeny. And how are we going to make them believe I'm authorized to deliver on the trucks?"

"That's where *he* comes in," Tarnofsky said, motioning to the other man sitting at the table. The older, well-dressed one.

The man nodded at Albright.

"Grosz," he said. "Bandi Grosz. How do you do?"

Albright had heard of Bandi Grosz. Everyone had. Grosz was a notorious figure in Budapest. He knew everybody, showed up everywhere, criticized everything. Though he was a German, he moved through various levels of Hungarian society, shuttling between factions and mortal enemies, invariably exuding charm, sophisticated wit, and a biting cynicism. And he did it openly, without hindrance, under some unspoken protection. He was, strictly speaking, employed by the Abwehr, the German secret service. But it was said that, at one time or another, he had worked for the SS against the Abwehr, for the General Staff against the SS, for Himmler against Hitler, for Eichmann against the Jews, for the Vaadah against Eichmann.

He stood now and shook Albright's hand. He was a small man, round-faced with twinkling eyes, thinning hair, and a habit of twitching his shoulders and back as if his underwear itched.

"I've wanted to meet you," he said to Albright. "You are a brave man. I look forward to working together."

Albright found it hard to suppress the impulse to wipe his hand against his side. To rid himself of Grosz's touch.

"Where do you fit in?" he asked.

"Where?" Grosz said. "I'm a realist. And the reality is that Germany's victims will soon be its persecutors. The time has come for me to hedge my bet. It's in my interest to be of value to the Jews."

"How?" Albright said.

"I can validate your credentials," Grosz said. "I can have an official Abwehr file on Eichmann's desk when he arrives tomorrow. Signed by Admiral Canaris, the head of the Abwehr. This file can say that the Abwehr has intercepted communications between you and the Message Center in Washington. This file can contain a complete dossier on you. This file can say that you have been authorized to open negotiations on the trucks. This file . . ."

"I get the point," Albright said. "But what's our guarantee that you won't blow the deal?"

"There's no guarantee, Captain," Grosz said. "Except that if I wanted to blow the deal, as you put it, I could just as easily have had this house raided tonight after you arrived. That's point number one. Point number two is that, as much as they'd like to, Hitler and Eichmann can't kill every Jew in this world. Some will survive. And after the war, they can testify that Bandi Grosz tried to help."

"There's just one other thing," Albright said. "Since there isn't a Chinaman's chance that Donovan will send us a truck, where do we get one?"

"We've been counting on Donovan," Tarnofsky said. "We haven't considered what we'd do if he doesn't come through."

"Well, you better start considering it," Albright said.

"Don't worry," Bandi Grosz said, twisting his shoulders. "I'll think of something."

It was this "something" that was on Albright's mind as Hermann Krumey's SS staff car turned off the mountain road and bounced across a large, flat field outside the town of Eger. The field was in a valley, surrounded by snow-capped peaks, and a stream meandered through it at roughly a right angle to the road. The driver got out and set up a table and three chairs. He brought a bottle of Schnapps, cold meats, and pumpernickle. A chill wind snapped the tablecloth.

"Here, my dear," Krumey said to Eve Kosytorz, handing her a glass, "drink this. It will warm you."

Krumey looked at his watch.

"It's three minutes of twelve," he said, pacing back and forth. "The plane should be coming soon."

"I think I hear it now," Eve Kosytorz said.

"Where?" Krumey asked, searching the sky with a pair of binoculars. "I can hear it but I can't see it."

"Colonel," the driver shouted. "Over there! A car is coming."

The engine noise had not been made by an approaching plane. It came from an enormous Silver Cloud Rolls-Royce, polished to a mirror brilliance, that swept up the mountain road at breakneck speed, swerved onto the field, and came to a halt beside Krumey's car. The chauffeur opened the rear door and out stepped the short, lumpy figure of Bandi Grosz.

"Heil Hitler!" he greeted them.

"Grosz, what are you doing here?" Krumey demanded.

"Bad news, Colonel," Grosz said. "An American C-46 transport plane was shot down this morning south of Lake Balaton. I just received word from the Abwehr that a search of the wreckage indicated that the plane was flying light. The only thing inside was a two-and-a-half-ton truck."

"*Dumkopfs!*" Krumey screamed. "I gave clear instructions that unescorted American transports were not to be fired on."

"What kind of game are you playing, Krumey?" Albright said. "I thought we had a deal?"

"We did," Krumey protested. "I don't understand how this could happen. Grosz, I want you to start an Abwehr investigation immediately."

"Of course, Colonel," Grosz said.

Grosz turned to Albright.

"Permit me to apologize for this unfortunate mistake," he said.

"Mistake?" Albright said. "You idiots just destroyed an American plane with its entire crew. You just sabotaged the whole deal."

"Herr Albright," Krumey said, "how can I prove to you that this was an accident?"

Albright shook his head.

"I'll have to contact certain people," he said. "They're going to be mighty upset."

"Anything," Krumey said. "Ask for anything. I'm ready to prove my honorable intentions."

Albright waited.

"*Please,*" Grosz urged.

"All right," Albright said. "Two of my people are being held in the municipal prison by the Arrow Cross. A woman and a man. I'll write down their names on this piece of paper. I want them released today."

4

Peter Hein was sweating profusely. He could feel his collar, damp and cool around his neck, where it had absorbed the perspiration. He knew he should have stayed home today. Only his sense of duty to the Arrow Cross had made him get out of a sick bed. He remembered reading in school that Napoleon had been defeated outside Moscow because he woke up on the morning of a decisive battle feeling sick. Yes, Hein was like his hero, Napoleon. Defeated by a bug. Worse. Humiliated by a woman!

"You failed!" the major shouted at him.

"Yes, sir," Hein agreed.

"We should hang you instead of the girl," the colonel said.

"Yes, sir," Hein replied.

"You are a disgrace to the Arrow Cross uniform," the general added.

"Sir, if I may be permitted a word," Hein said.

The general nodded for him to proceed.

Hein wiped his sweaty face with the sleeve of his uniform.

"I used all the customary methods," he explained. "I threatened to send her mother on the death march to Austria. I beat the girl myself—with my own hands. I let the men have her. Nothing worked. She will not reveal the transmitter signals. It's hopeless."

The three Arrow Cross officers stared at Hein from behind the long table. This was the twenty-first or twenty-second case that had been brought before their drumhead court so far today, and it was the first one in which a confession had not been extracted from the accused. The table was piled with documents relating to other cases that they were expected to dispose of before six o'clock tonight. But now, because of this sweaty, incompetent Hein, they had to stop and waste precious time.

"Bring her in," the general ordered. "I want to see this Jewess who can't be broken."

Peter Hein went out and escorted Ruth Bar-Adon back into the room. One of the women attendants had managed to clean Ruth up a bit and staunch the bleeding. But her face and mouth were swollen and discolored, and she had difficulty standing.

The general glanced at a thick, solid-gold pocket watch that lay open on the table.

"Two-thirty, gentlemen," he announced. "We can give this woman no more than fifteen minutes. Major, read the charge."

"This is an enemy agent, general," the major began. "British trained. Radio operator. Caught in the assassination attempt last July of Dieter von Wisliczeny. The depositions are in her file there in front of you. As you can see, we have determined that her name is Ruth Offenbach. Hungarian birth. Family, et cetera, et cetera. Jewish, et cetera, et cetera. It's all there. A traitor to the homeland. The charge is on page six, in the middle, second paragraph. Which, of course, carries the automatic death penalty."

The general flipped casually through Ruth's file, then looked up.

"Seems simple enough to me," he said to Ruth. "You have a right to say something, if you want. But keep it short."

Ruth stepped forward and lifted her chin.

"I . . ." she began.

Her lips were so swollen that she found it hard to speak.

She began again.

"I do not admit treason to my homeland. It is true that I was born here in Budapest. Here, I absorbed into my being an approach to life. My spiritual structure. Here, I learned to love the beautiful. Here, I learned to honor my neighbor. Here, I learned to respect the good.

"My father was a Hungarian author who left an inheritance to me and others—faith in the good and in laboring for the sake of goodness. Hungary was my first homeland, and for a long time I thought that the spiritual Hungary was the true Hungary. But as I grew up, I learned that as a Jew I had no place in this country. I learned that lesson in the streets of Budapest. And after the streets came the national leaders and each one voted in favor of race discrimination, deprivation of rights, the cruelty of the Middle Ages. I woke from my vain dream, the dream of my father and my father's father. I understood then. I had no homeland here. You canceled my citizenship with your hate.

"I went to Erezt Israel. The war came. Then you were for me an enemy. You had joined forces with our blood enemies—the Germans. But that enmity alone would not have brought me back to fight against you. The war was not enough for you. You raised your hands against my people. That is why I came. I came to rescue my brothers and sisters and children. And to save you, too, if you let me. Because every Jew who remains alive in Hungary will make the judgment against you lighter after your fall.

"So, it is not I who am the traitor. The traitors are those who brought this catastrophe on the heads of the people—and on your own heads."

There was a long silence.

"Is that all?" the general said.

"Yes," Ruth said.

"Then," the general said, "the verdict of this military court is that you be taken from this prison and brought to the place of execution and be executed by hanging. The execution is to proceed within the hour."

He looked over at Peter Hein.

"Do you think you can handle this?" he asked him. "Without . . . mishap?"

"Yes, sir!" Hein replied.

The general stamped Ruth's file: EXECUTED.

Ruth followed Peter Hein back to her cell.

"I'll come for you in half an hour," he told her. "Prepare yourself."

Stephan rushed to Ruth's side and hugged her.

"What happened, Aunt Ruth?" he asked. "What are they going to do with you?"

"It's nothing, sweetheart," Ruth said. "I'm just going on a short trip."

Frieda began sobbing.

"Why are you crying, Frieda?" Stephan asked.

Frieda shook her head but couldn't speak. Her chest heaved violently with each sob.

Ruth sat on the cot in front of Frieda and gently pulled the young girl onto her lap. She passed a hand over Frieda's forehead and the sobbing began to ease.

"Oh, Frieda," Ruth said. "I'm so happy that we met and that we've come to love each other so much. I know that you've always wanted to love me and that now that you can show your love, you will be able to love others, always, for the rest of your life. It is my gift to you, Frieda. My most precious gift."

Stephan stood watching for a moment, then said:

"I love you, too, Aunt Ruth."

"Oh, I know you do, darling."

And she enfolded Stephan in her arm, and the three of them placed their faces together and rocked gently back and forth.

After a while, Ruth said:

"No more composition lessons."

Stephan laughed.

Frieda tried to smile.

"But *I* have to write a kind of composition before I go," Ruth said. "May I borrow a page from your book?"

Frieda gave her a piece of lined paper, and Ruth wrote:

> To Joel Nathan, my dearest haver,
> Joel—Continue on the road. Never retreat! Carry on the battle until the end—Until the day of freedom comes—Until Jubilee! The day of victory and freedom for our people!
>
> Ruth.

And then she added as a postscript:

"Please tell our mutual friend that I love him dearly. More than my own life!"

She folded the paper.

"Frieda," she said, "I want you to hide this until the end of the war. And when you are freed, I want you to find the man to whom I have written this and give it to him."

"Yes, Aunt Ruth," Frieda said.

"Good," Ruth said. "Now I want to wash my face and comb my hair."

A few minutes later, Peter Hein returned and took her away.

"Good-bye, Aunt Ruth!"

"Good-bye, Aunt Ruth!"

Down the three flights of steps, on which she had borne the dead bodies of her fellow prisoners, and into the brick courtyard, Ruth followed Peter Hein. The sun was starting to sink beneath the roof of the prison, and a cold breeze bit into her flesh. Ruth looked around the rows of windows, three stories high, facing the courtyard. Somehow, word of her execution must have spread throughout the prison, for almost every window displayed a Star of David. Some cut from newspapers, some etched in soap, some simply traced by fingers in the dust.

They made their way to the far end of the courtyard, where three nooses swung in the breeze from the tall, wooden gallows. The hangman sat on the steps, biting his nails.

"I've got a little package for you to tie up," Hein said to the hangman.

The hangman spit out a nail and said, "You're too late."

"What's wrong?" Hein asked.

"New orders," the hangman said. "Just arrived a few minutes ago. From now on, Jews aren't allowed the honor of being executed by hanging. They've got to go on the trains to Auschwitz."

"That can't be," Hein said. "There aren't enough trains anymore."

The hangman inspected his nails.

"Don't ask me," he said. "I just do what I'm told. If the Germans want to kill them in Auschwitz, it's all the same to me."

5

Shortly after six o'clock, Bandi Grosz's Silver Cloud Rolls-Royce pulled up in front of the municipal prison on Tatra Street. The sleek, vintage automobile immediately attracted a mob of curious spectators, and Grosz had to push his way through the crowd to the front gate. He was late. It had taken longer than expected to cut the orders for the release of Ruth Bar-Adon and Joel Nathan.

Grosz flashed his ID to the guard at the gate.

Damned red tape was worse than ever, he thought. *Now you had to go through the Arrow Cross as well as the Gestapo.*

As he entered the building, Grosz was in a mood of nervous impatience. He did not pay particular attention to the three Arrow Cross officers—a general, a colonel, and a major—who were on their way home for the night.

Grosz approached the sergeant at the reception desk.

"I have orders for the release of two prisoners," he said.

The sergeant glanced at the papers and yawned.

"Wait here," he said.

"Will it take long?" Grosz asked.

The sergeant shrugged.

There were no chairs in the dimly lit reception room and Grosz paced the floor. He looked up at a photograph of Ferenc Szalasy hanging from the grimy wall. Szalasy stared back from dark, heavily lidded eyes.

Ten, fifteen, twenty minutes went by. Finally, the sergeant returned with a seedy-looking man in shirt sleeves and an unbuttoned vest. He was carrying a file in his hands.

"Herr Grosz?" he inquired in a high-pitched voice.

"Yes," Grosz said.

"My name is Zoltan Szurkebarat. Deputy director of the records department. I'm afraid I have disappointing news. A thorough search of our files shows no record of a prisoner by the name of Joel Nathan. Of course, he may be here under a different name. That happens all the time. Complicates our keeping accurate records, you can be sure."

"What about the woman?" Grosz asked, twitching his shoulders.

"Yes, the woman," Szurkebarat said. "I'm glad to say that we had no trouble finding her. I remembered her name. Or rather, her names. Bar-Adon/Offenbach."

"Well, where is she?" Grosz said sharply.

"Here," Szurkebarat said.

He handed Grosz the file. Ruth's file.

Stamped in red on the cover was a single word: EXECUTED.

6

The priest put down the phone.

"No answer," he said, biting into a piece of garlic.

"You sure you have the right number?" Albright asked.

"This is the number Grosz gave me," the priest said.

He showed Albright the slip of paper in his hand.

"Something must have gone wrong," Albright said.

"It's only eight o'clock," the priest said. "Have patience."

"It shouldn't take this long," Albright insisted. "Ruth and Joel should be out by now."

He got up from the table and began pacing the floor of the stuffy attic. The exhaust fan in the window moved sluggishly in a breeze from the window. The murmur of low voices drifted up from a room below. The Vaadah Ezra va Hazalah was holding a meeting.

All at once, the conversation stopped. There was a commotion outside. Then someone rapped on the wall. The priest opened the trapdoor.

"What is it?" he asked. "Are they here?"

It was the girl with the thick, dark eyebrows.

"No!" she shouted. "It's a raid! They've surrounded the house!"

The priest looked at Albright.

"How is it possible?" he asked.

"I told you something went haywire," Albright said. "It's that fucking Grosz. He's betrayed us."

There was more noise outside. Screeching tires. Boots pounding on cobblestones. Rattling tank treads. Doors slamming. Then a man's voice amplified through a megaphone.

"Members of Vaadah! Come out peaceably! Unarmed! No harm will come to you. We want the American. Send him out and we will let the rest of you go!"

A brief silence. Then a different voice spoke through the megaphone.

"Albright! This is Bandi Grosz! Your girl friend is dead! Exe-

cuted today! Your other friend is missing! You are alone! Your
position is hopeless! Come out!"

Albright and the priest exchanged looks.

"Dead?" Albright said, unable at first to absorb the meaning.

"Maybe he's lying," the priest said.

Albright considered the idea.

"No, I don't think so," he said. "If they've killed Ruth, Grosz
knows that'd tear the deal for me. I wouldn't be useful to him
anymore. She must be dead."

He put his face in his hands, gasping for breath.

"The Vaadah won't let them have you," the priest said.

Albright straightened.

"Tell them to stall for time," he said.

"What are you going to do?" the priest asked.

"Do what I say!" Albright demanded.

He went to the window and examined the exhaust fan. It was
hung on four rusty screws. He grabbed the protective frame,
pulled, and the screws began to come loose in the old, rotting
wood. With a few more tugs, the fan came away in his hands.

He looked out the window. An alley, about eight feet wide, sep-
arated the slanting roof of the Vaadah safe house from the black
slate ledge of the next building. It was a twenty-five-foot drop to
the ground.

He ducked through the window and stood on the narrow sill.
Then he slid down the steep slant of the roof until the heels of
his shoes were braced in the drainpipe.

Eight feet.

He crouched.

Jumped.

His body was perfectly balanced as he landed on the overhanging ledge. But the slate was old and brittle and it cracked under
the sudden force of his weight. He slipped and began to fall. He
grabbed at the razor-sharp pieces of broken slate, dangled for a
moment by his arms, lost his grip. He fell.

His right foot hit the ground first, absorbing the full weight of
his fall. He tried to stand and almost cried out in pain. The ankle
felt broken.

"Your time is up!" the voice boomed from the megaphone.
"We're coming in!"

Albright heard the crunch of the wooden door being broken open.

And he hobbled away down the long, dark alley into the dying city of Budapest.

CHAPTER TWO

WASHINGTON
Thursday, November 23

1

There was a story that Bill Donovan liked to tell whenever he invited a few of the boys from the broom closet—as the internal security unit was known—over for dinner. The raconteur in him was at it again tonight.

"Back at the beginning of the war," he said, "my wife realized that I'd be spending a lot of my time traveling back and forth between New York and Washington, so she rented this town house here in Georgetown. She's from old Buffalo stock and she got this idea into her head about setting up a kind of social salon—you know, *chez* Donovan, that sort of fancy thing. So she ups and hires this little pansy of an interior decorator to fix up the place."

A sip of tomato juice, a mischievous glance around the table, then he continued:

"Well, remember, this was in the days when we were still known as the Office of War Information—before the OSS—and you boys were using those 'Green Hornet' speech-encoding telephones with electronic key signals. So, comes the day the installers show up, and the pansy decorator takes one look at this big black mother of a contraption and says, 'You can't put that thing in the bedroom! It'll ruin my whole color scheme!' 'Where do you want

it?' they ask. 'Put it in the pantry,' he says. 'Nobody'll see it
there.' So that's where they installed it."

Another pause.

"And that's why I freeze my nuts off every night sitting on the
goddamn washing machine, waiting for you guys to send me the estimates over the phone."

Many of the brooms had heard Donovan tell that story before,
but that didn't stop them from laughing. Now, hours later, as he
was returning a far-more-sophisticated model of the "Green Hornet" to its cradle, an unsettling thought occurred to Donovan. It
was he, not the homosexual interior decorator, who was the butt
of his own story.

Appearances meant a lot to Donovan. Sitting here like this,
with his hairy legs dangling from the washing machine, he knew
he probably looked ridiculous. And he didn't like to be an object
of ridicule. That was why he continued to live under the same
roof with an unloved wife. Why he placed so much stock in getting the better of an opponent. Why he dressed with such care.
Why he was so pleased by a recent Hollywood movie called *The
Fighting Irish* in which the dashing actor George Brent portrayed
"Wild Bill" Donovan on the screen.

But, Donovan reflected bitterly, people were rarely what they
appeared to be. Not even him. Perhaps especially not him.

He resolved, once and for all, to get the goddamn phone moved
to the bedroom where it belonged. That made him feel a little
better. He began an entry on a note pad.

Code Blue. Cabinet B. Drawer 1.

Midnight November 23.

Albright from Budapest.

*Request for assistance to aid mass escape from deportation train
bound for Auschwitz.*

EOS 1–99 chance of success, verging on zero.

*Risk. OSS involvement in failure would be major blow to or-
ganization's image and appearance of invincibility.*

He made a mental note to phone London in the morning and
speak with Alex Albright's father. He owed it to his old friend to
break the bad news personally. If young Albright got on that
train, he was signing his own death warrant.

He tore off the sheet of paper and immediately began another entry. This time, his normally neat handwriting seemed to deteriorate as his fingers moved down the paper.

Code Red. Cabinet L. Drawer 4.
Midnight November 23.
Jojo in Washington.
Security check on Philby, final phase.
EOS 5–95 chance of his being a double agent.
Risk . . .

Donovan's pen hovered uncertainly over the sheet of paper.

What was the risk now?

He had been using the best brooms in security, the kind that could sweep up evidence against your grandmother, and the brooms had come up spotlessly clean. There wasn't a shred of evidence against Harold Adrian Russell Philby. Not a scintilla.

Only two weeks ago, Jojo, the chief broom, had urged Donovan to call off the sweep, close the file, and apply the overburdened resources of the internal security unit of the OSS to real threats. Not imaginary ones like Kim Philby. Just one word from Donovan and Philby would have been given a clean bill of health.

But Donovan refused.

Why?

Because he couldn't make up his mind.

Donovan prided himself on being a man of swift and certain decision, but this Philby investigation had brought out all the latent ambivalence in his Irish character. On the one hand, there was a part of Donovan that *wanted* Philby to be a Russian spy. It would prove what Donovan had been saying all along. That the fucking Communists were everywhere, penetrating the west at the highest levels, preparing the destruction of America. And it would prove that William J. Donovan wasn't some kind of anti-Communist nut.

But the trouble was that Donovan also liked Philby, admired the man for his manners, his mind, his capacity. And *this* part of Donovan did not want Philby to be a double agent. He wanted Philby to be what he was supposed to be. An ally.

Donovan knew that the Philby sweep had become something of a joke in the broom closet. The notion that Kim Philby, the head of Broadway's anti-Communist Section IX, was a Russian agent struck Jojo's men as absurd. The more they learned about Philby, the more convinced they were that he was just like them—just one of the boys. A straight arrow when it came to work, a normal healthy male after hours. Since he arrived in Washington, Philby had begun a casual affair with a secretary in the OSS library. A mousy girl with skinny legs, boney hips and astonishingly big tits. Silly name too: Rose Flowers.

The bug planted in Rose Flowers' apartment had picked up nothing more incriminating against Philby than the fact that he liked to screw while listening to popular records. And that his favorite was "Into Each Life Some Rain Must Fall."

That, more or less, was the "evidence" against Kim Philby.

Yet Donovan wasn't ready to give up. He wouldn't listen to the snickers and the snide remarks. Not yet. Not until Philby was put through one last test.

He slid off the washing machine and padded barefooted into the bedroom. Ruth Ramsey Donovan was curled up under a patchwork quilt that was part of her dowry when they married thirty-one years ago. It had been handed down from generation to generation and one day it would have been given to their daughter, Patricia, had she lived.

He crawled in next to his wife, lay back, his eyes open, thinking. . . . For a moment, he saw himself as George Brent, a dashing young officer in World War I. Then, once again, he pictured himself as he had really been in the trenches of Landres and St. George. Scared, uncertain, ambivalent, and . . . yes, a bit heroic, too. *As spurts of dust went around him and shells broke in the vicinity, Donovan cried out: "See, they can't hit me and they won't hit you!"*

Today, Donovan himself would rally his men. He would take over the broom himself.

Then, and only then, would he know for sure about Kim Philby.

2

It was a few minutes after noon when Kim Philby stumbled into the phone booth. He was struck by a foul odor. He looked around for the source of the smell, then recognized that it came from him. He stank. Like a distillery.

"Bloody cossacks find out I've been hitting the bottle, they'll dock my pay."

He fumbled in his pocket and a handful of change cascaded onto the grimy floor. He bent to pick up a nickle, lost his balance, and fell onto his knee.

"If I *survive* till payday," he giggled drunkenly.

He managed to insert the nickle into the slot and get a dial tone. He hesitated. Was he doing the right thing?

The emergency number was for emergencies, not for amateur histrionics. Maybe his controller would think that he was overreacting. This Sunday brunch that Donovan had arranged at the last minute might mean nothing. Just shoptalk among spies. That sort of rubbish.

But Philby didn't believe it was nothing.

He smelled a rat.

The phone buzzed three times. Though he had never used the emergency number before, he remembered the procedure. He hung up, waited for his nickle to be returned, then dialed again and let it ring once. He went through the routine a third time. Another of Gorky Street's outmoded games.

But Philby didn't mind. He had been careful to play by the rules ever since he had arrived in Washington five months ago. He had decided then that he had no choice. His sort of double life was chancy enough back in London where he knew the ropes; here, in a city of strangers, the risks of discovery escalated dangerously. That was the first reason he had not wanted to come to Washington. The second reason was even more compelling. He sensed that something like today was bound to happen.

It had been a hunch. But back in June, when "C" had called him in to tell him about the Washington assignment, Philby instantly felt he shouldn't go. And he remembered what "C" had said.

"Can't be helped, old chap."

Stewart Menzies had changed dramatically since his heart attack. He didn't look like the vigorous old "C" anymore. His face was drawn and pale and he had lost a lot of weight. He was sitting behind his mahogany desk scribbling a note in green ink on blue paper.

"Sort of reverse Lend-Lease, don't you know," Menzies continued, signing his "C" at the bottom of the note. "Chaps in OSS want to borrow you for a while. Seems that Donovan wants you to do for the Yanks what you've done so brilliantly for Broadway. Help set up a special anti-Communist section."

"If I g-go, it'll m-muck up all th-that I've worked f-for here," Philby stammered.

Menzies got up and sat on the edge of the desk, facing Philby.

"My dear boy," he said, "it would be terribly bad form to say no. In any case, the brutal truth is that, at this stage of the game, we need the Yanks far more than they need us. And you know the reason as well as I do. Old Hitler has apparently caught on to our little 'Ultra' decoder, and he's abandoned the use of wireless for communications between his main army groups. So our trump card has been snatched away. The PM is worried we don't have much to offer the Yanks now. If we can do them a bit of a favor by sending you over, it'll help set the balance right between us. Keep us in the thick of things."

"With all d-due respect," Philby said, "I wonder if this is j-just some excuse t-to sh-shove m-me out of the way."

"*Out of the way?*" Menzies said. "What on earth do you mean? You don't think you're being passed over? You don't think . . ." Menzies paused, then added, "You don't think it's this bloody business with the Jews, do you?"

"What b-business?" Philby asked.

"Some stuff and nonsense I've heard about a chap in Mossad," Menzies said. "Bloody Italian name. Peculiar name for a Jew. Slipped my mind. Been going about saying things, you know."

"DeVita?" Philby said.

"That's the chap," Menzies said.

"What's he b-been saying?" Philby asked.

"I'm surprised at you," Menzies said. "You should know me better than that. Never pay attention to people who say beastly things about my men. What kind of an organization would I be running if I did that?"

Standing in this Washington phone booth now five months later, Kim Philby recalled the hurt expression in Menzies' eyes.

The simple, decent soldier meant what he said: he couldn't conceive that anyone in Broadway would ever betray him. Or that they would even think that *he* would think such a thing. No, Philby was safe with "C."

Guido DeVita was something else. What could it be that had aroused his suspicion? For five months, Philby had been searching his mind. The only thing he could think of was . . . *Hungary*. Yes, it must be something to do with those bloody Palestinian parachutists who went into Hungary. The Albright team. It had to be. Philby had helped lay on the mission and DeVita had trained the team. That was the only point where their paths ever crossed. But for the life of him, Philby couldn't figure out where he slipped up.

If he slipped up.

It was always possible that DeVita was after him for a different reason. In Philby's work, one could never be sure of motives. It was often difficult to sort out the information from the disinformation. Maybe Mossad had decided to discredit Philby because it didn't want him to inherit "C"'s job. Maybe Mossad had its own candidate, someone who might be more sympathetic to the Jewish cause in Palestine after the war. Maybe . . .

Philby could think of half a dozen maybes.

But there was only one certainty. He wouldn't feel safe until he found out what Guido DeVita was up to. Philby had to follow the trail on which they crossed paths. And that trail led from the parachutists back to Donovan and then to Washington.

So he had gone to America.

The last five months in Washington had helped put Philby's mind somewhat at ease. At first, Donovan had seemed a little distant and cool, but gradually he began to take Philby into his confidence. Here at the tail end of the war, while everyone was talking peace, while holiday packages mailed from the States were being returned because the boys were expected home by Christmas, in this atmosphere of victorious euphoria, Donovan was secretly laying the groundwork for a new spy network. Targeted exclusively against the Soviet Union. Against Gorky Street.

The opportunity offered to Philby seemed too good to be true, and occasionally a chilling thought crossed his mind. Was Donovan giving him just enough rope to hang himself? Was the OSS chief waiting for Philby to make a mistake?

Philby had been careful. Very careful. Or at least he thought so until today. Now he wasn't so sure. And that's why, for the first time since he had come to America, he was using this emergency number of his controller.

Someone picked up the phone at the other end.

"Hello," a man's voice said.

As soon as he heard the voice, Philby panicked. As always, speaking into a phone filled him with a stomach-churning dread that he wouldn't be able to form words.

"M-m-m-may I p-p-please speak with M-miss Flowers," Philby stuttered.

A pause.

"Who do you want?"

"Rose Flowers," Philby said.

"Oh, I'm sorry. This is her brother. My sister isn't here right now. Can I take a message?"

"Y-yes," Philby said. "Would you p-please t-tell her that M-mr. Philby c-can't see her for lunch t-today. I have another ap-ap-pointment."

"Of course, Mr. Philby. If she wants to reach you, is there a number I can give her?"

"She c-can reach m-me at the Hay-Adams Hotel," Philby said. "I'm m-meeting two gentlemen there."

"Any names I should give her? In case she wants to have you paged?"

"N-n-names?" Philby said. "Y-yes, you c-can g-give her the n-names. D-donovan and D-d-d-deVita."

3

Even on a Sunday afternoon, the bar at the Hay-Adams was charged with sexual energy. Most of the customers were service-men putting the make on an oversupply of available women who were drawn here for just that purpose. The small talk was defi-nitely not small.

Very American, Guido DeVita thought.

DeVita himself hadn't touched a woman in eight years. Some people might have thought him peculiar, but his voluntary renunciation of women, cigarettes, wine, and his psychoanalytic work had been part of his decision to put aside all personal pleasures in favor of a higher ideal. And, in truth, he hadn't thought much about his celibacy until the last couple of weeks. But here in Washington the flood of attractive young women made him aware again of his sexuality.

He found the American capital irresistibly seductive. The clean, orderly boulevards throbbed with traffic. The sparkling marble buildings filled up and disgorged thousands of workers twice a day. Every man seemed to be with a woman. The two sexes dressed alike in military colors. They looked alike, young and trim and short-haired. And they hurried across the lawns and through the parks with an air of expectancy. Nothing seemed beyond their reach, their power, their . . . desire.

Here in Washington, the war affected him like an aphrodisiac. DeVita wondered if Kim Philby felt the same way. He hoped Philby caught the itch. Sexual desire clouded the conscious mind. It had the force of a zetz from the soul. It made men careless.

DeVita looked at himself in the bar mirror, thinking about his eight years without a woman. Had it been a punishment for breaking with Freud and for his wife's death? He began analyzing himself. Then suddenly he saw the reflection of a young man standing directly behind him. The man looked exactly like his photograph in the Mossad file. Dark and melancholy, yet appealing. It was Kim Philby.

"Mr. Philby?" he asked, turning around. "I don't believe we've met. My name is DeVita."

"How d-do you d-do," Philby said. "I've heard s-so m-much about you."

They shook hands. Philby didn't ask how DeVita had recognized him.

"I'm glad you could make it today," DeVita said. "General Donovan is waiting for us upstairs."

"Lead the way," Philby said.

As they waded out of the crowded room, one of the bartenders picked up a house phone.

"They're leaving," he said.

"Check," Jojo replied.

Jojo stood stiffly behind the reception desk in a rented morning coat that was one size too small for him. He watched DeVita and Philby emerge from the bar and walk across the small, wood-paneled lobby to the elevators. The austere, gray-haired Mossad man and the tall, nonchalant agent of Broadway. They looked like a professor chatting with a favorite student. Jojo had bet one of his men ten dollars, even money, that Philby would pass his test today. Then Jojo could at last close the file on Philby.

The elevator stopped at the fourth floor and DeVita searched along the corridor for Room 405. He rang the bell. A bodyguard answered the door.

"Yes?"

"General Donovan?" DeVita inquired.

A door across the hall opened.

"Over here." It was Donovan, alone, looking sporty in a loud checkered jacket, tan slacks, and penny loafers. He ushered them into a spacious room with tall french windows that overlooked the White House. Most of the leaves had fallen from the trees and the window framed a bleak, autumnal scene of the presidential mansion. Though it was only one o'clock in the afternoon, lights were burning in the upstairs family quarters.

Donovan noticed Philby gazing out the window.

"If I know our President," Donovan said, "he's probably glued to the telephone calling his political pals around the country, trading favors for favors."

"I d-dare say, he's a remarkable m-man," Philby said. "One of history's g-great winners, d-don't you think?"

"No question about it," Donovan said. He turned to DeVita. "How about some grub?"

They sat at a table that had been laid with cold cuts and soft drinks. For a while, they ate in silence.

"Remarkable j-job you chaps have b-been doing at that t-training b-base in Egypt," Philby said to DeVita.

"We couldn't do it without you British," DeVita said. "It's your base, your equipment, your planes."

"Y-yes," Philby said, "b-but it's your g-guts. C-can't b-borrow g-guts, c-can you?"

DeVita glanced over at Donovan. How long should they go on with this empty chitchat? He looked for a sign, but he couldn't interpret the expression in Donovan's pale-blue Irish eyes. His sixth sense told him that he and Donovan were thinking along the same lines. This was some threesome! Like a meeting of the blood royal: three aristocrats of the spy family gathered around a table in mutual fear and mistrust.

And frustration.

It had been the frustration, the long-simmering frustration that had been building up in Donovan and DeVita, that finally boiled over yesterday when they met in the general's E. Street office.

"Dammit, General!" DeVita had said. "Do you realize that I've been here in Washington for almost two weeks trying to get people to listen to me. I've talked to everybody. Henry Morgenthau at Treasury. Ira Hirschmann at the War Refugee Board. John McCloy at the War Department. Each one I've told the same thing. Something must be done to save the Jews of Hungary! Bomb the rail lines to Auschwitz. Bomb Auschwitz itself, for heaven's sake. Ransom the Jews with trucks. Do something! Anything!"

"Listen, DeVita," Donovan said. "I feel for you, but the kind of thing you're talking about isn't up to me. That's in the province of the War Department and the White House."

"General, you're abandoning not only the Jews when you talk that way," DeVita said. "You're throwing away eastern Europe, militarily and morally. You're turning the entire area over to the Communists. If you refuse to make some kind of stand, all those countries are going to have to accommodate to Soviet power."

"That may be true," Donovan said, sighing, "but you've got to try to see the big picture. The Russians have five hundred and fifty-five divisions along the eastern front, and if you think we can do anything about that, you're crazy. We'll be lucky if we can beat the Reds to Berlin. Sure, it would be swell if I could pull off a few covert operations in the east. But, believe me, I shot my bolt with the President when I got him to agree to that one parachute mission in Hungary. And you know what happened to Albright's team. They fell flat on their asses."

"That mission was doomed before it left our base in Egypt," DeVita said.

"Holy Mary, Mother of God!" Donovan said. "Is it that again? You still think Philby tipped off the Russians."

"That's right," DeVita said.

"*Balls!*" Donovan said. "We've done the most thorough security check on Philby that I've ever seen done at the OSS and do you know what we've turned up? Nothing. Nada. Zilch. *Zero!*"

"General, you're shouting," DeVita said.

"Me, shouting?" Donovan said. "I never shout. I never lose my temper."

And then DeVita knew.

He had one of his uncanny premonitions. Insight, intuition, a sixth sense. Whatever. He knew that he had Donovan in the palm of his hand. DeVita was absolutely convinced that Donovan agreed with him that Philby might in fact be a double agent. Maybe *agreed* wasn't the right word. *Wanted to agree.* That was it. Somewhere in Donovan's complex, ambivalent character, he *desired* it, *yearned* for it, *craved* it. The feeling was almost sexual.

"General," DeVita said soothingly, "we must be very careful about making a final determination about Philby. Think of it! There's so much at stake. In our business, facts aren't everything. Sometimes, we have to depend on our instincts, our feelings. We can't listen to what others say."

"You said a mouthful," Donovan agreed.

"Then why not put Philby through one final test?" DeVita said. "Go with your gut feeling. You owe it to yourself."

Donovan searched DeVita's icy, hypnotic eyes. He thought of the snide remarks that had been coming from the broom closet. They thought he was some anti-Communist nut. Well, at least DeVita understood.

"Okay," Donovan said. "What's there to lose?"

"A lot," DeVita said. "But it's worth the risk."

Now, as they finished their lunch of cold cuts in the secured OSS suite in the Hay-Adams, DeVita was calculating the risks. Seven thousand condemned souls, not to mention Ruth Bar-Adon, Joel Nathan, and Alex Albright. It was Mossad's biggest gamble of the war.

"Mr. Philby," DeVita said, "there was something in particular that I wanted to discuss with you. A message came in today from Budapest. You remember the group of parachutists that you and

General Donovan sent into Hungary. The Tchaikovsky Circuit. Their mission was a failure and two of them were killed. Three survived, including the American, Albright. Today's message says that those three parachutists are on a deportation train that left Budapest this morning for Auschwitz. Along with seven thousand people, mostly Jews. It is probably the last German train that will reach Auschwitz before the Russians break through."

"T-tragic," Philby said.

"A tragedy that can be averted," DeVita said.

"I d-don't receive your m-meaning," Philby said.

"Follow me for a moment, if you will," DeVita said. "Albright's message says that he is planning a mass escape from this deportation train. He has requested that we send a team of parachutists to aid in the escape. Drop them at the junction near Tarnow in Poland before the train is shuttled off onto the Auschwitz trunk line."

"It's n-never b-been d-done," Philby said. "Sounds like a f-fantasy t-to m-me."

"Perhaps," DeVita said. "But I still have more than a hundred trained Palestinian Jews at Camp Jubilee. They're ready and willing to take part in this operation. There is a British Liberator plane waiting on the airstrip at Jubilee, doing nothing. There would be no diversion of military resources in this operation. The Americans can supply aerial reconnaissance since they're flying over that area anyway. We can supply the men. But it's up to you and the British. It's your base, your equipment, your plane."

Philby looked at Donovan.

"What d-do you think, G-general?" he asked.

"I think it's worth the old college try," Donovan said. "I couldn't get it past Roosevelt, but if you Brits can pull it off, jeez, it would be one hell of a show. Maybe the most spectacular operation of the goddamn war. And think of how we could stick it up old Stalin's behind. A successful operation like this would be the biggest morale booster to the anti-Communist underground in Hungary and all over eastern Europe. It would really show those Bolshevik sonsofbitches that the west still has the will and the muscle to play right under Uncle Joe's nose."

"We're ready to go," DeVita said. "All we need is the word from you."

"Fascinating," Philby said. "Let m-me think about it."

"Frankly, Kim, there isn't time to think about it," Donovan said. "If we're going to move, it's got to be pronto. Today. Right now. Otherwise, we might as well forget it."

Philby walked over to the french windows and looked across the park at the White House. Somewhere behind those windows was Franklin Roosevelt. The bloody champion of the bloody free world. Counting his favors. Savoring his fourth term. His victory.

The trail that Philby had followed had led from the parachutists back to Donovan and then to Washington. And now to this.

The trap.

Everything depended on his next move.

CHAPTER THREE

THE TRAIN
Friday, November 24

1

"Upsy-daisy!"

Meyer Lipshutz boosted the boy onto his shoulders and grasped his ankles for balance.

"So, *nu?*" he asked. "Whaddya see, kid?"

"Nothing," came the muffled reply from the boy, whose head was poking out of the small, square window.

"Whaddya mean, 'Nothing'?" Lipshutz said. "You gotta see *something*. You're a smart bar mitzvah *bucha*, ain't you? Open your eyes and look."

Lipshutz was a burly, red-headed man with faded blue tattoos of naked women on both of his thick forearms. He had a coarse face jutting out of a long slanting neck, and arms that reached down to his knees. Which accounted for his nickname: "King Kong." At various times in his life he had been a butcher's assistant, a merchant sailor, a veterinarian's helper and, just before he was rounded up for deportation, a bouncer in a Budapest dance hall. He also had a sweet tenor voice and a lopsided smile so full of tenderness that it could melt your heart.

He had been through this routine with the boy before. Hoisting him on his massive shoulders so that the kid could take a look out of the window of the boxcar and report what he saw. Usually he didn't see much. Lots of beech forests. Here and there a farm. Once in a while a gang of peasant women in shawls and high boots repairing the tracks. And when the train was moving, a few brave men throwing themselves out of the windows of other cars, hitting the ground, running, stumbling, falling—most of them stopped dead in their tracks by the machine guns of the sentries posted on the roofs.

The boy turned back to the window. He was a handsome lad, sinewy, short for his age, with the fuzzy promise of a beard growing down his sideburns and across his top lip. None of the people packed shoulder-to-shoulder in the boxcar knew his name. He was "the kid." Or "the boy." Or, to some of the older women who prayed that he would bring them a miracle, "the *mashiach*." The messiah.

"I can't see much," the boy told King Kong Lipshutz. "It's pretty dark. A kind of glow in the sky. Just a lot of train tracks going off in every which way. And a little wooden house over there that looks like a train station. And a guard. I can see a German guard. About ten yards away. He's . . . he's playing with himself."

"It should fall off," Lipshutz said. "Now, look, try to get him into a conversation. You know, tell him we've got three stiffs in here and a few more people ready to croak. Tell him there's crap all over the floor. Smells like a zoo. Ask him for some water."

The boy looked down.

"Go ahead," King Kong ordered. Then he smiled his lopsided smile. "But go easy."

"Hey," the boy whispered loudly out of the window. "Hey, you! Over here! How about some water. *Wasser, wasser.*"

"What's he saying?" Lipshutz asked.

"Nothing," the boy said. "He's zippering up his fly but he won't look my way."

"Try him again. Maybe he's embarrassed you caught him with his pecker out."

The boy tried again. Still nothing.

King Kong Lipshutz swiveled around, still balancing the boy's legs on his shoulders. He looked forlornly at the man standing next to him. The *meshugener* who had boarded the deportation train willingly. The one who had a crazy plan for an escape. The American. Alexander Albright.

"Forget it, pal," Lipshutz told Albright. "It ain't no use. It won't work. Those motherfuckers are made of stone."

"I know," Albright said. "But we've got to keep trying."

"*Wait!*" the boy shouted from the window. "I see something else. Someone's coming out of the station. An officer. The one who limps."

"*Des Teufel's Stellvertreter,*" Lipshutz said, pretending to spit on the floor. "The Devil's Deputy. Lehndorff."

"Lehndorff," Albright said, repeating the name of the German officer who was in command of the train. "Dammit, that's the one thing I didn't think of. Finding out something about Lehndorff."

"What's there to know?" Lipshutz said. "He's a Nazi, ain't he?"

"Sure," Albright said, rubbing his ankle which still ached. "But if we knew something about him, what makes him tick, it could be helpful. Later on."

"You still harping on that 'later on'?" King Kong Lipshutz said. "Brother, let me tell you something. There ain't going to be no later on. You're just dreaming."

2

Christian Lehndorff slammed the station door behind him with his one good arm and limped stiffly across the coupling yard toward the waiting locomotive. A big black monster of an engine silhouetted against a silvery horizon. Sunrise was still an hour or so away, but the whole eastern sky was flushed with metallic colors. An aurora borealis courtesy of the Red Army's artillery. The Russian guns sounded to Lehndorff as if they had moved a couple of miles closer during the night.

Under the sky-glow, things gleamed. The skull and crossbones on Lehndorff's SS lapels. The clamp that held his empty left sleeve. The crushed stones between the tracks. The metal fittings on the locomotive—lamps, fender, boiler, exhaust ejector, chimney, bar frames, cylinders. Even the steam glowed. To Lehndorff, the great black shape of the engine seemed to float on a cloud of luminous steam that gushed between the mammoth driving wheels. Hissing, knocking, coughing.

Over the sounds of the artillery and the live steam, Lehndorff could hear yet another noise, this one low and haunting, like a fading chord struck by a church organ at the end of a hymn. It was one long continuous moan coming from the line of sealed boxcars that stretched behind the engine tender into the black infinity of the chill November morning.

The train had been sitting there, on a siding, for hours. Waiting. Hissing and waiting. Moaning and waiting. Since leaving Budapest almost two days ago, the train had made it only as far as Miskolc, a provincial station halfway between the Hungarian capital and the Slovakian border. It was already a day behind schedule. And at the rate the Russians were advancing toward the rail line, it might not make it through at all.

There was nothing much he could do. Every time a German military convoy came thundering down the track—on the way east to the front with fresh cannon fodder, on the way back west with the dead and the wounded—Lehndorff's seventy-car train was shunted aside. It had a Priority Four on the *Deutche Reichsbahn's* scale of five.

Running Jews from Budapest to Auschwitz wasn't Christian Lehndorff's idea of how to fight a war. It was a shit detail. Especially for the grand-nephew of one of Germany's most illustrious military heroes. His Uncle Erich—really his father's uncle—had been Christian Lehndorff's model ever since he could remember. General Erich Lehndorff, deputy chief of the World War I High Command, a hero of Tannenburg, a prime mover behind Adolf Hitler's rise to power in Bavaria, a soldier whose picture turned up in every German schoolboy's history book. The Lehndorffs *were* the German Army.

But young Lehndorff knew he couldn't complain. Not quite twenty years old, he was only an *Untersturmführer*, a lowly second lieutenant, whose bad luck it had been to lose an arm in a freak ammunition depot explosion at brigade headquarters in Romania. He still had enough shrapnel in his legs to build a battleship.

Someone else might have used the wounds as an excuse to get out of uniform. But not Christian Lehndorff.

He had waited all his life for a chance to go to war. To fulfill his Lehndorff dream, his Lehndorff duty.

At least here on these deportation trains he was still near the front. He was in charge of forty men. Most of them were pretty raw kids, sixteen and seventeen. But that was all the Fatherland had left to send. Some of these kids were squeamish about transporting human cargo to the slaughterhouse. Christian Lehndorff couldn't understand them. The job of a German soldier was war. And so long as business was good. . . .

As he approached the locomotive, Lehndorff heard a commotion coming from the engineer's cab.

"Hey, what the hell's going on up there?" he shouted.

The engineer stuck out his head. Moustache, eyebrows, hair, greasy face—all melded into one color. Mocha java. Except for little ovals of white skin around the eyes where his goggles had kept out the grime. He wiped his hands with an oily rag.

"Just me and Mr. Know-It-All here having a little difference of opinion," the engineer shouted down. "That's all."

Mr. Know-It-All turned out to be the fireman. He was a little younger. No moustache. But the same grime-encrusted face. Same white oval mask.

"I've been trying to tell this dummy that this locomotive is a Hammel," the engineer explained to Lehndorff. "But he keeps on insisting that it's a Gölsdorf."

"It *is* a Gölsdorf, you asshole," the fireman said.

"Yeah?" the engineer said. "Then if it's a Gölsdorf, how come it doesn't have a Krauss-Helmholtz bogie? Answer me that, fuck face."

"A Krauss-Helmholtz bogie!" the fireman said, slapping the palm of his hand against his forehead. "Listen, if this is a Hammel, then how come it starts steaming simple, then goes over automatically to compound expansion as the engine accelerates? Huh? *Huh?*"

Lehndorff stood there with his one good arm resting on a hip, not understanding a word they were saying, but enjoying the argument. As far as he was concerned, these were fine men who cared about their machine. They didn't give a shit about the contents of the cargo. If anybody could get this train through to Auschwitz, they could. Ram a hole right through the Russian lines if necessary.

"Listen, you two," Lehndorff said, "we've received orders to start up again. Let's get this train back on the line and see if we can make up some lost time. I don't know a Hammel from a Gölsdorf, but I know this isn't a refrigerated freight train. We've got a lot of rotting carcasses back there. We don't want to deliver spoiled meat."

The engineer laughed and ducked back into the cab. In a few minutes, the pressure gauge indicated that the boiler had built up a full head of steam—two hundred pounds per square inch. The three pairs of coupled driving wheels, six-foot, six-inch Hochbeinigens, began scratching sparks off the tracks. The horizontal low-pressure cylinders on the outside of the engine emitted a retching noise, like an old man trying to bring up phlegm. The train shuddered forward, squeaking, and began to move.

The steam whistle screeched.

Down the line, the SS guards scampered in different directions. Some toward the forward Einsatzkommando car directly behind the engine tender. Others toward the rear Einsatzkommando car in front of the caboose. Still others clambered up to the roofs where they paired off behind machine guns that were spaced ten cars apart.

Christian Lehndorff stood beside the track as the train slowly lumbered by. The door of each boxcar was bolted from the outside and had two numbers on it. Stenciled numbers went by in consecutive order and signified the proper placement of the car in the line. Chalked numbers indicated how many people were packed inside, the body count.

11/168. . . 12/106. . . 13/101 . . . 14/99 . . .

Lehndorff half limped, half jogged toward the front of the train and the forward Einsatzkommando car. As he passed by car 10, he glanced up. The two machine gunners on the roof threw him smart salutes. Not bad for young kids. Good discipline. Maybe they'd be all right, after all.

Directly beneath the barrel of their gun was the window of the car. Christian Lehndorff was dimly aware of a face staring at him through the window. The pale smooth face of a young boy.

3

"Tell me again," Joel Nathan said.

"I've already told you," Alexander Albright said.

"I want to hear it again," Nathan insisted.

"Okay," Albright relented. "I'll tell you."

They had to shout to be heard over the racket. The hollow clickityclack of the train. The yelling. Cursing. Arguing over scarce food. Shoving fights over a place to rest. Screaming over who had a right to stick his nose next to a crack in the wooden side and get some fresh air. Debates over their destination. Yelping children. People being sick.

"Ruth is alive," Albright said.

Nathan shook his head. His eyes were as hard and dry as pebbles in the sun. No emotion there.

"Ruth is alive," Albright repeated. "That much I know for sure. The man who hid me in Budapest, the priest I told you about, the one who saved my life—he found out. Two days ago. He came and told me. The Arrow Cross stayed her execution. They put her with a bunch of people to be sent to Auschwitz. She was supposed to leave on this train. With us. That's why I'm here."

Albright gazed at Joel Nathan, wondering whether his words were getting through. He had been over this before with Joel. Twice, as a matter of fact. But it didn't seem to stick. Nathan couldn't make the connections. His eyes weren't focusing. Every time he opened his mouth to speak, his tongue seemed to get stuck. He looked like he had suffered a stroke.

Albright was afraid to ask Joel what they had done to him in prison. And Joel had not volunteered. But all the signs were there. Burn marks on his hands. Missing teeth. Broken cheek bone. A raw scar circling his neck just below his prominent Adam's apple. He was so disfigured that it was hard to look at him. Hard to believe that this was really Joel Nathan. And yet Albright was convinced that if he could only break through Joel's mental and psychological block, none of his physical wounds would matter.

In a way, Nathan had been the toughest of them all in the

Tchaikovsky Circuit. Tougher even than the rock-solid Dan Gur or the hair-trigger Saul Patir. The toughest, the smartest, the best. The natural leader. The one they all looked up to. And loved. Especially Ruth. From the day he arrived at Camp Jubilee, Albright tried to pretend that this didn't bother him about Joel. But he realized now, with a sense of delayed guilt, that he had been jealous all along.

"There's a good chance that Ruth is on this train," Albright tried again.

"A chance?" Nathan said. "What's a chance?"

"*More* than a chance," Albright said. "A high probability."

"We'll never know, will we?" Nathan said.

"Listen, Joel," Albright said, taking Nathan's disfigured face between his hands, "you've got to snap out of this. I need your help. We're *not* going to Auschwitz. I told you that. We're going to make a break. The whole frigging train."

A vacant stare from Joel Nathan.

"I'm going to go over it with you again," Albright said. "Try to follow me. This is important. Okay? Like I said, I figure two things have to come together for a successful escape. The first thing is we've got to work out a way to communicate with the other cars in the train. So we can get word to them about our plan. The other thing is that, once we've got ourselves organized and ready to make the break, we'll need some outside help."

He leaned over, his hands sliding down Nathan's face to his scarred neck, and drew him closer. Their noses almost touched.

"I've worked out the second part," Albright said. "Before we left, I sent a message to Donovan in Washington asking him to keep the train under aerial reconnaissance until we reach the Polish border. At Tarnow. That's where the train stops so Lehndorff's transport unit can be relieved by the special company of guards from Auschwitz. The transfer should take an hour or so. That's where Donovan comes in. There at Tarnow. During the transfer of guards, we make the break. Donovan drops a unit of paratroops. The Krauts are taken by surprise. We bust out, link up with the paratroops. . . ."

He was wasting his breath.

Albright dropped his hands. He felt a terrible sense of defeat. His plan was a million-to-one shot. During the entire war there had never been a mass escape from a deportation train. Listening to himself explain it to Joel, he realized that he had made a dozen preposterous assumptions. Communicate with the other cars in the sealed train! *How?* Organize seven thousand sick and traumatized people! *How?* Break out of the train at the appointed place! *How?* Link up with Donovan's paratroops!

Donovan?

How could he depend on Donovan?

It wasn't a plan. It was a fantasy.

And yet. . . .

They were all condemned souls—he, Ruth, Joel, and the seven thousand others—and what did they have to lose? Somehow, he felt that he and Joel together had a chance to make the fantasy real. If only he could get through to Joel.

One look at Joel, a ghost of his former self, and Albright wanted to cry. And then he realized that he *was* crying. He could feel the hot tears on his cheeks. He couldn't believe it. Him crying! Why, he hadn't cried since . . . since he couldn't remember. Since his mother died and his father started taking up with those flashy Hungarian women who looked as if they owned beauty salons. Albright hadn't known that the pain was still there; he had buried it so deep that he had forgotten. He felt ashamed, stupid. A grown man crying, grieving for his mother and father, for his own past.

The hell with the past! It was time he put it where it belonged —behind him.

He wiped the tears away roughly.

And then he did something that shocked him. He slapped Joel Nathan across the face. Twice. Hard.

Nathan's eyes flashed. There was a spark.

"I'm not letting you get away with this," Albright told him. "You're not going to screw up my plan. You can't give up. You've never given up before. Joel, listen to me. Guido DeVita told me about you. About the polio and everything. How you felt ashamed for being a cripple and how you refused to give up. You've beat the rap before and you can do it again. But you've got to try. Damn you, you've got to try!"

Nathan's eyes, those hard, dry pebbles, began to focus.

"Try!"

From behind him, Albright heard a voice, a sweet tenor, repeat, "Try . . . try . . . try." He turned around. It was Meyer Lipshutz. King Kong. Towering over him. His coarse face jutting forward, concentrating on Joel Nathan.

"Try!" Lipshutz said. "Stay alive, man!"

And Joel Nathan began to speak.

His tongue still thick, his words slurred, his voice flat, he began to talk about his time in prison. He talked on and on, and Albright and King Kong Lipshutz listened, nodding, just letting him get it all out, the helplessness, the humiliation, the degradation, the shame.

". . . And then I was put into a cell with a group of Hungarian Jews who had been arrested for carrying forged papers identifying them as Aryans. Each morning, a secret police officer of the Arrow Cross, a mean bastard by the name of Peter Hein, would order us to line up outside the cell, and he'd march up and down the line inspecting us like we were troops on parade. These prisoners were practically falling down from lack of food and water and medical care, and this Arrow Cross officer, this Peter Hein, would make us stand at attention, and then he'd say: 'Who here is a Jew?' And his question was always followed by total silence. The prisoners would just stare at the stone floor, too frightened to speak and admit their Jewishness. That's just what he wanted; it gave him a sadistic satisfaction. None of them had the courage to assert their true identity. And I couldn't stand it, so the first time this happened I stepped forward and said, 'I am a Jew.' And you never saw anything like it. He flew into a rage. He ordered me taken away. They tortured me.

"And the next morning, the same thing happened. The question, 'Who here is a Jew?' No answer. I step forward. 'I am a Jew,' I say. This time he goes completely berserk and he takes me into the room and works me over himself. And on the third day the same thing, and the fourth day, and the fifth day, until I wonder how long I'll be able to keep it up until he kills me with his bare hands. And on the sixth day we're lined up and he asks, 'Who here is a Jew?' And the prisoners know that I've just about had it, that maybe this one more time and I'm finished. And before I can say anything they all step forward, *every last one of them*, and they say, almost in unison, 'I am a Jew!' And that's what saved my life. Those four words. 'I am a Jew.' A number of the others were tortured, but Peter Hein never played that game again. . . ."

While he talked, the train kept stopping and starting, starting and stopping. Military convoys rocketed past, leaving the boxcar shuddering in their wake. Nathan talked on. . . .

"I heard that Ruth was being held in the same prison. Everybody knew her name. Talk of her spread throughout the building among the prisoners. This beautiful, sensitive poet who had come from Palestine by parachute, from the sky, who had been caught and tortured and yet continued to defy her captors. She was like a saint to the others, an inspiration. If she could stand up to the torturers, so could they. And then on the day we heard that she had been executed, we lost all hope. I have never seen people in such despair. . . ."

As he talked, they could hear the Russian artillery drawing closer, ever closer. After a while, Lipshutz had the boy round up some food for Nathan—for King Kong's friend, the boy explained, and no one dared refuse. He brought a hard-boiled egg, a tomato, a piece of bread. Nathan talked while he stuffed the food into his mouth. Now that he had opened up, he was like a burst dam and the words spilled out of him in torrents. Finally, the train ground to a halt in another station.

"The sign says Hidasnémeti," the boy reported from the window.

"Hidasnémeti?" Joel Nathan said. "That's funny. When I was a kid, my parents used to rent a little cottage up here in the summer. To be close to the hot springs. The water was supposed to have some medicinal benefit and they thought it might help cure me. I bathed in it, I drank it, I soaked in it, I practically lived in it. Dreadful stuff."

He laughed. That ruined face with the missing teeth actually broke into a wide grin.

"More food?" Albright asked him.

"No thanks."

"Some water?"

"I'm not thirsty."

"You ready to listen to *me* now?"

"Go ahead."

And Albright started all over again. Ruth was alive. . . . He

had a plan for an escape. . . . Two conditions were necessary. . . . Donovan had been messaged to send paratroops. . . .

"Whoa!" Nathan said. "Back up a little here. How are we
going to get word to the prisoners in the other cars?"

"Welcome back to the land of the living," Albright said.

"The land of the short life expectancy," Nathan said. "So how
are you going to do it?"

"Okay," Albright said. "Here's how it goes. There are eight stations between Budapest and Tarnow at the Polish border. Hatvan,
Miskolc, Hidasnémeti, Košice, Presov, Plavec, Krynica, Muszyna.
The train always stops at these stations to give the crew and
guards a rest and to take on water and coal and provisions."

"So?"

"So, this train is a floating gold mine," Albright said. "Look at
the people in this car. I mean, really look at them. Look at their
fingers, their ears, their wrists, their necks. They're wearing every
damn piece of jewelry they own. That's negotiable currency. The
best kind in wartime. That's how we bribe the guards."

"We do the what?"

"Bribe the guards to open the doors," Albright said. "We've got
to convince the guards to open the doors. To let us clean out the
car of the excrement, the dead, to get some water, whatever. Most
of these guards are young kids. They're not really the hardened
old SS types. They can hear the Russian artillery just as clearly as
we can. They know the war is lost. They can be bribed. And once
we get the door open and we're outside, we bribe them some
more. To get another door open. And then we switch people from
car to car. And that's how we spread the word."

Nathan looked at Albright, then at King Kong Lipshutz.

"I think he's lost his marbles," Nathan said.

"Indubitably," Lipshutz said, pronouncing the long word with
great relish. "But then I ain't heard a better plan since I came
aboard."

"It'll never work," Nathan said.

"It can work," Albright said. "Our problem isn't going to be
bribing the guards. That's going to be the easy part. Our problem
is Lehndorff."

"Who's Lehndorff?" Nathan asked.

Albright explained who Lehndorff was.

"Lehndorff may put a stop to the bribes," Albright said. "I don't know anything about him, so I can't say for sure. But a one-armed second lieutenant in the SS who's still on active duty when he could be home licking his wounds—that bothers me. For all we know, he may be one of those fanatics."

"Let's assume for the sake of argument that we get a couple of the doors open," Nathan said. "Then what?"

"Look at it this way," Albright said. "We've got six stations left —this one and five more. Say we succeed in getting the doors open during only four or five of these stations. Each time we'll double the number of cars that know about the escape plan. Two, four, eight, sixteen, thirty-two. We can end up with anywhere from sixteen to thirty-two cars prepared to make the break at Tarnow. Thirty-two cars is almost half the train. And that's not half bad."

"I don't know," Nathan said. "It sounds crazy to me."

"I left one thing out," Albright said.

"What's that?"

"If Ruth is on the train, we'll have a good chance of finding her."

Nathan thought for a moment.

"True," he said. "Okay, let's go back over this. Especially the part about Lehndorff. Tell me again what it is about him that bothers you."

Just then, they heard the sharp, flat sound of small-arms fire, and then suddenly from the roof overhead the deafening roar of the machine gun opening up full blast.

"What's going on, kid?" King Kong asked.

"They're shooting," the boy said. "*At each other!*"

4

Christian Lehndorff was sitting on the toilet, reading *Die Front*, when he heard the first crackle of automatic weapons fire.
More Jews trying to escape.

Then the jackhammering of the machine guns. At least three of them. An unholy racket. An explosion. That was a grenade.

Shouts. Screams of pain. Another, louder explosion. This time a mortar.

What the fuck was going on?

The toilet door flung open.

Corporal Juergen Hoeffel, a green kid from Lübeck, stood there. Blond and blue-eyed, an Aryan stereotype right out of a Nazi recruiting poster. Except for the expression on his face. Utter astonishment. Hoeffel stared in horror at the mass of red scars welting Christian Lehndorff's naked legs.

"What is it?" Lehndorff demanded.

"Russians!" Corporal Hoeffel said. "A Russian scouting patrol."

"Gott im himmel!"

Lehndorff had trouble hitching up his trousers. He left his tunic hanging on the hook, grabbed his Walther P-38 from its holster, and limped-ran outside.

He couldn't believe his eyes.

Men spilling out of the lead Einsatzkommando car. Some sprawled right in front of the opening of the car on the grading, already dead or wounded. Others clustered around a mortar behind the engine fender. Bullets *pinging* and *ponging* off the boiler. The forward machine gunners on the roof of the train blasting away through the smoke gushing from the chimney. Their fire seemed to be directed at a clump of trees near the water tower.

"I don't see them," Lehndorff said to Corporal Hoeffel.

"Over there!" Hoeffel shouted. "Behind those trees. They've got sharpshooters."

"Got to get out of here before they radio in reinforcements," Lehndorff said. "This place is going to be crawling with Russians. Follow me!"

Hoeffel looked at Lehndorff as if he were crazy. A strange sound, a peeping bird sound, came from Hoeffel's throat. Then he turned on his heels and fled back to the safety of the station.

"Come back!" Lehndorff yelled after him. "Coward!"

There was no time to worry about Hoeffel now. Lehndorff headed for the engine. Heard the bullets buzzing through the air all around him. He kept himself straight, stiff, erect, so his men could see that he was not afraid. A bullet tore through the fabric of his empty left sleeve.

He felt good. Exhilarated.

This was more like it!

Just as he reached the engine, the sergeant operating the range-finder on the mortar slumped over the tube. He was pulled away—shot through the stomach—and replaced by another man.

"Get this train out of here!" Lehndorff shouted up to the cab.

"I can't," the engineer said. "Mr. Know-It-All here hasn't been keeping up the boiler pressure. I've only got a hundred pounds of steam."

"Hundred and ten pounds, you asshole," the fireman corrected him.

Lehndorff climbed up the side of the engine, in full view of his men and the Russians, and waved his arm, his one good arm.

"*Back!*" he yelled. "Get back in the train. Get back. . . ."

A Russian sharpshooter's bullet slammed into his right shoulder, spinning him around so that he had to grab on to a bar frame with the stump of his left arm. Another bullet took a bite out of his right thigh.

He hung on. Looked down. His men were watching him. Amazed. Frightened. Awed that Lehndorff, hit twice, stubbornly refused to fall.

The men began scrambling back into the Einsatzkommando car, dragging their dead and wounded with them. Lehndorff wheeled on the engineer, managed with painful effort to lift the Walther P-38, pointed the barrel at the man's head.

"Move this train!"

The engineer looked over at the fireman, shoveling coal into the firebox, then down at the steam-pressure gauge. One hundred thirty-five. Still fifteen pounds shy of the pressure required to move the massive Hochbeinigen driving wheels.

Bullets ricocheted off the cab.

The engineer shrugged. He yanked the brake lever, releasing the air in the train line and causing a great whoosh of steam to escape between the drivers. He shoved the reverse lever in full-forward position and reached up and gradually pulled open the throttle.

The Hochbeinigens spun on the tracks but the train didn't move.

"Use the sanders!" the fireman yelled.

The engineer unscrewed a valve, sending compressed air

through the sandboxes on top of the boiler and automatically piping sand on the tracks under the Hochbeinigens.

Sluggishly, the train crept forward, moving directly into the line of Russian crossfire.

Lehndorff glimpsed the figure of a Russian officer behind a tree near the water tower. He was astride a dappled horse and held a sword in his hand. He looked like a statue from a bygone war. Lehndorff began firing his Walther.

This was the moment he had been waiting for. His Lehndorff dream. The real thing. *Battle.*

He never once considered what his dream amounted to. Saving the train so that all seven thousand of its occupants could be murdered later on at Auschwitz. As the train churned on, he was thinking only of one thing—his grand-uncle, Erich Lehndorff, the victor of Tannenburg, the picture in the history book. . . .

Then, split seconds apart, two Russian bullets pierced his groin and ended Christian Lehndorff's short, happy life.

CHAPTER FOUR

THE TRAIN
Saturday, November 25

1

The long train snaked its way slowly toward the border.

By fits and starts it passed through rolling foothills, around deep, wooded hillsides and into a devastated country. All along the line there were ghost villages and abandoned wine distilleries. Smoldering vineyards. Burning stacks of wheat and maize. The bloated carcasses of animals. Weary columns of refugees trudging west, away from the earth-trembling artillery, away from the advancing Russians.

Hour after hour. Until the train chugged through a long tunnel and emerged on a broad plateau. Here, the sounds of the artillery grew fainter, muffled behind the low mountain range. At the next stop, while a military convoy sped by, a loudspeaker was mounted on the engine, and when the train lurched forward again it blared out "The Horst Wessel Song," the official anthem of the Nazi party.

"I'd rather hum to the tune of the Reds' guns," King Kong Lipshutz said.

"Don't worry, they're whistling in the dark," Alex Albright told him. "Remember, these SS guards are just kids. They've been shot up badly and they've lost their commanding officer. They must be pissing in their pants."

"*They're* pissing in *their* pants!" Lipshutz said. "Brother, you're still a dreamer."

Albright ignored the sarcasm.

"Does everyone understand the plan?" he asked Lipshutz. "Exactly what they're supposed to do? Have you explained it to everybody in the car?"

"Everybody over nine and under ninety," King Kong said.

"Have you got the pieces of clothing I asked for?"

"I've got them," Lipshutz said. "One bright red scarf, one large dark babushka, one man's felt fedora hat."

"You went over how to use them?"

"I went over," Lipshutz said.

"How about the arsenal?"

"An arsenal you call it?" King Kong said. "*Some arsenal!*"

To begin with, the "arsenal" consisted of fourteen suitcases. The handles, stripped of the leather sheathings, supplied fourteen steel frames which, wrapped in cloth and tied around a man's hand, made effective brass knuckles.

These same suitcases turned up eight elasticized pouches for toilet articles. The long rubber bands in these pouches were useful as slingshots. So were seven garter belts. Together, these fifteen slingshots were capable of firing such missiles as the nails from nearly one hundred pairs of shoes.

The shoes provided another weapon. Forty-eight pairs of shoelaces, tied into lengths of four, doubled and knotted, could be used to garrote an enemy.

For knives, there were twelve fountain pens, four hatpins, and about sixty spoons sharpened to a cutting edge.

More than forty belts with their metal buckles were turned into bolas.

Socks weighted with shoe heels, loose change, paperweights, and other heavy objects made blackjacks.

The stuffing from pillows and toy animals, lightly dampened with urine, rewrapped into sacks fashioned from underwear, could be lighted and tossed as smoke bombs.

The spiral binder from a boy's stamp album made a short stave.

The contents from three bottles of cologne could be thrown into the eyes of an enemy to temporarily blind him.

Two baby bottles, each filled with two and a half inches of whisky and stuffed with rags, made Molotov cocktails.

Such was Alexander Albright's "arsenal."

"Do it again," Albright said.

"What?" Lipshutz asked.

"Go over everything again," Albright said. "I don't want any mistakes."

"Okay, folks," King Kong called out, "rehearsal time!"

It was pitch dark when the train pulled into Košice, the first station across the Slovakian border. By then, five more people had died in car 10. Two children, two old men, and a consumptive woman whose left hand sparkled with a diamond ring the size of a silver forint.

Everyone agreed that it was the most valuable object in the car.

"I can't get it off," Albright said.

"Here, let me see that," King Kong said, tugging and twisting at the ring. "You're right. It's stuck. I'll have to cut her finger off."

"You can't do that." This from the woman's husband who held her head in his lap.

"Diamond rings ain't going to do you much good where we're headed, pal," King Kong said. "And, believe me, *she* won't know the difference."

He took a pen knife from his sock and began sawing away at the dead woman's finger.

"I used to be a butcher," he said, flashing his lopsided smile at the horrified people watching him. "Like they say, you live long enough, everything you know comes in handy."

He severed the first knuckle and slipped the ring from the bloody stump. Wiped it off on the front of his shirt. Squeezed through the mass of people over to the boy. Handed him the ring. Hoisted him on his shoulders.

"Okay, kid," he said, "do your thing."

The boy peered out of the small window into the darkness. He looked up and down the train. Shafts of yellow light spilled from the open doors of the two Einsatzkommando cars. Laughter drifted across the tracks from the station. There was no one on duty.

After a while, a blond SS guard appeared at the station door, his arms around two women. He tripped, steadied himself, then stumbled across the tracks toward the light of the forward Einsatzkommando car. As he drew closer with the giggling women, two guards jumped out of the car.

"Hey, Hoeffel!" they called to him.

"Where you think you're going with those dames?"

"Men up front here, boys in the rear."

"You got your mother's permission?"

"He don't have no mother. He was scraped off the whorehouse wall."

They made vulgar smacking noises with their lips.

The boy inside the train could not see what happened next. The men's voices grew louder, angrier. One of the women cursed in Slovakian. There was the sound of fists smacking against flesh. Someone fell onto the cinders. Then the two guards reappeared back into the shaft of light, each with a woman on his arm. They were greeted by a roar of drunken approval as they lifted the women into the waiting arms of other guards.

Moments later, the boy heard shuffling footsteps and spotted the figure of Corporal Juergen Hoeffel, blond head bent, hands in his pockets, approaching car 10.

"*Psst!*"

Hoeffel looked up, taken by surprise. A worm of blood leaked from a nostril. An expression of despondency was etched on his young face. He had just suffered his second humiliation in as many days.

"Here!" the boy said.

He tossed the diamond ring out of the window. It landed near Hoeffel, who picked it up.

"Wasser," the boy said.

Juergen Hoeffel held up the ring, twirling it in his fingers.

"Wasser," the boy pleaded.

Hoeffel dropped the ring in his breast pocket, gave the boy the finger sign, and walked on.

The boy told Lipshutz what had happened.

"Okay, dreamer, what next?" Lipshutz asked Albright.

Albright had lifted a gold watch from the vest pocket of one of the dead men. He reached out to hand it to Lipshutz and felt someone tugging at his arm. It was a woman with wide, sad eyes

set in an oval face. A poignant El Greco face. She reminded him
of Ruth.

"Here," she said, "take this. It's more valuable. It belonged to
my grandmother."

She dangled a large gold locket, studded with diamonds and
worked by a sapphire clasp.

"Thanks," he said, and gave the locket to Lipshutz.

"Try again," King Kong told the boy.

The boy waited. Half an hour went by. An hour. No sign of any
guards.

"They're all inside their cars," the boy reported. "Sounds like
they're having a party up front. They could go on all night."

Some of the older women were praying for the boy. Their
mashiach. Low, droning voices, heavy sighs.

"Keep your eyes peeled," King Kong said.

The boy felt sleepy. He pinched his cheeks to keep awake. His
eyelids grew heavy. He was nodding off when he heard a noise
drawing near.

It was the blond guard, Juergen Hoeffel, returning with a
friend. The other guard was taller, with the gangling look of a
youth who still had some growing to do. They stood under the
window, looking up at the boy, their mouths hanging open.

The boy swung the locket back and forth, like a talisman used
in hypnotism. Two pairs of eyes followed its arc. Finally, Hoeffel
slung his machine pistol off his shoulder and jerked it at the boy.

"Drop it," he said.

The gold locket fell to the ground and the gangling one
scooped it up. Then the two guards ran off.

"They'll be back," Albright told a disappointed-looking Lipshutz.

They were.

This time there were four of them. A change had come over the
blond guard who led the way. Corporal Hoeffel seemed cocky. A
smirk played on his face.

"Cough it up," Hoeffel told the boy.

Inside, Albright tapped Lipshutz on the shoulder.

"Get the boy down," he said.

"What?" Lipshutz asked.

"Take the kid down from the window," Albright said.

Lipshutz lowered the boy.

"Everybody quiet!" Albright whispered.

The women stopped praying.

From outside, Hoeffel's voice: "Hey, kid, where'd you go?"

From inside: silence.

A stone bounced off the side of the wooden car. Then a barrage of stones. Then banging. Fists. Rifle butts. Then yelling. More banging. Then a long silence.

Then the door was unbolted and slid open.

2

Albright stood alone in the open door.

He felt the cold rush of the night air vacuuming out the fetid odors from the boxcar. The sudden supply of oxygen produced a coughing fit among some of the passengers who were pressed back in a semicircle behind him.

The faces of the guards, gazing up at him from outside, were rigid with adolescent anxiety. There were only three of them. The fourth guard seemed to have fled the scene.

Albright calculated the odds in his favor. Why not make the break now? He, Joel Nathan, and King Kong Lipshutz could easily overpower three scared kids and release the people in car 10. It was a moonless night. They'd have a chance in the dark. But what of the other cars? What of Ruth and the thousands of others? He could never get them all out in time.

He jumped off the train.

The three guards immediately stepped back, machine pistols at their hips.

"I'm the representative of this car," Albright said. "Which one of you is in charge?"

Juergen Hoeffel came forward. He pointed his gun at the middle of Albright's chest.

"We want all your valuables," he said. "Are you going to turn them over?"

It was clear to Albright that Hoeffel was frightened and confused. He had already made two mistakes. He shouldn't have let

Albright get off the car. And he shouldn't be asking; he should be telling.

Albright motioned to the open door and said, "You want to go in there, sonny boy, you go right ahead."

Hoeffel looked up at the solid wall of bodies in the door. His eyes fixed on the menacing form of King Kong Lipshutz.

"Let's get the Dobermans," the gangling one suggested.

"No," Hoeffel said, turning to Albright. "You get them for us."

Mistake number three. He accepted Albright as the go-between.

"We want to make a trade," Albright said.

"Don't let him put one over on you, Juergen," the gangling one said.

"No trades," Hoeffel said.

"All we want is some water," Albright said. "And the chance to clean out the car of our dead and the filth."

"We don't bargain with Jews," Hoeffel said.

Just then, they heard a high-pitched scream coming from the front of the train and saw a woman leap through the shaft of light out of the Einsatzkommando car. She was wearing a long skirt and a white chemise undershirt. Seconds later, she was followed by a guard who ran after her and brought her down with a flying tackle. They rolled over and over on the ground, hissing and cursing, until suddenly they stopped.

"That's the bastard I told you about," Hoeffel said to the gangling guard. "The one they call Willi. He's the guy who decides who can go in his car."

"Forget it, Juergen, will you?"

"I'm not going to forget it," Hoeffel said.

He watched as Willi and the barefooted Slovakian girl got to their feet and returned to the party, laughing as though nothing had happened. When Hoeffel turned back to Albright, his face was puffed with anger.

"Back inside!" he ordered Albright. "I've got some business to attend to. I'll get to you later."

"Oh, for crissakes, Juergen, let him have his fucking water." This from the third guard who had remained silent until now. He was a round-faced boy, slightly cross-eyed, with subcutaneous acne stippling his forehead just below the hairline. "If those bastards up there are getting their birdies licked, why shouldn't we take what we can here?" he said. "What's the difference if you give them a little water?"

"What are you, crazy?" the gangling one said.

"Who you calling crazy?" the boy with the acne shouted back.

The two of them fell into a loud argument and Juergen Hoeffel had to pull them apart.

"I'll make the decisions around here," he said.

He looked toward the front of the train, then at Albright.

"All right," he said, "you can clean out your pig sty and have some water. But we want half the jewelry first. The rest later.

Mistake number four.

3

Standing there in the dark, Juergen Hoeffel was astonished by his own audacity. Dizzy drunk with an unaccustomed sense of power.

All his life—or at least for most of the seventeen years of it that he could remember—he secretly felt that something was wrong with him. Something missing. Something that made him inadequate. He had entered first grade in the year that Hitler came to power and so his mind, if not his heart, was a product of the Third Reich. He was indoctrinated with all the Nazi myths and paranoia. With his perfect blond Aryan looks, he was expected to live up to the model of the Nazi superman. His spirit was willing but his flesh was weak, and things didn't work out that way.

It was to cloak himself in a bravery he never felt that he had joined the *Schutzstaffel*, the black-uniformed SS. But he believed that this only proved he was a bigger fraud. It never occurred to him that many of the other young men who flocked to the SS felt exactly as he did.

He thought of the orgy going on in the lead Einsatzkommando car and wished that Willi, the leader of that bunch, could see him now. Taking charge of a whole car of cowering Jews. Giving orders. Making important decisions. He had the sudden urge to collect an audience for this grand performance.

He sent his tall, gangling friend to the rear Einsatzkommando car for reinforcements, and his friend returned with a small army. Ten new guards. Ten frightened kids. They stared at Alexander Albright as though he was an apparition.

"What's going on?" one of them asked.

It was almost three in the morning. The guards were groggy from interrupted sleep. Their commanding officer was dead, and in the dark the thudding Russian artillery sounded closer than it really was. It was a cold, black night and here was this Jew, wandering like a ghostly specter, *outside* the sealed train.

"Yeah, what the fuck's going on?"

Juergen Hoeffel tried to explain. While he talked, Albright did some fast arithmetic.

From the description of the boy in the train window, Albright figured that Lehndorff's transport unit had suffered heavy casualties when it ran into the Russian scouting party back at Hidasnémeti. It sounded like maybe fifteen men, dead or wounded. That would leave around twenty-five guards capable of active duty out of the original forty.

He could account for thirteen of them. They were standing right here, glowering at him over the barrels of their machine pistols. Nervous boys with nervous eyes and nervous fingers.

But there were at least twelve others. Most or all of *them* were probably up front getting their jollies.

So much for simple arithmetic. The psychology of the situation was a little more complicated. Since the death of Lehndorff, this SS unit appeared to have split roughly in half. Willi's group at the head of the train; Juergen's group in the rear. Why?

Albright thought he knew. If these kids were like soldiers in other armies, they fell into two broad categories. The guards up front with the women were the bully boys—older, tougher, meaner. The ones here were younger, less sure of themselves. *But not necessarily less dangerous.* These kids still had to prove their manhood. If they ran true to form, there was only one thing that mattered to them: to be accepted by Willi into his exclusive club. For that, they might do anything.

So there was no time to lose. The moment had arrived for Albright to try to switch passengers from car to car.

Albright nodded to King Kong, who handed him a pillowcase stuffed with jewelry.

"Here's our deposit," Albright said. "Half now, half later."

Juergen Hoeffel emptied the pillowcase on the ground. He and some of the others examined the contents, poking at it with the barrels of their guns. One of the guards let out a long whistle.

"I think we got ourselves some Rothschilds in there," he said. Hoeffel appeared to be satisfied.

"You can take the bodies off now," he said.

Joel Nathan jumped out of the car.

"Who said he could get off!" Hoeffel yelled. "No one else gets off!"

A few of the guards cocked their weapons.

"Easy, easy," Albright whispered to Nathan.

King Kong kneeled at the door with a corpse in his arms. It was the body of the woman whose finger he had severed. With great gentleness, he slipped the body into Joel Nathan's waiting arms. Joel took her shoulders, Albright her feet, and they carried her to the rear of car 10, over the coupler and around to the other side of the train. A dozen or so yards from the tracks was a clump of bushes. There, Joel put a stone on each of the dead woman's eyes.

Under the nervous gaze of the guards, they went back to their cars and took off one of the dead children.

"Snap it up!" Hoeffel said.

Each body had to be lifted over the coupler connecting cars 10 and 11. As they passed between the two cars, Albright and Joel could hear voices beseeching them for help through the wooden planks of car 11. The lamentation grew louder each time.

On their fifth transit, the voices suddenly fell silent and they heard someone whistling. A sad, dirgelike melody.

Nathan stopped, the shock of recognition on his face. But he didn't say anything until they got to the clump of bushes and were laying the body to rest.

Leaning over Albright, Joel Nathan whispered:

"It's Ruth! Ruth is in that car."

"How do you know?" Albright said, placing the stones on the eyes.

"That tune she's whistling," Nathan said. "It's the Stern Gang's anthem, the one she used to whistle before their radio broadcasts."

"It could be somebody else," Albright said.

"It could be but it's not," Nathan said. "I'm certain. *It's Ruth.*"

4

Ruth Bar-Adon removed her face from the tiny air crack between the wooden planks. The words of the tune she had whistled echoed in her mind. *We serve our cause for the length of our lives.* . . . Had the other prisoners heard her? Who were they? What were they doing outside the train?

Outside.

Strange, but she could no longer clearly imagine the feeling of life on the outside. What must it be like to breathe and move freely? For her, life had become—after how many hours on this train?—totally absorbed in the experience of being *inside*. Trapped in a long, sealed, airless coffin.

Ruth's car was no different from the sixty-nine other cars in the train. Except in three important respects. The bars on the window beneath the ceiling could not be removed, so escape was impossible. The single pail of drinking water that was part of Eichmann's meticulous regulations had somehow not been provided. And car 11 contained one hundred and sixty-eight people, each with approximately one square foot of space to stand in. There was, quite literally, no way to move. Even the dead had to remain upright.

Ruth pulled a bandana over her mouth and nose in a futile effort to keep out the foul stench of one hundred and sixty-eight sweating bodies. The reek of vomit. The stable stink of urine and feces. The sticky-sweet aroma of decomposing flesh. In this hot, suffocating car, just the thought of the putrid odors was enough to make her gag.

They were sealed in a somber twilight. A kind of shadowy inferno of shapeless forms undulating in a jellylike mass. In the gloomy miasma, each face was indistinguishable from the others, each personality soaked up in the blob of them all. Ruth could barely make out the slight, hunched figure squeezed up against her.

She reached out and touched the flesh.

"Frieda?" she said.

"Yes, Aunt Ruth."

Her young prison mate. Once so resilient and defiant. Now, having gone without a drop of water or food for more than two days, Frieda was dying from dehydration.

Frieda, Stephan, and Ruth. The three of them had been reunited in prison after Ruth's stay of execution, sent to a depot, and put aboard the deportation train. On the first day, Stephan died, crushed to death, a rib stabbed through his lung. And now, if there had been enough light, Ruth would have seen that Frieda's face had turned blue. As it was, Ruth could only feel Frieda being shaken by the painful death rattle.

Ruth and Frieda had come to love each other, like mother and daughter. They shared a common bond. Belief in survival. Frieda, the tough prison brat, and Ruth, the visionary, could not even comprehend the idea of surrender. They talked about it during their last few days in prison. Ruth confessed that she felt nothing but contempt for the millions of Jews who failed to resist the Germans and allowed themselves to be led meekly to an ignoble death. She felt an even deeper scorn for those who turned their backs on their fellow Jews and escaped with their lives. The survival of the group, the community, the race was all that mattered.

All this time, until the moment they boarded the train, Ruth had believed that. And believing it, she had tried to respond to the voices of her people calling for salvation. She didn't want Frieda to think of her as a saintly person. The pleasure of life— the *poetry* of life—was too sweet for her to aspire to that. No, she had simply followed her cause with unswerving faith.

There was one thing that she had not told Frieda. For some reason, Ruth did not tell her of the day that she and Alex Albright had visited the desert ruins of Crocodilopolis where the ancient Egyptians had worshiped the dead. "There is no grandeur in death," Ruth remembered telling Albright. "Not anymore. Not in our time. Not since Hitler began *peopling* the world with the dead. I believe in survival."

And now Frieda and everyone else on the train was going to die. Horrified, Ruth realized that she had nothing left to believe in. But how could a person go on living, even for a short while, without faith?

She hugged Frieda, crooning that same mournful melody. As she came to the part about *a service which ends with our breath*, she sensed a disequilibrium among the bodies massed around her, as though the jelly of flesh was reforming itself into a different shape. It was impossible for people to move, and yet she was certain that a new person was standing next to her. She felt his hot breath. Somehow, she knew it was a man.

"Pardon me," he said. "I couldn't help hear this girl call you Ruth. You don't happen to be Ruth Bar-Adon?"

"Yes, I am. How do you know my name?"

"Everyone in the underground has heard of you," he said. "The stories of your resistance in prison reached us outside."

"You were in the underground?" she asked.

"Yes," he said. "In the Vaadah Ezra va Hazalah. My name is Tarnofsky. I knew one of your fellow parachutists. Captain Albright."

Ruth felt herself stiffen. She couldn't speak.

"He tried to save you, you know," Tarnofsky said.

"Did he?"

That was all she could manage to say. For some reason, she couldn't bear to ask anything about Alex Albright. Not even what she wanted to know the most. Whether Alex was alive.

"Who tried to save you, Aunt Ruth?" Frieda asked.

"A man," Ruth said.

"A very special man," Tarnofsky said. "A parachutist who came to Hungary to help us."

Ruth asked Tarnofsky: "Is he . . . alive?"

"Yes," Tarnofsky said. "He escaped a German roundup."

Then a prisoner standing beside her said: "Listen! Over here. Someone is speaking to us."

Ruth put her ear to the tiny air crack in the boards.

"I don't hear anything," she said.

"Wait. Listen."

Then she heard the voice.

"Ruth," it said. "It's me. Alex."

She pressed her lips to the crack and said, "Alex, Alex, Alex . . ."

"Thank God it's you," Alex said. "Listen, throw the jewelry in your car out to the guards."

"Alex," she said again.

She listened.

Was he gone?

"Alex?"

"This girl is dead," she heard someone in car 11 say. And she knew that it was Frieda who was gone.

"Another one dead?" someone else said. "How many is that?"

"Who knows? Who can keep track?"

She stood there, overcome with a rush of conflicting emotions. Frieda dead. Alex alive. Stephan dead. She herself alive. Who knew how many dead? Who knew how many still alive? Who knew how many were living dead—uprooted from their homes, herded into ghettos, abandoned by neighbors, starved, marched off at gunpoint to relocation depots, disinherited, beaten, told lies of farms they were being sent to in Poland, of factories where they would work in Germany, of a new life, of hope, of a last chance, an only chance.

Who knew the answers?

Not she.

She suddenly could no longer feel contempt for the millions who had gone meekly to their deaths. Or even for those who had tried to save their own lives. Who was she to judge?

Who, after all, was she?

She was Ruth Bar-Adon. She remembered her first meeting with Guido DeVita, Mossad's chief recruiter, a psychoanalyst who wanted to know everything about her. There wasn't much to know. She had told him: "Those of us whom you choose to send back into the flames of the Holocaust will be messengers of hope."

That was all. That was enough.

5

Two buckets of water were waiting for them when Albright and Nathan got back to their car.

"We can't clean it out with all these people inside," Albright said to Juergen Hoeffel. "We've got to make some room. You've got to let some people off."

Hoeffel stared stonily at Albright.

"Hell," Albright said, "you've got all the hardware. A few Jews aren't going to bite you."

"Five," Hoeffel said, holding up the fingers of a hand. "Five people can get off."

Albright jumped back inside the car to make the selection.

"This is it," he said. "We're going to make the switch. You all know what to do."

He turned to the woman with the wide, sad eyes and the El Greco face. He bent over, whispered something into her ear and then tied the bright orange-red scarf around her neck.

"Good luck," he said.

She jumped off the car.

Next, another young woman. Also dark-haired, oval-faced with chalky-white complexion. He said a few words to her while he fastened her hair in the dark babushka.

Then a middle-aged man. He got the broad-brimmed light gray fedora along with Albright's instructions.

King Kong Lipshutz leapt off next. A looming, bareheaded, apelike figure that immediately captured the guards' awed attention.

And finally the boy.

Albright joined the group in front of the car.

Seven were now outside the train.

The buckets of water were handed up.

And then they heard what sounded like raindrops—*plink, plink, plink*—hitting the ground.

"Look at this," one of the guards called to Hoeffel. "A ring."

Pieces of jewelry came flying out of the skylight of car 11. Ruth's car. Rings, broaches, earrings, watches, necklaces, bracelets, tie clasps, cigarette cases . . . A shower of gold and silver and precious gems.

Guards scrambled on the ground like beggars.

And still more treasure fell to the ground. Silverware, Stars of David, jade cufflinks, gold cigar cutters, money clips, candlesticks . . .

"Wait!" Hoeffel called to the men, who were scattering to retrieve the valuables. "This has to be done"—he paused, looked around, searching for words—"with *discipline*."

That seemed to impress them.

"We can't act like a bunch of stupid kids," he said to his two friends, the tall, gangly one and the round-faced boy with a fore-head full of acne. "There's seventy cars on this train. That's a lot of loot. Let's talk this over."

The three of them walked away from the others and huddled in the darkness.

"All right, I'll do it," Albright heard Hoeffel say after a few minutes.

"Good," the gangling one said. "I can't wait to see their faces. You'll show the bastards."

"You want me to come with you?" the round-faced one asked.

"No," Hoeffel said. "You two keep an eye on the Jews. I'll han-dle this myself."

Then he turned and began walking slowly toward the head of the train and the shaft of light coming from the bully boys' Ein-satzkommando car. Corporal Juergen Hoeffel was going to redeem himself and join Willi's exclusive club.

6

It was a long wait in the bitter cold.

The boy's teeth began to chatter and King Kong Lipshutz put a tattooed arm around his shoulder. The woman with the orange-red scarf and the one in the babushka stamped on the hard ground to keep their blood circulating. The middle-aged man in the fedora hugged himself, his hands tucked beneath his armpits. Joel Nathan stood stock-still, his ruined face betraying no emo-tion.

And Albright kept watch.

A faint pinkish light appeared in the east. It was hard to say whether it was the Russian artillery or the first glow of the morn-ing sun. Too early for sunrise at this time of the year, Albright de-cided. It must be the Russians. On the move again.

Behind him in the open door of car 10, the passengers were ex-haling puffs of frosty condensation. In front of them, the guards were smoking, slapping the sides of their arms and passing the time. Stopping when they saw a flash of artillery.

"With lightning," one of the guards said, "you can tell how far away it is by counting the seconds. One-one thousand, two-one thousand, three-one thousand. Each second is a mile."

"That doesn't work with artillery," another said.

"How do you know?"

"I know. My father told me. He was in the last war."

"Things have changed," the first one said.

"Yeah, the Russians haven't surrendered in this war," said the other.

Albright looked over at Ruth's car. Number 11. It was quiet. No voices of lamentation. No whistling. But now, even as the rumbling artillery grew louder, a stir could be heard coming from the car in front, number 9. A hand appeared at its window, holding a gold pocket watch. For some reason the hand wouldn't let go.

More artillery. A staccato thud echoing off the mountainside. It sounded as though the Russians had launched a major offensive about fifteen miles away. They were probably that close.

Suddenly, the fingers of the hand in car 9's window opened and the gold watch dropped. As soon as it hit the ground, objects came catapulting from other cars—8 and 12, 7 and 13, 6 and 14. . . . Soon, the ground in front of the train was strewn with a path of gold and precious gems.

Then a chorus of voices reverberated along the entire length of the train. All seven thousand condemned people were aware of what was happening. A contagion of hope and fear spread throughout the seventy cars. The prisoners were finally communicating with each other. Contact had at last been made!

And at that same moment, one of the guards yelled: "Here comes Juergen!"

"Who's he with?"

"It looks like Willi."

It was Willi. Pug-nosed, crew cut, high shiny cheek bones. A genuinely wicked-looking pig-faced young man. He walked splay-footed. A huge pigeon-breasted torso, short stubby legs. His uniform was wrinkled and stained. He was unarmed.

He was talking with Corporal Juergen Hoeffel as though there had never been any trouble between them, as though they had always been the best of friends. Laughing. Slapping him on the back. Enjoying the surprised looks from the other guards.

Willi stopped in front of the line of prisoners, put his hands on his hips, reared back his head, and spit extravagantly on the ground. The gesture of contempt silenced the passengers inside the train.

"Watch this," he said to Hoeffel.

He pointed to Albright and motioned for him to step forward.

"I want to talk to you," Willi said.

He had a velvety voice and he aspirated heavily as he pronounced each word.

"You hear those Russian guns?" he said. "Pretty close, huh? So close you're probably thinking to yourself, boy, if only those Red Amazons everybody's heard about—you know, those six-foot-tall Russian women soldiers—if only they'd get here in time and cut off these Germans' balls."

Willi smiled. He hadn't brushed his teeth in a long time.

"You know about those big Russian women, don't you?" he said. "Amazon shock troops. Carry special knives just to lop off German *shlangs*."

"Can't say I do," Albright said.

"That right?" Willi said.

He turned to Juergen Hoeffel.

"This one says he's never heard of those big Russian babes," Willi said.

"Everybody's heard of them," Hoeffel said. "Maybe he's lying."

"Juergen thinks you're lying," Willi said. "Me, I don't think you'd try to pull a fast one like that. So, who's right? Juergen or me? You say Juergen, I'll beat the shit out of you. You say me, Juergen'll work you over. Which way you want it?"

Albright couldn't believe this was happening. He felt as though he were caught in a time warp, transported back to a junior high school playground, facing a classic no-win bully's game. Is this what the thousand-year Third Reich was all about? Not Lehndorff's ideal of military duty. Not Hoeffel's perverted lessons in racial purity. Just this. A weak, worthless punk named Willi?

"You're both right," Albright said. "I've heard talk about Russian Amazons, but I never believed it."

It was as if he had poked Willi in the solar plexus. His mouth fell open. He tried to recover with a smile of contempt. But it wasn't convincing. He was thrown off balance.

"No more fun and games," he said. "Me and Juergen have been talking things over. Like pals. Share and share alike is what we decided. We want all the valuables on this train. No trades, no bullshit. We start at the front and work our way back. Nice and orderly. Two or three cars at a time. My boys and Juergen's boys working together. Right, Juergen?"

"Right, Willi," Juergen said.

"We're going to keep an eye on you while you clean out the train for us," Willi continued. "You and your friends here. In and out of each car real quick. You take up a collection. Like in church. Which you Jews wouldn't know about. But you got the drift of my meaning."

"I got it," Albright said.

Willi turned to Juergen again.

"Okay," he said, "the Jewboy here's got the message. Let's get organized!"

Willi went back to the front of the train and barked out an order. His men spilled out of the Einsatzkommando car in various states of dress, followed by half a dozen women. In the dark, Albright was able to count eleven guards, one fewer than he had guessed. With Juergen's group, that made a total of twenty-four.

Now Albright knew the exact odds: seven thousand to twenty-four. He was beginning to feel encouraged.

The guards were ordered by Willi to spread out in a single line in front of the first three cars. Then Willi unbolted the doors and slid them open. He clamped his fingers on his pug nose.

"*Phew!* It's like a sewer in there. Jews really stink."

A few nervous giggles from the guards.

"All right," Willi said to Albright, "you wait outside. I want to keep my eye on you. The others go in, two at a time. I pick who goes."

As he spoke, Willi's pigeon-breasted torso heaved up and down, as though it was an effort for him to catch his breath, and his words were expelled in syncopated puffs.

For a moment, no one moved. Not the guards. Not the people huddled in the open cars. Not the seven prisoners outside. Then, splay-footed, stubby-legged, Willi strode forward and began making the selections. King Kong Lipshutz and the woman with the babushka were sent into car 1. The boy and the middle-aged man in the fedora into car 2. Joel Nathan and the woman with the orange-red scarf into car 3.

Sputtering artillery lit up the sky.

"We don't have much time," Juergen said to Willi.

"Yeah," Willi said. "Go tell the engineer to start steaming."

A few minutes later, they could hear the rhythmic hissing from the engine cylinders.

Moments after that, the prisoners began emerging from the boxcars carrying sacks and suitcases bulging with jewelry.

King Kong, the boy, and Joel Nathan.

And three others.

Three different people wearing the babushka, the scarf, and the fedora.

The kettledrums of artillery boomed in the dark, sending a fluttery quaver down the line of guards. The locomotive's steam whistle shrieked impatiently. The jewelry sluiced out of the sacks and suitcases onto the ground. Willi let out a yelp.

He rushed forward, a crazed gleam in his eyes.

"You see," he yelled, spreading his arms over the piles of jewelry. "Look at this stuff. A fucking king's ransom. It works. My plan works!"

The guards broke rank, gathering in a large circle around Willi, who danced a stubby-legged jig in front of the piles of golden jewelry.

In all the noise and commotion and fear and triumph, no one noticed that three different people had come out of the cars.

The exchange had worked.

CHAPTER FIVE

THE TRAIN
Sunday, November 26

1

In the cab of the locomotive, the engineer and Mr. Know-It-All were arguing. They had never really stopped. But after four days, their bickering had turned savage.

"Blow the glass clean," the engineer ordered.

"Blow it yourself," Mr. Know-It-All said.

"It's the fireman's job to blow the glass," the engineer said.

"Who says?"

"I say," the engineer shot back. "I'm in charge here and if that water-level gauge limes up, you're in big trouble."

"*I'm* in trouble!" the fireman said. "For somebody who doesn't know the difference between a Hammel and a Gölsdorf, you should talk."

The engineer grabbed a wrench and brandished it at the fireman.

"You stupid sonofabitch!" he screamed. "If you don't keep that gauge clean, the water level could fall and we'd melt the fucking crown sheet. The whole damn boiler will go up."

"Serve you right, asshole," the fireman said.

The engineer moved toward him with the menacing wrench.

"All right, all right," the fireman said.

He moved over to the glass meter, which indicated whether the steam-operated water injectors were maintaining the proper level of water in the boiler. He immediately saw there was a problem. The hard water they had taken on at Muszynia had deposited a brown scum inside the glass. Limed up like that, it was impossible to get an accurate reading on the water level.

He looked up at the engineer, who had put away the wrench and was peering out of the cab down the tracks.

The fireman turned his back and fiddled with the gauge. *Pretending* that he was blowing the injector pipes clean of the lime. He mumbled under his breath, "Serve the asshole right."

2

In the forward Einsatzkommando car, the radio operator slipped off his earphones and glanced up at Willi.

"HQ at Tarnow says incoming artillery has reached as far as co-ordinates 3P-64 and 3P-65," he said.

Willi consulted the map on the table.

Leaning over his shoulder, Juergen Hoeffel watched as Willi's stubby finger stopped at a place on the map only nine miles from the rail line.

"We'll never make it through," Hoeffel said.

"We'll make it," Willi said. "The Russians aren't that close all along the line. Just here. All we have to do is get past this stretch of track"—he tapped the map with his finger—"and we're home free."

"Either way it's a losing proposition," Hoeffel said.

"What's that supposed to mean?" Willi asked.

"Either the Russians get us," Hoeffel said, "or we're going to land right in the soup when we get to Tarnow. We can get court-martialed for opening the doors to the train and taking all that stuff."

"They'll never find out what we did," Willi said. "We only opened six cars."

"I wouldn't be so cocky," Hoeffel said.

"Listen, we agreed that six cars wouldn't make them suspicious," Willi said.

"Yeah, but they happened to be the *first* six cars," Hoeffel said. "That's where they're going to look first."

"This is a hell of a time for you to think of that," Willi said. "Why didn't you tell me all this back at Košice?"

"I didn't think of it then," Hoeffel said.

"*You didn't think!*" Willi said.

He grabbed Hoeffel by the front of his tunic and shoved him back against the edge of the table.

"You're a fucking idiot!" he said. "I knew I shouldn't have gotten mixed up with the likes of you."

"Wait a minute," Hoeffel said. "Calm down. Maybe we can pull over on a sidetrack and put the first six cars at the end. I once saw a movie where they split up a train like that."

Willi released his grip on Hoeffel's tunic and sat down. He ran a hand back and forth over his high, shiny cheek, as though he was rubbing a bruise.

"Nah," he said. "That won't work. It's too complicated."

"Incoming on 3P-65 and 3P-66," the radio operator said.

"Shut up!" Willi told him. "I'm not scared of the Russians and I'm not scared of our officers. Nobody pushes me around. Let them find out. Who cares? Back home, I got out of worse fixes than this."

They felt the train slowing, then switching over to another track and screeching to a halt.

"Another military convoy's coming down the track," the radio operator said. "Our guys must really be getting chewed up at the front."

"Quiet!" Willi said. "I'm thinking of how we're going to cover our asses."

3

The train stopped again. A cone of light shone through the small window in car 10 onto the disfigured face of Joel Nathan.

"What time is it?" he asked.

"I don't know," Alex Albright said. "We gave away all our watches at Košice."

"Košice," Nathan said, his voice thick with bitterness. "That was a laugh."

Košice and the scorched earth of Slovakia were now far behind them. The train passed through the mountain stations at Presov and Plavec and crossed the border into the broad, flat wheatlands of Poland. It stopped for coal and water at Muszynia. It had been shunted aside a dozen or more times to let priority military traffic rush by. It never shook off the pursuing hounds of the Russian guns.

And not once in all this time had any of the doors of the train been opened. Nine more people died in car 10. Many of the others were turning blue from dehydration.

"Look at it this way," King Kong Lipshutz said. "At least we made the switch in six cars at Košice. That's something to be grateful for."

"Six cars isn't thirty-two cars," Joel Nathan said. "What happened to the big plan? Two, four, eight, sixteen, thirty-two you were talking about."

Just then, the train gave an abrupt jolt, throwing everyone off balance.

"It looks like we're moving again," the boy called down from the window.

"I still don't get it," Albright said, as the train slowly began to grind forward. "Why did they stop at six? They could have cleaned out the whole train by now."

"Cold feet?" King Kong offered.

"Not that guard Willi," Albright said.

"Well," Nathan said, "we should know the answer soon. The station at Tarnow can't be too far from here. That's where the special company of Auschwitz guards takes over, right?"

"That's right," Albright said.

"And General Donovan lifts up his staff and parts the Red Sea and delivers the children of Israel from bondage," Nathan said.

Albright and Nathan stared coldly at each other.

"I'm sorry," Nathan said after a moment.

"It's okay," Albright said. "I know how you feel."

They embraced.

"Hey, someone's jumping off the train," the boy said.

They waited for the sound of the machine guns.

"There's another one," the boy said. "And *another*."

"Why don't they shoot?" King Kong asked.

"Because they're not ours," the boy said. "They're Germans. The guards are abandoning the train."

4

"When it comes to emotions, every man is a millionaire," a parole officer once counseled Werner Moll. But like a lot of advice given to the young, it wasn't until years later, when SS Captain Moll arrived at Auschwitz, that he understood what the parole officer meant.

Moll loved Auschwitz! He loved it so passionately and so persistently that it penetrated even his dull, brutish nature. He became fervently attached to everything about the extermination camp.

The well-tended lawns and flower beds. The fresh linen, pressed and neatly tucked every morning under the thick mattress of his bed. The good food—pickled duck's liver, chicken, roast pork, potatoes, red cabbage, stuffed tomatoes, delicious vanilla ice cream. The soap flakes. The hand-tailored uniforms. The generous rations of Schnapps and cigarettes. The inexhaustible supply of female flesh from the Birkenau women's camp. The gay tunes of the camp orchestra, eighty musicians in perfect harmony playing selections from "The Merry Widow" and "Tales of Hoffmann." That special bond of comradeship among men and officers, forged by the knowledge of their secret work. The pride of belonging to the hardest of the hard core.

Such was the pull of Auschwitz on Werner Moll that he hated leaving it even for a few hours. He always felt a pang of melancholy as he drove through the camp gates and left the towering chimneys and that indescribable smell that pervaded the air. Though his IQ measured in the low nineties, though his conscience was untouched by the brutal whippings, the public hangings, and the *Sonderaktions* that gassed two thousand people at a time, Moll's emotions were able to register the pangs of separation anxiety. He wasn't the type to examine his feelings. But after spending most of his violent life as a convict in many of Germany's maximum-security prisons, he knew he belonged as a gaoler at Auschwitz. He belonged to Auschwitz.

So it was that today, as he led a motorized convoy down the winding highway from Auschwitz, SS Captain Werner Moll felt more than just a sense of transitory melancholy. Ahead was the station at Tarnow, a huge switchyard abuzz with rolling stock being marshaled through a vast delta of tracks, where the deportation trains arrived daily with Adolf Eichmann's "sausages" from Budapest. Behind him was the "meat grinder," the greatest killing factory ever conceived by the mind of man. And in his pocket was an order from Heinrich Himmler, the head of the SS, the satanic genius who selected men like Moll and found them the perfect home.

Himmler's order had arrived this morning for the commandant at Auschwitz, and Werner Moll had been given a carbon copy, which he was carrying in the pocket of his great coat. His staff car bumped over a set of tracks and entered the station. As it headed for a remote corner of the yard, well out of sight of the main terminal, Moll unfolded the piece of paper and read it once again.

"Surrender is out of the question. The camp is to be evacuated immediately. No prisoner must fall into the hands of the enemy alive."

There it was in black and white. The commandant at Auschwitz, Josef Kramer, who had replaced Rudolf Höss, had confirmed the message with Berlin.

Himmler had ordered the destruction of Auschwitz.

This was the last trip that SS Captain Werner Moll would make to Tarnow. The last train he would ever meet.

He got out of the car, his radioman scurrying after him, and saluted the guard at the barbed-wire enclosure. He entered the platform and looked down the glittering stretch of track in search of the train. He heard his men taking up their positions down the long platform, the nails of the attack dogs tapping on the pavement.

He was reminded of a winter day from his childhood. He had come home on leave from a particularly brutal reform school and heard the voice of his father and the bark of their dog in the back yard. It was really young Werner's dog; he had found it in a woods on the outskirts of Waldbroel, and it was perhaps the only living thing that had ever shown him any affection. While he was away at reform school, the dog had bitten the postman, and when the dog was tested for rabies it was found to be infected. Werner, of course, knew none of this, and as he came around the side of the house under the trellis of withered grape vines, he saw that his father had trussed and tied the dog to a tree. His father had an ax in his hand. Werner rushed down the stone steps, shouting for him to stop. His father brought the flat end of the ax down on the dog's head. Werner had grabbed the bloody ax and tried to kill his father. . . .

The locomotive came into sight and hissed along the platform. SS Captain Werner Moll did not notice the faces of the Jews sticking out of the windows of the boxcars. He did not even notice the absence of the sentries behind the machine guns on the roof of the long transport. He forgot all about the message that had arrived two days ago informing Auschwitz that Untersturm-führer Christian Lehndorff, the commander of the transport unit, had been killed in action during a Russian ambush at Hidasnémeti. It did not strike him as strange that the boiler of the locomotive was enveloped in a mist of steam, or that the fireman jumped from the cab before the train came completely to a halt, or that none of the guards were visible in the open door of the forward Einsatzkommando car. He did not see any signs of trouble because he was not expecting any trouble from this last trainload of Jews. The relief of the guard at Tarnow station, as with everything connected to the smooth operation at Auschwitz, was strictly a routine matter.

And so, as the train pulled in, SS Captain Werner Moll was lost in a swirling fog of emotions that had been stirred up by Himmler's order to destroy every last trace of Auschwitz. The memory of his father bashing in the skull of his dog flashed through his mind, and he was seized by that same murderous impulse that had made him try to kill his father.

What if his dog had had rabies? What if Auschwitz was discovered by the enemy?

Was this any reason to betray him? To take away his home, his refuge, his sanctuary?

5

The train stopped.

"Tarnow," the boy at the window said.

"How many men do they have on the platform?" Albright asked.

"Lots. Sixty, maybe seventy. And dogs. And machine guns."

"Any sign of the airplanes?"

"Not yet."

"You sure?"

"I can't see anything but a flock of buzzards."

"Look again. The planes have got to be there."

"I'm looking, but I don't see any planes. . . . Wait!"

"What is it?"

"They're opening the doors."

From the front of the train, Albright could hear the sounds of the bolts being drawn. Shouted orders. Dogs snarling. Shrill screams. "Throw out your dead! Throw out your dead!"

The boy looked down expectantly at Albright.

"Now?" he asked. "Should I give the signal now?"

Albright felt the sweat dripping from his armpits and coursing down the sides of his chest. The anxiety triggered a memory of his meeting last spring in Shepheard's Hotel with Donovan when they first discussed the parachute mission. "It'll be your show," Donovan had said. "You'll be able to call the shots from start to finish. All the shots. You'll have complete control."

Complete control!

Albright had never felt *less* in control in his whole life. He also never felt more involved. Now, the boy was waiting for an answer. King Kong and Joel Nathan and the prisoners in car 10 were waiting. Hundreds of people who were part of the escape plan were waiting.

And Ruth was waiting.

He had learned that with Ruth he could not have a fleeting, impermanent, don't-count-on-it-forever kind of thing. With Ruth, he could have neither control nor detachment. He felt bound to her but, at the same time, wonderfully free. Love like this wasn't a burden. It was a liberation.

He looked up at the boy.

"Now," he said.

It was the first time Albright had seen the boy smile. And he realized he didn't know the boy's name or where he came from or who his parents were or what he wanted to be when he grew up. And that now it was too late to ask.

The boy stuck his arm out of the window as far as he could reach. He felt the cold November air on his skin. He opened his fist, and dropped a crumpled piece of paper. It sailed to the platform. Then he pulled in his arm and peered up the line of the train.

More than seventy yards away, the lookout in car 6 saw the speck of white bounce off the platform onto the tracks. He immediately dropped his crumpled ball of paper. Cars 5, 4, and 3 followed suit.

The hand in the window of car 2 withdrew without dropping the paper.

In car 1, the door flew open and the prisoners were handing over their dead to Jewish *Kapos* in striped pajamas. Out of sight of the Kapos, in the shadows beneath the window, stood a young woman. The one who had worn the dark babushka during the switch of prisoners at Košice. Her chalky-white complexion was flushed with anger.

"Why didn't you drop it?" she said to the teenaged boy in the window. "They're counting on us. Don't you understand?"

The boy's eyes were full of fright as he looked down at a man standing next to the angry woman.

"What should I do, Father?" he asked. "Car 2 didn't do it."

"You know what I think," his father said. "This woman wants us to risk the lives of everyone in this car. I want this to be a good car. I want us to maintain our reputation as a cooperative, reasonable people. After all, we're Jews in here, aren't we?"

"You mustn't listen to your father," the woman said. "I've explained what will happen to us at Auschwitz if we don't escape."

The boy looked from his father to the woman.

"I don't know what to do," he said. "Why should it be left up to me to decide?"

By now, the doors of the first eight cars were open and the platform was teeming with Kapos hauling away the stiff, bloated corpses in wheelbarrows. The removal of the dead here at Tarnow was another Eichmann innovation; it expedited the unloading of the living at Auschwitz. The corpses were thrown onto the wheelbarrows like cordwood and piled high. One of the overloaded wheelbarrows tipped over in front of SS Captain Werner Moll, and the offending Kapo cringed in anticipation of a lashing from Moll's whip.

But Moll did not seem to notice the accident. He was cast into such despondency at the thought of leaving his beloved Auschwitz that he failed even to hear the lieutenant who had approached him.

"Captain."

"What is it?" Moll replied at last.

"We can't seem to find any of the transport guard," the lieutenant said. "There's no one in the Einsatzkommando car."

"Oh," Moll said vaguely. "I forgot to tell you. They ran into an ambush down the line. They're probably all in the rear of the train."

"But, Captain . . ."

"Don't bother me!" Moll said sharply. "Go look for them in the rear."

"Yes, Captain."

The lieutenant made his way down the crowded platform, passing car 10. The boy in the window spotted him going by.

Inside, Albright said to the boy: "You must be blind. Those planes have got to be there."

He felt a hand on his shoulder. It was Joel Nathan.

"Donovan isn't coming," Joel said. "We're on our own."

Albright searched Joel's face.

"You're not really surprised, are you?" Joel said.

"No," Albright said. "But listen, Joel, there's something I want to tell you."

"There isn't time," Joel said.

"I've got to tell you," Albright insisted. "That night on the hill when we tried to assassinate Eichmann. Well, that wasn't part of our mission. I had specific instructions from the head of the underground not to go after Eichmann. It was my decision to go ahead. Gur and Patir are my responsibility."

"You did what you thought was right," Joel said.

"I never had a chance to tell Ruth," Albright said.

"She'd understand," Joel said.

"I hope so," Albright said. "I've been thinking about it. It's like a thing, a great distance, between us."

"Soon, you'll be telling her all about it," Joel said. "Just remember, she's in the next car."

In car 11, Tarnofsky, the youthful leader of the Vaadah Ezra va Hazalah, was struggling with the bodies. By carefully arranging them piggyback three abreast in front of the door, he had created a potential avalanche once the door was opened. In the suffocating heat, sweat streamed down his face as he lifted the last body. Ruth Bar-Adon. He placed her on the back of a dead man and threw her arms over the corpse's shoulders.

"There," he said, "it's done. An army of the dead."

There was no reply from Ruth.

Tarnofsky wiped his face with a sleeve and heard a Kapo shouting, "Throw out your dead!"

The door of car 10 rolled open on its rusty casters. A Kapo stuck his head into the car. He was a gaunt young man with olive-gray complexion and dark rings around his eyes.

"Throw out your dead," he said. "If you don't, they'll use the dogs."

Albright looked up at the boy one last time.

The boy shook his head slowly.

"Without Donovan's paratroops, we don't have much of a chance," Albright said to Joel.

"We *never* had much of a chance," Joel said. "Not from that first day you walked into the parachute rigging hall at Jubilee and gave us that phony speech in Hebrew."

"It was a pretty good speech," Albright said.

"It was a *great* speech," Joel said.

Albright's face broke into a smile.

"You know something?" he said. "You're right!"

He glanced over at King Kong Lipshutz, who stood in front of the open door waiting for the prearranged signal. Albright drew his finger across his neck and King Kong flashed him his best lopsided smile.

The escape was about to begin.

"We ain't got no dead bodies in here," King Kong told the Kapo.

Albright found himself mouthing King Kong's words like a prompter at a performance. Everything had been rehearsed. They had tried to anticipate exactly what might happen in the next few minutes, even though they knew that was impossible. What was it that Dan Gur used to say during the field-craft exercises at Jubilee? "It's only when you don't know exactly what to expect that you're in trouble." Albright wished that Gur were here to help. And he wished for something else. That the Kapo would respond to King Kong as they had anticipated by calling for the dogs.

"Have it your way," the Kapo said, looking up at King Kong from his raccoon eyes. "But don't say I didn't warn you."

He turned and shouted. "Dogs! Dogs in car 10!"

The bodies inside the car parted, making a path for Albright and Joel Nathan so they could join King Kong in the doorway. They watched as two guards approached with their growling attack dogs.

Albright searched the platform for the commanding officer of the Auschwitz unit. He spotted him. An SS captain. As expected, the captain was trailed closely by a noncommissioned officer carrying a mobile radio unit. Albright nudged Joel Nathan and motioned to the captain and his radioman.

"I see them," Joel said.

But something struck Albright as strange.

SS Captain Werner Moll appeared to be wandering on the platform in a fog, lost in his thoughts. He wasn't paying attention to the operation. His indifference to this life-and-death moment worried Albright. It could be a sign that he knew all about the troubles on the train—Lehndorff's death at Hidasnémeti and the mutinous guards and perhaps even the escape plan—and that he felt supremely confident he could handle any difficulty. Then, again, the captain's lack of concern could be a sign that he didn't expect any problems. A sign that Albright's escape plan had at least one thing going for it. The element of complete surprise.

The dogs bared their teeth as they drew near.

Joel Nathan put his hand behind his back and a prisoner handed him an unlit Molotov cocktail.

Albright and King Kong each had a makeshift pair of brass knuckles tied around their fists.

"*Mazel*," King Kong said.

He had barely gotten the word out when the dogs were unleashed and sprang into the car and Albright and King Kong vaulted over them and hurled themselves at the guards.

Inside the car, prisoners pounced on the dogs.

Joel Nathan spun around, held out the Molotov cocktail and other prisoners lighted the wick. Joel jumped out of the train and landed running and heard the stifled cries of the guards and the gurgling sounds of the dogs being strangled to death with the shoelaces.

At that same instant, the door of Ruth Bar-Adon's car was flung open by another Kapo and the dead tumbled out like felled trees. Ten, twenty, thirty . . . It was hard to count. In all his months at Auschwitz, the Kapo had never seen a single boxcar produce so many corpses. He was momentarily staggered by the enormous task of carting away all this human wreckage.

Sighing wearily, the Kapo looked down at the inert shape of a woman lying on the heap of bodies. She had a bandana tied around the bottom half of her face and her open, almond-shaped eyes stared glassily into space. He bent to pick her up and suddenly felt one of her hands grasp him about the throat and saw the other hand, blurred in his peripheral vision, flashing the sharp point of a pencil.

Seconds later, Ruth Bar-Adon released the dead Kapo and scrambled to her feet.

"Go for their weapons!" she shouted.

And the heap of bodies came to life. In the inferno of car 11, Ruth had organized her own escape.

As she rushed forward toward the line of Germans, Ruth heard her name being called. At first, she thought it was Tarnofsky or one of the other prisoners from her car. She looked over her shoulder and saw a man coming toward her, *holding a machine pistol*.

It took her a moment to realize that the man was not about to kill her.

It was Alex Albright.

"Here!" he shouted, and he tossed the weapon to her.

"Alex!" she said.

"I didn't leave you," Albright said. "I'll never leave you."

"I believe you," she said.

Behind Albright, Ruth saw prisoners pouring out of car 10, hurling smoke bombs at the Germans, then peeling off in opposite directions.

She heard gunfire.

Prisoners began falling.

She curled her finger around the trigger, turned toward the German guns, and began firing her weapon.

Joel Nathan heard the sound of the guns at his back as he raced up the platform. He expected the noise to come from the front of the train. They had smuggled the other Molotov cocktail into car 1 with the woman in the babushka and, according to the plan, the breakout was supposed to begin with a diversionary explosion from there.

Supposed to. But now things weren't going as expected.

Joel caught sight of the commanding officer, SS Captain Werner Moll, leaning against the fence, one hand supporting his elbow and the other resting on his chin. Moll was looking down the platform, a bemused expression on his face. His radioman stood next to him, on tiptoes, trying to follow the direction of Moll's glance.

The sound of the gunfire, the smoke, the confusion had all captured their attention, and they didn't see Joel as he loped like a broken-field runner around the Kapos with their wheelbarrows of corpses. By now, Joel had reached as far as car 6. He fell to his knee, drew back his arm and lobbed the Molotov cocktail toward Moll and his radioman.

Just then, Moll noticed Joel Nathan and, with that same dull expression on his face, watched as the flaming bottle arced toward him. The bottle fell directly in front of Moll and smashed on the platform. But there was no explosion.

It was a dud.

Slowly, Moll removed his hand from under his elbow and pointed at Joel Nathan.

"Shoot him!" he ordered.

All at once there was a tremendous blast at the front of the train and the men around Moll turned toward car 1. Prisoners began spilling out of the train—except for car 2—and smoke bombs sailed through the air. The Germans opened up with their machine guns, raking the escaping prisoners.

Bodies were falling all around. At first, they were mostly Kapos and their corpses, but then there were prisoners, piling up in mounds of squirming flesh. Bullets tore into the dying bodies, jerking them in a kind of convulsive St. Vitus' Dance. Joel Nathan took cover behind the growing wall of the dead.

Through the smoke, Joel could see SS Captain Werner Moll barking out orders to his radioman.

"Prisoners escaping! Prisoners escaping!" the radioman shouted into his transmitter. "Send help!"

Joel was up again, rushing straight for Moll. He slammed into his hip, sending Moll sprawling onto the ground. Then he yanked the transmitter out of the radioman's hand, bent his wrist backward and snapped the joint of his elbow over a shoulder. The radioman collapsed beside Moll. Joel drew back his leg, kicked Moll in the fleshy depression of the temple. Drew back his leg again, aimed another kick, killing the second German.

He grabbed their pistols from their holsters, fell flat on the platform and began firing.

Now, hundreds of prisoners were pouring out of the cars, screaming at the top of their lungs, sending up a howling ululation, women and children and men, slashing away with their crude homemade weapons at the guards and the dogs. The guards fired point blank into the tidal wave of humanity, but the prisoners kept coming, overwhelming the outnumbered Germans.

The doors of cars 12, 13, 14 were flung open and more prisoners flooded the platform. They were without any weapons, but they tore at the guards savagely with their bare hands, gouging eyes, biting ears, stomping on the Germans as they pressed the attack.

In the hand-to-hand struggle, prisoners and guards slipped in the spreading pools of dark blood. A mixture of blood. German and Jewish blood.

Joel kept firing until he realized that both his revolvers were empty. He tossed them away and crawled over to the body of a dead German. He pried a machine pistol from the dead man's hand and, hunched over, began making his way down the plat-

form through the smoky melee. Suddenly, he felt something sharp
sink painfully into his neck. It was one of the attack dogs. He
tried to twist free, battering at the dog with the butt of his rifle,
but the animal clung tenaciously, tearing at his flesh. Then he
heard the dog give a piercing yelp. And as Joel pivoted around he
saw King Kong Lipshutz with his hand around the dog's throat,
squeezing a nerve that released the vise of his jaw.

"Used to work for a veterinarian," King Kong said. "Everything
you know comes in handy."

"Where's Albright?" Joel asked.

"Over . . ."

King Kong never had a chance to finish the sentence.

He staggered backward, arms flailing for balance, and tipped
over into an empty wheelbarrow. Lying on his back, his chest
heaving, he looked up at Joel, and his coarse face formed a lopsided smile. Then from deep in his chest he emitted a guttural
noise that sounded like a grunt of satisfaction. And he was dead.

Joel glanced around in panic, looking for the source of the
enemy fire that had struck down King Kong. And then he saw
them. German machine gunners all along the roof of the train.
Strafing the platform. Mowing down the prisoners in droves.

Where had they come from?

The lieutenant whom Moll had sent to the rear of the train had
found the remnants of the transport guard cowering inside the
shuttered Einsatzkommando car. Seven of them, including the
gangling youth and the one with the stipples of acne on his forehead, had remained on the train after the others jumped. The
lieutenant ordered them out of the car and around to the other
side of the train. There, at gunpoint, he offered them the choice
of either facing summary execution or climbing up onto the roof
and manning the machine guns.

Alex Albright and Ruth Bar-Adon were working their way along
the cars, unbolting doors, freeing prisoners, rallying them to attack when they heard the brassy rattle of the machine guns.

"The roof!" Albright shouted, and he threw his arms around
Ruth and pressed her against the side of the train, out of range.

They watched in horror as rows of prisoners collapsed under the
withering fire from above. The thousands of people swarming over
the platform broke into a wild stampede.

"We've got to stop those guns," Ruth said.

Albright's mind was racing.

"We can't take them from this side of the train," he said. "We'll take them from the other side. Behind them."

"That won't work," Ruth said. "They'll spot us. We have to do it from inside the train. *Beneath* them."

"Beneath them?" Albright said. "But we don't know which cars they're on."

"Look!" Ruth said, pointing up the line of the train.

Joel Nathan was rushing toward them, blood streaming from a wound in his neck.

"Joel!" Ruth called.

"Ruthie!"

Joel staggered against the wooden side of the car, gasping for breath.

"Their guns are spaced every ten cars apart," he said.

"Thank God for the orderly German mind," Albright said.

"The first one's on top of car 60," Joel said.

"Let's go!" Albright said.

Hugging the side of the train, he raced toward car 60 and leaped inside. Dead bodies littered the floor of the car, which acted like an echo chamber for the thundering machine gun overhead. Albright squeezed off a short blast at the ceiling and the machine gun fell silent. He turned toward the door in time to see the body of a German soldier topple to the ground.

Now he was running up the side of the train, Joel ahead of him, Ruth ahead of Joel, battering their way through the panicked mob of prisoners. Joel ducked into car 50, Ruth into car 40, and Albright finally pried his way through to car 30.

Dozens of prisoners had taken refuge inside.

"*Down!*" Albright shouted, and he let go with a burst from his gun. Above them, the machine gun continued to fire. Albright compressed the trigger and swept the barrel of his gun along the length of the ceiling, showering the crouching prisoners with large splinters. They heard a scream, the sound of stumbling feet, then the thud of the guard's body landing on the ground.

Outside again, Albright looked around. The frenzied stampede had stopped, and hundreds of prisoners were clambering up the sides of the train and taking over the unmanned machine guns.

They turned the guns on the remaining Germans lined up along the barbed-wire fence.

Albright sprinted toward the front of the train.

The Germans had abandoned the forward machine guns. Thousands of people were swarming all over the train. Albright rushed through the mob, through the pushing, shoving, ecstatic, crazy scene of jubilation. Strangers were thumping him on the back, hugging him, kissing him, blessing him in Yiddish, Hungarian, German, Slovakian, Czech, Polish. . . . He hardly heard what they were saying.

He saw the boy, who had been the lookout in car 10, leaning over a wheelbarrow that contained the body of a dead man. The boy was weeping.

He saw the woman who had first worn the bright orange-red scarf and the woman who smuggled the Molotov cocktail into car 1. They were embracing.

He saw the man who had gone into car 2 wearing the gray fedora hat. He stood, cowering inside the door of the car, afraid to come out.

And then he saw Ruth.

She stood beside the locomotive, dwarfed by the great Hochbeinigen wheels. Her gun was pointed up at the engineer, who leaned out of the cab with his arms raised in a gesture of surrender.

"Don't shoot, don't shoot!" the engineer blubbered. "I'm a civilian. I only drive the train. Don't shoot! I'm not a murderer like the others."

Albright came up to Ruth and gently put an arm around her shoulders. She was trembling with fury.

"Don't kill him," he said.

"Why not?" she said, staring at the engineer. "He's just as bad as the rest of them. Think of how many thousands he's transported to this place to die."

"I know," Albright said, "but we need him."

She turned to look at Albright. The beatings in prison had left their marks on the cameo beauty of her face. But Albright noticed that the change was deeper than that. Though she was still lovely, Ruth no longer had the face of a girl in the process of defining her inner character. That character had fully emerged, strong and definite and certain.

He felt himself falling in love with her all over again.

"Need him for what?" Ruth asked.

"To get us out of here on this train," Albright said. "The guards are bound to have radioed Auschwitz for help. We can expect an attack in force. We haven't escaped from the Germans yet."

6

Albright took Ruth into his arms.

"I wish there were more time," he said. "There're so many things I've been saving to tell you."

"You don't have to say them," she said. "It's not necessary to say them."

He kissed her and said, "I adore you."

"Yes," she said. Her fingers curled around his neck. "You are my love."

"I want to be with you always," he said.

"Yes, yes. . . ."

"And I'll cherish you for the rest of my life and never leave you and . . ."

"Alex, Alex, Alex," she said, moving her fingers to his lips. "There isn't time now. Later."

"I don't want to lose you again," he said.

"You won't lose me, my darling," she said.

He kissed her again and said, "If something should happen to me . . ."

"They can't get us now," she said. "We're beyond their reach."

"But if something should happen," he said. "I've never cared about dying before. But now, I don't want to leave you. You know that, don't you?"

"Yes, I know," she said. "But nothing can happen to us. We're not going to die. We'll be together, always."

He kissed her again and said, "I'm really pleased that you believe me. You're so splendid."

"We're both splendid," she said.

"Wait here," he said. "I'll be right back."

He was about to mount a ladder to the roof of the train when he spotted the boy from car 10 standing sentinel over the dead man in the wheelbarrow. He walked over to him and put his arm around the weeping boy and waited a moment before he spoke.

"You were such a brave fellow in the train," Albright said. "I could use your help again. Will you come with me?"

The boy glanced down at the rigid smile on King Kong Lipshutz's face, then back at Albright.

"He'll be all right," Albright said. "By the way, what's your name?"

"Noah," the boy said.

"Come with me, Noah."

Noah went with Albright and they climbed onto the roof of the train and surveyed the sea of people on the platform.

"What do you think, Noah?" Albright asked. "Can we convince them to get back inside the train? Will they listen to us?"

Noah smiled weakly at him and shrugged.

"Well, here goes," Albright said, and he raised a bullhorn to his mouth and his voice boomed out across the station.

For the next fifteen minutes, he tried to reason with the escaped prisoners, but it was no use. They wouldn't budge. Of the original seven thousand people who had been herded onto the train in Budapest, nearly a thousand had perished during the journey or died in the breakout here at Tarnow. Albright could understand why the survivors balked at the thought of boarding the death train again.

"You've got to listen to me!" he said. "Every minute we delay brings a German attack that much closer."

Albright lowered the bullhorn and said to Noah, "I can't get through to them. Let's go."

They climbed down and walked over to Ruth Bar-Adon and Joel Nathan.

"I don't know how to make them listen," Albright said.

"Perhaps I should try," Ruth said.

She took the bullhorn and climbed on top of the train. Her lips moved but there was no sound. She had forgotten to switch on the battery. She threw the switch.

"My name is Ruth Bar-Adon," her amplified voice reverberated. "Some of you may have heard of me."

A ripple of excitement swept through the crowd.

Joel's gaze wandered from Ruth to the faces of the prisoners and then to Alex Albright. It was obvious that Ruth had cast her spell. The American looked up at her with an expression that bordered on adoration. It was such an open, unfeigned expression of love that, for a moment, Joel was blinded by intense jealousy. He felt shut out, pushed aside. After all, wasn't this *his* Ruthie, didn't she belong to him? But this feeling was instantly smothered by a conflicting emotion. Shame. He knew that he had no right to compete with Albright. He had spent too much of his life overcoming his inner doubts to permit himself an unguarded, selfless devotion for a woman. This was the missing part of Joel Nathan's character and he knew it. He resolved not to get in the way of these lovers.

"The man who has been trying to talk to you is an American," Ruth continued. "It was he who planned our escape. He is a wonderful, brave man and we all owe him our lives. But he would be the first to tell you that his plan included outside help. Before he left Budapest, he radioed the Americans and asked them to send paratroops to aid us in the escape. Those paratroops never arrived. We didn't need them after all. We discovered that resistance to the Germans was possible all on our own. You had the will to resist and live. But now the Germans are mounting an attack to prove that you were wrong. If you remain here, you will die just as surely as if the Germans had thrown you into the gas ovens at Auschwitz. We are asking you to show that you still have the will to live. Get back on the train and come with us."

Ruth's words were received by the massed throng in total silence. She climbed down from the roof and walked slowly through the densely packed crowd, which parted as she made her way to the middle of the train. And there she climbed into a boxcar and turned to face the staring prisoners.

Then a voice called out, "To the train!"

And the cry was repeated, "*The train! . . . The train! . . . The train! . . .*"

A great roar went up—"THE TRAIN!"—as six thousand people flocked toward the train and slowly began boarding the box-cars.

Albright turned to Joel Nathan.

"We've got to reach the Russian lines at the border," he said. "That means traveling right through the German positions. We'll have to bluff our way through."

"What if the bluff doesn't work?" Joel asked.

"Then we'll blast our way through," Albright said.

They organized a company of prisoners and rounded up weapons from the dead Germans and from the two Einsatzkommando cars. They set up machine guns and mortars in the doorways and posted men in German uniforms on the roof. The stirring Nazi anthem, "The Horst Wessel Song," blared from the loudspeakers and SS flags fluttered in the breeze.

Albright inspected the train.

"Looks convincing," he said. Then he shouted up to the engineer, "Okay, back it out."

As the heavily armed train squeaked backward out of the station, Nathan boarded the locomotive, and Albright, followed by Noah, jogged down the line to Ruth's car. Albright held out his hand for Ruth.

"Jump, I'll catch you," he said.

"I want to stay here with the others," she said.

"No," he called up to her, "I want you to be with me."

"We'll meet at the border," she called back.

The train was beginning to move faster now.

"Ruth," he shouted, "don't!"

"It's only until the border," she cried. "I know you'll think I'm being silly, but I want to stay with the others until the end. You understand, don't you, my darling? It's what I have to do."

"Something might happen," he shouted.

"Nothing can happen to us anymore," she cried.

And suddenly the boy, Noah, leaped onto Ruth's car and called back to Albright, "I'll stay with her," and the two of them, Ruth and Noah, waved as the car receded down the line.

Albright stood there, his arms at his sides, a lone figure on the platform except for the hundreds of corpses of Germans and Jews, and when the locomotive came by, he swung himself onto it and stood there on its side, staring at the station at Tarnow growing smaller and smaller in the distance.

Once clear of the switchyard, the engineer reached the line that ran due east, away from Tarnow toward Przeworsk near the Russian border. The train lurched forward.

A few miles on, they chugged by a garrison. The German soldiers in front of the post were washing their clothes in a communal tub. They wiped their hands on the sides of their trousers and waved to the SS train as it passed.

After the train went by the second garrison, Joel Nathan began ladling coal into the firebox. Albright watched him heap the coal into the white-hot fire, then turned to the engineer.

"Can't you make this thing move any faster?" he said.

"If you knew anything about trains," the engineer said, "you'd know that an old Hammel engine with this kind of a load can't do much better than thirty-five miles an hour. And that's assuming everything's working just the way it's supposed to be, especially the water-pressure injectors."

"Where's your water-pressure gauge?" Albright asked.

"Over there," the engineer pointed.

Albright looked at the scummy glass meter.

"I can't see a thing," he said.

"Let me take a look," the engineer said. "Jesus Christ! The pipes are all limed up."

"What's that supposed to mean?" Albright said.

"It means that the water isn't reaching the boiler," the engineer said. "And if the water level falls below the crown sheet at the top of the firebox, we're in big trouble. The whole damn thing'll melt loose, releasing all the pressure in the boiler."

"Can the boiler blow up?" Albright asked.

"Can it blow up!" the engineer said. "Like a goddamn five-hundred-pound bomb."

"We'll have to risk it," Albright said.

"Look!" Nathan shouted. "Up ahead!"

Albright and the engineer rushed to the windows of the cab. A few hundred yards down the track, a German Army unit had set up a barricade by driving a tank across the right of way.

"Give it all you've got," Albright shouted at the engineer.

The engineer reached up with his left hand and pulled open the throttle the last two or three inches. The train picked up speed. Its whistle shrieked as it barreled down the track straight for the tank.

Albright saw the red ribbon spew out of the tank's gun, then heard its mighty blast. The shell exploded short and to the right of the onrushing train. The second shot was long. The machine guns on top of the train answered with a rattling roar of fire, and the tank suddenly swiveled on its treads and tried to lumber out of the way.

But too late. The train plowed into the rear fender of the tank, hurling it into the air, and it landed on its side and exploded in a great ball of flame. The locomotive was nearly derailed by the collision and it yawed crazily as it sped by the scattered German unit, then steadied itself and raced on.

They passed a sign, "Przeworsk 12 Km.," and the train leaned into a long, curving stretch of track. As it straightened out, Albright heard a loud grating sound, like metal straining against metal, inside the cab.

"What's that?" he asked the engineer.

The engineer pushed Joel Nathan aside and looked into the firebox.

"The crown sheet's pulling loose from its staybolts," he said, a look of terror in his eyes. "It could blow any minute. We've got to stop."

Albright jabbed a pistol into his side.

"We're not stopping until we get to Przeworsk," he said.

"We'll never make it," the engineer said.

Suddenly, a tremendous explosion rocked the train and the cab was showered with earth.

"Artillery!" Joel shouted.

"*Russian* artillery," Albright said. "We're near the front. Keep a lookout for German units."

Shells whistled in, landing on both sides of the track and pelting the train with geysers of shrapnel and stone and clods of earth. The force of the explosions buffeted the locomotive as it hurtled along a high embankment beside a swiftly moving river. Across the river, the artillery barrage had flattened the forest into acres of smoldering tree stumps. The train whipped past a kilometer marker, "Przeworsk 6 Km."

"Less than four miles to go," Albright said. "We're going to make it."

Then over the deafening artillery explosions, they heard a harsh, raspy crunch followed by a sudden thunderclap.

"One of the staybolts!" the engineer screamed. "It's blown loose from the crown sheet."

Gushers of steam flooded into the cab. A caterwauling screech came from the engine.

The engineer shoved Albright aside and hurled himself from the speeding train. Albright raised his gun but the engineer was immediately lost in the smoky pale of the exploding artillery.

Then another tremendous eruption rocked the locomotive's cab, which was rapidly filling with columns of steam.

"The whole thing's going to blow!" Joel said. "We've got to stop the train."

He reached up for the throttle.

"Wait!" Albright shouted. "We can't stop now. Up ahead. Germans!"

Joel Nathan looked out the window of the cab. At least two companies of German *Panzers,* a mile or so away, were advancing down the track straight for the train. Nathan counted a couple of dozen tanks and armored cars accompanied by scores of infantrymen trotting along their sides. As they headed for the train, the Germans were moving directly into the line of fire of the Russian artillery.

"They must be crazy," Nathan said. "They're retreating right into the artillery."

"They're not retreating," Albright said. "They're coming after us. They must've gotten a message that the train escaped. They want to stop us more than they want to stop the Russians."

Just then, the tanks opened up with their guns, and the train hurtled down the track through the bursting shells of the Germans *and* the Russians.

"I'm going to stop the train!" Joel cried, closing the throttle and yanking up the reverse lever. "*Jump!*" he yelled over the piercing noise of the locked Hochbeinigen wheels screeching along the tracks. "*Jump! Jump! . . .*"

And as Alexander Hamilton Albright stood perched there on the edge of the howling locomotive, with Nathan shrieking in his ear, "*Jump! Jump! Jump!*" he was again carried back for a brief instant to that crisp autumn day ten years ago when he made his first parachute jump from his father's Le Père biplane. And the thought of jumping, of leaping into air, of dropping faster and faster until he attained the region of terminal velocity, of hurtling toward the earth, of being attached to nothing, totally isolated, a falling body, a frail human feather defying the winds of destiny . . . this *idea of himself* as a parachutist no longer filled him with any joy or passion.

He was through with risking his life in order to feel alive. He was finished with parachuting.

He jumped.

For the last time.

His body was crouched into a tight ball, his neck tucked into his chest, his elbows gripping his sides, his muscles coiled . . . and at the instant he landed on the embankment he unleashed his tightly sprung body, and he bounced over onto his side, arms and legs absorbing the impact, and he rolled over and over, down the rocky incline until he came to a natural rest.

He tried to stand and a sharp pain stabbed through his arm. It felt broken. The long train raced past him, the speeding force of thousands of tons of momentum thrusting against the brakes, impelling the locomotive closer and closer to the German Panzers until it was almost upon them. And then in a tremendous explosive flash of blinding light the locomotive blew apart, shaking the ground, sending the boiler and cab and engine tender hurling through the air, gouging a massive hole in the German lines, flattening everything in its wake.

The first cars of the train jackknifed into each other in a crunching derailment, and the rest of the train shuddered to a halt. The Russian artillery barrage suddenly stopped and for a brief moment the smoky scene was gripped in an eerie silence.

Albright struggled to his feet and immediately saw that a number of the cars in the train had received direct hits from the Russian and German shells. He began running toward the train.

At least half a dozen cars lay on their sides, split apart. Dead bodies were strewn all over the ground. The survivors slowly crawled out of the derailed cars. Albright made his way through the scene of carnage, crawling over the dead and the dying, searching for Ruth.

In the confusion and panic, he grew desperate. The women in their tattered and blood-splattered clothing all seemed to resemble Ruth. He clutched at them, seeking her familiar face, then going on.

The middle of the train had received the worst pounding and one car had been entirely obliterated. The explosion had shattered the sides of the adjoining cars. Albright was afraid to look inside the exposed charnel house.

And then he saw the boy, Noah, kneeling on the ground.

There, lying beside Noah, was Ruth.

Noah had covered her chest with his jacket and was holding her hand.

Albright knelt next to Noah.

"Alex," Ruth said.

It was hard for her to breathe. He forced himself to look beneath Noah's jacket. It was horrible.

"Don't try to talk," he said.

"I'm sorry, darling," she said. "I left you."

"That's all right," he said.

"It was something I had to do," she said.

"It doesn't matter now," he said.

"I was worried about your leaving me, and instead I left you," she said. "Isn't that funny?"

"Yes," he said, "it's funny. Don't try to talk."

"I want to talk," she said.

"Okay," he said.

"Tell Guido what happened," she said.

"I'll tell him," he said.

"Tell him that I was very happy because you never left me," she said. "Tell Guido he was wrong. You didn't leave me."

"Okay," he said.

"I didn't think I was going to die," she said.

"Oh, Ruth," he said.

"But you were splendid," she said.

Around them, people were praying over the dead. . . . "Yisgadal veyiskadash shemei raba bealma divera. . . . And then, amid the murmuring incantation of the Jewish kaddish, there were excited shouts. Stunned and bewildered, overcome by death, people were standing and shouting and pointing to the sky.

Albright and Noah gazed up.

In the west, slicing through a bank of clouds, they saw the silhouette of a two-engine Liberator. From a door in its side, the transport was seeding the sky overhead with a line of blossoming white canopies.

Kim Philby had sent the parachutists from Camp Jubilee.

And as the canopies slowly floated to the earth, a formation of Russian soldiers emerged from the blasted forest and waded across the river, waving joyously toward the sky.

Albright bent down and gathered Ruth's body in his arms and, with Noah by his side, he went to join the liberators.